Around the World in Eighty Years

By

Sabine Joyce

ARPress
ILLUMINATING IDEAS,
EMPOWERING VOICES

ARPress
45 Dan Road Suite 15
Canton MA 02021
  Hotline: 1(888) 821-0229
  Fax: 1(508) 545-7580

Ordering Information:
Quantity sales. Special discounts are available on quantity purchases by corporations, associations, and others. For details, contact the publisher at the address above.

Printed in the United States of America.

  ISBN-13:   Softcover   979-8-89676-389-5
              eBook   979-8-89676-390-1

Library of Congress Control Number: 2025919975

Around the World
in Eighty Years

SABINE JOYCE

Around the World in Eighty Years
Traveling with Pepto Bismol

A story about my travels.
(Almost all my stays have been in Hostels or low-cost Hotels)

Traveling has always been my passion since I was a little girl in Silesia, (Oberschlesien) and I remember being tied to a tree on a long tether along with my pet lamb to curb my wanderlust. We both had a habit of going further away and the only solution for my mother was tying us together connected to a tree.

Then in 1946 we really got to "travel" across Poland going east as refugees to Germany with guns of Russian soldiers pointed at us to make us move faster. We were Refugees now.

We settled in the north of Germany. As soon as my age aloud it I joined the Youth Hostels and rode on my bicycle to see as much of Germany as my free time allowed. Sometimes it meant skipping school.

A two-year stay in London, England, as an au pair and cook followed. It gave me a taste of what was out there in the world. While I was there, I saw an ad in the London newspaper looking for a cook in Florida.

On September 11, 1960, I immigrated to the USA, to the land of all possibility. For my first year I chose to live in Florida because the weather was better than in Europe. I discovered endless places to visit, and I spent all my free time traveling all over the south. The Greyhound bus was my best transportation.

I settled in Washington D.C. after traveling up north and checking out possible places to live.

It was a great time in Washington then, living now where the Kennedy Center is built. We sunbathed on P Street beach and swam in the Potomac and visited all the sights in D.C. The Smithsonian was all free, what a great thing for me.

My first Salary in D.C. was $36 a week. Not much but enough to go to concerts and Theatre. By a good stroke of luck, I found reasonable prices for flying to other countries as well. My sister Petra worked for different airlines and could book relatives on planes when seating was available.

East Africa, 1972

My first trip was in 1972 to East Africa. I'll never forget it since they were still using propeller airplane that spit fire out of the engines, and one could see it at night. Scary!

Petra was employed at that time at the Nairobi Airport as a manager for Atlantis, a German airline.

Traveling in Africa required patience, especially in Kenya. Since the local transportation system was inefficient, to put it mildly, and for me, it was very inconvenient to waste travel time. Upon arrival, I just wanted to go, go, go.

I arrived at night and was greeted by smiling faces and a leopard skin capped hostess. A beautiful breeze awaited me. I will never forget that first aroma of Africa--all the cooking fires, the charcoal smell!

That was Africa, then a wait for my passport to be stamped. A speedy car ride to Nairobi made me think that I should have made a will before my trip. There was no speed limit.

Nairobi was a city of extremes different from anything I knew. It was old and modern. Bougainvillea the size of our oak trees surrounding a tall Hilton Tower Hotel. Miserable slums contrasted with fine residential areas with sumptuous Villas.

The Nairobi Corydon Museum was well stocked with African culture. Joy Adamson, the English writer who wrote Born Free, had contributed many paintings to the museum and made Kenya and Tanzania famous with her "Elsa the lion" stories. There were nightclubs and a casino, a snake house, a big park.

I passed the days following my arrival arranging tours to see the sights. Bargaining was essential to every transaction.

On a Wednesday, I finally took off in a rented car with some of my sister's friends. Togetherness is particularly good because it is cheaper and safer.

Amboseli Game Park was first. Game was so abundant that we covered very few miles as we stopped constantly to see the animals. It took my breath away to see a giraffe with a baby standing in the Road.

A stop at Kajiado brought me my first contact with Maasai warriors. They are nomads interested only in cattle and warfare. The Maasai's live on milk, blood drawn from a cow, and cheese.

At Ol Tukai Lodge in Amboseli we hired a park ranger and who showed us spots where we could see special animals. The first time we saw lions we drove very close, with windows closed, then we noticed that we were stuck in the mud right under their noses. For one hour we insulted the Lions until they got up very disgustedly and stood behind a tree, twitching tails and watching our attempts to get out of the mud. We managed it, but we learned always to look at the ground where we drove.

We had many flat tires and often no spares, which involved waiting for many hours until help came, with maybe a lion family settling down next to us.

While we were in camp, we could hear lions roaring all night. If we had to go to the bathroom after dark, we walked carefully from our sleeping tent to the lavatory. We just hoped carrying and flapping an umbrella would ward off any danger and keep us safe. The guards usually were sleeping safely high in the trees.

One day I flew to Mount Kilimanjaro, and Olduvai Gorge (where the Leakey family of archeologists found the oldest human fossils), Manyara Lake, Ngorongoro Crater and Serengeti. At lunch in Seronera, Serengeti, a Ranger pointed out the cliffs where Elsa the Lion lived and where the movie "Born Free" was filmed. That day we saw 18 Lions and three Leopards. I felt lucky to see so many in one day.

Landing a bush plane is challenging, as wild game loves the green runway and must be scared off before landing. The pilot must fly very low to scatter the herds.

Wherever one looks you see wildebeest, also called gnu, walking along by the thousands. They trek 500 miles every year from Kenya to Tanzania and return.

Taking the night train from Nairobi to Mombasa on the east coast was awfully slow as the engineer could see animals sleeping on the track only at the last minute.

Mombasa was very Arabic and medieval and is almost all Muslim. I became acquainted with a family there and stayed in their home to get to know the residents. The old town streets are only about five feet wide and very shadowy. Many family compounds were blooming with flowering jasmine bushes out front and inside the walls, another smell I will never forget. The friends just tucked a little flower somewhere on the body and one smelled very well for a long time. Chickens were everywhere. Finally found out how the people knew which chickens belonged to whom. The all had a distinguishing mark on top of their head to identify their owners.

The women wore the bui-bui outside their house over their beautiful colorful dresses.

We could not sleep late, as the muezzin's first call to prayer came from the mosque at 5:30 and then four more times throughout the day. The only way to get to know the habitants is to live with them.

Every morning, we shopped for fresh food. There was no refrigerator yet. And electricity was almost always off. Furniture was sparse but always there was a big bed and many pillows, easier to keep clean in the tropical climate. I was enchanted by the constant smell of cooking and getting used to many spices they used. I also had to learn how to eat sitting on the floor and using my right hand only, since I am left-handed. We spend evenings talking while the men chewed qat, a green plant stimulant.

A big wedding took place over several days. They go on and on. There is a Lady's day and I could not get over how beautiful everybody was dressed, covered with much jewelry on "Lady's day". More Food was passed around and dancing to the music of a drummer and clanging of metal lids. Then the bride came out and she was showered with money which was supposed to bring good luck. The bride was 12 years old!

Lamu, 1974

Looking for more adventure? Sail on a Dhow up the African coast to Lamu!!!

Finally, my Arab friends arranged for me to go on an ocean-going dhow to the island Lamu, which lies near the border with Somalia. Lamu is the oldest and best-preserved Swahili settlement in east Africa. The dhow, a Jahazi type, was sailing on the northbound kusi (a wind) blowing them home with fresh cargo to their home port. This was a difficult project because women never have been allowed on a dhow. And so, my adventure started. What was supposed to take three days took ten days.

Much has been written about dhows, but I had never met anyone who had ever traveled on one. To me it was an experience which I hoped one day to have. The opportunity came on my visit to East Africa.

A dhow is an ancient type of sailing vessel made from wood (Nambo Mgarti) and palm tree leaves. The large mast slant forward and supports a three-cornered sail which appears to be upside down when it is set, with the pointed end on the bottom.

At the Old Custom House in Mombasa, Kenya I persuaded the captain of the Dhow Zawadi, to take me on as a paying passenger from Mombasa north to the island of Lamu. I was told that the passage would take at least three full days depending on the winds. Since the crew subsisted primarily on dried fish, it was suggested that I bring along some additional provisions as well as a blanket and some limes. The need for the limes escaped me, but I bought them as well as fruits, canned food, a can opener, Kleenex, and so forth etc.

I watched throughout the day, as my dhow – 50 feet long with a 14-foot beam – being loaded with two truckloads each of cement and ground corn, as well as with additional cargo consisting of beans, peas, potatoes and furniture. I wondered how there would be room for me.

I boarded at midnight to try to get some sleep before sailing. I bedded down on deck under a palm leaf canopy on deck, where I kept sliding into the ship's railing. There was no other space anywhere on deck, and one had to hunt for a spot. I finally discovered some room in the matting on the floor.

Awakened at 4:00 am by the prayer call from the local mosque, we set off. Actually, what happened was that four of the crew rowed out of the harbor until we were able to find some wind.

At daybreak I was able to observe closely for the first time the crew of six who were to be my companions. They were quite a motley bunch. All were Arabic, and only one man could speak any English at all. My Swahili was just as limited as it came entirely from my book.

Two hours after sunup we encountered a heavy rolling sea. It was too much for my stomach. Following the Captain Zawadi's instructions, I held the lime to my nose and drank the juice. It seemed to help prevent certain bodily functions but not others. Where were the toilet facilities? This was something I had not checked out.

Outboard at the stern of the dhow was an armchair-like device with two footrests but no seat. One slip and you are in the ocean. I felt too embarrassed to use that throne especially with the captain stationed next to it, but nature prevailed. I soon discovered that the toilet was the entertainment center for everyone. It was hilarious when someone got hit by a big wave. Automatic flush!

I passed up the first day's breakfast and lunch, especially when I saw what was being served. The posho, a ground corn meal eaten at every meal, was palatable enough, but my nose never became accustomed to the smell of the dried shark meat that they ate. The first evening I shared my canned food to the delight of the crew. None of them had ever seen a can opener, and they kept checking the tin cans to see how neatly they were opened.

No one slept much that night because the sail had to be adjusted constantly.

The next morning, we were out of sight of land in heavy seas, with dolphins swimming all around our ship. It was a joy to watch these animals, truly friends of humans. I felt sad when they left us after a few hours.

By now the seas were very heavy, and I wondered how long our ship could last with all the rolling and battering from the water, especially with our load of cement below. They had no radio or lifejackets on board nor any other safety equipment except for the decrepit lifeboat which looked like it would not even float. And here we were in the shark-infested Indian Ocean.

Captain Zawadi decided to return to the coastal waters and did so without the benefit of any type of navigational equipment. There we anchored for the night. Later I was able to appreciate that the entire passage was navigated by dead reckoning. If I had known as much before we left, I am sure I would have remained in Mombasa.

While anchored, we fished. We caught two kingfish, or kiboma, about two feet long and weighing about ten pounds each and so we feasted. The crew even changed into new kikois, their traditional skirts.

After dinner it was a treat to hear the beautiful singing voice of one of the men. Afterwards the crew's storyteller took over and throughout the voyage he kept all the men happy with his stories. It was fascinating to see how they all listened so intently to what he said. I only wished I could understand him.

Another interesting aspect of the crew's routine was prayer session five times a day. They washed their hands and feet before praying, and spread a prayer mat. They always knew in which direction Mecca lay.

The next day was beautiful sailing weather. For the first time I saw sharks up close. Their fins were like knives cutting the surface of the water. Unlike the dolphins, they were not amusing.

Throughout the day everyone snacked on my provisions. The dry cereals were a big hit. However, any food that had to be cooked was prepared at the bow of the boat and often the ocean would douse the fire, and we would have to wait for our tea or whatever – heating again.

On the final day of the voyage, we navigated carefully through many coral reefs before seeing land again. The coast is lined with the ruins of ancient fortresses and long stretches of white mountains-not snow, but sand dunes.

Late in the afternoon we reached the island of Lamu. Then I began to dream how wonderful a nice bath or shower would feel. But first I had to get my land legs. For a while I could not walk straight, and that night I even had trouble lying in bed, as I felt that I would roll onto the floor.

Lamu is an ancient Arab town where life appears to go on much as it has for the past several hundred years. Its economy depends mainly on mangroves grown there to build furniture with its wood. Tourism is also important. Lamu is a holy place, and hundreds of pilgrims visit each year to celebrate the Prophet's Mohammed's birthday. The celebration lasts several days.

Usually, it is a leisurely place with no paved streets or motor traffic, and most of the "roads" are only three feet wide. I found it worth my while to devote ample time to wandering the maze of narrow roadways and observing the carved doorways which take about three months to create.

The food supply is extremely poor as very few staples are available. An ordinary dinner, as we know it served in the hotel, consists of a plate of rice, gravy, and one or two pieces of meat, enough to fill a stomach at any rate. But eating was difficult because I was surrounded by many village children watching me eat.

The seven-mile stretch of white sand dunes is a paradise for jaded city dweller. It is wild and open to the sea with no habitation in sight. If you climb a few hundred feet to the top of a dune, you can see the entire island.

My time on Lamu quickly came to an end. A one-hour ferry ride took me to Mokowe on the mainland, and from there followed a 16-hour bus ride mostly on dirt roads to Mombasa. The bus was full and had no air-conditioning! It carried lots of live animals and much produce for the markets or next buyer. Dust covered everything. The return trip itself was an adventure.

East Africa, 1974

My next trip to Arusha, Tanzania, where I met and became friendly with a Maasai family. I never will forget Subarbi, who wished to marry me, notwithstanding my husband in America. The Maasai's lives are very hard and staying overnight in their kraal home was an unforgettable experience. The house was built entirely of fresh cow dung and must be repaired almost daily with it. At night they close the boma, or farmyard, with thorn bushes to keep the wild animals from getting to the livestock.

Turkey on a German Airline called Suedflug, 1975

After many years of reading about Istanbul I found it a fascinating city. My one week there was short, and I tried to learn as much as I could about Turkey. As a single woman, I learned right away to stay near a family with children in order to be safe. And it gave me an insight to the families too.

East Africa, 1976

Returning to Tanzania two years later with my husband Kevin, I was eager to share with him the places I had seen before. I had a great reunion with my Maasai friend Subarbi, who still was not married. It did not stop Subarbi to ask again to mention marriage. Having two or more wives is customary with the Maasai and always a younger one is needed to help with the work. I guess Subarbi thought I should have two husbands.

A visit to Arusha National Park was especially important to me. The movie "Hatari" with John Wayne and Hardy Kruger was made there in 1962. Momella Wildlife Lodge was built in the shadow of Mt. Kilimanjaro just for the movie.

I knew I had to go up that mountain one day. We spent many days driving around to see the animals, and often were stuck in remote places because the rain made roads impassable or the little planes could not fly. I revisited Mt. Kenya to watch the animals at the waterhole from the lodge. I always had a hard time leaving the beautiful Rift Valley and the Flamingos on Lake Nakuru!

We took the night train to Mombasa and rented a car in Malindi for a beach vacation and luxuriated in feeling the beautiful sand under our feet. Along the coast north we drove and discovered old Arab towns, trying our proficiency or lack of, to speak Swahili to everybody. Most beautiful Nyali Beach Lodge was our favorite.

Getting stuck on the ferry crossing one of the Rivers north but the human manpower on the ferry just lifted our car up. Calling that thing a ferry was a joke. It listed so badly a wonder we did not capsize. Taking the train back to Nairobi in a sleeper compartment was great.

A Trip Around the World by Plane
November 1976

I saved some money from my cattle sale and decided to spend it on a great trip around the world.

Hawaii was the first stop. So much to see! Miles of sugarcane and pineapple fields. Impressive Waikiki and its beaches!

Philippine Islands

On to the next landing in the Philippines. A big Mabuhay-welcome. We did a lot of traveling there in my short four days.

First to the volcanoes Taal to stand on top and see endless rows of volcanoes. And I watched rice farmers at work.

Now by Bus to Pagsanjan Falls to experience the River where just the movie Apocalypse with Marlon Brando was filmed. Much of the movie structures were still there and even body's swaying in the wind hanging from trees. By bangka-a long dug out boat going upstream. Hard for the young man to push us upstream. Through the falls which was welcome in the heat. Going back was downstream, a fast trip.

Singapore

Singapore the land of perpetual summer. I fell in love with Singapore. (Have been back many times now) Orchids growing all over. From the top of Mt. Faber, one could see the famous Singapore straits of Malacca. At this time 350 freighters were waiting to be loaded or unloaded.

The visit to the Tiger Balm Garden was a must-do for tourists.

Having read so many stories about Raffles Hotel, it was my dream to visit. Naturally, I had to have a Singapore sling. It was not expensive then but now…

A day trip to Johore Malaysia and visit to a rubber plantation. Then to the palace of the Sultan, very beautiful. Next day a water tour with a Chinese junk and viewed life around the waterfront.

Hong Kong

Flying into the city, it seemed that our plane would land on the rooftops. It must be the tightest landing in the world.

Not much rest because again a place full of sights not to be missed. Aberdeen first. There the highlight is eating in one of the biggest Junks, (boats.)

Then a Chinese Farm. There was lot of explaining by the young farmer of raising Ducks and vegetables.

To the walled city of Kam tin. Many Peking ducks are raised there. It looks funny when the farmers walk the ducks with the long pole and a little cloth tied on the end.

To Lok Ma Chau to look over to Mainland China, Shatin heights to see Amah Rock. The legend goes: A mother and her child had waited there for her husband daily to return from fishing, but he eventually did not return, and she turned into stone and it is now a symbol of faith, hope and love.

And now Victoria Peak, exiting stairs to the top, got to be in shape to do all. The wonderful sight of Hong Kong, the busy waterway.

Afternoon tea at Repulse Bay Hotel. There I met Robert Mitchum, the actor. Yes, I ran into him by accident.

We went to another Tiger Balm Garden and in the evening shopping on Nathan Road.

Taiwan

We arrived in Taipei at night. We saw many temples on this visit. Lung Shan Temple was very crowded. Chinese Opera was seen in the evening. Awfully hard to take because of the high voices. But Taiwan was more Chinese then I expected. The tradition is strong. Especially in the National Palace Museum. There are exhibits stressing old China.

The Grand Hotel where we stayed was very much like a museum; I could not believe the treasures around.

Taiwan is also a destination for foodies. Everything tasted so delicious.

I met two of my former guests Yung-an and Pinan who had stayed with us in the USA. I learned a little about their home life. Spending two days in Taiwan whetted my appetite to come back again.

Japan

Again only 4 days but I tried to see and walk all over the city. Tokyo was interesting, especially the little noodle places hiding in the niches of buildings.

When I was a young girl, I read all story's about Mikimoto, the Pearl King. So now was my opportunity to visit the store. They must have thought my request for admission strange, because I was dressed as a tourist and did not look like someone who would buy a pearl necklace, but they made me very welcome.

A 2-day trip on the Bullet train to Kyoto. But again, there was endless history. So much to see there again, so many temples. I have always tried to come back to learn more.

Turkey, November 1977

Landing in Istanbul at night, I am sitting in the cockpit pretending I am flying the big plane.

I had good friends there now and quickly became acquainted again. It was the last day of Ramadan and sheep were tethered everywhere-to lamp posts, the stairs in my building-it was amazing how everybody got ready for the big feast day.

Istanbul was fascinating. There were palaces, churches, mosques and cisterns. The fishmongers on the Galata Bridge, the oriental Bazaar with 4000 stalls.

I cannot forget the movie "Topkapi" and had to see Topkapi Palace. The jewels were bigger than I expected.

The blue Mosque was incredible! I wandered the streets and discovered more treasures than I can describe.

A trip on the Bosporus was another highlight. Tasting Turkish coffee, the saying is: coffee must be black like the eyes of the girls.

There were dancing bears and for a few pennies one could watch them perform. I did not enjoy watching the Bears.

I loved the trip along the Bosporus. Ships from all over the world passing right and left.

The Gambia, 1978

Lucky me, I was offered a free trip to The Gambia. It is a very small country wedged between Senegal West Africa.

It became an adventure again. 40km wide and 450km long. It was an English colony before 1965.

Banjul, the Capital, very English looking still.

The Gambia River divides the country but provides travel by waterways instead of roads. Beautiful beaches abound. But Soldiers with Rifles had to protect tourist or anybody swimming at the Beach. Stealing and being robbed is a problem.

I decided to go to Juffure were the TV Movie "Roots" about Kunta Kinte was made.

It involved getting on a most broken-down ferry. Looked like we would sink anytime since it was heavily overloaded to the top with people. Crocodiles lounged along the River and I had no intentions to be their dinner.

Juffure is the homeland of Kunta Kinte, ancestor of Alex Haley who authored the best-selling novel Roots. My welcome in Juffure by the Mandingo Chief Sanjali Bojan was interesting. He still had 6 wives and 25 children.

This is an ideal African village, lots of vegetation. Since there had been no tourist for a long time the people followed me everywhere because they thought I would bring new money to the village.

Nearby is James Island where all the newly caught slaves were held in holding pens until being sold and shipped overseas.

After going there and seeing the old buildings intact I went back to Juffure. There I was introduced to the Kinte's family and was told all are related to him. On my way to the Ferry, I was accosted by a young man carrying a long knife, but I could run faster.

It is maybe now peaceful but at the time I was there the transition to a modern life was not readily done.

It was all interesting but not a safe tourist country. On my way to the airport, I got into a taxi and found out I was kidnapped by a couple who demanded all my money at gun point. After much talking and telling them I was poor they dropped me off near the airport and I was happy to get away from that country.

Aruba, 1979

To Aruba for warmth. I was so surprised how windy it is. Kevin and I had a first time Caribbean vacation. We delighted in fresh coconut and long hours on the beach, easy living. Driving around and discovering old places and the Natural Bridge.

Modern Oranjestad. Colorful and quite beautiful.

And we found a nice horse farm that had great Paso Finos.

Lots of sunshine and a place to return to.

(Which I did with my sister Petra a few months later).

We watched a very strange ritual of the feeding of the sharks. Much meat was thrown over a cliff and an abundance of sharks were waiting for it. Where all the meat came from, we never found out, since the Island is all desert and no cattle are raised here. It must have been the leftovers from the stores.

I found out that I could do scuba diving lessons and started right away. But not were the sharks waited. It was a reason from then on to make it my mission to dive all over the world.

Cayman Islands, November 1980

It is cold again and I must go south for my vacation. Cayman, a British crown colony and very English, is still very unknown to tourists. Driving on the left. Since there is no anchorage for big boats, cruise ships have not come yet.

My first rental in Boddentown was one of the many small cottages in the Caribbean style. Playing Dominos with the natives I can still hear the clinking of the Dominos. Even donkeys were still used. Boddentown was the oldest settlement and still had only little houses and a church. Graves were on top of the rocks since no earth to dig down. The island is all coral.

There was a turtle farm which released about 400 baby turtles a year. Some of them get caught by fishermen and sold as soup.

When it is stormy, sea water explodes from the blowholes, a grand show with water shooting high in the air.

Surrounding the Island are many wrecks of freighters and other of ships. Many are the best diving places for Divers.

Cayman, 1981

A visit now with my daughters Petra and Kara. We rented the little place in Georgetown. It was a cottage perfect for us. We could see "our" own wreck right in front. And could shuttle to it with our little outboard anytime. There was diving for me and snorkeling for the girls right outside. Since there is no sand nearby the water stays clear and full of beautiful fish. Many hours we spend just hanging in our hammocks.

One day an enormous freighter anchored right in view of the cottage. It was the "Hermy" from Holland. We took the little boat to talk to them and made friends and were invited to come on board. Climbing up the rope ladder was a feat for all of us. Lucky the sea was still. But we were scared, going down in the dark was better.

One morning our bathing suits were missing from the clothesline outdoors. We found out dogs had stolen them, and we had to get new suits in the little store. Yes, it was fun traveling then.

Tenerife, Canary Island, 1981

Another discover trip to Tenerife. Mostly spend soaking up the sun. sightseeing the beautiful old buildings. Food was great and a big nightlife place for German tourists.

Jamaica, November 11, 1982

Arriving at the Seawind Hotel was the greatest place in Jamaica. A Hotel run by Jamaicans. Situated on a small Island near Montego Bay. And lucky me that week the Sun Festival was in progress, and I got invited to sit in. I learned to appreciate good Reggae music. It was so perfect to listen there.

The Beach with its clear water was the ideal place for a warm spell. Lying in the sand watching hermit crabs running around, occasionally a good drink-what more could I want?

Jamaica was still wild, and you could buy anything from beautiful villas to ganja, a potent form of marijuana used chiefly for smoking.

I enjoyed short trips to Ocho Rios and the Dunn's River Falls. Saw the beach from were a James Bond movie was filmed. There even was a train called Governors Coach Diesel going from Montego to the other side of the island. With a stop in the Cockpit countryside. It was almost all looking like Africa then. Sugarcane fields for the Rum factory Appleton. There all got to taste the best rum.

A new friend introduced me to a very good horse at the Hastings Ranch. We had great rides, him explaining that long time ago almost all were coconut farms but not used now anymore, on riding around we found thieves taking coconuts, but we ignored them.

The Manor house was for sale, and I left for the USA trying to talk Kevin into buying it.

Jamaica, 1983

Coming with Gail to see more of Jamaica. We stayed in the Seawind again. And it was a fun trip. Gail took part in every contest given by the Hotel.

We took our first balloon ride; I felt it was going to take off. Went to Germantown. It was settled 150 years ago by German farmers. They have still the blue eyes and blond hair.

We visited Dunn's River Falls again. It is exciting when the water is running hard. But very slimy in certain places so it becomes dangerous when falling.

Went over the Blue Mountains, which rise to over 7000 feet above Jamaica Beaches. Also, the Blue Mountains are known for the best coffee in the world. We saw a lot of Jamaica again and it calls for a return trip soon.

Mallorca, 1983

One week in Mallorca Spain driving and visiting many historical places and the Beach. The Cathedral in Palma is imposing and close to the harbor with all the fishing boats.

It is very hilly and has been an Island for Poets.

Jamaica, 1984

For Kevin's second trip to Jamaica, we stayed again at my favorite Seawind Hotel. Kevin was happy here as there was so much activity for him. No Sunning for Kevin with his Irish skin. Had to show him lots of places like Appleton Rum distillery. The Bamboo Alley which is almost 4 miles long.

We dined on Ackee, a vegetable that grows on a tree. It is always served with salty Codfish. Went to Dunn's River Falls again and visited a bauxite plant in Colombia.

What a relaxing week it was for us. Could not convince Kevin to buy the Main Manor House I fell in love with when riding by Horse there. I had already dreams of living there.

Peru, 1984

In Peru I took up a new and different sport, mountain biking! Totally new bicycles came on the market. Never before have there been bicycles like that. Bigger tires, very heavy bicycles about 30 pounds. 15 gears! And I was off on the Bike trip to hell.

I answered an ad from an outfitter in Colorado and joined the group to go to Machu Picchu by Bicycle. We were 2 women and 4 men. Our Stump Jumper bikes came by Specialized Bicycle Co. I signed up. What could go wrong? I was in shape I thought. We could only travel with what we could carry on our bike. It was a challenge to downsize and still be comfortable as we had only a vague idea where we would sleep at night. It was all not very well planned.

The leader of the group had permission for us to bike along the trails and railroad tracks and had a signed document from the Government of Peru.

We began with two days in Lima, most interesting. Lima was a gray city of fog and desert while we were there. Learned quite a few new foods and loved Pisco sours made with a Pisco brandy distilled from corn. Ceviche made with raw fish, is not my favorite.

When we exchanged dollars, we got a big shopping bag of soles and coins. Where to put that? The people who saw the bags of cash thought we are rich in USA.

Arrival at the el Pueblo Hotel in Lima a big surprise. It was built like a Spanish village right in the desert. Every room was furnished with antiques. The hand carved doors are 600 years old.

The Hotel is a place for the Peruvians to go on weekends. So, a big barbecue was held with tables laden with food.

Cusco arrival

The people in the Cusco airport gave us a double take as they had never seen bike tourists before. The altitude of 11,000 feet hit us right away and drinking coca tea on arrival at the Airport helped. Drinking Pisco Sours helped too. I had many cups of coca tea. And I was ready.

Later, we learned the news of the day:" Por primera vez seis norteamericanos uniran en bicicleta a cusco y machpicchu."

So everybody who read the paper knew what we were doing.

Many Indian women wore the traditional dress with lots of petticoats under their skirts.

Touring around by bike was fun but difficult since the stone-paved streets are not level. Most people called us locos especially when we told them we are biking to Machu Picchu.

Something disagreed with my stomach, and I got sick. Lomotil did not help but Peruvian medicine worked well.

Biking to Sascayhuaman was all uphill and very tough and followed by 15 miles downhill which was great. On top, a talented group of wandering minstrels was performing, and it gave me a good feeling. I recorded the music quickly.

The Scenery is unbelievable. Viewing snow-covered mountains in the background and cliffs next to us on the Road.

More beautiful scenery as we left for Pisa. What a mountain to ride across-12,000 feet up, and down again to the Urubamba Valley. Passing Donkeys, Llamas and people, mostly women, carrying heavy loads. Getting to Ollantaytambo one of the Inca fortress and to the Pisac Ruins. Sitting magnificently on the Mountainside.

Our first stop was a meadow in a private Hacienda Albergue Turistico, shaded by many eucalyptus trees. The Owner invited us 2 ladies to stay inside to spend the night in the real bedrooms. We loved it and took advantage of it. The four men out there in tents did not have the luxury. Our beds were stone slabs covered with thick sheepskins and blankets. And we slept.

In the morning the owner served a delicious Breakfast with food from the farm only. The Hacienda is 350 years already in the same family.

We did pan for Gold in the Urubamba River, but I had no luck. We are now in the Valley of the Suns. Maybe there was a lot of Gold long time ago.

Our next overnight was at the Sacred Valley Inn, Naranjachayoh. Again, very beautiful. With many Inka treasure exhibited throughout.

On the road, met Donkeys and Horses but they are not carrying much as the men we saw. They were the burden movers.

Today we stay in Alberque Inn, rather primitive, but we were getting used to traveling rough by now. The toilets are usually located above a little creek, and flushing is fast. We are near Ollantaytambo. The most magnificent ruins.

After that we had only a path to ride on from here alongside the river.

It is mostly work; this part of the ride was grinding work with many troublesome incidents. My bag strapped on the back of my bike kept rolling off. The pack on my back was getting heavier, even with no food in it. I needed to get rid of some stuff and no more Beer or coke just water. Some of us fell and rode with a few bruises. I still had to check my balance to prevent falling. I did not want to go down a cliff into the raging river.

There is a saying in Peru: A mother must have 12 children, or she is not doing her good for God (12 stations).

In the evening hours I could hear music in the hills, and we guessed it was wandering musicians singing for their food.

We are not happy about the high grass because the night snakes like it. The Bushmaster is nocturnal and likes to crawl into warm places. Our sleeping bags? As I lay there and looked at the stars, I thought of the Vampire bats flying around. We crawled into our bags and covered up against mosquitoes. Our Dinner was a slice of cheese and one Oriole cookie Bar.

The next morning birds started to sing, and we were hungry. Having now only 2 Granola Bars left for 6- not much to eat. Several varieties of hummingbirds with very long beaks were all around, feeding on a plethora of flowers.

Wild Geraniums were in bloom, about 10 foot tall. Zinnias, orchids, Gladiolus, Lupines, Canna lilies, Castor plants, Mimosas, Carnations, Strawberries and more flowers I cannot name.

Green Conure parrots flew over us screeching. We are tired and stopped making photos. But there is always Water, the River flowed below us.

The Railroad track fizzled out and it is a lot of pushing on the tracks. Finally making it to KM 88. Shortly after that we arrived at the small Station Pampaccahua, where the Stationmaster confiscated our bikes and locked us in a room. He could not read our official papers and even held them upside down. By evening we sneaked out took the bikes and quietly crept along the Railroad track hoping he was not coming after us.

We reached a little Indian cottage and bought some corn, all there was to be had. We were starving and willing to eat anything by now. Finally settled near the track in some bushes. By now we had only a chocolate bar.

Progress was slow, it took an hour to cover 3 KM. Beautiful birds and flowers everywhere. We are tired hungry but at least there was plenty of water to drink.

At last, we were approaching Aguas Calientes, with a major train station and Hotels and restaurants. Even the town Mayor, on crutches, was waiting to greet us.

We pushed on to our next stop at Banos Calientes where we

delighted in warm water and plenty of food. Big storms that night, it was spooky to see the lightning flashes on the walls of the cliffs.

The next morning after a good breakfast we were back onto the bikes again. All uphill now to Machu Picchu two hours to the top. Fifteen kilometers of a steep uphill serpentine road.

I just wanted food first and then go and see the ruins.

What a great sight is this wonderful place on the top. Especially after all the tourists left, it was ours alone. Whoever built this city knew how to do it, without tools or wheels. We explored every corner. The rain starts around 4pm with an eerie mist.

I kept asking myself how did the Incas get this city built?

That will never be answered.

In 1984, the Hotel Turistas, were we stayed was then $70 a night. Since then, it has increased to about$400 a night. It had a great Bar with good Pisco Sours, but sleep was needed for the early sunrise over the ancient city.

There we are at 6am waiting for the sun to rise. And then walked through all the little passages and up and alleyways. I was awed at all the exquisite workmanship.

Last night's rainstorm was again dramatic, lightning the walls of the mountains and crashing thunder!

A particularly good lunch and down the Mountain by bike eight km. Saw a few Alpacas on the downhill. Very elusive animals.

I cannot have enough words to describe the views.

We took the train back to Cusco, an old train full of tourists and natives and musicians playing. Paid about $3 for first class the trip back. From the train we saw a rainbow which was called by the people Arco Iris, 7 colors. There are 3 classes on the train, and we got the premium!

I did not get to see the famous switchbacks up to Cusco because it was dark; it is another feat of train building.

Arriving in Cusco we had to argue with the Stationmaster as he refused to let us get our bikes and locked the doors on us. After he reread and understood our documents, we got the bikes back.

Once again in Lima, my stomach is giving me trouble again, must be something in the house where I stayed in Cusco.

Staying on the 10th floor with a view of the ugliest grey Ocean I have ever seen. I was happy leaving for my trip to the Amazon.

Now off to the Amazon.

Destination Iquitos, its former oil and rubber booms are almost forgotten. They have a saying here: If you ever wondered what became of the trusty teller in your hometown bank who left with a quarter million dollars, check in Iquitos phone directory because they are here.

Iquitos is 2300 miles from the Ocean, and the Amazon is still wide and deep enough for big ships to get here. No roads lead anywhere. Casa de Fierro (house of Iron) built by Gustav Eiffel of Paris was shipped by a rubber tycoon here.

I soon left on a little outboard boat for the Jungle with my little guide David. The camp was somewhere in the jungle. We frequently left for the jungle to discover animals or whatever came across our trails and stopped on shore to take short hikes and meet native people and fauna. There are two seasons on the Amazon, and it was dry season for me. The water can come up 30 feet higher in the rainy season.

My best friend at the tent Camp was a little marmoset monkey. My head was his sleeping quarters. He was the size of a rat. A wooly monkey was my other companion. With all the animals around, I thought I was in heaven. It was an exciting place.

After a few misses, I learned how to shoot a big spider with a blowgun. Many Tarantulas spend the nights hanging in my screened bedroom all night.

A day came I did not expect I ran out of tampons but was told not to worry. The next day David, my guide, produced a package with old fashioned tampons for me. What a surprise! I never knew where he found them as there was no store and the nearest town was many days away.

It was another exciting experience.

Back to Lima and a few more days of touring and visiting the Gold Museum and a farm where Paso Finos were raised.

Took a trip to Pachacamac, the sacred city of pre-Columbian period.

Poland, 1985

A trip into my lost youth in Poland with my mother.

My mother "Mutti" and I wanted to see our homeland again and what a joy it was for us to see it together. Driving was difficult through East Germany. One had to follow exact driving directions through East Germany. Needed coupons for Gasoline and gas stations were hard to find. Most were closed and out of Gas. All this had to be arranged before going across East Germany.

As we were driving and passing the little East German car Trabi we felt bad about it. Usually, 6 people were squashed in it and we had a big German car just for us alone. It was a luxury the East Germans could never afford or had a future for them. Whoever would have thought the wall would come down soon and a United Germany.

Crossing the border into Poland! We stopped in Hirschberg now Jelenia Gora. A town we went as children to visit. Naturally, we stopped at a lot of Horse farms. Which are almost all run by the State.

Then we reached the Riesengebirge, Krummhuebel, now renamed Karpacz, where we had learned to ski. Snow kept falling during our visit as we drove up to the Schneekoppe, Sniezka. Here are all the sagas about Ruebezahl, the Giant of the Riesengebirge.

Getting colder now we needed a warmer place and on we went to Ottmachau to see old friends. And finally, our town Bad-Ziegenhals in sight. (Glucholazy), the town I was born in.

What a strange feeling it was after 40 years to be back.

Our house remained just like we left it. Nothing had changed. Not a new paint job, just the property seemed to be smaller in my eyes. I still remembered it as a child size. Down in the valley the big swimming pool lay in ruins as it was bombed in the war.

But meeting some of our old friends was a great event for my mother. And the River Biele is still flowing as always.

The town center was redone in front but in back all the buildings were falling apart. The Church is the centerpiece of Ziegenhals. It has been standing since 1428 and was not destroyed totally.

Stores had food, but mostly bread, so one could buy lots of it and cakes. Sugar and flour were the staples at that time.

The storks are still in their nests in trees or housetops. It means the grounds are still healthy and frogs are their dinner.

Traveling to Krakow is a center of Polish history, with its famous architecture and ancient churches. It was not damaged in the war, and the medieval city is still in its glory. The story of the trumpeter in one tower which is still played every hour. It always ends very sudden in the melody to commemorate "The Trumpeter of Krakow". The Trumpeter was killed playing it by an arrow.

The excessively big Wavell Castle! Market Square with the Draper's Hall. Many old medieval Buildings. And then one can see crumbling buildings in the next block since there is no money for repairs.

Next to Zakopane. The foremost sports center and resort in the Tatra Mountains. It seemed crazy to go in this cold weather, but Mutti wanted to see the places she went skiing in her youth. We rode the Horse-drawn wagon up to the Five Lakes. A little cold but we had blankets to ward off the cold to Morskie Oko Lake. Quite a few people were ice fishing.

Driving now in the lowland again. Passing through Racot and home of one of the largest stud farms in Poland, maintaining 700 Stallions, Mares and foals. The Farm is from the 17th century and built by an Italian builder. It made us feel princely in such opulence.

We continued north to Wolin, where we used to spend our summers and I have great memories. Swinoujscie now, was Swinemunde. Nearby there is the little town of Miedzyzdroje, Misdroy then, with our summer house next to the convent. Our great Aunt Blandina was Mother superior in the Convent. Taking flowers to her grave was good for Mutti. The Grave is still the most interesting place in the cemetery because of stories told by the Nuns about what Sister. Blandina did when the Russian soldiers invaded the town. She painted signs for the outside of the convent: Smallpox dangerous. Then she painted boils on her body and answered the door when needed. The Russians never entered the convent or hurt a Nun. It was a trip into the "Vergangenheit" And I was glad having had my mother on this trip to explain many things for me. (I have a tape of us talking. Kept it next to our seat in the car.)

Rhodes, Greece, May 1985

With Hapag Lloyd to Greece! Petra, my sister, Klara my sister-in-law to the warmth of Greece.

We set off in a rental car to discover a quite different Island. Lindo's is the prettiest city there I ever saw. We stayed in a magnificent hotel called Steps of Lindo's. That was pure luxury. The town's main attraction here was its Acropolis with a great view from the top. The houses in Lindo's are mostly from the 15th century. The women in town specialize in exquisite needlework in lace and needlepoint.

Driving with a manual shift was challenging to me. The roads were too narrow to allow passing in either direction or often we had to back up in very dangerous places. Naturally when we saw a Taverna first thing we had to do was stop to have a drink to get our nerves in shape again.

Jamaica, January 21, 1986

In Jamaica with Kevin again, our first stop was the Seawind Hotel. After check-in we drove off in our rental car to the wilds of the Island. We stopped a lot for good Jamaican food: Ackee was again in season, and I loved it.

We revisited the blue Grotto and Rick's café in Negril. And to Richmond Hill Plantation.

And the old Villa at Hastings Farm we fell in love with years ago to check what happened to it. Why did we not buy it? We debated too long. It had the most beautiful view of the Caribbean Sea. By the time we decided to buy and called, it was sold.

New Zealand, 1986

When it is cold in Maryland, I look for destinations south of the Equator.

Off I went with my oiled and tuned up bicycle to New Zealand, a long flight! Biggest surprise was being sprayed for insecticide and on arrival being told that I must let out the air of my tires before going into the Airport. They want to keep New Zealand safe from invasive flora and fauna: there are no sparrows or starlings. Only animals native to the country are allowed to live here. Auckland, North Island was my first stop.

From Auckland I flew on to Wellington where I started biking. It was surprisingly hilly. With stops at little tea-rooms, hills are easy. I discovered Scones filled with Jam and topped with real cream. Wellington was full of Chinese Take-outs. Incredibly good prices and affordable.

Maoris, the natives of New Zealand surprised me with the strange tattoos in their faces.

Fruit was for sale everywhere. Have eaten more Kiwis and Apricots. It does rain more than I expected and had to take my rain coat off and on. Butcher shops looked interesting with big leg of lambs hanging. Lots of Venison is raised like cattle in big fields.

On my walking tour I noticed that houses had been built close to the steep hillsides and using electric cable chairs to reach their doors.

I knew that there were big sharks close to shore, but people were swimming unafraid at the Beaches. The water is very cold.

Biking on the way to Masterton which is the sheep shearing Capital of the world for the Championship for the sheep shearing championship There are 60 million sheep or so.

On to the Ferry to the South Island.

Which I thought would be warm, oh no it was windy and cold. But so close to Antarctica.

The Ferry passengers relaxed in reclining chairs. It was a very stormy crossing, and I worried about getting seasick.

On arriving in Havelock, the wind was blowing, and I had to get used to it. It never stopped. Cycling through the most beautiful Fruit growing country for 26 miles brought unending surprises-a charming little teashop or an ice-cream seller. Plants and Bird life, I never had seen before. The roads are paved quite different and are called "metal". These metal roads were not smooth, more like bluestone. So, a lot of mountain climbing. I was happy to have 15 gears. There were no bike trails, but no traffic either. A big herd of Sheep or cows occasionally blocked the road, making it difficult to squeeze through.

At night I trekked up a mountain to see the Glowworms, Spooky to look at all around me. A lot like Christmas lights.

One day, like a gift from heaven, I found a bag of fresh bread on the road and ate most of it. It must have fallen out of a car, a gift from heaven.

At the beach near Nelson I stopped for a swim, (cold!) Even in bright sunshine. I acquired a nice sheepskin saddle pad for my bike, and it felt good.

Restaurant food was exceptionally good. Venison always on the Menu and for dessert Pavlova. The national Dessert of N.Z.

All through the fruit growing region on the South Island, I could not help eating fresh peaches and Kiwi fruit. I finally learned how Kiwi grow. It was then a new fruit on the market.

Then through the Marlborough sound to the west coast, passing the Buller Gorge which is famous for the White river.

It continued to rain and sometimes I hitched a ride on a truck or a Bus.

It rained so much all my clothes were damp and I hung them from my handlebars to dry. It was the southern winter; the lodges had no heat, and it was cold.

Reaching the Greymouth area and saw the Sea Lion Colony with the sun again.

Pancake Rocks was next, a different Rock formation with big Blowholes. Again, the scenery was beautiful.

Arriving near the famous Franz Josef Glacier. And as usual the scenery by bike was beautiful. Except on one of the Railroad bridges I had my first spill. At my next stop I went to the Chemist and had myself cleaned up.

At the Franz Josef Glacier, I started trekking the great Bush tracks up the hills. And later tried Helicopter hiking in the snowfields. On the way up saw the strangest Goat type animal called Thar or tahr. Big and beautiful with exceedingly long hair.

But at the bottom, again it rains, it does make biking difficult. And having to go over three mountain passes in the rain again wore me down!

Now on to Fox Glacier where I parked my bike to view the scenery. There we were warned that the Mountain parrot called Kea loves tires or anything they can destroy. So luckily my bike was not lunch since there were enough cars in the parking lot to be torn apart.

To Haast Pass in a sunny sky and in sheep grazing country of central Otago. For miles one never sees stores or any place to get food. Farms had driveways 10 miles long. I carried much of my snacks in my bags. The west coast people looked very hardy since they spend a lot outdoors with the sheep.

The Hotels I stayed had all Restaurants and the food was always excellent. Always was particularly good wine served with dinner. In the rooms always was hot tea or coffee with real cream. But no heat. So again, one started biking with wet cloth. Lots of Rainforest to see too. And many Mosquito's and Sand flies are in attack mode.

Many times, a truck or car would offer a ride, but it was ok to bike.

Then inland to Wanaka along deserted Roads again to famous Queenstown, the town with every sport available.

It was hard to decide what to do first. I enjoyed beautiful scenery during a horseback ride way up into the mountains. The Horse was a standard bred, which gave me an exceptionally smooth ride. Not enough time here.

An Excursion on the TSS Earnslaw built in 1912 a vintage steamship, on the lake below Queenstown. On the return trip I watched the stoker working by hand to fill the boiler. The ship had a speed of 13 knots. It took us to a Sheep station, called Mt. Nicholas, 100 000 acres large. Where they raised 250 000 Merino sheep and 2000 head of cattle. There we could watch the sheep dogs working and the sheepshearers as they clipped the fleece.

Back in Queenstown I took a train ride on the Kingston Flyer, built in 1900, all first class.

Both the ship and train had come from Europe disassembled and had to be put together in Queenstown.

And then off to Milford Sound. The southern Fjords! Trekking a place, I have had read about and now within my reach. On the final stretch by boat. The Mountains go straight into the sea with lots of waterfalls. The high point is Mitre Peak at 1694 meters. It is so called because it resembles the head of a Bishop's formal head piece.

In Queenstown, the most delicious dinners can be had on top at the Skylight Restaurant. It is famous for their Pavlova dessert, which is served in 30 different types.

One gets there by lift, which is one of the steepest lifts in the world and took only 4 minutes for 2400 feet.

On the road again over the Lindi-pass, a very deserted-looking land. Stopped at a cattle drome to see many different breeds of cattle.

Stopped at a sheep station (farm) with a 5-mile driveway and thought I never would get there and did have an interesting time. Not many visitors come by bike, never did, and I was very welcomed. Many men were shearing sheep; The shearers worked so fast, each animal was done in no time.

The headwind on the road to Twizel made biking very tough.

At Lake Pukaki and Mt. Cook we stayed at the Hermitage. A historical Hotel, a skier's paradise in the winter. The Bar at night entertainment was listening to climber's tales about the mountain.

At last, I had some easy and fun biking along Tekapo Canal. 25 miles and only a 3-foot elevation rise alongside a canal cut through the mountains. I reveled in great weather and the constant view of snowcapped mountains. At the end of trail is the little Church of the Good Shephard.

A little stop at a winery called Barkers Wines.

Arriving in Christchurch. Everything was going on at one time. Saw the band Dire Straits-wonderful sound. Christchurch looks like a very beautiful English city, with the Avon River meandering right through town. With big Willow Trees hanging above the water.

Full of bicycles traveling along tree lined Roads next to the Avon River.

One of the most interesting Museums in the world had an exhibit of the 1912 Antarctica Exhibition of Robert Scott, even his Tent and his diary. One could really feel the pain of the men in the frozen state in which they were found.

New Zealand was exceptionally clean.

Fiji

To Fiji on my trip eastward again. Arriving in Fiji from New Zealand. Spending time in Nadi, a town. And I am ready for the Islands and choose Malololailai Plantation Island by speedboat. The place to be, to relax, lots of clear water and lots of fish. Palm trees to sit under and once a while having a good coconut brought for drinking the juice.

The Lovo, dinner, last night was delicious. All food grown there. Lots of fish.

There is another Island which can be reached at low tide by foot and forded the sandbar. I did try to go and saw only wilderness. Not enough time to hike too far that late.

There is lots to do at the Hotel. Crab races, Volleyball, Frog-races. Fijians are very friendly, natural and fun loving.

But I had to try the next Island again at low tide, three hours of walking brought me to a village where the chief invited me to partake of tea.

On my walk back home, I stopped at a home and was again invited by a couple who are trying to grow pineapples for the market. It did not look very prosperous, as rain is sparse on the Island and it is hot. But I made lifelong friends with them. The Sovas.

That night everybody went out to see Haley's comet.

Swimming at night and just lazing in daytime what a life!

"Bula" we all say to each other. It can be used in many ways. "Hi" or" happiness". The accommodations are thatched roof Bures,

Longhouses. Many people fit into, but it is cheap. The only bad part is the snoring. We saw lots of Lizards crawling all over. They keep the mosquitoes in check. Sometimes a Lizard would fall from the ceiling and land on top of a sleeper producing a scream and funny moment until we all fell asleep again.

Once more, at low tide to the little Island again to say goodbye to my new friends the Sova's. We have become very good friends and have visited each other since then in the USA or Australia.

Next day I went on a little plane, a Britten Norman Highlander to Sigatoka. The passengers were weighed on a bathroom scale-not the luggage, the people only.

Took the Bus around Viti Levu and stopped at many places. Loved the "Hide-a way Hotel" and went back again there on my next trips. At night we had a Meke, which is the Fijians entertainment, lots of singing and trying to drink Kava, which to me taste awful.

The saying here is: There are two reasons for drinking: one is when you are thirsty to cure it, the other, when you are not thirsty to prevent it…prevention is better than cure.

The ever-changing landscape is sugarcane. Palm trees with nuts on it. Since Copra used to be the economy of Fiji but is changing more into Agriculture.

Suva is the Capital. Getting there was not easy since the Bus had a leaky Radiator, we had to stop constantly to refill it.

Suva is hot and humid. The town is busy and full of people. The men wear skirts! It must be a leftover from the British.

Went to the Grand Pacific Hotel for afternoon tea and air-condition. It was built in 1913 and very English style.

My last dinner in Suva was a big crab with taro and coconut sauce. Very tasty and eaten with fingers.

By Bus to "Sea Shell Hotel" to Sciatica, a beautiful place, but the open sea was too hot there to swim. It was killing all the undersea world.

We cooled off in the pool.

There are Gecko's all over and they talk to each other and whipped their tails to express themselves.

As usual Dinner was fish fresh from the sea. And if you did not watch out Geckos would go right into a beer bottle to have a drink. So, lots of fun here but I was slowed down by a bad cold.

I have the worst cold here and hope it will be better soon.

There was a Beach nearby called Nataldola. Miles of Beach, sand and no people. The clearest water. I wonder now how many Hotels are there.

Israel, March 11, 1986

A quick trip to Israel on Hapag Lloyd. A wild arrival since I had not planned of time. I used a people taxi filled with 8 persons but room for 4 only. And driving in the direction to Jerusalem was a surprise seeing so many tanks and military vehicles by the roadside. Later I learned that these left as a memorial from the previous conflict.

The land was so rocky I wondered what possible grow could there. I wondered how many plow blades broke all the time.

My travels took me to Nazareth, Tiberias, Galilee, Golan Heights, Capernaum, the Jordan River, which is so small I would call it a creek.

Then to Massada. Ascent by cable car. Unbelievable place. So much History there.

Next to Ein Gedi for the Spa and a dip in the very salty Dead Sea. So salty!

Jericho, the oldest and lowest city in the world was next. And then back to Jerusalem. I did a lot of walking. That is the only way to see all the old buildings, the eight Gates of the old city, David's Tower and the Citadel. And the old Jewish Quarters with the Wailing wall. The City is full of life with Pilgrims from all over the world and the Vendors trying to sell anything. It was a cacophony of languages.

Outside the Gates I saw beautiful Horses, beautiful Arabians. And then home again.

Jamaica, March 24, 1987
South America
Chile, Argentina, Uruguay

On our way south Kevin, my Husband, and I flew over Jamaica and decided to stay there a few days. We rented a villa in Montego Bay on the Ironshore and luxuriated in the warm breeze wafting through the house. We have started to practice our Spanish which we need now on the next flight to Peru.

Arrival in Peru

Lima again was interesting as I could show Kevin places I had been before.

On the flight to Cusco the pilot decided to fly over Machu Picchu. What fantastic view especially for me since I had bicycled it three years before. We could clearly see the steep Road I biked on to the top of the mountain

Hotel Picoaga in Cusco was our rest stop. An old hacienda furnished with Antiques. From there we set off to Sasquehunan to see the workmanship of the Incas.

I noticed that the Indian population was not working the terraced fields anymore. Their new occupation was standing beside the Roadside with llamas posing for tourists' cameras, bringing a better income than growing maize (corn).

So many woolens can be bought in the stores in Cusco. Can all this be made in Peru?

We had our altitude headache today. I guess we did not drink enough coca tea. We filled ourselves with all the medicines and dragged ourselves to wander around the city.

Next morning, we took the train to Machu Picchu. Not the public train I used a few years ago; but the luxury train. Then from the station up to the ruins we rode a minibus.

I enjoyed it more this time since I was rested and had time to think how hard it was for the Inka's to build it.

We stayed overnight in the Hotel next to the ruins. We were the only tourists there after three o'clock. And we had the ruins for us alone to see.

Daylight came late when the sun finally rose over the mountains. We were alone again to enjoy the silence.

Kevin climbed Waynapichu by himself as it was too slippery for me. I have great memories now thinking about this place.

On the way down we could see the Urubamba River running along and through all that wilderness somebody built the Railroad, with switchbacks all the way to Puente Ruinas.

We returned by train to cusco where we fought our headaches with tea. The 400-year-old Hotel Picacoaga was nice, and the beds were new.

Trying to return from Cusco to Lima was frustrating. Three times we were send back to the Hotel because the Airplane from Lima could not land.

Finally, we landed in Mira Flores, a suburb of Lima. At sea level again we were able to sleep better. Visited the Gold Museum, full of treasures the Spaniards missed in their looting.

Then we sat through another delay because of the Pope's arrival. So, we started to enjoy a few Pisco Sours. We finally got our plane to Pachacamac for more sightseeing. There I saw a few of the famous hairless dogs.

Santiago, Chile

What a different place from Lima! Santiago looked and felt very European. We stayed in Vina del Mar, a big beach town, and picnicked in Valparaiso.

Something made Kevin sick enough to stay in bed. I went to see the Pope, who just arrived in Santiago. If only I had known what I was getting into- a walk of eight km, always uphill, to catch a Bus for another mile, then walked again two more miles with a throng of 300 000 people. Police on Horses kept everybody in line.

Kevin was lucky to be sick.

We went north to Marbella to visit the hacienda of Don Miguel, who greeted us in his Vaquero outfit. Many Chileans are of German descent, and it was no surprise that we spoke German while at the Hacienda.

It is one of the largest avocado Ranches and exporters to the USA. Next to the old hacienda is a German Fachhaus brought from Germany by ship and is over 500 years old.

We went sightseeing in Valparaiso again. It is built on very steep hills with lots of Elevators to reach the different levels of the city.

Then we returned to Santiago. This time, a lot of smog in the air. Pollution is strong and the sand from the desert blown in on top of it.

It was hard saying goodbye to Kevin as he is still not well and will have to visit a doctor soon. And my plans are going on to Argentina.

Argentina

I continued on my adventure to Argentina, and was very glad to learn that Kevin got good care in USA on arrival.

It was a beautiful flight over the Andes to Buenos Aires. From the Air, Argentina is green.

At the airport I shared a taxi with a pilot and a passenger. The passenger was on a business trip and paid for our taxi. Lucky again.

Walking around town trying to find a backpacker place which was right next to the Waldorf Hotel in the best area of Buenos Aires.

Florida Avenue reminded me of Paris, France. Street performers making music everywhere all over. The finest stores, and so much to enjoy.

Buenos Aires has had no significant earthquakes, and all the old Houses are well preserved. The city is filled with very big old trees, like a European city. A great place for walking!

Uruguay, 1987

Tomorrow off to Uruguay. It is raining again and by Hoover craft to Colonia, Uruguay across the Rio de la Plata. It was very stormy, and I was ready to use the "seasick bag" provided by the Stewardess. Took 1 1/2 hours.

From Colonia by Luxury Bus along the coast to Montevideo. Which again took 3 ½ hours. On these beautiful roads I wished I was on a bike because there was no traffic at all, many Horses and old cars from the 30's. A very hilly country and very green with lots of cattle in the fields. It reminded me of North Germany. And found out lots of Germans settled here for that reason.

The Hotel Lancaster was very reasonable and old and nice and had great food.

Montevideo, again, a walking city. The Capitol was very impressive, like the Capitol in Washington, D.C. Seeing the famous monument "La Carreta" (Covered Wagon).

I was only a few days there and returned to Buenos Aires by Hoover craft on a most beautiful day with a very quiet sea this time.

Argentina

Buenos Aires again, so exciting. Eating Steak like an Argentine at 11:30pm. I spend my time walking around the town listening to music, not resting much.

April, and the Pope is now here too. I am avoiding the crowds now and taking trips out of town—Rio del Mar. To see the countryside there. I had dinner at an estancia where they basted whole goats on the spit for hours. I admired the beautiful buildings and the cemetery Recoleta where Evita Peron is buried there since her death in 1952. It is still a holiday for all Argentines of her death.

Iguazu Falls is the meeting point of Argentina, Brazil and Paraguay. Trying to catch a plane from Buenos Aires to Iguazu resulted in another tangle with the Pope. I had to hike five kilometers, no taxis, because the Pope was leaving, and no other plane could take off before his. I finally got away and arrived at Iguazu and thrilled to the great views as the plane flew low over tea plantations and trees and more trees. The tiny town of Puerto Iguazu is on the Argentine side of the falls. Right above the falls I found a cliff restaurant overlooking Paraguay and Brazil, an interesting junction of three countries. We diners toasted it with a great drink made with fresh pineapple.

Frogs so large, jumped all over. At least 20 inches around. Toucans flew over and many other strange birds. Butterflies were everywhere. I called it the Mariposa place since the restaurant was called Tres Frontera's.

On April 12. after a good sleep and good food, I was off to Las Cataratas de Iguazu, passing many tea plantations, a national Park belonging to Argentina. The guides spoke extremely fast Spanish and in the noise of the Waterfalls I could hardly understand anything.

And again, a good dinner with the most beautiful view.

Next day I went to the Brazilian side of the falls, not an easy venture. I had to meet the Brazilian Ambassador who was living near the Border to get a visa. On my way I stopped quickly in Paraguay and on the biggest Hydro plant I have ever seen and stopped quickly in Paraguay in a very uncivilized border town. Everything on the streets was for sale. I was told almost all cars there had been stolen and then brought quickly into Paraguay. I bought great stuff cheap. I went to see the Paraguay Zoo because I was told it had the biggest Eagle there. A Harpy Eagle.

The view of Iguazu falls on the Brazilian side is better to see from the bottom up. It is higher here than Niagara and it is 275 different Falls, the largest system of falls in the world. The Devil's Gorge is 200 feet deep, and the noise of the waters can be heard for miles.

I stayed in the Hotel Esturion, very large and beautiful.

The flight back to Buenos Aires was a very rough ride again because of storms. I swore I am not going to fly again.

So now I am on my Quest to reach Esperanza in the western part of Argentina, Cordoba is the biggest Town there, by train from Buenos Aires. I have had a wonderful great- aunt living in Esperanza. She was Mother Superior of the Convento Christo Ray. She had been a very guiding light for our family after the war. I had stayed in touch with one of the Sisters Hermana. Adelaide (G.Schastok my great aunt).until she died 26.10.1975.

I promised her I would visit her one day, but she died before I could take my trip. For my first Communion in the 50s a beautiful dress arrived in the mail from her when I was little. The nuns of the Convent invited me to come anyway.

Argentina is a huge land, and I am on a long train ride! We had to pull down the iron shutters to prevent bandits from smashing the windows. It was supposed to take six hours to Santa Fe, but after eight hours I was told maybe three hours more, but eight hours have gone already by and was told maybe three or four hours more. I did not bring enough food and was starving since I had not eaten breakfast and only candy in my bag. Fortunately, then people on the train noticed I had no food and was offered food from my seat mates.

Arriving in the middle of the night, everything in Santa Fe was closed at that hour. But everybody helped. I was helped onto a taxi now to find a Hotel and my "new friends" instructed the driver not to drive in Circles with me just straight to the Hotel Zavaleta. It still was difficult to wake somebody there to give me a room, difficult for me to make people understand since my Spanish somehow got lost so late at night in my brain.

The next morning, the taxi came as arranged to take me to Esperanca, an hour away. The Driver knew where to go, and I was delivered to the door of the Convento. All the nuns greeted me in German. And I was made to feel at home.

I slept and ate well and strolled through the gardens to see Sister Adabalda's grave. She died in 1975 at age 86.

The nuns told me what my great-aunt was like and what she did, to help the poor. I recognized their old Silesian dialects as most of the nuns came from Ratibor, now named Raciborz in southern Poland.

The young nuns were Argentines and already learning German. Sister Leomitis took care of me and introduced me to everybody.

We had good food, and I was told wine usually was only served on holidays and all were happy to drink it because I gave the occasion to celebrate.

In the afternoon, everybody had mate tea. I never learned to like it funny to see the Nuns in their habits drinking it from a silver cup through a silver sipper.

I slept well and deeply and at 6:30am it was beautiful to awaken to the singing of the nuns and organ music. And again, good food. A walk one more time to say goodbye. Sister Leomitis, my unofficial tour guide, made me feel so very welcome.

The nuns insisted that I eat a huge breakfast so I would not go hungry on the train, and they packed bags of provisions to keep me on my long trip back to Buenos Aires.

Back in Buenos Aires and enjoying once again Florida Avenue. The Music!

Now it was time to visit friends nearby. My friends did show me a little different culture of the working people. Francisco, the head of Labor Union at that time, gave me a very good tour of what they have accomplished.

We stopped at Estancia El Mangrullo which has been owned by the same family over many generations. A Restaurant is there and many fine Horses.

The owner showed me a most wonderful trained group of Horses. Standing in a big field, he told me to remain still. When he called, ten black Horses came galloping toward us, then stopped and stood still in line right in front of me. How did he do it? Training and practice. I was offered a very nice Horse to ride, so smooth.

In the meantime, a small revolution in the suburbs of Buenos Aires and everybody was a little nervous but calm came overnight. Was told by the American Embassy to collect at the Airport for needed transport but it was all false alarm.

Chile

On April 17 I returned to Santiago, Chile again. My friends picked me up at the airport and we went to a Picnic in Valparaiso, having a great time letting kites' fly.

We went to Portillo, which has been on my list to see for a long time. I was still skiing at that time and wanted to see the bleakest ski resort on earth. The drive to get there is all hairpin curves, and scary to drive.

Skiing there was scary too. Straight down hardly any intermediate grades-not for me. There was plenty of snow, average 60 feet a year, but the altitude was hard on the lungs.

From the town I walked up to San Cristobal Hill for a great view of Santiago.

I took my time walking the streets looking for the places I have read about, in all the stories of Isabell Allende's books. She writes so clearly you can find all the places she describes. It is a city of poor people. Nothing flashy like Buenos Aires.

But the wines are so good, and I enjoyed lots of fish which is so fresh from the lakes and Ocean.

Today I went to Concha y Toro's vineyards. The white wines did taste good to me. It was founded in 1883.

On my way back I saw the place where the dictator Augusto Pinochet was ambushed last autumn. A big stone is marking the spot.

I returned home via Lima, Peru. Compared to the other cities I saw it is very dirty here, but it has great Pisco sours, which I enjoyed while waiting for my flight to USA.

Switzerland, November 1987

A business trip of my husband Kevin turned into a very great sightseeing trip for me.

Nine days of driving around and discovering this beautiful country. It was my first time there and I was astounded by how pricey everything was. Only problem was instead of snow lots of rain. We tried to drive almost to all the little villages and drove through many Tunnels. There were trains going in all direction and I wanted to be on them to see places they could go. I never forget when we stayed in a small Hotel near a train track, which turned into a surprise for us to see the trains going in many serpentines up and down we could see from our window. We did not get much sleep that night.

Guatemala, January 23, 1988

My short visit to Guatemala was to learn Spanish.

The plane is full of returning Guatemalans. It looks like I am the only tourist. A lot of helpful places to visit were given to me. I arrived but my luggage did not. My driver did not come either, I felt I am starting out with trouble to come.

I was enrolled in a school in Antigua. So, I had to bargain for a taxi ride to Antigua. A beautiful 45 minutes' drive.

The countryside was interesting. Green, lush and very hilly.

Antigua is old and so full of history. There are 32 churches, and one was more beautiful than the other. The 1775 Earthquake pretty much destroyed the city. And many buildings after all these years are still lying there in rubble. Antigua was once the capital of Guatemala, built in 1543, but now Guatemala City is the seat for the Government.

The people who stayed behind in Antigua rebuilt only needed homes and left the churches and monasteries to the weather.

In 1976 another Earthquake destroyed the city again and only one-story buildings are in existence. My walking around showed me the grandeur of old Spain in the ruins.

The weather is always eternal spring and autumn. Flowers are everywhere. And cool at night. Did not have the right cloth for this and had to acquire some pullovers. I was too thin dressed for the nights. I checked out the school today, seems to be run by nice people. All teachers are Mayans Indians.

A few days later my suitcase came finally, good old Eastern Airlines.

Wherever one walks in Antigua one can see the big volcano. Maybe I will find time to climb it.

But first I had to find the school and enroll and meet my teacher. Lessons are taught one on one. There are many nationalities here. Any age of students.

The teacher Miriam is very patient with me and never rolls her eyes even when I forgot what I knew 30 minutes ago. I am not used to sitting so long and was happy when the first break came. The classrooms are open to the air which I love. There are birds singing all over the school.

At lunchtime I left to go shopping in the market with my teacher. Everybody speaks slow Spanish to help me understand. Great. But the nights are so cold, never was I so cold before. My residence ran out of blankets. But was told by noon it will be warmer.

Classes have become exceedingly difficult now. Verbs...

A big bird, Great Curassow, is sitting on school fence, almost like a peacock. The sound it makes is like a bell.

At night, the town was quiet. Little electric lights but I felt walking around safe. In the daytime I try to investigate the courtyards. Behind the big walls are beautiful Gardens with so many flowers. I love the walk to school, meeting a lot of people and everybody says nice greetings. "Buenos Dias". And the men tip their hats.

Now I can have a conversation and feel I am getting into the Spanish language. I have a heater now and more blankets. The cold is here to stay. Stomach problems have bothered a lot of the students. I am still ok.

I got a bicycle now from a new friend I met on the plane, he brought it to me all the way from Guatemala City. I cannot believe sometimes how lucky I am. It is a little difficult biking here since all the roads are cobblestone.

Traveling for a few days to Tikal. It is important for me to see that area too. I will miss school for a few days.

As I looked around all the Spanish schools are filled up with tourist to learn. Amazing.

Flying now from G.C. to Tikal, a short flight. But a cloudy sky, too bad. At Flores I am staying on the Island, situated on the Lake del Peten. Called the Maya Intl. Hotel Santa Helena. All built on stilts over the lake reachable on walkways over the water to Bungalows.

There are always fireworks going off and I think it is shooting. Why do people like it? It is a deafening noise over the water.

My Dinner was great.

Bird life is fantastic and so many strange ones.

By Bus to Tikal, 65 km on a dirt Road. Wild countryside and meeting a few soldiers carrying Rifles.

Tikal is the first Mayan structure I experienced. It is so impressive to just look at it on entering the place. There are many Structures of the Mayan's in Central America. Monkeys in the trees are staring at us.

Climbing up the Temple was a bad idea, I could not get the nerve to go down again, it was too steep for me. Finally convinced by a soldier to go backwards and holding on to a chain, 96 steps slow. As I walked around, I found many more temples but never climbed again.

Back again at the Lake Hotel and I went to a smaller Restaurant. Food was delicious but a filthy place. An Ocelot (small wild cat) was walking around, and a Raccoon kept climbing on every table. Parrott's and Monkeys hung around too. I loved all the animals.

By boat to a little Island on the lake where there is a small Zoo. Black shiny and sleepy Jaguars in pens and lots of Birds. Then to the Caves Acun Can. I do not like caves, but this one was big on the inside.

Back in Guatemala City, being hassled by everybody and the last Bus to Antigua left already. The usual bargaining again for my ride to Antigua.

So now school again but with a new teacher, we did seven hours of conversation if only I could understand the different verbs!

Of all things I got a tooth infection and starting antibiotics.

Today, February seventh, the day when all Christmas trees are taken out of the houses for the big burning fiesta.

In the meantime, I finally climbed the Volcano Cero de la Cruz. Good exercise and great views from the top. But a very dusty climb.

Walking around Antigua again to see all the beautiful churches like San Francisco, built in 1543 destroyed in the 1773 earthquake and partially rebuilt.

The middle Plaza is the social center of Antigua with a beautiful fountain—La Serena, built in 1738. And all-around people with firecrackers making noise. The start of the fiesta, first preaching and prayers and many candles are lit. And now with music, more noise.

Another day trip to Chichicastenango, an enormous open-air market, it is the largest in Guatemala, noted for its excellent produce as well indigenous arts and crafts.

My time is almost over, and I try to cram as many classes into my days. At the cemetery in Antigua, which is known for elaborate designs, I enjoyed a few hours. It is almost like a city.

Now almost everybody is sick in school. I think it is the sandwiches we eat. No refrigeration is used.

I still can go swimming and feeling better.

I am doing better in school, and it is amazing the many languages spoken one can hear from the people in the school from all over the world. I loved the Classes and people and especially the teachers.

South Korea, Hongkong, China, April 25, 1988

At check-in at Korean Air, plane was overbooked. But the problem was solved. And we are off finally on our planned bike trip through China with a stop in South Korea first.

I met my friend Gail and her friend Sol. I sat between two babies, a horror, but could finally change seats.

I collected as much information from all my seatmates who were going to South Korea what we could do in three days. 14 hours of reading and talking on the plane and on top we lost a day.

Kimpo airport just opened three days ago, a big beautiful place.

My chosen Y or backpacker stay place was luxury. Even bellboys who carried our luggage, so clean and all this for $7 a night.

We ate at a real Korean family place but needed help in translating what we wanted to eat. I knew noodles. They are the best in Korea.

So little time here, we walked all over Soul, took the subway to some places. Everybody tried to help. One looks at a map and right away help is there; people even crossed the street just to show us which way.

Somehow, we ended up having eye examination and bought reading glasses which I still have. To the big market for Tampopo soup.

Anything can be bought at this enormous market. From clocks to noodles. Even snakes, cats and dogs which are supposed to taste like chicken.

To the Samson Tower next up by cable car. But no photos since it is Government property. Up on top a very good Beer was for sale.

Then I had to go on a little hike since Gail and Sol were a little tired.

There are many temples and still traditional dress are worn there. The traditional dress is very colorful.

I noticed that the country was exceptionally clean. People always were out cleaning or using the broom. Too short a time because so much to see but had to get ready for our 5am flight to Hong Kong.

Hong Kong

Another stopover. On our flight to Hong Kong, we had Knockwurst! German food? So now we gained one hour again on arrival. Landing was so exciting. Right and left the houses almost touched the wings. It felt like flying along a street. And hot after cold Korea—90 degrees.

Just getting to know the city is fun. It is a walking city; I had been here before and knew my way around pretty well. We took ferries, buses, taxis and subways. My friends are tired by now.

Went to Aberdeen to look around on the double-decker Bus. And then by a sampan to the "Jumbo" Restaurant. A fairytale boat.

Having eaten particularly good food, back to Kowloon to our "Y" which was perfect, next to the Peninsular Hotel. The Peninsular Hotel was a most luxury Hotel and was connected by a little Ally to our very reasonable priced "Y".

It must be the rainy season, so much came down today. But then after reviving Sol, who needed his sleep we walked Nathan Street, which is all shops for 3 miles long.

Had a hard time sleeping with two snorers', slept in the Bathtub the remaining hours. Today I am trying for my own room. Great food and then walking off at Nathan Street again.

There is the Jade market and vegetable market and tanks full of fish. The city does not sleep, always something going on. We used every minute to see more of the outlying places too.

People say here "If you cannot find it in Hong Kong, then it does not exist.

China, April 30, 1988

Flying now to Beijing China. Going through so much security, it took a toll on my photos. From now on we fly China Air.

The pilots must have been Air force fighter they way the fly.

At security's many questions are asked: Diarrhea, Jaundice, Lymph-gland swelling, vomiting, Fever, Rash, Cough, sore throat, bleeding, Psychosis? Leprosy, Aids, Venereal disease, active pulmonary tuberculosis and other diseases, having all this who would say yes?

Flying over China not much to see just fog. There was no order or standing in line, getting off the plane was all pushing.

In the arrival Hall could not recognize our guide I hired, since everybody was Chinese. Chen finally connected with us. We were not difficult to pick out of the mass of people.

Driving into Beijing was interesting. The 20 miles of long straight streets were planted with flowers and beautiful trees on each side. All other spaces were vegetables. Many fields of rice.

And then there was Beijing, gray. Our Hotel was nice. The Restaurant had the best food and delicious.

Visited my friends that day, the parents of one of my exchange students. They were surprised since they did expect me a day later.

There is a coaldust in the air and the yellow sand from the Gobi Desert gets into the eyes. Not good when wearing glasses. By 8 am we had our first big sandstorm. It went into eyes and teeth. But people are used to it, life goes on here. Told there are 250 million bicycles. We went to see Mao in his open shrine. Long lines and us foreigners stood out.

Tiananmen Square is supposed to be the biggest public square in the world. Standing in line everywhere we had to finally find a toilet. No such thing. Just a wall to go behind. And what a stink, but it is used as fertilizer and not flushed away.

I noticed there were no dogs running around. It was against the law to own one.

And next to the Palace of Heavenly Harmony, another palace to impress the next emperor.

Finally, to the Forbidden City or Imperial City, so much to see there. One great Building after another, courtyards and Halls. Even a clock museum with the trickiest Clocks I have ever seen. The last Emperor was a clock collector and always had to have the newest clock. It is a lot to see in one day.

Had tonight our first roasted Duck in the "Roasted Duck Restaurant". So good!

Food is very good, but it is served very fast. From the kitchen to the round wheel in the middle of the table and one must snatch the food fast or it is gone. My favorites are all kinds of dumplings.

Table manners are next to none. People do spit a lot and cough. At the table smacking, open mouth eating, picking the teeth or spitting on the floor is expected.

There are many spittoons everywhere, but they look disgusting.

Today I went to my friends the Wei family. Everybody was waiting. A ridiculously small Apartment with too many people. But everybody was happy and thankful their daughters found a good home in USA with me. Mrs. Wei did not speak one word of English, but she talked to me all night and somehow, I knew what she was saying even without translating help. Old Grandmother sat on a perch and smiled all night never said a word. I was allowed to see her bound feet. Amazing what the custom was doing to a woman to look beautiful. Anytime "Old lady" had to go to the toilet or anything she wanted she had to be carried because her feet were totally useless.

We are biking now and are very hungry in the evening. Chinese food does not make you fat. Even the noodles were never enough. We almost always stormed the dining room or food table on arriving. But not all food was what I liked. One had to watch. There were French fries which turned into chicken toes, deep-fried.

Mayday in China! Red flags everywhere and 11 million bikes on the Road and we are too. What fun.

Today we went to the Great Wall; since the days are long, we can do a lot in one day. We did see from our Bus a dead cyclist hit by a car. That is unusual, I was told bikes have the right of way. Fruit trees and food is growing on both sides again along the Roads. Ponies and Mules are pulling heavy loads.

At the Great Wall I was surprised how big and fat the Camels were. Two humps. Seeing the Wall was impressive. Having read a lot about it and was surprised how wide it was. And so steeply built right on top of the Rocks.

But every human who had a day off must have been there too. It was like a shoving match. And all the Humans made photos and hoped to get us into a photo too. I wonder how the Mongolian young men explain when they get home, how the encountered us. Especially Gail and I were a head taller than anybody and blond hair.

From talking with people there, they had only good feelings for America. "Love America" was the saying. And slowly we picked a few words out to understand each other.

At the Ming tombs I was surprised again how much underground was there just for Mausoleums for each Emperor.

Biking in Beijing again, there are special Roads just for bikes, Cars are not important. (Different now). There is a certain speed, all move in unison. Always looking at what is in front never back. One stops, everybody falls on top. Which happened to Gail when she decided to take a photo. Nobody got mad many Apologies!

The Wei family came to pick me up with an extra bike and gave me a private tour. Then lunch, 15 different dishes all cooked in a mini kitchen. Mr. Wei cooked especial fish. And it tasted fantastic.

Out on the street, parents were walking their only child dressed in the best cloth just to show off. If it was a girl she was all dressed in red.

And I noticed that there were no old trees, only in the palace. All of them were used to heat or cook. But now millions of trees have been planted.

We are catching the train now in the huge Beijing train Station and then to find the right compartment. Nothing is written in English. And the train left at the minute.

We were assigned 1st class bedrooms. Silk bedspreads, lace curtains on the windows, fresh flowers and hot water under the table for tea. There are Slippers next to it. The cleaning is not so good somehow, soap is missing.

The dining room is full of activity with lots of strangers. We had steam Engines pulling our train. And again, the food served for Dinner was the best.

The beds were wonderfully comfortable with down beds and lace pillows. I acquired my pillows for a certain price to take home after the finish.

Gail and Sol's bedroom companions was a Chinese General who was very sick, and our guide Li was in their top bed with the flu. Sol was very unhappy. But the General was getting better with his wife's herbal compresses.

I slept beautiful.

I love the sound of a train, puts me to sleep.

Morning awaited us again with a very good breakfast which was Chinese. There must be 1000 ways to cook vegetables.

Nanjing

Getting on our Bicycles at the train station and an exceedingly long ride through the hills. Who said there are only flat Roads?

The City Walls of Nanjing are about 30 meters, or 90 feet high. How much labor went into that? Nanjing Hotel was nice with nice Chambermaids who brought us hot cloth to get the sweat of our faces.

Tried the dancing Hall in evening but too tired and off to sleep.

From Nanjing we took a Bus and then started biking in the

countryside again but then the Rain came.

Many times, we could hear loudspeakers in the Distance along the fields. They are the communications to the Country-people and workers in the field. The news, weather and I am sure propaganda.

A Farmhouse off the Road looked inviting and I suggested we stop there. Incredibly surprised Farmers welcomed us into their "best" room. No, we did not understand them and neither did they. But we got along using hands.

The room was concrete Floor, big but cold. There was a big bed a chest and a bench.

The Kitchen was the storage for farm food and for all the other vegetables which could be kept. As I understood it, they can grow as much as they want to and sell it for profit. I showed the Lady my supply of Candy which she finally accepted. At least we got out of the rain for a while.

Did the final stretch by Bus. We biked only 25 miles. The Bus was very good and our service Truck we had hired was always somewhere behind us. We are told there are no dangerous animals on the Road or fields. And no mice, no rabbits, no squirrels because everything is food and has been eaten.

As we pedaled again the next day, we noticed that we always had a new guide added, telling us about the new towns We followed the Yangtze River from Nanjing, Lheiying, Changshou, Wuxi, Huaxie, Sushou to Shanghai.

Our Bus is owned by the Bike provider, so we are in great hands. We got new bikes called Gia Dao Bikes, not the flying Pigeon which we had tried already. Brakes were Disk.

To a Lake called Slender Lake-Shouxi, and the biggest bike traffic we encountered here, to a Jade Factory.

There was a Garden, which was once owned by a Salt Merchant who spend so much money to build this elaborate place. All four seasons growing were planted.

And many Pagodas this day we passed.

That evening we had instructions on Chinese painting. Tried to do a Horse...

Then some Chinese music, Mandolin, Flute, Guitar with one string, a drummer and a big violin.

We all got dressed in old Chinese outfits. Like an Empress and Sol made photos, as we felt very regal.

And later I had a very good massage by a young man, but he did not do toes. Wonder why, I love toe massages.

We are now in Zhenijang in the Jinshan Hotel. It is beautiful. Palm trees, vegetation like Florida. And many Birds finally. There is the sound of Pigeons outside I always enjoy.

We biked 18km, it felt longer; Streets are a cacophony of bleating trucks or Bus Horns. Ringing Bicycles horns, bells and a fall, which Sol was involved. He is not doing so well with so many people.

We passed Rice fields, many fishponds and endless wheat fields. Yellow Frogs Calling for mates all along the dikes on the canals. Females are black and twice as big.

Then we saw the Farmers herding their Geese and ducks. Water Buffalos doing heavy work. But the men do heavy work, the loads they carry on their backs!

The traffic is always the same since it is staggered on off days. No Weekends.

They Yangtze River is in sight many times; the whole area is called the" Land of fish and rice" and how true. That is what we ate a lot. The fish is always alive to the last moment before cooking.

Now we crossed the Yangtze River. So much like the old paintings. Boats everywhere, small, and big and made out of wood.

The only new boat was the Ferry as I could see.

Off on the bikes again after Lunch. Zhenjiang is a city for biking.

There is an old Buddhist Temple. It has a pagoda 98 feet high. Many of the Monks are young and old and I was told no shortage of young men to join. All Monks posed for us, and we had to pose for them. I left my signature in the Guest book under Lady Bee. Outside was a camel and I asked for a ride just around the circle. What fun.

I noticed the absence of cemeteries. Sometimes one can see a cone like shape in a field that is an old family cemetery. But the graves disintegrate and turn into dust and that is it.

Visited the Museum which was till 1929 the British consulate. It is situated on a hill and the best scenic spot in town.

One can hear the Horns of the boats on the river all over town. On a walk after Dinner, I needed another helping of noodles. I looked for a noodle kitchen again. Miantiao I was told to order.

They were delicious in a broth simply perfect. By the time we started eating we had about 50 Chinese people watching us eat. They told us there had been no foreigners ever in their favorite noodle place. And we were the entertainment for them how we ate. Since we had a hard time getting noodles on our chopstick, they all fell into laughter constantly. And some of the men tried their English on us which was: Hello, just a minute, and ok.

Changzhou

Breakfast was not enough food. We are always hungry.

Biked to Changzhou on a very heavy populated bike road. So many people and the streets are not as wide. Lots of Canals and crossings for us. It was very scenic again. If we stopped everybody behind us had to stop or had a pile-up. Since we wanted to take photos, we created many traffic jams.

Visited a Comb factory, interesting. Just making combs!

Then to a Hospital and where we started in the Acupuncture section. The Acupuncture was very primitive. Many people were lying on beds, pregnant women, needles sticking out of their bellies, and others ailing people all mixed gender. Ashes all over the beds, since the medicine gets put on top of the needles and then lit. It smelled like Camphor.

There was a big room just for massages and we got to try. But for me trying Acupuncture was a no no.

The Pharmacy was interesting; it was strictly herbs and animal products. The care is free to all.

Stopped at another Monastery with an afternoon ceremony.

Wuxi

And now to Wuxi by bicycle. We have crossed the Grand Canal, built 2400 years ago, which connects to the yellow River, Yangtze, and Qiantang River.

I was told it took the lives of over 5 million people to complete in 6 years. It is the longest manmade waterway.

It is now a little hilly and since we have no gears, we have to work at pedaling. Could see what was growing in the fields, Lima beans almost everywhere. One of my favorite Beans.

We stayed at the Canal Hotel. Quite simple and dirty. Most everything was broken. But the food was delicious. I did have an interest in what we were eating and after asking what was on my plate? the answer "very delicious" is all I got. The Chinese always answer yes or no. Very polite.

Afterwards I found out I was eating shredded Jellyfish !!!!and fried Octopus.!! Not something I like. I started checking the food more closely.

Today we took the Bus to see a silk factory in Wuxie.

There we learned the whole procedure what the little worms do.

Wuxie is like Silicon Valley, many factories surround the town. Lots of Canals and little cement Boats transport all the freight. No Cars just bikes and small Busses.

The grown adults are all still wearing the Mao outfits and gray colors, but the children do look more colorful.

The bicycles are the transport for almost everything except by boat. Many Chickens, even pigs, geese. And all pulled or driven by little Chinese Men.

The parks are beautiful. Flowers are all over and many Benches. But again, too much spitting! And nobody picks up the garbage. The toilettes are bad and as I was saying it is all collected for Fertilizer.

After a two-hour drive, we went to visit Huaxie Commune. There are 1300 people living here. And everybody is happy and making enough profit to live particularly good. At the time I was told $4000 a year was a good income. But all of it was dirty and needed paint. Naturally there was a store where we could shop. And we did.

Our rooms in the Commune faced another Canal. Beds are big and 4 poster beds all around with Mosquito Netting.

Dinner was not my liking. The Chicken and Duck came whole on the table and had to be torn apart by hand. And fish soup was served but is not my taste. Snails cooked and raw were served yuck.

I ate the vegetables.

A walk afterwards through the fields to the village center. And did get invited into one home. Very bare, not much luxury. Nothing extra like a carpet or pictures.

In the Kindergarten the children performed for us, and they were very cute. I was thinking if they all become so educated who is going to work in the fields?

That evening we went to a movie. The projector was ancient, the movie too. It was almost funny because the sound was so bad, and the picture kept disappearing. I think it was from 1920.

Our beds looked good, but the mattress was a surprise, it was just a blanket awfully hard. Not much sleep there.

Breakfast was Tofu, horrible. Some baked stuff. A glass of milk was 1 teaspoon of carnation powder, 1 teaspoon of sugar and topped off with water. I am still hungry. So little and nobody complained.

Then we had to see all the factories of the Commune. Aluminum is the moneymaker but the noise! Nobody was wearing safety gear or earplugs. Life is cheap and labor too.

Lunch again bad and waiting for the Rice which is always served last. Frog legs, chicken heads but then the dumplings and vegetables came. And a good soup finally.

Back to Wuxie again with stops at a beautiful Park and an Oyster pearl raising factory. One pearl had 30 pearls inside a 40-year-old Oyster.

Saw a lot of fishponds with many dead fish floating on top. Took my appetite for fish away. Now I am buying chocolate and bananas. One almost dreams about potatoes. Which are not obtainable.

So back to my noodle dinner. And everybody is pouncing on the bowl. Meat is not important to us we need noodles! The waitress was horrified at our manners.

Suzhou

To Suzhou by Train. And first class. Lace Doilies on all the furniture, flowers. Really nice and clean. Drinking a bottle of Fen Chiew. Ingredients are cereal, oils, and another foodstuff.

Watching the rain from the train is good. There has been only little sun on our trip so far.

Hotel Dongfang is good and quiet. Up on the 7th floor.

Suzhou is a garden City. We had to see all the Gardens and got very tired. All of them are beautiful with exquisite ornaments and fishponds. Souzhou is called the "Venice of the East".

Went to a silk dying factory and had a little fashion show.

The models looked beautiful but very skinny and small it was fashion for Chinese.

More Parks and Gardens. Beautiful Markets. We biked all around the town. Had Dinner in a Pavilion with a sunset finally.

There are huge Koi in the Garden Ponds. At least 3 feet long.

Today's exercise was playing Frisbee and then off to the next Adventure.

At the Train Station as usually, we had to go into the foreigners Lounge before getting on the train. Many little Bonsai Trees decorated this Lounge.

Our Compartment is called Soft Seat Again or 1st class.

Shanghai

Finally, a City I have been dreaming and reading about, especially after I saw the film "The Sand pebbles" with Steve McQueen.

The Train Station was all new, but nothing stays here long that way. It gets dirty so fast and always their spitting on the floor makes it filthy.

Hotel Hai Hong is nice. And clean. As usual in all Hotels is hot water ready for making tea. We all bought our own chopsticks now and feel better when we eat somewhere. Sanitation is still not what we are used to.

A lot of toilets still empty into the streets and it smells. Then in certain Streets the Slop wagon arrives daily to empty the containers from the night.

I am told there are 12 million people in Shanghai, wonder if we can bike in this city?

At breakfast not much food was served, and we left very hungry for the sightseeing day. The guides are following instructions what foreigners can see, and we do not want to follow anymore. We have seen many parks and temples. So, a carpet factory was good where we got to see how silk carpets are woven. Such beauty but expensive for sale.

At the old shipyards we got to see some of the old history and went to a Restaurant there, everything served was delicious and eaten fast again.

Now the Bundt!! How much history I have read about it. The Germans built most all the beautiful Buildings, and all are a pride to look at still. There is a little look of Paris. Looking inside of Buildings much of the old splendor was still there. Lots of Marble was used in building the Bundt.

Behind the Bundt are still the little streets to walk, not many tourists or foreigners come here. Old men have their cages hanging outside with songbirds. And the Birds get judged on singing and loudness. The cages are small, and I wonder how long a Bird can last in it. When the sun comes out the men take the Birds for a walk near the Bundt where there is a Park.

Frenchtown is next; it was built for the French concession. Looks very much like Europe with a lot of trees and Gardens.

Had to stop at one of the Dept. Stores Nr. 1. Floor after Floor of goodies.

An exceptionally fine Dinner at the Park Hotel built in the Palace style of Europe. Lots of Marble and exquisite Woodwork all around. After Dinner we saw a Panda Bear perform and a Baby Elephant with 6 Lhasa Apso's Dogs doing a skit.

Later went to a French Bakery to get a cake for a Birthday the next day.

Shanghai has beautiful weather for us. We even got a western Breakfast today and lots of coffee.

A long walk today through the city, with many people shopping. Saw the Jade Buddha Temple and then to the China Exhibition in the former Russian Embassy. Chinatown was remarkably interesting. It looked like time stood still there. Still all the little alleys and people dressed in the old Chinese outfits.

Guilin

We are leaving by plane to Guilin. Our tickets could not be found, a desperate search by the guides and then a 7-hour delay, we took off.

In Guilin at the Jia Shan Hotel, we settled in for the night. It was hot but no Air-condition. We had the windows open but were advised to close them, visitors might come in at night.

Guilin is surrounded by the Osman tree which flowers in October and fills the air with a sweet orange smell. It would have been a disaster if anybody were allergic to the Osman tree.

Guilin means: Forest of Osman thus tree.

Electricity was scarce, a lot of candles were used and illuminated the Karst Mountains in dark shades.

The Karst Mountains, which jut straight up out of the earth, have been the attraction for a long time to many artists to paint them.

In the morning with the rain and mist on the mountain it all looked just like a painting. Again, beautiful Gardens all over and many Birds singing. But then the tranquility was over, when a Chinese man came by and did his spitting, disgusting.

At breakfast, again, there is not enough food. Noodle soup! And so, the hard candy and chocolate I stashed in my bags had to help.

Today on a boat down the Li River with many Chinese tourists. The Scenery was difficult to describe! Too beautiful. The boat even served food.

In Yangshuo we stopped, and I finally found my cricket cage. I had been hunting all over for an old cage. When the Revolution was on, all pets had to be killed, and Crickets were kept in these cages as pets. Since my Chinese was almost zero, I had a hard time explaining to old people what I wanted. The old Lady finally understood and went into her house and came out with the cage.

For the last Emperor crickets were his passion.

We came back by Bus through wonderful Scenery and very winding roads. Always flat and around the Mountains so in old times the coolies could carry their burden easier.

Rice paddies, Tobacco, Melons, Corn even some cotton growing.

This evening, I went by bike into the countryside and ended up in a little village. There was a temple with a big Dragon Statue. Some villagers invited me to come in and to have tea and some praying afterward. As I understood from the farmers, they grow mostly corn, sweet potatoes, rice, and peanuts. And then trade most of the food. Making about $190 a year.

The Rain is still coming down. No biking, by Bus to Elephant Hill and the Zoo. The Zoo was very depressing all animals were starving.

By now all Roads are very muddy and our trip to the Dragon Cave in the Seven Hills was still to be done. A must on our list. The explanation for the Cave is that the Dragon inside got mad and shot out of there and blew and made the huge opening. There were 1000-year-old writings on the walls and was told it was poetry.

We are ready now for a one-hour flight to Guangzhou (Canton). Felt like the pilot had seen too many supermen movies. He banked both sides. I guess he wanted everybody to have a close view.

Our local guide Jimmy was excellent, the best of all. We did have some lousy ones! Especially the ones who thought we were stupid since we did not know anything.

Jimmy let us see things we wanted to see. And he took us to the best Luncheon in the finest Chinese Restaurant we ever been.

We did stop at an Ivory carving place. It is sad to see the Elephant teeth used for it still being used.

The guide there was telling us that all elephants drop their teeth and bury them and then people find them and carve them. How gullible did he think we are?

Afternoon spend at the Qinglin Market. What a place!

Anything what could crawl, fly, or walk was for sale to eat. Snakes in Baskets by the pound. Horsemeat. Kittens fresh cut up or alive. Owls,

Pandolins, Lemur, Raccoons and all kinds of Birds. Special table with Testicles from anything. Deerhorn's. Fungus of all kinds, Bear paws. Anything… The owl was $200. Bought by a man for a believing in long life.

Off to see more fine Buildings and an old school.

Our Hotel, Bai Yun, was just across from the Garden Hotel. An unbelievably beautiful place. We went to see it, and I was speechless at such splendor. There were artworks all over and carved woodwork all around us. Many copies or real, of the soldiers of Xian standing around.

We went to a seaside Restaurant for Dinner, a very romantic place and a little bit more affordable. The food was outstanding. And the service is so good. Always a servant waiting and just watching.

Had to go to the Friendship store for more shopping and was surprised at a little Robber trying to dig into my handbag. I am towering 2 heads above him. I grabbed him and gave him an understanding that I was going to chop his head off if he does not stop this kind of stealing. I am sure he did not understand a word but knew what I meant because he clasps his hands in the air but then was taken away by security. Too bad I was not finished with him yet.

Back at the Hotel our last night and on the 26th Floor.

Dim Sum Breakfast was not very good. There was liver on the menu. Again, yuck.

Leaving China today.

At the train station problems, so many people, custom was very nosy wanted to know what we bought.

At least for our 3-hour train trip to Hong Kong we had comfortable seats and air-condition, the track was new and the train station in Hong Kong very new. But immigration and customs picked us again apart. This is still 1988 with a border between the 2 countries.

Hong Kong is alive.

Night and day. There is no other Harbor like this. Busy with so many boats, ferries, and big ships, just watching all this is fun. There is Blake Pier with good Restaurants, and we had incredibly good Samosas.

The Korean Restaurant Place was quite different. No fats or grease is used, and all food is cooked on an open fire.

Had to walk after that to the Poor Man's Market. There again a vast array of little stalls offered different foods. Good to look at but not my taste.

Took the Bus to Stanley Market. I think the Bus Driver was thinking he was on a race. And that on a double-decker Bus. And all on the left side driving.

Stanley is a shoppers Haven. I bought quite a few things but put down my shopping bag to check on something and my bag was gone.

On our way back we stopped at Repulse Bay. I remembered it as an old Romantic Hotel where I run into Robert Mitchum in the 70'. All gone. It is a high-rise of 60 stories now!

We are in the best Hotel in Hong Kong. It is the YMCA next to the Peninsular Hotel again. And the Star Ferry one block away.

Except this night my friends made a snoring concert, and I moved into the Bathroom again to sleep. Forgot all about from the first time to get my own room but I think they "Y" was sold out.

We are going to Lantau Island today. It is an outlying Island. Very hilly and much forgotten. Great. 22 km long, no traffic, no roads really.

A Bus to the Po Lin Monastery. The Bus was old and had many problems. We checked into the Tea Garden Inn for the night. It had Air-condition and we could keep the windows closed. Many Mosquitoes are hungry. There is chanting from the Monks for hours already. And the smell of incense lingers. We ate with the Monks Vegetarian Dinner which was mostly cabbage.

We went on a hike. Lantau is known for very good, marked trails. There are even huts to go under should rain surprise. And toilets too.

But on returning from hiking it was difficult to find the place since no lights were used.

And we accidentally squashed many frogs under our feet.

Many dogs are there, since the Monks do not believe in killing anything so that the dogs have found a haven.

There are some Horses in the stables, and they look beautiful. Too expensive to ride.

Morning surprised us with a very heavy fog. We made our own coffee and ate cookies for Breakfast. Could not take another soup again.

And then we hiked to the top of a hill to see the view of the lower valleys in the sunshine. Very peaceful. Just birds singing. And the chanting of the Monks.

But we must go on to explore the Silver mine Bay. It is hot and there is a little Beach town.

Back to Hong Kong by Hovercraft now. We got a bigger room now and hope to sleep better tonight. Overlooking the Bay from the 8th floor. Next door at the Peninsular people pay much more for the same view. What a bargain.

But we went to the Peninsular for high tea, it was very elegant with music playing on the upper Balcony "Tea for two" …

Went to the city by Ferry and the train up to Victoria Peak. A wonderful view especially with the evening lights.

One more time on Nathan Street. Fascinating street.

And the 30 days are over in China.

Copper Canyon, Mexico, December 4, 1988

American Airlines to Tucson Arizona. A quick one day stop in Tucson, driving to the Sabino Canyon.

Another flight to Hermosillo, Mexico. Changed then to a smaller plane for Los Mochis, Mexico.

It looked like Kevin and I were the only tourist in town. Everybody else was gone home for Christmas.

This is the most interesting Train trip in the world, and most dramatic train ride. Books have been written about its sights and feats of the building such as trains.

A long Bus ride to the Station, and there waiting for us a most classy train! First class. There were few people boarding the train, departure was at 6:03 and on time.

Around curves forever. The Scenery was constantly changing. From sheer cliffs to Bridges and many Tunnels. Some short and some very long. Could hardly decide which way to look. It is a feat for the people who built it, there are no switch backs at all. Somehow the train worked itself up the Mountains.

A particularly good Breakfast was served too.

Our first overnight stop was Bahuichivo at 11:45am. We were the only ones getting off the train. An old rickety yellow school bus was waiting to transport us for 50 minutes, 8 miles down into the Canyon. I was happy we were going slowly. I was wondering do we have good brakes.

Arriving in Cerocahui without problems. Cerocahui is an old Mission still in use and we were booked into the Hotel Misiones.

In the back yard I could see meat hanging on a laundry line. Maybe to dry it?

The Hotel is an old Convent, but I saw no priest or Monks around. Much poverty in this place. All the old Indio's who were sitting outside, were hoping to get food from the kitchen. As I was told the young people do not stay around and try to get jobs in the cities as fast school is finished.

We ate food grown in this place like corn, but most was now canned or dried food.

After Lunch we were driven over the Mountains to meet some of the natives. I had to close my eyes in some places it was scary driving. There was not much room on the pathway for a car, just steep cliffs.

Stopped at a family of Tamara Indian who lived in a Cave. They had nothing but seemed to be happy. All the animals lived in the same cave too. Everything inside was black from the smoke of the open fire. How many centuries had they been living there? Even the skin of the people was almost black from the fires.

That place was the famous Urique Canyon.

At the Mission we had a nice and cozy room heated by an open stove, very flimsy, and was homemade. I could not figure out how our stove was lit. Wood first, pour petroleum and throw a match on it. It worked without us being burned.

A Dinner again from the farm food. We joined singing with a German group who were hiking. And electric generator switched off at 10:30pm.

In the morning back on the old Bus up to the Train station again. But now it took one hour to get up the Mountain. We certainly could feel every bump in the Road. I do not think the old Bus had any shocks and wondered how old the Bus could be.

Then at the station we waited and waited and no train. Finally, somebody got the news our Train derailed near Agua Caliente. We had to take the old Bus again back to Misiones.

There we had Lunch of fresh fish! And then took a hike for 6 miles to the Waterfalls.

On returning we are told to go back up the Mountain to the train again to see if a train would come this evening. There are no telephones and I do not know how anybody communicated. It is becoming an adventure by now.

Since it is Kevin's Birthday, we are waiting with a nice bottle of wine we had with us in an old Rail Wagon hoping the train will come.

We have a good fire going because it is cold outside. There were wood pieces lying around.

As we finally saw the train and it stopped for us, we got all the news from some travel agents who were on board.

Near Agua Caliente a freight train derailed so when the tourist train arrived near there with 30 American travel Agents it was a disaster for them. For 7 hours the train just sat there. Toilets were locked, no food. And just wild countryside.

Finally, people were told if they need to continue to get off with their luggage and walk to the other side of the accident where another train had arrived to pick them up. One elderly Man could not continue because his suitcase was much too heavy. He died right on the little footpath. CPR was done but did not help. So dead Senior was brought on the new train and put into the first train wagon on the floor covered by a white sheet. His wife was seated next to him.

Slowly this train now was coming to our station, and we finally got on. With a slow pace we chugged along. Kevin needed to go to the Potty and decided to go forward to the toilet, he was not told where Senior was. Well, he almost stumbled over him.

In San Rafael we stopped for a new Locomotive. The Observation car with all the Travel Agents was right behind the Locomotive which got unhooked and the Observation car was all alone sitting next to us suddenly. One could only see the faces of the Agents when they noticed what was happening to them. They scrambled off so fast not to be left behind. Now all this is playing out at 11pm in the darkest night with not much lights at all. They sure have a story to tell when they get home to tell about the Train trip.

By now we were ready for a rest and got to Divisadero Barrancas by midnight. We had reservations there and got off the train.

This now is midnight everybody was asleep there or left for home. There was a cook asleep, and we dragged him out of bed to cook something for us. Got my Blanco Cheese with Tomato. Our beds were very comfortable, and we slept very good.

In the morning, the view, again, was too beautiful to describe.

Unbelievable! Our Hotel wash hanging right on a canyon wall, one almost felt the Hotel would slip over the cliff. But it is so cold. Winter is here for sure. After a good breakfast we felt better and even went around the plateau for a hike to the Indian village in the Caves. There was an Indian Woman who told us she danced with Pancho Villa. She was 95 years old.

The food was excellent in this place. That was the only good thing as it turned out for the next hours no more food was available. Our next train was to arrive at "4pm possible" . Saying it in Spanish sounds good.

Now we wait again. 3 hours have gone by. Nothing is happening. We are waiting in a nice place and we have good company.

But now it is 12:30 midnight and no train in sight. We are 20 people and have played games, told silly jokes, good jokes. But we cannot relax. Every time we hear a train, we race outside hoping it is ours, but it is always a freight train.

Everybody from the Hotel has gone home. We are hungry and getting cold.

We have 3 more pieces of outside furniture for the fireplace! This is a night to remember. By 2am we started burning the railing from the outside Patio. We refrained from burning the inside furniture. And now it is snowing on top of it. We still are a good group and try to keep our spirits up. I will never forget the couple who pulled a bag out of fortune cookies. We all had a few laughs there. We did change seats by the fire, so everybody got some warm heat.

By 4:15am we all felt like we were forgotten. And when we heard a train, we were slow to jump up and just saw the taillights of the train disappearing. Everybody run outside and started screaming, swearing too. Our voices were thrown along the canyon walls very loud. After waiting for 15 hours, we all had a sinking feeling seeing the train go by. But our screaming helped and was heard on the train. It stopped and backed up. So, we climbed through the snow and ice up to the train and just fell into our seats and slept. Till Creel was announced, where we got off.

Here it is 5am and our Driver was still waiting for us, he just slept in the car. Everything was now white, the big snowstorm still going.

Our Taxi Driver was good in this snowstorm, 1 hour to the Copper Canyon Hiking Lodge.

Our room had a big roaring fire and Kerosene Lamps, and we slept we needed it. We feel good again, filled with incredibly good cooking.

I see still lots of poverty around, it is very cold, and the Indians have only lean-tos. There is a lot of coughing, and I think tuberculin is common. We had ourselves checked when coming home for TB.

This is the Sierra Madre Weather, snow at its time. I did not have snow boots, just sneakers. Still today it looked incredibly beautiful with the white blanket. A good hike was needed.

At night, very good food and wine was served and we slept by the fire soundly.

Today the sun is shining, and we are sightseeing to the Caves of the Tarahumas, the Valley of the Gods, and Ignatius Valley.

We did buy tickets for the ending of our trip on a Bus to USA. We had enough of the trains. But then we found out the Bus stopped everywhere. At least we got to see some of the Countryside.

In Chihuahua we stayed at the Hyatt to take the next morning train to El Paso. I was looking for Chihuahuas dogs. None around.

Again, a very luxury train, all first class.

If only there would be no smoking.

(At that time, it was still aloud) 1988

Good viewing from the train. Coyotes running along, saw my first ones.

Yes, it was an Adventure.

1989 2-2 Australia, Fiji, Tahiti, Australia!

I have read almost everything I could get my hands on this big country. The History of it is so much newer than the USA.

And I am getting to a warmer place, for many people to hot.

On arrival the plane gets sprayed with insecticide to keep all bad bugs out of Australia.

Sydney finally! My Fijian friends Lola and Timocy picked me up and introduced me to the brilliant Sunshine and great food.

The houses are beautiful, small, but have red tile or blue tile roofs. And so many birds! So many cockatoo's and parrots, so many parakeets.

I like to get to know Sydney, so first up the Sydney tower to orient myself. Beneath the Queen Victoria Building with all the Restaurants and stores.

And finally, The Opera House. It is magnificent as I always hoped it be. It looks like a Butterfly.

Rock city, the oldest part of Sydney. Which used to be full of boats from all over the world. But now converted again to stores and restaurants.

The food is excellent especially my favorite dessert Pavlova Checked out a place about Opals. The quality, colors and the values. With an excellent transportation system, I found my way around easy. In Parametta I went to the Governors House for Devon shire tea. Love to sit outside and enjoy the warm air.

There are trees full of yellow crested Cockatoos! And people call them a pest. They do empty a fruit tree in minutes. Which I watched to a plum tree next door. When the owner came screaming outside, all was eaten.

Today, a trip to the Sydney Zoo. Famous for natural big pens. But to get there: Bus, Train, Ferry across the harbor and then on the gondola to the top of the Zoo. It took 5 hours to walk down because of so much to see there.

I fell in love with the Dingo's and Wombat's.

When people talk to me the first question is always: "are you trekking about?"

I will do that soon.

By car now to Goulburn and Canberra, traveling through Eucalyptus forest for many miles. Stopped at a "Blue and white" Restaurant and was told the chicken salad is very good. So that is what I ordered. It entails a half a chicken on a bed of Lettuce surrounded by fruit and vegetables covered in a Salad Sauce. It could have fed 4 people. Too bad had to leave most of it.

Canberra in view. A totally new built city and now the capital of Australia. Except not many people living there yet because it was too far from Sydney. (1989)

Toured all the embassy's, American Embassy looks just like the governor's house in Williamsburg Virginia. It even had a TV Tower and a fine view we had from there.

There is a saying: No Aussie is happy till he has his own home. But it is expensive to build so their houses are small, and very seldom 2 stories. And if possible, as close to the coast.

There was a bicycle museum too. And a pub with good food.

Back in Goulburn again to see the big Marino Sheep Show in the Aerodrome. Interesting. The sheep products were too expensive, but I bought 2 Opals and found out later they were only chips nothing worth. My first lesson.

There is Horse country too, called Moss Vale and Bowral.

And now to the Blue Mountains Katoomba. There I visited the 3 sisters Mtn. And Echo Point. And took the steepest Railway in the world straight into the Gorge. It was used to carry miners into the Mines.

I am getting ready for my long trip into the heart of Australia.

Melbourne

Flying to Melbourne and was served with the most delicious Riesling wine. Melbourne is expensive. Had a hard time finding a backpacker place. Lived on Chinese take-away. Never saw a small sink like I had here 10 inches about round. But better a sink than none.

Did go to the Science Museum to look for one of the most famous Horses in Racing. There he was! Phar Lap, stuffed and very lifelike. Even his blister marks on his legs one could see. He was 17 hands. In 1932 he raced his last race in the US.

Now to Phillips Island along the coast by Bus. With a stop at the Giant Worm farm. Worms are 4 feet long.

Across the San Remo Bridge onto Phillip Island to see Koalas which are plenty there but get run over at night by cars.

Watched Seals and Fairy Penguins and their baby's. They are very tame and ignore humans on the way to the burrows.

On the way back to Melbourne we watched the Movie "The Man from Stony River" How appropriate.

Got to touch a Kangaroo today at a park. It was very tame, Emu's who wanted to be scratched.

Adelaide

Arriving in Adelaide on the 16th of Feb. A 10-hour bus ride. Wonderfully comfortable. And found right away $55 a week room in a Hostel. Through the Hostel I met more people who wanted to go to the same places as I. It is nice to have company. We went to the wine country, called Barossa Valley. Visited a Mclaren Vale winery, very good. Chateau Yaldara a good wine. There are so many good wines and in beautiful settings. The Maslin Beach here is very cold water but clear and lots of warm sand.

At night, the Mayland Pub for food and folk music. Many historic

Homes are in Adelaide. And many Germans have settled around in this part of Australia.

Again, a trip for the day to "Wispering Wall" built 1898 and it is the largest reservoir in Australia. Its retaining is enormous.

Lyndoch, Angaston and Angas Park fruit factory. A stop at Dorrien winery at Siegersdorf and Gnadenfrei which was settled in 1840 as Seppeltsfield and now Marananga. Then Saltram Winery, started in 1859, one of the oldest. It all resembled the Silesian Countryside, (Schlesien) in Germany. I was born in Silesia.

Back through Gawler Horse country.

There was still a corner I had to see near Adelaide, Hahndorf, a very German Town with Fachwerk Hauses from 1840. Everything was in German even the stores carried German food. Many Blackberries are growing in hedgerows and free for the picking which I did.

Noticing the men are wearing ridiculously small shorts, wonder why?

I did see my first Kookaburra, a very strange looking bird. And a funny sound it makes.

Tomorrow I will get on the long Bus to Coober Pedy. It is supposed to be extremely hot there, 120. I have now an Aussie-pass which I should have bought in Sydney. It is great, one can get off anywhere as long it is in the right direction the pass is made out. This will be a 30-hour Bus trip.

Train ticket cost a lot more. But the buses are clean and on time. No juice or fruits can be carried. Would make the bus sticky, one is told all that before boarding by the drivers.

A long haul now. We stopped in Port Pirie. Just a Roadhouse like many along the long Road. The food is always bad, and it is becoming more and more the outback. The few houses or cabins I see from the Bus have only tin roofs and look forlorn.

Movies were shown but nobody watched. Movies were exchanged by the Bus Driver when heading the opposite way. Both Busses stopped and the only talk one could hear from the drivers, and each changed a pack of videos. The most boring one was shown first so we all would quiet down and not make noise because one driver was always sleeping.

Coober Pedy

Arrived after many hours in Coober Pedy, the Opal mining Capital in the world at 5am. Deep in the earth a backpacker place was my night reservation. At $9 for 2 nights, great. The town is underneath because of the heat. And one usually sees only the front door or a sign and then climbs down. The deeper the hole the cooler it is. Dugouts really are the houses. Since daytime temperature go to 120f, it is the only way life is bearable there.

The big Hotel is a luxury place but all under the earth, it even has a movie theatre. Many Dugouts are 4 stories deep or below deeper. One pays a bulldozer to enlarge a place.

The water to Coober Pedy is brought from a borehole 20 miles north and then sold by the liter. Our showers were cold but if you put 20 cents into the Little thingy, hot water came for 2 minutes. Flashing toilets is a waste with so much water used each time. I did bring my own toilet paper; how lucky I was.

Saw my real first Aborigines. The one is I saw in the towns did not count. Expected more but the ones I saw early already were drunk and looked like lost animals. Alcohol is a big problem since there are no jobs for them.

The miners stay to themselves and are remarkably busy digging in the Mounds for Opal. I found out when asking friendly at a Mound: "could I noodle please"? I had always permission and did bring beautiful Opals home.

My favorite Restaurant was the Dugout Café. Owned by a Croatian man who made his money with Opal digging and decided to stay and feed people. And it was the best food. Wine for $1 a glass. Lamb roast was great. And I never ate Lamb or liked it before.

Now by Bus again north. A stop at Marla Station but here prices for Food are expensive!! So, I am digging in my bag for the last food I brought from Hahndorf.

Looking out of the Bus window the red earth flies by miles and miles of bush, cows, Kangaroos, parrots and run over animals.

I wanted to see the famous Dingo fence but was asleep when crossing. The vegetation is like Arizona but no Cactus.

Stopped to look at Mt. Conner by the Salt flats. 200 miles distance between Stations now. And more dead Cows along the road. They stand in the Road, but the big Road Trains cannot stop for them.

And now a view of Ayers Rock or Ylara, so red. And the Olgas. The heart of Australia is here. And only years ago people walked here or rode Camels.

Here are Aborigines walking around. They have a very upright statue, no shoes always barefoot, their eyes are very deep-set. It has a reason because of the flies who do not like it. Communications between them is a lot of shouting.

Hired a taxi with more Backpackers to tour Maggie Springs and the Rock! It really does look close-up like fish skin, very flaky and it is the sacred stone for the Aborigines.

At night doing the Moon and star walk with a Ranger and learned a little about the stars on the "other side".

5am to Ayers Rock to climb for sunrise.

I did not feel like doing after arriving there and walked around.

There is a chain going up to the top and the wind was blowing very hard. And coming down again was nixed by me.

On the bottom of Ayers Rock are plaques dedicated to the people who have fallen off the "Rock" and died.

My walk around was very peaceful, not a person in sight. Many Caves with paintings can be seen. By the time the sun came up it gave me the chills. So beautiful are the colors. No civilization around just that big Rock. Nothing spoils that place. It is a holy place for the aborigines.

Relaxing a little at the pool and doing laundry. It dries in an hour with the dry heat. And as usual lots of parakeets and finches.

Going on to the Bus to Alice Springs. At the Bus station many job offers to everybody since not many people want to live for a long time in Alice Spring.

I checked into the Melanda Lodge for $9 a night. The Backpacker special.

Alice Spring is very pretty. Lots of old Buildings. And water is used to make flowers grow and bloom.

At the Camel stable I hired a Camel. Capt. Morgan. A wonderful Camel. What an experience! My ride was what I was dreaming about. And now I take any chance to ride a camel. I love them.

There are big stores, Woolworth, K-Mart, Malls with fantastic Garden arrangements. Food is as usual expensive.

Went off on my rented Bicycle to discover the Town.

When the Todd River has Water which is very seldom, it destroys sections of the town and nobody rebuilds it.

Now I travel to Glen Helen, a Homestead with lots of History. Will experience the outback there. Glen Helen has 600 000 square miles of land. Supposed to be the second largest Landowner in the world.

Stopped at Pine Hill Station and learned how to make Damper there. One of my favorite recipes now.

This stretch of land is interesting. Very dry, but lots of birds hit the windshield.

Stopping at the first waterhole of the 3000miles highway, 2000 unpaved. Went swimming at a waterhole to cool off. Crossed Ellery Creek and stopped at Orniston Gorge. Beautiful. Soon arrived at Glen Helen a trip of 133 km from Alice Spring.

The temperature was about 120 by now but very dry and I did a lot of hiking to see this part of Australia.

Redbank gorge and walking in the river for 30 minutes carrying my bag on my head. On the way back I was not so lucky and went under with my Camera included. But it still worked afterwards.

At Glen Helen I watched the wildlife. A 4-foot lizard suddenly appeared in front of me. And small Kangaroos. A different breed.

A young Japanese tourist is playing the flute under the trees. It is unreal to be here and listening to her classical music.

The night was hot, there is no air-condition. There was little sleep.

Hiked to discover a new place the next day. One had to swim across a river again, they call it a waterhole. The water is not clear, and I was wondering what could eat my feet or bite me. Lots of crayfish. But it was worth it.

There was a dry riverbed with black Swans, Iguanas and black Ducks on the other side.

Going back met some Aussies camping who had Beer. I was offered a can. And that was good. Even warm beer is good. One seems to drink more and never sweats.

Back to Civilization over the McDonald Range. And got a room at the Red Centre Resort in the backpacker section for $9. Everything was included just like the people who paid the high price. And sleeping in Air-condition tonight!!

Today some historic places in Alice Spring. Visited Telegraph Hill. The Pioneers had a hard time here since water was scarce.

Then to the Flying Doctors. They still do their work, and it was exciting for me to talk with everybody.

Right and left of the Road huge Termite mounds. 10 feet or taller now.

On the Bus again to the next stop- Mataranka on the Steuart Hwy. About 500 miles from nowhere. Another Homestead with lots of Mineral Springs.

This was a busy stretch of highway. Road trains back and forth. Usually, 3 trailers and they drive extremely fast. Each train has 60 tires! And they are packed to the top. But they take Hitchhiker's too. Have not needed them yet. Again, we arrived early, 6am. But the Station was waiting for us. An Oasis in the middle of the Desert.

The historical Station is called Elsey Station and is now immortalized by Jeannie Gunn's Novel "We of the Never Never" and one of my favorite Movies was filmed here. "Never, never Land." When walking around I found in the Sand a 1916 Australian penny. Big and made out of Copper. What luck! Always wonder who lost it and how it got there. I still have the penny and a photo of the place and can feel the heat and sand.

A long walk to the back of the Land are thermal pools which I enjoyed and could have stayed there forever.

And one can do bushwalks all around. Many Kangaroos are there.

Sitting now on the Bus north I noticed my reading glasses and shoes were left in Mataranka. The Bus driver told me they will be there on my way back. (2000 miles later).

On to Darwin after a good rest. Have a date to meet Crocodile Dundee. Luckily, the Busses cannot speed, they are controlled by a blue light, a ringing sound came on right away when going over speed limit.

The countryside is changing, it is getting very tropical. But still Beef Cattle in the countryside. There are never fences on this Highway.

Darwin is HOT!!!
It rains here a lot and the humidity is high. The Chinese and Thai

food is supposed to be the best but, I have had better.

I am sweating.

I am going to meet my first real Aborigines, family and all. But I need different shoes in this weather. Flip flops! So off to shop for flip flops. Learned today that Darwin was bombed in 1942 240 times. By whom?

It is a very strategic place. Even Americans have their landing strip rights. It is a very unpleasant town. Too hot. One cannot swim, too many Crocodiles. Sharks and a most poisoned sea nettle. One touch and you are dead.

Back to my Aborigines. My Guide's Toni and Mata-Mata picked me up. The Aborigines language always doubles all words. Toni looked like the man from Dundee and lots of fun to be around. Went first to Kakadu National Park to see Buffalo and big Croc's. The Park is the size of Switzerland yet very little known. Unspoiled outback and bush. Then there are known 5000 rock paintings in caves like Galleries that record life from as far back as 50,000 years.

Our lunch at the Beach was different, had to keep our eyes open for crocs. Would have loved to go swimming. But no way. We even had a fire between the sea and us to keep the croc away.

Mata Mata cut wood for spears, he needed new ones. And even played the didgeridoo. Great sound. He finally found a waterhole where I could swim but I declined. Did not trust it because I could not see the bottom.

On our Bushwalk leeches glued themselves on our legs all over. Strange Birds, the same with the fruits. Mata Mata knew what we could eat. Tony pointed out the biggest tree frog I ever saw. As we were watching it, a snake came and swallowed it.

But to feed us took a lot of looking and digging for food. At our fire, Tony made Damper, Billy tea was boiling and the Jams (potatoes) we found tasted very good.

Even when we walked Mata-Mata did not see the snake in the path and almost got bit. We all had only flip flops on our feet.

Now I am looking forward to my 33-hour Bus trip to Cairns. Shopping in the market for food and drinks. Anything fruity is expensive but meat is incredibly low priced. Never can have enough provisions.

In Adelaide River Station we had Hamburgers. The video on this Bus is broken. Finally, I have peace. Always is a Movie playing usually to keep passengers happy.

And we stopped in Mataranka for refreshment. Quick to swim there and some good pot pie.

I Just mentioned that I lost my glasses and shoes the week before. Yes, they were right there, could not believe it.

Our first blowout tire. Everybody is watching and making photos of the Drivers trying to change tires.

Soon on the next stop I must get off and wait for my connecting Bus to go East to Townsville. A big highway of 1000 miles mostly dirt.

At Mt. Isa Station for Breakfast. Should have stayed and looked for Silver. There is a mine shaft going 1 ¼ km down to the silver mine. 5000 miners are there digging. But I like Gold.

On the Bus again. Lots of small lonely towns fly by in the heat. Hoping to be in Townsville soon.

On arrival in Townsville checked right out how to get to Magnetic Island by Ferry. Great place to go to and booked a room in a backpacker Inn on Magnetic Island.

There is a safe bay called Alma Bay. I still watched and looked when I went swimming. The crocs are fast.

Magnetic Island is 80% Park and has a lot of wildlife. And rain.

So, I went trekking and again saw a lot of Animals. Even many Koalas'. And I saw 500 Rosella's Parrott's. I counted.

There are Horses to ride but to skinny, so I rode a Camel which was very good looking.

But snorkeling is out because of the weather, too much rain and wind.

Trying now in a new day full of sunshine to swim in Radical Bay, the warm water is always good.

It is time to move north now because Kevin will arrive in Cairns and time is flying. It is already March 8.

Townsville is beautiful with houses being restored to the old glory. Towering over the town is Tower Hill. In the Second World War, Americans tried to build a Bridge from the hill to Magnetic Island, but it was only a dream. Again, the Town has lots of History.

Caught the Bus to Cairns now. Through Sugarcane fields for Miles. Mango Plantation, many, but not in season yet. Pineapple fields everywhere. And more rain. The Bus had to wait a few hours till the Road got clear again from flooding, Passed Tully, the wettest town in Queensland.

Cairns is flooded. More rain than ever. But made it to a "Gone Walkabout" Inn. Nice. When the rain let off, I went to inspect Cairns. Found the city beautiful because flowers growing everywhere.

Checked into another place for better convenience and now to the Airport to pick up Kevin.

It is great to share now with him my impressions of Australia. Except we had to get a place with Air-condition.

We are going to Kurunda with the Tourist train. I do not understand why the train was built under such difficult condition. Tunnels, deep cliffs, erosion next to the track. There is a Road which goes right around the Mountain.

Kurunda is a little town on the Plateau with no Humidity. A very big Aborigines Theatre is there and performances every day. The music they play with the Didgeridoos is fascinating.

With have rented a car, to see more of the Hinterland of Queensland and drove up to the Tableland to Mareeka, Timaroo and rested at the

Beulah Homestead. Had our tea and watched the cows getting milked.

I do like the idea in Motels and overnight places having a little closet outside of the room. In the morning fresh tea or coffee and toast and the small things one needs for Breakfast are sitting there. Even real cream.

The weather is very good up in the Tablelands, without humidity and cool at night.

We met a lot of people and got to talk to everybody except the Aborigines who are always standing on the sidelines and do not talk.

Timoro Lake is manmade and the irrigation system for all the Valleys. It waters the whole Valley.

Then off to see the fig trees at Yongerburro and Malada. And tried to find a paved Road to Heberton. Which did not exist.

Stopped at the Fosters Winery and tried their Riesling. A little sour but good in the evening.

At the Green Spring Homestead, the most perfect place, we decided to stay. With very good hiking trails we saw a lot of animals, Wallaby's and lots of Kookaburras in the trees.

Greeted by Rusty the Bull, a pure Brahma, Horses and dogs.

Last night we were entertained by readings of Poetry and aussie music. And I finally had long conversation about the history of Australia.

Stopped next at a Banana Plantation and got to taste a lot, even papayas. For Lunch at Migilla Falls Homestead for the Plowmans Lunch. Damper and Corn beef.

At a tea plantation of 1000 acres, we learned a lot about the products. And having lemon scented Eucalyptus leaves makes it taste better.

On to Innisfail to see the sugar Museum which was on the coast surrounded by smoking chimneys burning the sugar cane.

Arriving again in Cairns to take a trip to Green Island. Which we did by a Catamaran called Quick Cat. We stopped at Michelmans Bay to snorkel and watch the Birds in the Sanctuary. 10 000 Birds right next to us on the Sand. And very noisy with so many birds. One could almost touch them. They did not move when walking by.

And then a 30-minute fly over the clearest water at 25 knots to Green Island. The snorkeling was fantastic, so many fish and big ones. Only one Resort is allowed on the Island, and the fish never get disturbed, it was fun staying overnight and just going out in the water anytime.

I kept thinking of the "Thorn Birds" a lot, what Island was it filmed on? The Love Scenes!

With a new rental car to Daintree. A beautiful coastline. Constantly changing scenery. Stopped at a big Crocodile Farm and looked at their pet Dingo's.

Port Douglas is the jet set city of Australia. Country clubs and Resorts. And then sugar cane fields again with a Mill in Mossman for processing the Sugar cane.

Across with the Daintree Ferry over a rain filled River. From now on only dirt Roads again but we turned around after 10 miles. It was very muddy and getting stuck was not good for us. From here it is still 1000 more miles north to the Torres Straights.

In Cairns we watched the Aborigines give a Korribiri in the Plaza which is seldom seen. They dance like in a trance, and every move is learned by their ancestors. Since there is no written language.

After that the Aborigines got drunk, and we watched them beating each other up. And there is no stopping them. Except native police can do that.

Driving south with our rental car, not on sandy roads we were told, but almost all Roads are unpaved.

Townsville at 5pm. Great Pubs and good food. And plenty of take-outs.

It is raining but we still made it to the Flinders St. Market to look at all the craftsmanship. Very beautiful pottery.

Going to Charters Towers, a gold mining town, with a filled car for food and drinks, 180km, and nothing between. We always pulled over when traffic came at us. Did not want any windshield broken or damage to car. The Roads out there are all one lane.

A stop at Beyands, a service Station and again nothing for another 170km just cattle grids and big holes, deep sand. As we stopped trying to get a cool drink, we came onto 4 guys just sitting outside and inviting us to get what we want ourselves. As it turned out the generator was broken, and everything was stale, sour or not good anymore. But the Beer was cold. It was buried deep in the sand.

Many Kangaroos, wallabies are sitting in the middle of the Road.

Clermont finally and late, lucky a Lodge had room, and good pizza.

In the morning off to the Emerald Area and Sapphire Fields. A small Road led us to Anakie. There are no signs, and all without telephone or GPS. It was lots of luck us ending on the right Road. Rubyvale, near Anakie is known for beautiful stones and lots of Emeralds.

Sluicing the stones is hard since the stones look alike of the color of the earth. One buys a bucket full of dirt and starts washing. I was told 80% of the world supply comes from here.

In Emerald we had great Steak Dinner by the beautiful Railroad station. Very ornamental on the outside.

We passed Planet Downs Station, an expensive overnight stay. We are now in a very dry country where it had not rained for 5 years and saw many Kangaroos dead lying around. And crossed the Dingo Fence and stopped in Miles. Where we stopped at the Knights club and became honoree Members for the evening. Again, lots of history here. The houses are all built in the 1800's.

Jondaryan Woolshed was our next destination. We learned a lot about sheep there. And Kevin got to shear a sheep, not as fast as he thought, since he did not have a good hold on the sheep.

Fortified with fresh fruit and Damper we had a great pick nick near a waterhole.

Brisbane, staying in the "Kangaroo Hotel"! With many Music places and beautiful weather, I can understand people love it there. Sightseeing is great here. The Botanic Garden a Jewel. Since it was

Easter week a lot of celebrations were going on.

South again to Beenleigh Rum factory. Good Rum. And now to Surfers Paradise. The longest Beach and lots of apartment houses looking at the sea.

Murwillumbah to the Mt. Warning Lodge to nowhere. Up in the Hills with a lot of hiking trails. Saw a lot of wildlife and very good-looking Horses. At night strange sounds. Never found out what it was.

Tried to find Koalas but rain stopped us. And we helped bringing in the sheep with the dogs doing most of the work. All dogs here have Dingo mix. The wild Dingo are killed because of killing the sheep.

The sound of the Outback all night with the Kookaburra Bird.

Now to Kyogle on unpaved Roads again. The Scenery is so beautiful, and we soon came to Glen Innes on the New England Highway. To a sheep station May bole, 40km. Lots of sheep, nice Bunkhouse. Except we had to catch our own dinner on the Lake. A Trout! And then some children showed us how to catch Jappies which we stewed. They tasted just like Lobster. Jappies hide under big Rocks in the water.

Long drive today to the Hunter Valley and in pouring Rain again and at 5000 feet. At a Fossil dig I found two zircons. They are a kind of diamond.

This is Horse country. Many beautiful Farms. Easter Sunday now. Maitland and Scone with wine country.

Supposed to be 76 Winery's in the Valley.

Wanted to see Morpeth. But where the hell is Morpeth? Have read about it. Found it. And it is alive. A City built by convicts in the 1800's.

Katoomba is next when we get there. Still many wineries. Then again for 100 miles no town till the Blue Mountains. Driving for hours through Gum tree Forest's. And it is getting cold. Driving along the Canyon to Megalong and hiked there along the trails. Saw two Lyrebirds! Every kind of parakeet and Lorikeet. Birds all over.

In Katoomba we took the Skyway and train. And had Pavlova in the Hydro Majestic Hotel at Medlow Bath.

With more rain forecasts, we took advantage of a sunny morning and went to an old private home called Notre Dame. Spend 5 hours there because so much history there again. Had many Andalusian Horses.

Acquired a Drizzabone Coat in Parametta. Everybody has to have that coat!

Sydney

My friends the Sovas had a nice welcome for us and for me it was like coming home again. Having slept for almost 2 months every night in a different bed but I liked it all.

Kevin must leave soon. Went to Sydney with Kevin to see something of Sydney. We walked for 2 days all around.

Did a pub crawl at night for his sendoff. It was the best 3 weeks in my life, and we promised us to do it again at our 50's wedding anniversary which did not happen because of Kevin dying of Cancer at our 48th wedding anniversary.

Sydney is now colder and Melbourne too, I must catch a plane to Fiji. I can hardly wait for warmer weather.

Fiji

Why is it that planes land in the middle of the night for arrival in most places? It is 3:30 am. But my driver from the Seashell Cove in Fiji was waiting for me. Rainy season!

All Roads were mud. Driving was difficult and the Rains have been heavy. At the Seashell Cove everybody was trying to keep dry. Since the wind was drifting in all directions and the rain came into the Buildings. It has changed since my last visit 2 years ago. There was a coup with the Government and Fijians are doing more of the menial work. Before only Indian workers did the menial work.

Kava drinking is still going strong. At 7:30 at night before Dinner the ritual starts.

Now the sun is shining again. Cleaning up now from the storm and many trees were blocking Roads. At the Village I was invited to the Kava drink. Do not really like it and take small sips. The Elders kept watching that I did not miss to drink.

Tahiti

After Fiji a stop in Tahiti and again a 5am arrival. Here I had a small problem with my French so early in the morning. The Tahitian people are nice and helped me finding the right Le Truck to Papeete. There I met a Tahitian woman who could understand my trouble with my little French, she told me, she would take care of me and put me on a Bus to my destination and gave the driver strict instruction were to drop me off.

Mahina Beach, black sand and the perfect place to hang out. I have a lovely room called the blue room. The Ocean is right out in front of my door. What is surprising is the black sand. One always thinks of Tahiti's white Beaches. But the black sand comes from the Volcanos a long time ago.

The real Tahitian do not want to speak French, they have their own language. I am using Le Truck for all transportation now. Fun.

Sleeping at night is a delight with the water lapping on the shore.

Today I went around the Island. Stopped at the Gauguin Museum with a fantastic ground. Many Orchids are in the trees, and one could swim there too. It all looked like the paintings of Gauguin.

At a River I crossed some very heavy Ladies were washing the laundry and invited me to join them too.

There was a good feeling talking with the Tahitians. They are big people, and the women are built big but very elegant in their moves.

Tetiaroa Marlon Brando's Island

TETIAROA is always on the news because of family trouble of the Brando Family. Having read about this Island so much and I knew Marlon Brando owned it. I had a chance to visit for a day trip. Almost missed the departure to the Dock because of many traffic jams at 6am! However, by the time our "Le Truck negotiated the heavy morning traffic, the boat had left.

At the Dock I got my biggest surprise. Thinking I would be on a luxury Cat or Quicksilver Boat with showers and toilets I was sad to have missed it.

2 Tahitian men promised me for a certain amount of money they could catch up to it with their speedboat. A good deal I thought, if only I would have gone home.

By the time we caught up with the excursion boat well out to sea, the calmness of the harbor had given way to waves so high that direct boat-to-boat transfer was impossible. Instead, I had to scramble into a rubber dinghy to be hauled to the boat which turned out to be ancient and small compared to the luxurious little boat I just left. What was I thinking?

It was a horrible transfer. One boat always was up and one down in the waves. I could not get on board. Totally wet by now I was pulled into the "Yacht". All this should have been filmed. I suggested a few times to go back to Papeete was falling on deaf ears. I saw my yacht was just a wooden bucket. Totally primitive. Should have been firewood long time ago. There were 5 Tahitian fishermen on board to handle this "Bucket". They knew what they were doing at least.

That we completed the remaining three hours of the passage is a tribute to the skill of the Tahitian fishermen crew who maneuvered the boat through the enormous waves and finally over the reef which shelters Tetiaroa.

I was holding onto anything and noticed I had white knuckles by now. Such big waves I just have never seen.

Tetiorea came in sight surrounded by a big Reef. How to go through this?

No problem for the Guys, shooting right through it. I closed my eyes.

Once inside the lagoon we switched to another old boat but very safe since the water was protected.

Tetiaroa is a ring of small atolls which have remained nearly unaltered since being purchased by Marlon Brando a number of years ago. The old village of the 19th century owners is deserted and overgrown. Heavy vegetation, but a sanctuary for a wide variety of colorful birds. It is surrounded by pristine beaches from which fantastic snorkeling can be enjoyed. Between periods of swimming, walking and listening to our crew's music, we all stuffed ourselves with breadfruits, salads and fish the crew had caught. The food was provided by the young men on the Island.

Two big Frigate Birds were walking around us trying to steal food. The birds had no fear.

With a rubber motorboat we sped off to another place on the island. The driver explained that in his free time he was a motocross driver.

Now we walked for 2 hours visiting all the Birds who had no fear of Men. Booty's and lots of Terns. The Booty is a funny looking Bird. Duck feet, Chicken body, and a long beak.

At the old Village we saw the graves of the last Owners Marlon Brando bought the Island from. It is now all left for nature to take over.

And it is protected very much by his sons who were our guides on the Island.

Snorkeling was fantastic. Lots of fish. Which was served again for Lunch with breadfruit, salads and lots of fruits.

Late in the afternoon we had to get ready for our 60-mile return.

I knew the storm was still out there. The seas were heavier than we previously experienced. We finally got onto the "Old Bucket" again after the crossing of the Reef! 60 miles of this again! My more religious companions on the boat said a rosary as the boat pitched over waves which frequently exposed the engine's propeller. And watching the Captain losing control of his wheel did not make me happy. He was always drinking Beer.

Some people were bailing water hoping that kept their mind on something else. I held on to anything like a vice.

By the way, no life preservers were on board.

The crew kept drinking Beer through the whole trip. But our prayers must have helped, for we finally reached the safety of Papeete's harbor, wet and tired.

Arriving in Papeete the Captain steered the boat to fast into the Harbor and hit first a railing, then backing, hitting a boat leaving a big hole in it. I got off as fast as I could and left this group of drunks. But it was a memorable experience I will never forget. I really thought I would drown on this trip. I swore I would never go in a storm on a boat again.

At the Hotel showers and getting ready for a 2:30am flight to the USA.

My impression of Tahiti: anybody with Tahitian blood and ancestry is nice.

It is not a clean country; trash is not collected.

Nova Scotia, Canada, July 21, 1989

By Air Nova, a propeller plane up to the north east of Canada.

We flew very low to enjoy the scenery.

Yarmouth was my first town on arrival. Many old homes and each one is different built.

Had Haddock and strawberry rhubarb pie for dinner. So good what else can be better? It always will be my favorite desert.

There is a big Herring fishing fleet in the Harbor and it all smells of it.

The season of long days are now here, and the sun does not go down till almost 10pm. It will be great for bicycling.

Our wakeup call by a Foghorn. Fixed my bike and went on a tour of Yarmouth and the lighthouse with my friend Evalyn. Talked to the fishermen and found out there are no Lobsters till November in Canada. Now is Scallop season.

The big ship, "the Blue Nose" arrived from Bar Harbor Maine with more of my friends for our bike trip around Nova Scotia.

We will do 57 miles today. First through a lot of woods but then along the Ocean. And lots of Wildflowers blooming and the perfect weather.

Our first breakdown happened on a very deserted road with Gail's bike. We had no tools and would have known what to do anyway, a nice fellow in a pickup stopped and fixed the bike. But soon Gail had the same trouble again. She had not learned how to use all the gears and had trouble because of it. And is using now only the smallest gear. Our leader, who disappears often, thinks we are pretty stupid on gears. He was supposed to help in trouble and show us the trails. Following the lighthouse trail or trying to.

I noticed that in many driveways strange colored weed looking, was lying on the cement. It turned out it was Moss from the sea. It either gets raked by people or by Horse off the bottom of the sea. Then dried in the sun and packed to the cannery's for eating. Who eats it? And supposed to do other uses.

Today, along the Barrington Passage after a good sleep. We overnighted in a Commune in an old Schoolhouse. Very neat and good cooking. There seemed to be lots of Baby's there.

And a new day, to Shelbourne for 52 miles after a good pancake breakfast. I am biking alone so I can see some wildlife. A desolate countryside without any stores. Deer crossing in front of me. Watching in the river 4-foot Salmon jumping to get to the spawning fields.

Just before Shelburne we encountered hills, lot of climbing. And the great Mill River invited us to cool off.

Liverpool for 60 miles next. With a lot of up and downs now along the coast but then arrived in Sommerville were we stopped at a bakery for nourishment. By now some of the Riders are getting tired. Evalyn had a big blowout but a new tire was found.

Liverpool had a Quilt Exhibition which was great to see artistry on some of the quilts.

Our Dinners consisted mainly a lot of Haddock and Halibut. And I could eat them every day. And the Beer is very good.

I find biking near the Road a lot of Raspberry bushes and try to eat my fill.

Lunenburg for 51 miles. The hilly countryside is still with us, but we are now in shape and bike faster not because the wind was blowing us in the right direction.

Lunenburg was built by German Settlers 150 years ago. Big doublemasted Sailboats are being built here. Even the replica of the "Bounty" and the "Blue Nose" came from here. Lunenburg is the most pristinely preserved 18th century fishing village in Canada.

Went to the county Fair that night and had a lot of fun. Sleeping is difficult since the beds are very old and creaky.

After the fog lifted the next morning Evalyn and I biked Mahone Bay. Very pretty like a Postcard photo.

Later after Gail had a flat tire fixed, again, she and Marriel joined us for tea.

Trout tonight for Dinner.

That night we could not sleep, since it was very hot, no fans or air-condition. It is unusual to have heatwaves up north.

Caledonia is our next stop today, but the rains came. Gave us reasons to stop for more Bakeries'. They are very good, and we all eat the good scones because we are biking. That was always our excuse.

Back to Yarmouth now, we have done the circle of Nova Scotia. On a very lonely forested Road again. So our bike trip was over.

I rented a car for our remaining hours, and we went to see some more of the places we did not see. Stopped at a small Restaurant where I had my first Rappiepie. It is Potatoes and Chicken as the main ingredients. We rehashed our trip lying on a hill in the grass by the lighthouse. Good memories forever.

Gail and Merriel left for the "Blue Nose" and I flew home.

Brazil, 1990 Stopover
South Africa and Beyond, January 20, 1990

Had just been for a week in Cayman Island and packing now for my trip to South Africa, via Brazil. It was a long flight to Rio de Janeiro. I like stopovers and try to see some of the places then.

On the plane I got lots of advice what to do in Rio and what not to do. Do not wear any Jewelry or a watch or anything. At the Airport I was given instructions on what to do and be safe again.

Great arrival, no hassle and a nice taxi ride into town. I went out for a long walk heeding all the warnings. The city is very dirty and very rundown. People do not wear much clothing. Women wear the tightest outfits. And the men all are scratching their scrotum or whatever was itching them there and many bellies protruding above their belts. Must be too much beer drinking. There was a woman who was in a stupor lying on a bench with the tiniest baby on her side almost rolling off. So sad. Finally, another woman put the baby closer to the drunk mother.

There is a lot of street dancing; it is Carnival, so most people are practicing for the marching of the Samba Bands. All this in 90-degree heat.

I am having trouble deciphering the money. Some of the paper money is so shredded. Food seems to be very cheap. I had a steak dinner for $5.00, and a chocolate Napoleon which was out of this world.

When I ordered some of the famous small pancakes I ended up getting a glass of milk. My Portuguese is not so good.

Hotel Savoy is nice, and I am 2 blocks from the famous Ipanema Beach. It looks good but it stinks. No toilets anywhere in sight and people just go anywhere for relief. A mass of people in the water and it is Sunday morning. Everybody must be here to cool off.

Tried today to get into a Samba place but it does not start till 10pm. Too late for me.

A very good breakfast, Papayas!! That is really all I want. But cannot live on that alone and had some of the homemade cheeses and good bread. Starting out on a daytrip to Sepetiba Bay to Itacuruca, Costa do Sol by car. Could see many Islands off the coast. There are 36 Islands. Then transferred onto an old 2 mast ship. It is called a Saveiro ship.

I had to stay under the sunroof Did not want to get burned. And we stopped at a Beach called Jaguamum. The Mangroves are plenty and vegetation grows right down to the water.

The water is not very clear, and I skipped swimming. Then to another Island called Machin?

There was a great Restaurant with fantastic food. Fresh Frisch! And the best Beer.

Now a good swim in the warm and clean water.

Back to Rio by boat and Bus. With great thunderstorms along. Rio has many trees making it easier to overlook the dirty walls which all could use a good paint job. The police have power to fine if your storefront looks dirty, but I never saw any action taken.

I have the coffee in the morning and it tastes like lubricating oil. It is so strong!

My Bus arrived late which is not unusual to be late. I am going to the Natl. Forest Tijuca. But having a little stomach problem, not because of food because of the drive along the Mountain road and what speed the bus is going. There were some people praying on the Bus.

We drive through jungle like forests. Eucalyptus, mahogany,

rosewood and many other trees are towering above us. It is a rainforest which almost disappeared in the 19th century. Then the last Brazilian King Dom Pedro II, decided to reforest again. Over 110 000 seedlings were planted, by slaves mostly.

Many Butterflys flitting around. Tijuca is one of the largest urban forests in the world. The famous Christ the Redeemer statue is perched on the summit of one of the dozen peaks in the park.

At the tram station Iasajeiros, it was wild, everybody pushed on to get a seat.

I had a wonderful view, and we traveled at least through 30 tunnels before climbing up to Corcovado for Lunch in a meat restaurant. The waiters are walking around with 3-foot-long skewers full of meat then come to the table and slice off what one points to.

On Corcovado's Summit, at 2300feet, the Christ Statue was built in 1931. It is 120 feet high, and weighs 700 tons. The head alone weighs 30 tons.

It was built by a Frenchman Paul Landowski. (It is now one of the 7 wonders of the World in 2007).

And now to sugarloaf Pao de Azucar. A cable car goes up in two stages. First to Urca and then the top. There I had Maracuica Juice, Passion Fruit. Thirsty after the meaty Lunch.

Saw the soccer stadium with 250 000 seats! the new Cathedral which looks awful but with a lot of stained glass. The top of it was supposed to be a heliport but the roof is not strong enough. It was a bad design.

Catching a late 11pm flight to South Africa

Johannesburg, South Africa, January 24, 1990

There is again that beautiful smell of charcoal all over the air. I love it, it is Africa to me.

On arriving in Johannesburg my friend Will toured an interesting place, Soweto! It is so different from what I expected. Teeming with life! It is a collection of shacks made out of anything to keep them from falling down and beautiful houses. I was used from TV seeing a different view.

A typical "Barbie" dinner with Lamb and delicious wine for my first night. I do feel the height of Johannesburg knowing it is at 6000 feet elevation.

All night we had rain and storms. But the morning there was again blue sky. Traveled through the countryside by bicycle and found it beautiful.

Now we left for Nelspruit and then Kruger Park. Established in 1884 by President Paul Kruger and opened in 1898.

The Roads are very smooth. Driving on the left side is no problem. I have done it in other places I have visited. I loved the many flowers growing near the Roads, Cosmos mostly.

At the first Gate of Kruger Park a Warthog family was rooting around, like a nice welcome for me. Loved how their tails pointed straight up. From then on it was slow driving because of so many animals to be seen.

The next 8 miles we saw so many animals, many Impalas, Hyenas, Duikers and many different birds.

The first Lodge Berg-en-dal was beautiful, situated in rolling hills. And my first Dinner was Kudu steak, it tasted very good. And always the famous Boerewurst. Meat is very important on the Diet of Afrikaans.

On a short walk around the Camp only a frog was in sight. We were fenced in, so we do not have any surprises at night. 6 am is opening of the gates again.

Awakened by birdsong at 5:30am some of the birds sound like

children crying.

Red billed Cowpecker, black headed Oriole, namerkop, Francolin, Garmine Bee eater, Bateleur Eagle Grey Hornbill, Yellow Hornbill, black Hornbill.

A very good breakfast of porridge with Papaya and the Wurst and eggs and Bacon.

And on to Skukuzu at the lower Sabie River. Took all day to get there but always is so much to see. We wanted to be at the waterhole to watch the wildlife at 8pm, if to decide what is more important.

Driving along the jungle like big trees and along the Crocodile River. A very lush area.

Satora

The first animals seen in the morning: spotted Hyana, Steinbock, squirrel, snake, warthog, Impala, Partridge, Guinia hen, Kudu, Zebra, Wildebeest, Cervet Monkey, Baboon, Crocodile, Bushbuck, Elephant, Klippspringer, giraffe, Mongoose, hippos, and a Leopard Turtle. I am making too many photos. We drive by a lot of Elephant Dung on road. Keeps the Dungbeetle busy. I had to watch them how they rolled each pebble, the size of a marble, wherever to.

5am, first trip out again for a game drive. 2 Elephants standing right by the gates, big! Since we can only drive on the gravel road, we have to wait for them to move. Our car looks so little next to their bodies.

We have driven and stopped at beautiful waterholes and by 8am we must turn back. It's too hot already and most animals will rest under the trees. But we saw Dwarf Mongoose, Red crested Kohaan, Walberg Eagle, saddle billed stork which is unusual I am told, African fish Eagle, buffalo, Hartebeest, Waterbuck, Knob billed Duck and a Lion female with two males.

At Lunch time, we made it to Tschohwane to Satoka and checked in and drove the Roads around near the fence to Mozambique. We encountered a Lioness who just killed a Zebra. She was out of air and had to recuperate first before starting to rip apart her dinner. She did look like she got kicked in the face by the Zebra too, we could see a big cut.

By now about 200 vultures are waiting in the trees, a jackal sniffing about and all the tourist cars arriving for photo options. The poor lion was so exhausted and now she was not happy to start eating, too many tourists watching.

We had to get back to camp because Gates do close at certain times and don't know what would happen if we are locked out of camp.

Our Rondell is beautiful, and that in a state Park. There is nothing like this to compare in USA. Built in the African Style with hammocks to watch wildlife. And great Dinner served at the Lodge. Impala Steaks!

Satara

4am Game drive! 6 Lions are outside the Gates sleeping.

On Rt. S100 to Skibotwana now and we meet up with more Lions who are eating a Buffalo. It stank! As we kept looking and making photos, suddenly a Lioness came up next to us. And closed our windows very fast.

Driving to Oliphant's. It is known for Elephants. checked it because it is so beautiful situated on top of a Mountain with views to the Oliphant River below. Yes, many Elephants are standing in the River.

Again, we got another beautiful Rondell there. And drove around to find out what I could discover next. Ground Horn Bill, Reedbuck, Marabou, black switch Plover.

We had to watch crossing the River. It has been raining the last few hours, and the river is getting higher. Do not want to be stranded on the wrong side. I noticed that the Impala like to stay on the paved road; they do not like the wet grass. A big Baboon family crossing in front of us.

Again, a very good Dinner at the Lodge.

Phalaborwa and Branddraai is the next stop. On our way there 30 wild hunting dogs just lying on the paved Road. The puppy's started playing and it was so much fun watching the wild Dogs. When 3 Hyenas tried to come close the Large dog Male attacked them right away. The Hyenas only wanted the poop from the Dogs because it was fresh and that is what they like to eat.

At the exit Gate from Kruger Park at Phalaborwa was an Ostrich standing like a guard.

We are on our way to the Drakensberg passing a lot of Mango Plantations, lots of fruit trees. And we passed through a few Homelands. Very poor, overgrazed and very dirty. Garbage anywhere. Tin sheds all over. No sanitation or electricity.

Passed through the Abel Erasmus tunnel, which took 16 years to be built. But everywhere one stops somebody is trying to sell something. Very pushy, and if we did not buy, we got screamed at us.

Arrived at the Blyde River Canyon Lodge called the Oorde Resort Odendaal. Situated on the Canyon rim. Very beautiful and very plush, I think 5 servants for every customer.

Went hiking the Mountain trail but I picked up a long stick after I was told about leopards attacking people, but saw only Baboons.

Great Dinner and went to sleep after the best wine and Mangos.

It is raining today; all this area is known for Mountain views, waterfalls, Gorges. Next time. I will be back.

Back to Johannesburg

Went sightseeing on the double-decker Bus. Never saw so many

Guard dogs in all the houses I could see. Little poodle types.

Went up the Carlton Tower and had very clear views of the City. Went to the American Embassy to leave a copy of my papers since I was going off to travel alone into unknown places to me.

Johannesburg is interesting with so many tribes living there.

A trip to Pretoria first. Had to learn about the history and Pretoria is the Capital of South Africa.

Much history in Pretoria. Samuel Marks House first built in 1884. I would call it a farm. Every piece of furniture was imported from England and only the best. Even his 30 English servants too.

Then to the Cullinan Mine of de Beer diamond fame. Everything underground, it is like a city only 60 miles from Pretoria, but it has everything. So much money comes from a shiny stone. Diamond! And the digging is still going on. 4000 employees, always 2000 underground. I went down as far as possible. Afterwards I had to go through a strict search by lie detector and a sense detector. Not a piece of dirt can be picked up.

Back to Pretoria again to see the Union Building. It is like the Capitol in Washington DC. But it is built on the highest point of Pretoria with a view over the Valley. Walked to the Krueger House which was beautifully built too. Krueger lived here till he died in 1901. So, everything is real, no copies of furniture. The town is a living Museum.

I went back to Johannesburg, and I stayed in the Linden Hotel. It is owned by a Lebanese woman from Harare, Zimbabwe. Complaints were that there is no good help anymore.

Zimbabwe Former Rhodesia, February 2, 1990

There was a strike in Johannesburg. But I got somehow onto Air Zimbabwe. It flew only to Bulawayo, which is the entry for the country now. Hoping another plane will go to Victoria Falls. I was in luck. A small plane was available. The view from the plane was green trees, many Rivers and no Roads.

We stopped a few times on grass strips but I could not buy anything since I did not have enough Rands and $ were not taken. Great views over the Victoria Falls. The pilot loved giving us a tour. On landing I checked into the Rainbow Hotel, very nice, looked like a castle. Now I could swim and drink castle Beer.

Getting ready for tonight's Village Dance at the Victoria Hotel. A beautiful old Hotel.

For Dinner a Braai at the Rainbow Hotel.

Many Mosquitos are attacking me. Always me.

Victoria Falls

All night I could hear the falls. And with Thunderstorm and rain it should be a sight. They are called the "Wet Falls". One has to wear a raincoat or something like it. Cameras have a hard time staying dry. It is all left alone like a Jungle. Even on the long walk the litter cans are hidden in hollow trees. One cannot see too much with a lot of Water in the air. The falls are 913 meters high, it is very humid too.

I decided to walk 3 miles along to the falls in Zambia.

The Border guards were very nice. I walked over the famous Bridgewater Bridge. What a view from there. And then to the Falls to see from the "other" side. There was a big difference. In Zambia, no tourists or any commercial building. But many Monkeys playing around. The people are very sweet and very proud. Nobody has money.

I was offered a ride back to the Bridge Border on a pickup truck with 4 Zambian young men who worked in the copper mines. Well spoken, educated. I remember Steven Knanga. We kept in touch for a while. His only request was to send Battery's for his Radio, which I did. And photos of us all together.

In the afternoon I went to a crocodile farm on the River and then on a Boat trip on the Zambesi River. History again! Dr. Livingstone was here before me.

Hippos in the River and I was told they could turn our boat over easy. But luckily it was rest time for them.

I could still see a lot of bombed out houses on the hills from the civil war. Many Hotels are sitting empty and since there is very little Money in Zimbabwe and no tourist business. All the white Farmers have left and moving to South Africa. Fields are going into jungle and undergrowth.

Today I rented a bicycle and pedaled all over. Along the River and through the village. I could enjoy it a little more, since I could stop were I liked. Just sitting on a Bench and watching traffic go by. And always the thunder of the Falls. Along the River a Warthog surprised me or I surprised it. One Antelope in a hurry and an Elephant just standing in the middle of the Road. I had to wait till he lumbered off.

I walked around and talked with some young street sellers. I was told all the artist of Zimbabwe come here hoping to sell something. Small figures they carve out of Malachite. There are no other jobs.

At the Victoria Train station I noticed a Steam Train getting ready to leave I started talking to the Engineer because I love trains. The Engineer invited me to come up into the front. There are 140 Engines still in use in Zimbabwe and all use coal. 13 Wagons is the average. This Engine was built in 1943, and the Engineer has been on it for 23 years. In this heat and stoking the fire.

But I had to go catch my little plane to Hwange. For 100 of miles the plane flew over forests, no house or anything and landed at Hwange Airstrip.

Hwange Lodge

The Hwange park is supposed to be bigger than Ireland. Never saw so many wild animals and at least 200 Elephants in one herd. When driving with a jeep it was strange that the Elephants did not move off. The surrounded us and just wanted to smell us. Counted Buffalos but gave up counting after 200. Sable Antelope a very elegant animal. Spurwinggeese with lots of Babys.

There has never been any hunting in that area, all animals love to be close to the Lodge and take advantage of the biggest Waterhole there. Lights are shining at night, and one can see a moving show of different animals coming for their drinks. Even the Owls are almost tame and do not move when pointed at. There was no fence, and a constant flow of animals went through the open foyer.

Dinner was very good. I love eland Steak.

5:30 game drive with Eden, the guide, it was still dark. Many animals were sleeping in close range for us to see, maybe it is the safest place for them.(There was a Lion in 20002, who always was nearby and named by the tourists Cecil, but got killed by an over eager Hunter in 2015.)
I finally saw a white Rhino and joined by a small baby, there are so few left. The get poached for their Horns. 5 hunting dogs got a baby Impala right in front of us. Not much was left of it after 5 minutes.

Had to change my room because the Mosquitos just got to me there. I look like I have the measles. Now I have Air-condition.
It is hard going to sleep at night just watching all the Animals. Don't want to miss anything. The Zebras are watching from the waterhole. The monkeys are a problem one has to watch, the steal anything. Saw again a Rhino and a secretary Bird, a Jennet Fox with two babies.

All Lodges have the best food. One has to watch the calories since very little exercise.

The evening "performance" at the waterhole was so great again. 60 Elephants showed up. A honey Badger.
The Hwange park has been in existence since 1926 and with the lodge another 40 000 acres were added.
One more day and again an early game drive. There are always Impalas to entertain you. They show of, are full of life, back and force like a dance for us, beautiful.
I sit later by the waterhole just watching the animal's parade in and

out. Game drives are almost an extra. And the weather is so pleasant.

Can there be snow in USA?

I am flying in a very small plane, stopping in Kariba, juice was served, had to fly over the runway twice to clear the airfield. Then to Harare, and we even had food served. Lots of wildlife viewed from the plane.

The drive to Harare from the Airport was very interesting. One could see long lines of people standing and waiting for maybe one loaf of bread, then into another long line for the next product.

There are no cars, stores looked empty. But a lot of vegetables were growing almost everywhere. The President wanted that everybody plants food and not flowers.

I am staying in Hotel Mowoti on the 16th floor. I think I am the only guest. With my money I could afford now anything. Food in the Hotel was cheap. It is a 5 star Hotel. My first ever. Was not used being addressed "Madam this and that". Very nice.

Sightseeing in the City. I think it was the cleanest city I had ever been to. It was pointed out that the buildings are being built after independence and are the better? As much I saw they all were empty.

The TV station is built on the highest Hill in Harare.

There is a tale told by a person to me that some Medicine man, a shaman, is saying one can only be cured of Aids if sleeping with a white woman. So there have been 8 rapes last week of white women. The witchdoctor is the most powerful man in the country and people stand in line to see him. More powerful than the President.

And I am reminded to take Malaria pills all the time.

Malawi 7th

Arrived in Lilongwe, Malawi. A small country and then only known for taking many Refugees from Mozambique. I wanted to get to know it more because it had history of Livingstone and the Lake

Malawi with burial places of the Missionaries from that time.

Many forms had to be filled before leaving the airplane. Sloppy dressing and long hair was not excepted.

Finally my ride to Nkopola Lodge. A 5 hour drive, I thought we would never get there. No public transportation at all for all the natives standing on the road hoping to get a ride.

Everybody is walking and carrying heavy loads. Their cloth are torn or shredded, children have cloth made out of flour sacks. Since driving close to the Mozambique border almost all the people I saw are refugees from that war torn country.

Nkopola Lodge surprised me. As usual no customers except me. It is one of the most romantic places I ever saw. Malawi lake is warm and clear, it is very deep.

The fish for Dinner was caught fresh right out of Lake Malawi.

Some of the people living in the village heard I was visiting. I big welcome in the evening with a performance by four old Riflemen, who at least were over 75 years old. Very serious faces and medals pinned to their coats.

My room is right on the Beach. Cooler and relaxing. Very good food again was served.

Next day an Excursion to Cape McLear. A Road with big potholes and a lot of water crossings. The little Suzuki car is a workhorse. Arrived at Dr. Livingstone's first settlement. But it was not taken care off, very overgrown by the Bush. I was seeing living History right there. The Graves of the Missionaries who died of Malaria and other ailments can be visited. The ruins of the old Hotel, which was used only 5 years, are still there.

A most beautiful Bay for swimming right there. Hoping the park service will take it over one day again.

Lake Malawi is a strange lake. Nothing grows in it except very large fish. Very warm water.

Next to my Hotel are 3 fish eagles just waiting in the tree. Big rocks are there to climb on. Where did the Rocks come from?

The village youth invited me to play Volleyball with them. They are very good and did not like me holding the Ball too long.

I think this place is lovely. I am still the only guest and get spoiled by the help. I like the weather and always have been a friend of warmer climates.

Dr. Livingstone complained about this place of the heat and the Malaria problem. On my walk through the bush I encountered monkeys, Baboons and Hyrax and many Butterfly's. Then I spend hours just in the warm lake water relaxing again.

Malawians work in the South African mines. When they make enough money they bring a new car back. One cannot buy a new car in Malawi, there are no Dealerships.

I am a big fan of the writer Wilbur Smith and reading "The Sunbird" by Wilbur Smith who is describing almost all the places in that story I have seen right now.

Went today to Mangochi, crossed the Shire River and all on dirt Roads with the Suzuki. Saw a beautiful Pottery called Malawi Pottery.

Women wore a beautiful wraparound with the president's face on the behind. I wanted one too. But no store sold it because it was out of style by now.

But I saw a woman taking her laundry off the line and "my wraparound". 30 Kwacha and it was mine. I was the happy owner of a president Medallion now.

This all called for a nice long swim again on coming back. English tea was served and a later Barbecue with a different tribe from another Village dancing for me.

The whole village was invited too. And everybody tried to explain the different dances to me. The Chief Chipoka of Mangochi was sitting next to me. He was born 1914 I was told.

Today there is a stormy see. Feels like an Ocean, I was told sometimes big storms come and is not always peaceful. And it is raining now.

In the village I had a little box made for me and picked it up. All handmade with a little lid. It is very funny.

At lunch I met the village chief again, he brought his 2 wives and 8 children. He is the absolute power here. We exchanged some presents, but mostly he wanted to know how single women can travel alone and why.

Wonder if the Peace Corps ever made it here. So I learned a lot of their lives and we talked.

Crocodile for Dinner! But too salty for me. Did it taste like chicken, I don't think so.

The big news today, Mandela is released from prison. He was a terrorist but so where many other big leaders of African countries.

I wish I could have been in Cape Town but I will get there.

Driving to Lilongwe the capital of Malawi. Having not slept much last night. The bats on the roof kept me awake. And the Monkeys woke me up just when I was ready to sleep.

4 hours again of pothole roads but I was the first passenger at the Airport. There are 3 flights a day. That is busy for this little country. Reservation are not necessary, first comes first.

Durban, South Africa

Found a great place to stay. A 2 bedroom Apt.! Clean too, and a very good night.

The language here is English and Zulu. Zulu is a clicking speech.

One does not notice anything of Apartheid here. It is always been a very integrated city. And Durban is surrounded by Zululand.

Everything is Mandela News. Many happy faces. The city is beautiful too, pots with flowers all over. Out in the Harbor many ships are at Anchor, it is the biggest shipping town for South Africa.

Had tea in the botanical Garden.

Then the Beach! Warm water! But many shark nets for the swimmers.

I have to get used to the Zulu women having heavy white cream on their faces. They look like Ghosts. I guess it is for the sun. Watched TV and saw a Coca Cola commercial in Zulu. Then listened to Mr. Mandela's speech, which was great.

Books I am reading now "Dick King: Sandpiper and Somerset". All stories about South Africa. And on TV Dallas in Afrikaans!!!

There is a shopping mall nearby. 8 floors, 12 movie theatres. But I went to the History Museum of Durban. And now I notice that almost all people here speak 3 languages.

As I walked 3 miles to the Indian Market this morning I met many kind of people. The market was horrible. The smell was putrid. Wherever one looked Lamb heads were hanging. For sale many Spices.

Durban has one of the biggest Mosques in Africa it looked to me like a shopping center.

The old Rail station is converted into a beautiful Mall. But again it is off season so no tourists in sight. At City hall Zulu Music was performed, they called themselves "Colenso Alabama".

To Zululand. I finally got to see Shaka Zulu.(a impersonator) He was very famous. This was his land. Called the land of the 1000 hills. Always houses are built on top of a hill. The big town is Kloop, very beautiful with flowers blooming all over.

Here again is a place I read about in one of Wilbur Smith Books

"The Swallows". Looking now for Shakas Gate, I wonder if it still exists.? The Zulus do not have telephones but flagpoles and each has a different flag which can mean: party, Birthday, death or anything.

In the village some of the Zulu Girls danced. They had no problem having no tops on. Very natural.

The men are strong looking and many carry an assegai which is a mixture of a knife and spear.

In the evening gone to eat Indian food. Very spicy.

Cape Town

Arriving in Cape town and have credit card trouble. Not good when one needs to rent a car. Had to call USA to Kevin to see what was wrong, he fixed it.

Rented a very nice place for 25rand a night. Breakfast included. Only bad part, window faces the street. We will see.

Cape Town is either up or downhill. Beautiful. I can see the Mountains and the Table Mountain is right above me. All old houses are beautiful restored and very colorful painted.

A lot of homeless and drunks seem to sleep in the bushes. Alcohol is a very big issue. If you pay a black worker before Friday he or she is gone to drink. If it is a good worker and increases the salary, it is even worse. Then they do not come back for 2 weeks till the money runs out. They just don't get the idea of saving ahead. Only today is important.

There is an old Master Captain who told me the ship I immigrated to the USA, "Berlin", sunk at Francis Bay. Which is near Cape Town. Everything was dismantled for scrap except the bottom. I always wondered why I never saw the ship again.

My night was noisy no sleep, and I changed to the Palm Court Lodge for 35r a night. Very clean too.

Went today to the Cape of Good Hope by Bus. The Road looks very dangerous to drive. On each side a different Ocean. The architecture of the houses clinging to the hills is beautiful. Houses are painted white with green window frames. Somebody told me that it was the law because a lot of green paint was in abundance and had to be used???

Stopped on my way back in Groot Constantina. A very good wine was served there, it is situated next to the Botanical Garden which was once Cecil Rhodes home and Farm.

Finally that night a long sleep and Breakfast in bed. It is raining anyway and very foggy on top of the Mountain.

Walked over to the famous Hotel Nelson. It is so English. The outmost luxury.

A walk to the South Africa Museum and having tea there. Got into big discussions there with a lot of people what will be next for the country. It was great to listen. Politics, School system everything came up.

I did not like how big whaling used to be here. How cruel it was.

Now to the Old Castle Fort to look at. That used to be the old prison and was being restored as a museum. The way it looked I don't think many prisoners ever made it alive out of there.

Coming home, my Lodge had the best Apple cake for me, I liked the place even more.

In the evening, I met all my new friends for more talks and very good wine drinking from the Nederberg winery.

A trip to Stellenbosch on a rainy day. Stellenbosch was settled by Dutch and French Huguenots. The wine area is known for very good wine. But then the sun came out on arriving in the wine country. For many miles just winery's. No country can drink it all alone and found out that a lot of wine is being shipped to South America and from there to North America.

Hartenberg Winery was the first stop. Wine is too dry. Next please.

Stellenbosch is beautiful and I will return.

Now to Franshock, more wine region. "Boschendal" not my taste either, to dry.

Lunch at Lancerot a beautiful Estate in the countryside.

And always the Valleys are surrounded by Mountains. The little Roads wind through curve after curve. It is Grape picking time.

Then a stop at the Hugenot Memorial, a small cemetery from the old wars. There is a poem on the big stone.

"Not dead but soared from human sight
To God in closer Bund.
Not dead, but passed from darkest sight
To realms of Bliss beyond."
1836-1892

There are dairy Cows, vegetable fields and lots of fruit trees. I cannot understand how anything grows in this rocky soil. Stones are plenty.

Moving again because my room is needed, everything is full but found a place at Mr. Morris on the Hill. Have tried getting a car but hard to get.

It still rains again but got an automatic car. I got my visa for Namibia and reservations and especially in Etosha. Which I will visit after I come back to Cape Town.

Went to see the Movie Shirley Valentine. Great!

Ate Apple pie with lots of cream and then went on a hike to work it off. Going up to the Reservoir and got a view of 2 Rainbows and of shiny Cape Town underneath me.

Finally, my rental car arrived. A BMW, but no other choice.

So, I am off to the northern coast.

Paarl, first to see the Nederberg Winery.

Then on to Tulbagh. A Town not to be missed I was told. One of the oldest settlements of the Afrikaans. And what a surprise it was. Every house is prettier than the other. The 1969 Earthquake destroyed a lot, but everything was rebuilt in the old look again.

The Drostdy built in 1805 a beauty.

But there were no Hotels or B&B's. It was too late to drive back to find a Hotel anywhere. After asking around, I was told up in the hills is a farm, who take sometimes Guests. And that is where I found my new friends. The du Plessies Family. There was Johann and Leta, parents, and children Marilie, Charl, Daniel and little Johann. On my first night there I babysat and liked it.

It is a big surprise to me how fast I was like a family member. The next day I was shown the Farm. Johann proudly explained the work they do and how good everything was running with help.

The big Sheds all were used for drying fruit. And big Baskets filled to the top sitting in the sun for drying natural. Prunes on racks to dry. Many Fruit trees laden still with prunes. I love Prunes.

Then we went to the winery section where I tasted the Drostdy-Hof. Adelpracht and old Sherry. No South African Wine has sugar added. And are not so sweet like California wines.

At the Dinner table, heavy discussions on what my impressions are. And the future of South Africa. It is now the big question on everybody's mind.

There are 3 little dachshunds as house pets. The love to snuggle. On my walk the following day I almost stepped on a puff adder snake. The dogs saw it first. One of the workers came running and chopped its head off very fast. The color of the snake was no different from the earth.

Tonight, Johann on his walk found a still in the vineyard and it was destroyed right away. The workers make them for quick alcohol.

My time here was great. I enjoyed all the learning of the farm. I will never forget the place. Surrounded by a Mountain Range and very peaceful. With the perfect weather everything is growing. Found out it is about 1000 acres of fruit trees.

One can see a lot of the workers in the fields, picking or in the sheds with the fruits.

Johann found some time to take me to the top of one Mountain. There is a little house for a perfect getaway.

Now I am sitting on a Rock just watching the animals that come out in the afternoon on the big Rock piles. Looks like two Meerkatz looking at me. Wild Guinea Fowl running around.

I see Johann inside next to his computer. Which is opening the water allowance in different areas. 3 days a week, he is allowed to fill the Reservoir.

The only problem is when it is dry in the Karoo—fire! And it can come over the Mountain to the Farm.

This morning the children went off to school and I am getting ready to leave. Marilie is a very talented 15y. In Tennis, piano and straight A's. I am told to visit the Family Beach House in Janfontaine if I have time. That is a great invitation.

(The peace did not last long in the Valley. 2 years later the women in the family got assaulted and Johann had many stab wounds in his Belly from the attack but recuperated.)

I am driving through Ceres. Many Juice factories are there, and I always see the juice in the USA now and it reminds of my time there.

For 50 miles I have not seen a car. I am in the Little Karoo. Mostly desert. But getting to Montague with the famous warm springs. It is supposed to be radioactive healing waters. Feels so good. Staying in the Hotel Avalon, hope the Disco will not make too much noise at night.

But before darkness, I went on a hike called Lovers Walk. Saw

Klippspringers, a big Turtle and lots of Lassies.

A good tea and some poppy Bread have revived me again. My stomach has a problem, but it will settle.

Driving is very nice here. People pull over to the right if somebody wants to pass.

I drive through Barryvale, Ladysmith and then to Outhshoorn. Crossed many passes and Valleys. And more Winery's. Many Ostrich Farm's. Thousands of Ostrich, they are raised like cattle. Ostrich Steaks are really good. The heads from the butchered Ostrich's go to Crocodile farms. The feathers for products plucked every 6 month alive.

The legs give 4 pounds of Biltong and the steaks are coming from the shoulders. The skin brings the most money, for shoes, handbags and so on. The eggshells are so hard one can walk on them. Many useful parts of one bird.

I did ride an Ostrich, had to do it. Very uncomfortable. Visited the Cango Caves, very big and an Organ music was playing in there. The seating for concerts is for 5000 people.

Staying now in Klainplaas Holiday Resort. 45rand a night. Beautiful sundown today over the Mountains.

Leaving early gives me more to see. Came to one of the Vortrekker trails. Very tough road and all had to be done with Oxen. The Boers were a tough people. Curve after Curve again. Woods and there was the ocean.

Brenton on Sea and I started looking for a rest here.

Knysna

Another beautiful town. The Ocean is pounding below with a noisy surf. My room is closest to the Ocean I could get, should be good for sleeping.

Driving around to see what is growing, fields of Hops! It's grown for Beer. Majestic Mountains in the background. And long sweeps to the beaches, and all beaches are empty.

Driving the famous Garden Route, so much to see. I have to stop constantly.

Stopped at "Wilderness" another historical place on Mossel Bay. There is an old wreck the "Caravelle". But the attraction is the most interesting tree. It was used as the Post Office for ships going or coming this way in olden times. The tree is still there and is called the Milkwood tree. Sailors left their notes by the tree. It was Documented already in 1500. It was a place to bring fresh water on all the ships.

Then crossing the old Bridge over the Gowits River, it was a building feat.

And Stillbay near Janfontain in sight. A long drive through Dunes and Hills and I found the du Plessis House. The caretaker opened it for me.

Not a person in sight at the Beach or Village. I had the place for myself.

The caretaker seems to be the only person living in the Village. He told me his wife died last year.

I left the seaside unwilling but had to move on. Janfontain is a long way from Cape Town and that is where I am headed now.

A totally different countryside now. Grain fields for miles, sheep and grain again. 400km to do.

Stopped at the Bontebok Natl. Park. The only existing place for Mountain Zebra and I saw 2. Gray, Rhebok and Red Hartebeest.

Swellendam

A beautiful old town. With a big Drostdy (Magistrate) erected in

1746.

Today, a self-drive to Cape Agulhas, to the most southern point in Africa. Fantastic Lighthouse. It is better by tour bus, too many curves and cliffs.

Cape Town

Lucky, I got the last room in the Carnaby Hotel. A nice pool and again nice owners serving scones and tea.

The old Harbor in Cape Town is being redone. Right now, it is still a place for seals to rest on the old piers.

Trip up to the Tafelberg. (Tablemountain). Took a double-decker bus to the Station. The Bus can hardly make it up the hill. Wheezing and slowing down. I could have walked faster.

Then by Seilbahn to the top. It started out fine but when we went over the big cliffs, my stomach did not like it. Such a steep way! Arriving on top, I had to get used to the height first. Quickly ate something it helped. But was not looking forward for the way down. I lingered as long as long I could one cannot stay overnight.

The view is fantastic with a very clear sky.

In town again had a few films developed, but it is very expensive. And relaxing by the pool with tea and just talking to people.

In the evening, I have my favorite wine from Nederberg Stein 1989 semi sweet.

Saved one of the Doves by the pool from the claws of a cat.

Namibia, 1990

My flight today to Namibia over the beautiful Tulbagh Valley. Good memories from my stay there.

Windhoek the Capital. This is a country I read about a lot in grade school because it was once a German colony. And I was into the history of that country very much. It made little sense a country so far away from Germany. Windhoek was founded in 1890. It calls itself city of Harmony.

A 40 km drive into town and never a house in sight. My Taxi took me to the Pension Handle. I was surprised how much everything still had the German names. But the town can be seen walking in one day. Could not find any Bus service going to the places I wanted to go.

Black and white people talked to me in German, and I found out it is still the main language. There are bakeries and stores with the German names of 100 years ago.

Then I noticed very tall and most statuesque people. They are the Herero tribe. Very proud. They do not do manual labor and love to dress in very beautiful outfits. Many layers of petticoats, like 10 skirts. Their hats are made from the finest material too. Long time ago a missionary told them to dress like that, and they have kept that tradition.

The average woman is about 6 foot tall. It is very interesting to see so many different races in this country and all getting along.

The first Independence Day is celebrated on the 21 of March so a lot of exiting things will happen.

For Dinner I could have been in Germany only the food here is better. But I had Leberkase, yummi and Sacher Torte.

I met some people who were tourist too and had a car and invited me to join so we went to Gross Barmen which has very hot Springs. It was so good to just soak there in the Sulphur water. Again, was told healing power.

Why is it raining again? It never rains here. Driving back 100km in the rain to Windhoek.

Just thinking: made it to the highest in the Andes by bike to 14000 feet.

To the deepest point of the earth: The red sea in Israel.

To the southernmost point of Africa, Cape Alguas.

Anyway, Windhoek is populated by the UN. Most every car is owned by them. They are here for the celebration of Independence, that everything will go smooth.

The Pension Handle is very good, but I cannot sleep. Mrs. Handle is so motherly and cooking so German how can I go anywhere else?

The town is very hilly and as I walk I find out it is "breathtaking" I am out of shape. I found out the city is at 3000 feet.

A very good museum is one of the German forts. So now many new buildings are seen too and a lot of high rises are planned.

Again, it is raining; I am bringing rain to every place I go. And we are in a Desert! Inland it seldom rains.

The Konditoreien are my downfall. How can I stop this good eating?

My Hostess took me shopping and explained about politics and what is going on here. She immigrated 6 years ago to Namibia at 74 years old from Germany. She is doing tourist business and hopes to do good.

Going for drinks to the "Fuerstenhof" on the Kaiserstrasse. But a quite night there. The people I met there had me in deep Discussion right away and we exchanged books by Wilbur Smith. They are a great reading.

Watched some TV and do not like the commercials at all. They promise black family's the moon. Nobody mentions that one has to save money to get all this.

Now to Etosha finally with the first night at Waterberg. It has been a Baboon day, there are so many.

Waterberg again has warm springs which I think are very important on trips. Then we all climbed up to the Plateau and viewed a lot of Birdlife. Fantastic Birds I have never seen before.

Waterberg was a German Fort and Police Station of the Schutztruppe. The big war of 1904 was fought here against the Hereros. And now we tourists can enjoy this beautiful place.

Still one can see the old Orchards and canals the German built to get water there. It is all left to go into old growth now. The Germans I meet now are already 4 Generations here. And it was called South West Africa then. It is now Namibia which means nothing grows here?

Wie man einen Loewen faengt? Erstmal dreht man die Fernglaeser um. Dann schaut durch, sieht den Loewen. Makes no sense to me but was told to me by an old man.

Our little houses faced the Mountain and all night one could hear noise from Baboons barking. And other strange sounds, the rain on the roof. A wild place.

Today's walk is to the old German Mission from 1800's and the cemetery. Most all the people buried in the cemetery where about 20 years old at death. They had a very short life. But everything was very orderly, and the Graves are kept clean and so far in the countryside away from any town. When I talk to a German descent person, they speak wonderful high German, and they are very proud of their ancestry.

Otjiwarongo, a small clean city for refreshment and on to the Etosha Hotel in Okankuejo. We are in the endless plains of Etosha. The Hotel is an old Fort and has a big waterhole. The tower, which was an outlook for the German Army. Climbing up one can see for miles. I could not even describe the sunset. Colors!

And now the stars are so clear and a full moon. Since there is no electricity for hundreds of miles it feels like one can reach the stars.

At the barbecue at night 3 Jackals are sitting nearby hoping something for them to eat.

Morning trip to see animals. Not much to see. The Grass is too tall from all the rain. And the animals do not need the waterholes, and we have to look for them now.

There is a large fat Lion resting on the Road. And we are sighting now the Jackals, Onyx, Zebra, brown or red Impala and lots of Springbook. Many ground squirrels and Birds. And it is an endless stretch of flat land.

In this dry heat the Pool is welcome at the Hotel, and I enjoy it.

The afternoon drive was again full of Animals sights. And suddenly standing there, two Rhinos, very large. A great finale for the day.

Namutoni

My wakeup call was a Lion roaring, gave me goosebumps. We left early since we have to drive 150 miles till the next stop.

Lunch at the Etosha Sands. But not a night stop since it is not Elephant or Lion safe.

There are Mirages in the front. From the heat it looks like there are many lakes. Nothing, not a drop of water. But still Animals are in sight. But no other Human. It is different from Krueger Park which is very civilized.

We are trying to see Desert Elephants. They are known for being very elusive. Zebras are good to view too and there are many.

Namutoni Fort again with a very beautiful pool for the night. Our Hotels are old forts which I had requested. This was a very strategic place for the soldiers and was defended in 1904 against 300 Womba warriors. Now the Fort is a very nice Rest camp. And very good wine is served here. Bellenhan from the Johannesburg area.

Back to Windhoek. 530km. Long drive. After the bugle call at 6:40am we were off. Much to see and time went fast.

In town Windhoek everybody is excited and there are no taxis at all. 6000 guest are expected next week. Where are they going to sleep?

On the street I noticed people selling big white Mushrooms about 1 foot big and wide. I am told they grow in the termite hills and are a delicacies. 1rand a piece. Did not try them.

Johannesburg

An uneventful flight to Johannesburg and checked into the Reef Hotel in Hillbrow. Except it is not a nice area for walking. Lots of Robberies.

So I am going to see more of the country by rental car. First Pretoria again since I only saw little of it the first time I went there. The wonderful Vortrekker monument is very impressive.

Next into the direction by car to Numbi and Sabie. The Roads are empty of traffic. Great driving. Making many detours through Mountains and countryside.

At Krueger Park magnificent weather. Checked into the Numbi Hotel at the Gate. Tomorrow I will do a 200-mile circle I can do all day at 60km an hour. That is the law. Had to drive through one homeland but was told not to stop for anybody, going through.

Next day, 7am for another game drive. I liked a sign by the River: Beware of Hippos. Many Hippos congregate and I know they can be fast.

As I was just sitting in my car watching some birds, the most beautiful Cheetah suddenly jumped on my Hood. Staring at me and trying to show off. 15 minutes just watching her and suddenly she was gone. I was very excited for this moment with the wild cat.

No cars all day, fantastic. The north of Kruger Park is just too far up for tourists.

There is a pride of Lions, Impalas, Giraffes, Zebra, Gnu or Wildebeest, Sable Antelope, Buffalo and a big Elephant with long tusk. Some Druiker running across the Road, Baboons and Monkeys and the Warthog, always the tail up.

Stopped at a farm rented room. For 18rand a night. But did not like the sign "Whites only". This sign was from before Apartheid but still up.

At night, 9 German shepherds patrolled the grounds. I stayed close by the house and did not want a run it with the watchdogs.

On my roof all night was a playground for Bushbabys and Francolins. Hard to sleep but finally got used to it.

Pilgrims Rest

Leaving early to drive over Graskop, a very scenic Road. Had coffee at the Panorama Lodge.

Over Kowyn Pass and later DeBerg Pass which was 10,000feet high. Everything was very green.

At Pilgrims Rest I walked around looking at all the little stores and the Mansion of the "Gold King". It is still a mining town.

Lunenburg, Belfast and on N4 back to Johannesburg and staying at the Reef Hotel again.

Went to the Gold Reef City and took the tour.

Down we went in a very fast Elevator. Had to wear a Hat with light. Went to the level 5.226 meters.

Here are some statistics:

The deepest shaft is 3000 meters. 9000feet!!! Built in 1949.

There is an emergency stairway with 1600 steps. But now seldom used.

There is a mercury rectifier. ?? Supposed to be only 2 in the world working. One in England. It converts electricity from AC to DC whatever that means.

The tunnels are Dolomite rock.

The language spoken down is called Fanagalo from the Zulu.

There are a 500 000 mine workers in S.A.

It takes 4 gram gold for 1 ton of stone and earth.

The 5 level tunnel is 60km long

We went to the top again 3meter per second.

Some facts. 1849 gold worth $16
1900 worth $20
1990 $399
2000 $1500
Lifting a Gold Bar was exciting, 12 pounds heavy

I did buy a Zulu hat as the only souvenir.

Today, I walked one more time through Johannesburg. After 2 months here I felt pretty much at home.

London, 1990

Flying to London and meeting my sister Petra there for 5 days. London was crowded. We saw a show called "Shadowlands" very sad. More sightseeing now with the double-decker Bus. I had lived in London in the late "50s. So it was nice to visit Windsor Castle, Runnymeade and Hampton Court again.

And then the rain came. And our trip was over anyway.

Germany biking, May 1990

This trip I called biking, hiking and kneiping----A bicycle tour of North Germany.

Having returned annually for many years, Germany is not new to me, it was once my home, but this year's trip was different because my regular bicycling companions, Bobby, Susan, Nancy, accompanied me on a bicycle tour of the north of Friesland, Germany. My sister Petra and five German women friends from my hometown of Bad Zwischenahn joined us for the week.

Equipped with German rented bikes (three gears, since the only departure from flat terrain would be the dikes we would climb).

Our plan was to travel by train from Bad Zwischenahn to Emden, a city at the Dutch border in the northwest corner of Germany. From there, we would bicycle eastwards towards Wilhelmshaven along the North Sea.

We met at the train station with hangovers from the get-together party the previous evening. When the train arrived, we stowed our bicycles and broke open our first bottle of wine for the 1-hour trip to Emden. Drinking early in the morning is understood by everybody.

From Emden we bicycled to Norden enjoying the beautiful villages, churches, Friesian Horses, huge Holstein cattle and many windmills which are ever present in the north.

Our arrival in Norden was late, but because daylight in late May and June lasts until about 10pm, no one was concerned.

For the next few days, we bicycled along the dikes in generally fine weather. The headwinds encountered were our excuse for frequent stops for cakes, beer or whatever refreshment got us going again. We especially enjoyed the fresh white asparagus, strawberries, and fish and, of course, the wonderful breads. At night, we stayed in comfortable Hotels or pensions, sleeping in big feather beds.

For a side trip, we ferried one day to the North Sea Island of Norderney where I had worked in a Pension, when I was a young girl. We spent the day hiking the Island and maintaining our policy of no-diet eating and drinking (kneiping).

Our Ferry ran aground on our return that was exciting to watch how the ship got floated again. Fortunately, it did not take us the several hours it sometimes does to become afloat, so we returned to the mainland at a reasonable time.

Although our German friends jokingly referred to us as "wet blankets" because we could not sustain their pace in attempting to consume all the available beer, wine and schnapps in North Germany, we nevertheless had many laughs together as we enjoyed the charm and beauty of this part of Germany which is little known to most American Tourists.

Venezuela, January 18, 1991

Went to Venezuela to see and climb the Roraima Mountains in the Sabana Grande. My experience in climbing is nil.

Arrived in Caracas and a very good Taxi-driver took me to the Hotel San Sabana Grande. He spoke very good English.

As usual I had many questions for him.

Caracas is built on hills. Up and down. Walking to get the feeling for the country. Having food at cheap prices and everything is fresh. Even fresh orange juice pressed by a street vendor. I had one day to see Caracas only because needed to fly to Ciudad Bolivar to meet my guides.

At the Airport I found out Airplanes do not fly till they are full. So a long wait, 2 hours now of waiting and finally departure.

Met my guides Ceasar and Louis and another couple who joined for the trip. Louis is the cook for the trip.

Our Hotel for the night is very beautiful right next to the Orinoco River. I am told the River is full of Piranhas. Hope not to fall in it. The town is a colonial river town.

Had a wonderful time by the pool and knew it would be the last civilized day.

Sunday morning, we are packing and hope to have bought all the important things. We have stocked up with apples and other fruit. Meat! There will be no more stores for a while. Our Land rover is packed to the fullest.

Passing many Oil refineries.

At km 70 we had to stop and show our passports and find a toilet and some Rum.

We have camped every night near some river or waterhole.

The Road is good and paved so far as we get closer to the Brazilian border. Passing some waterfalls, many Palm trees, and small Rivers. Going always south to the Gran Sabana, the Amazonas's territory. The Landscape has changed now a very green land.

Our Journey is to the Lost World made famous by Arthur Doyle. That is Roraima. Flat tabletop Mountains.

We are close to the jungle and arrived at the last outpost St. Elena. Brazil and Venezuela has one small border crossing there. I have tried to see and meet people. Not possible. There are no friendly faces. Most everybody is a goldminer, and we could be completion in looking for Gold. Still looking for the el dorado.

Then we lost our extra gas Tank, gas spilled on most of our bags, but all our wine bottles are ok. A slow leak in the rear tire is not helping much either. Checked the extra spare, it looks like new. We have driven 8 hours by now again and are tired. I do not like driving in the dark. First of all, I like to see the countryside.

With a Natl. Guard help we found a camping place.

I tried to convince everybody to eat bread and some soup. The cook was tired.

Beer or Rum as dessert. I stayed away from Alcohol because I took a lot of Medicines for my back.

I did sleep pretty good in the tent. Having the River run next to us was great soothing noise.

A sunny morning turned into rain very soon. Louis is doing breakfast. Scrambled eggs with everything. Mostly garlic.

Lois I found out was no cook.

We are driving now on a dirt path and did not know what a car could do till now. Such rutted Road. And many big water holes to cross. We did get stuck right in the middle of one and worked one hour to get the car going again.

Getting close to the mountains was an Indian village. They made us pay for the drinking water we needed, it was Indian land, but government water. Still pay. From now on it was hiking, no car could go further. We hassled for porters to carry our luggage. Small guys and one would think how could they carry anything. But they were strong. The charged $20 a day each. And no more than 30 pounds a bag. They were Pemon Indians.

Lots of parrots flying in the trees.

Now we are ready to go up to the "Lost World" or "Islands in time".

We have arrived at para Tepui at 9000 feet.

Mt. Romaina in front of us we will be climbing. A beautiful sunset at night. But since we are still in the village the Roosters and dogs are barking all night.

Early morning starts because of the sun. Looking at the porters bags I felt my bag was bigger than the porter Adolfo. We were moving fast. The path is baked like cement. The Grand Sabana is so desolate. No fences lots of green grass. Which is burned by the Indians for watching for snakes. They insist it keeps the snakes away.

We are resting our feet at a river. I have no blisters I cut out my sneakers in front, and they toes have freedom.

Leftover for dinner tonight. Bad Gnats all around. They go deep into the eyes. And I have a sunburn too. We rested at the Rio Tek. Beautiful. Soup and vegetables and something like a Paella. Horrible tasting. Cesaer and Louis ate it all. They put cuttlefish in it. By now I look like I have the measles. So many bites.

The Indians supplied us with wood but it is wet and we just have no fire. Their staple is Sardines and Yucca. We walked today from 9:30 till 5pm. I eat fruit and cookies.

Rio Tek

We camped by the Rio Tek, but I could not sleep tonight. Knowing what I have in front of me made me anxious. Should not have read "Lost World" before.

I am wearing long pants in this heat but it keeps me safe and no sunburn.

Never saw 5-inch spiders before. And many bullfrogs, birds with long tails, and lots of other birds.

Hiking at 8:30 again. Always up and up. My feet are like lead, but going on. Crossing the Kukenan River today and many waterfalls.

Kamaija-Meru or Mt. Ronaima- mother of the waters. Looks tough, very tough ahead.

At the lunch stop I needed a rest. And then off to Base camp by 2pm. And that was a hard hike, I revived in the cold River.

Dinner was cooked again and a long rest. The wind came up and had to hold down the tents. Then the rain started.

Today, I woke up with a very swollen face. Wonder what I am allergic to. We are contemplating the Wall how to climb up. First the small trails through the woods and always up, up. Climbed through a waterfall and everything got wet.

5 hours of climbing and hanging onto branches and roots never looking back it was too steep. Never thought I could do this. Over Rockslides, slippery Rocks, and thinking how am I going to go down again? I was very exhausted. The ascent had taken two long days, up from the gloom and tangle of the jungle, along slippery ledges hardly wide for a toehold. Many times, I'd thought we'd reached the summit, only to peer through fleeting holes in the clouds and see the rock face rising up endlessly.

Saw a lot of strange plants, Birds I never saw before, and the biggest Hummingbirds. And then we reached the top onto a Rockledge.

We are on top of the Tepui Roraima at 9900 feet. That is going to be our home for a few days.

On the Rockledge is barely room for 3 tents, we will be climbing over each other.

Ceasar snores so loud. He did hit his head already on the Ledge and has a big headache. I feel an altitude headache coming on. Tylenol and Pepto Bismol are taken right away.

Dinner was soup, rice and tuna. Now everything tastes good. Weather-wise we are lucky. The Tepui is known for rain. But it has stopped to rain.

6am and freezing. Eating heavy food, rice cheese and black beans. We have a 9-hour walk planned today.

I cannot get over this strange world up here. The summit was a barren black wilderness of worn rocks. A landscape from a different world.

There is a little black frog called Oreophynella or mini monster. There are new flowers I have never seen before, and plants and trees. Every minute is a different scenery. We stopped at the 3 corners monument. Or Punto Triple. Venezuela, Guyana and Brazil.

Our feet get sucked in black mud and pink mud. We look pretty bad already.

A big dragonfly I never saw before, little crayfish in the puddles. And the little monster frog, they crawl not hop.

At camp, tired, the guys are cooking, and I try to clean up myself. Rice, soup and pineapple is Dinner.

Again, a freezing morning. And cold rain all night. Our camp looks like it is going to swim of the ledge. Cutting it short and are finally packing for the downhill climb. I was glad with the heavy fog I could not see the bottom or I would be still up there.

1000 feet straight down. It took 2 hours with a kind of rappelling or sliding. Never thought I would live to the days end.

At the bottom we walked along the Kukenan river and then along the Rio Tek. That was not as good as going there.

Now are in Indian country and see burned almost all the green fields and it is a very dirty hike in ashes. Gnats are crazy for us. They stick around the face.

Stopped at the Indian village Para Tepui . Dogs running around looking like skeletons, horrible.

At the River, we washed ourselves but the water was ice cold! And always the Gnats. Black walls of them in front of our faces.

Finally, after a long hike had a good dinner of Spaghetti and Melon.

My toe is rotting from all the water we walked through.

This morning the sun is shining but all the Gnats are out too. Cut more out of my shoes so my toes can breathe. And off we went walking and always through some burned sections which made it dusty and dirty. The Indians have been told not to burn but it is their custom and it is hard to break.

Snacks now were Bananas and watermelons which we bought from the Indians.

Finally, we came to our car again and drove to Sta. Elena. The Frontier Hotel had a nice room and "clean". I did not want to sleep in a tent. The Owner made me a sandwich because I looked like I needed it.

Our Dinner outside was excellent. The meat was tough but still good tasting. One could not be choosy, this is nowhere and whatever was available, we ate, dessert was papayas and passion fruit, so good.

It was grand to sleep in a bed again. Even the lumpy pillow felt good. The Mattress was well used I did not care.

The next day looked very good. Ate in a Lancheria with lots of passion juice. I walked around Sta. Elena alone and met more people finally. This is the only town in a radius of 400 miles and not many new faces show up. There was a newspaper in town but not for sale. One could read it and then return it to the shop owner. Not much to do here.

Tried to go across the Brazil boarder but it was denied. So, we are heading north again.

Stopped at the Jasper Falls. Miles of beautiful Jasper and water flowing right on top polishing it.

It rained in the Gran Sabana, so we kept going to Claritas, since we had still daylight we kept going to Tumereno and found a nice little Hotel Miranda. Had my favorite, shredded Beef for dinner. Slept pretty good except could not find a light switch to turn off the light. Had to find my facemask.

Empenadas for breakfast, very good. Fresh Orange juice and coffee. What else do I need? By 1pm we reached Ciudad Bolivar and checked into Hotel Universo on the Orinocco River.

The best Arepas for Lunch and rested at the pool. Bought on my walk 2 Hammocks to take back to USA. Not much room left in my bag.

Booked a trip to Angel Falls and had to be at the Airport, at 7am no plane was waiting. By 10am finally a little Havilland arrived and was ready to board. It was supposed to be a sightseeing trip to Angel falls but the plane had to turn around because too many clouds. This is the only way in the dry season to get there. Since all small Rivers to Angel falls dry out and there are no Roads.

A second try is made this afternoon. And we landed by Angel Falls and had to celebrate with good Beer.

First comes a canoe trip, then a big tunnel to walk through and then through ice cold water to get to the Kavak Waterfall. It was fun and returning to the village and eating there a good dinner.

The pilots look like they are 18 years old. They are daredevils. And up we go to the Angel falls. Quick turns and trying to show us the falls from all directions. Angel Falls are the highest Falls in the World.

This is the Lost World one does not get to see easy except by hiking to it or flying over it.

Merida

From Ciudad Bolivar to Caracas and a next day flight to Merida. At the Caracas Airport the plane was late as usual. And then everybody is trying to run through the gate to get on first, what a scramble!

Many people cannot read and don't understand seats assignment. So when I got to my seat, I had to throw an old man out of it. While

I tried to sit down an old lady jumped right in my seat. The poor Stewardess had to persuade these people to move. It was really funny.

So now I am flying over the Andes to Merida. That is the most exiting Airport in the world. Since the city is built on a Mesa and the Airport just squished right in the middle of the city. There is just enough for one plane to arrive going uphill. And only if there are no clouds. The plane stops at the last minute, and I almost hit my head at the sudden stop. The turnaround is 30 minutes. If the planes leave, they go downhill and very fast in that half-hour of clouds.

I was awaited by Jerry, my Mountain connection. And then Louis and Casear arrived by car too. They drove all the way from Ciuad Bolivar.

I am staying at the Hotel Chama. We all went to the country club for a relaxing swim and dinner. My bike trip is planned the next day.

Hotel Charma was good. But no Breakfast included or served. So had to look for a bakery.

We went with our Fisher bikes on the Road to El Morro. That is Mountain biking! Only Donkeys have gone there before. Downhill for 4 miles now to El Morro. Breathtaking scenery and unpolluted air. A beautiful old town. Having lunch in the old plaza and then up biking again. Very difficult now. Lots of pushing at this altitude. So we hitched a ride on a pickup for a few miles.

Stopped at a bodega were a woman just made fresh bread. Pastries filled with cheese and then fried and a good Beer with it. Yes, that was very good.

In Merida, I had time to walk around the streets and see the city by myself. It is full of young people. The University of Venezuela is here.

Dinner at an Italian Restaurant was awful. So, we went to a street vendor to get dessert. He had fresh Flan. Love it.

A new day and ready to bike again. I was told it would be hard. Altitude at 10 000 feet. And it was hard, but I got used to it. Bought Empanadas and other snacks for a picknick. And then up and down in the Mountains. Saw a cow being killed in front of the little Bodega for fresh meat for sale. Took almost my appetite away. And on to an endless road to a farmhouse way up in the Mountains.

There, Father and three sons were playing a bowling game. But when they saw me, everything stopped. Open gazed mouth of the sons was funny. They never had seen a blond woman and especially coming on a bike. The stared at us and we pretended it is all very usual. We took a lot of photos, and it made them very relaxed. I fed the sons candy, and they loved it. One son proposed to me and the father had to convince him I was married.

We were at 12 000feet and my head did not feel too good. But from now on it was all downhill but still my head was dizzy from hard breathing.

Passed a lot of little Horses and Mules and Oxen. It was amazing how little people need to live. And everybody had been friendly to us.

Went to a Glacier lake Mucubaji for our picknick.

At night dinner at a Chinese restaurant which was very good. A new fruit to me Nispero was served as dessert. It was delicious.

Morning at the market for a breakfast.

Arepas filled with the special cream I love so much. It is a cheese and sour milk combination.

And then to try out the Funicular.

It is the highest and longest in the world. 8 miles!

At 15634 feet elevation. At the top I felt like I was drunk. Had to move very slowly. A quick hot chocolate helped. There was Oxygen available, but I did not need it.

We went down one station to walk to Los Nevados. I made it to the cross and I was ready to give up every 20 feet. It was ecausting at this height to walk, the young man kept pushing me. It was worth it. We were on Pico Espejo.

Lunch a station lower and a hike then to the Zoo. I love to see Zoos in other countries. But all animals were in small cages not good. And children were teasing them.

A visit to another Mountain now to see a farm which is a Dairy farm. They raised Schnauzer dogs too. A beautiful place like a dream world. Everybody in the family is artistic with weaving. 5 Loons are being used.

Carlos took me to the Grand Balcony for Trout dinner, I love being spoiling by a bunch of young guys.

The big surprise was meeting Cesars parents who invited me to come back and stay with them after I did my tour.

Now to San Fernando by plane. A farewell to all my new friends who I will see soon again.

From San Fernando flying with a Cessna 182. Dr. Hugo Estrada was my pilot. He and his son run the Hato Dona Barbara. 95 000 Acres! Saw a lot of the green Llanos and lots of Rivers. Landed right in the yard of the Hato.

There was an Airplane upside down in the trees and I was very interested how it got there. One of the trips back from San Fernando Dr. Estrada landed upside down in the tree. Both, his wife and him did not get hurt but had to climb down somehow.

Anyway, his wife and son Francisco were waiting for us.

The Hato was owned by Dona Barbara a long time ago and long stories have been written especially one Book by Romulo Gallego which I have and have read before and wanted to see this Hato.

The Hato was going to be my home for a few days. But everybody is talking English not much for my learning to speak Spanish.

Dinner is all meat, yuck. I ate a lot of noodles. There was a beautiful sunset by the Orinocco River.

Not much sleep, the mattress was so creaky and finally took the mattress on the floor. Lots of strange noises at night. Different birds, monkeys barking and howling. And boats going by on the Arauca River. The Palm trees are full of Ibis, and they were chatting all night and in the morning they were screaming.

Arepas for breakfast and turtle eggs. Did not like the eggs will stick to the Arepas.

Later Francisco saddled Horses. They are small but look tough.

And what a ride. No slow speed here.

Saw a lot of wildlife since no hunting or trapping is aloud. It is a birders paradise. Animals are tame. Pigs and Armadillo, deer.

Lunch was not my style again. Brains and meat. Had noodles again. Lots of Tamarind juice and star fruit juice is served.

A rest in my Hammock.

At my afternoon walk I learned a lot about Dona Barbara. She must have been a tough woman to have lived here alone and doing things only men did then. She died in 1923.

Dinner again was plenty and lots of fruit.

Studied the bird book so I can add to my "seen" collection.

I tried sleeping in the Hammock but changed again to my mattress. It is an art to sleep in a Hammock.

I was told the llaneros of the Hato left at night to catch a bull. The saddles have no horn, the rope is tied to the tail of the Horse.

This morning the Birds were very loud early. No sleep for me so I went out to see the sunrise.

Arepas for Breakfast, love them.

We went by boat today on the Arauca River. Big Iguanas sunning themselves on the banks and River Dolphins came to see us. And then we started to fish Piranhas. And I caught a catfish. Knowing all this will be Dinner.

So Francisco and I sat in our Hammocks with a Beer waiting for a cooked Dinner.

3 times a day Francisco gets on a phone they work from generators on the roof catching the sun, to call to San Fernando.

The wind is now blowing and very hot air with it. I can understand why 2 hour siestas are good. It is just too hot.

Llaneros only caught 2 bulls last night.

Senora Carmen Estrada is just cooking her heart out for me. All the meat is raw. But she finally hit the jackpot. She made Roastbeef and beet salad.

The two Anteaters are pets and are as big as a small pony. One is trying to lick my feet. Their tongue is everywhere real long.

Did go to a waterhole by jeep, so many birds!

Our Piranha Dinner was great. One has to spit out the bones a lot but the fish taste very good.

In the evening, we sat by moonlight on the Veranda and watched the stars. Two of the farm pets kept us company. One was a vulture and a baby deer.

Another sleepless night. All the screaming of the animals keep me awake. Now some dogs even barked keeping company with the Monkeys. I guess that is why they are called Howler monkeys.

With fortified Arepas we left for the Dairy Farm section. Had to get cheese and I got to milk a cow. But the cow had to be tied on her hind legs or she would have kicked me to heaven. They are really wild, the head was tied by a rope, and we had to rope them before we even could get close to them. And that is a routine every day for the llaneros.

On the Hato is a Christ Statue. Some children saw Jesus there and now pilgrims come to see and pray. Now this is in the middle of 100000 acres. And no roads. People just walk for miles.

There are waterholes and one can get cooled in them. Lakes are dangerous because of the crocodiles, and some have piranhas.

Then suddenly there is a grey fox right in front of us, very bushy tail. When we came back the bad news, baby Bambi and capybara run off. But there is so much space for them why not?

Stopped at a fishing camp, was very interesting. The men do that all day fishing and dry the fish for other times on the Hato.

Down by the House is a white Beach but I cannot go close. No swimming, hungry animals in the River. Big electric Eels and stingrays.

But on the sand is a black stone which people collect and carve for jewelry, I took some home.

Good news Bambi is back again but alone.

Senora Estrada has constantly new recipes and I am still using them. Wrote them down. Usually after eating Dinner not much to do except count the stars.

Which we did.

At Breakfast a new dish Cachapas which are made out of corn and filled with cheese and cream. Called Natillo. More fresh Tamarind juice.

And then Flying again in the little plane with Dr. Estrada, piloting, to San Fernando. As usual, the connecting plane to Caracas was not there, did not even exist. How the airlines here stay in business is a question. Later found a plane to take me on to Caracas. In Caracas my friends were awaiting me. Very good feeling to see a familiar face. One has to change always planes in Caracas for any place in Venezuela. And this is my 5th time now in one month.

Driving to Choroni over the Mountains in the direction to Maracaibo to a Beach house. A very pretty old home we are staying in, very luxuries.

Visited Pt. Columbia an old fishing town. The population is all out dancing in the streets. Carnival is starting and it will be wild.

I finally slept! The cool sea wind and the 100-year-old house made me feel good. It is built in the old Spanish style. 20foot high ceilings. Many Hammock hooks are ready for ours. There are 5 people to take care of us. Great.

The Beach is beautiful. Very clear water. Had wild ginger Beer made in the Village and fresh Parchita juice. My favorite. Our cook is only 17years old, but can he cook!

So we had to climb up a few mountains to get some exercise. Stopped at a sugar mill where they made the favorite drink Papelon for people here, made out of cane sugar.

Looking down to Pt. Columbia in the blue waters.

Well now I slept great again. Fresh Arepas and down to the Beach for a swim. All this is over now because we are driving back to Caracas. These few days were like going to heaven.

Rented a car for the next weeks. I feel I own the car now, it cost so much.

Kevin came from USA to join me for a while. We are driving through new places to Colonial Tovar. Looks like a German town. It was settled by Germans.

Near Morrocoy we stayed in a Hotel to see the area. Just so many tourists, I am told because of Carnival it is so crowded.

We decided to fly to Margarieta Island. Good choice. A beautiful Island with the most beautiful Beaches. Stayed at the Karibe Hotel in Playa de Cardon situated on top of the rocks.

Camerones de Gundia what a dish. My pants are getting tight.

Waves are high at the Beach but fun to swim. At night had to sleep under the Mosquito net. Many Mosquitos wanted my blood.

Polamar is a shopping town, not very interesting for me.

The pounding surf put us to a heavy sleep. It silenced even Kevin's snoring.

Different food here. Rice cakes stuffed with ham for Breakfast.

Now again at Caracas Airport saying good bye to Kevin, and hi to Cesar. And Gail my friend, arrived from the states, and we took the next plane to Pt. La Cruz. Too bad I did not go with Kevin here. I was so surprised how beautiful it is and the many flowers there. We stayed in the Hotel Melia. Luxury. Our lounges are under the Palm trees. The Pool is right there and the Beach in walking distance.

At night we did go to the Paseo Colon and did what everybody was doing. Strolling along and showing their best outfits.

Again a good breakfast, croissants and fresh orange juice.

We hired a fisherman to take us to a swimming cove. Snorkeling was not good because the water was very cloudy but what I saw was beautiful. The water was very cold too. Why? Lunch was fresh caught fish, Arepas and vegetable salad. Our trip back was a wild and stormy sea. We got drenched but it was fun. And now we want to go to Margarita Island and are taking the Ferry.

Morning at 4:50am to catch the Ferry! A flying boat. A Hovercraft.

But when we got there the Ferry had trouble and was not going to leave. So to another Ferry which had a class section. We took the 2nd class, looked better. This was a heavy boat and was very silent. I fell asleep for the 3-hour trip.

Margarita arriving in the rain! But by the time we settled in, the blue sky came again, and we had lunch at a little Beach hut. And Hotel Karibik is very relaxing.

We made friends with a Doberman from the Beach hut. He walked with us wherever we went. Great Guard dog.

There are many Huts with things for sale. Found out Margarita is tax free, so people come just to shop.

At the Hotel a very good Band was playing Venezuelan Music, and we settled with our Rum drinks for the evening.

Breakfast was too much food. It always looks good. Had to walk the Beach for exercise. Watched the fishermen fixing their nets. A little sunbathing and then off to the airport again.

In Caracas we stayed at the Kings Inn right downtown. We could walk around and see some of the city before Gail had to leave tomorrow for home again.

Today after taking Gail to the airport, I am alone for the first time in weeks.

But I have to catch now a plane to Merida.

This will be different living in a family home.

The Qintero family is a large family group. But very small built people and I am towering above all of them.

I am told right away by the Quintero's: me casa su casa. So polite. Many friends have come by to meet me.

My new home is an old farm or Hacienda in Merida. Now surrounded by the city. The house is at least 300 years old.

My first morning was going with Elsa to the market at 6am. We stopped at many places for meat, fruits and vegetables. Fresh food is bought every day.

Then I enrolled in the language school for one week first.

At the house is a beautiful German Shephard Max, but he barks all the time. He is so sweet but why does he sit under my window?

Have walked the city which is interesting. There is only one street from one end to the other. With a big Cathedral in the middle. And the usual Plaza or Park.

Dinner -Arepas again. I love them but they are bad for a weight problem. Must walk a lot.

Today many Relatives arrived because it is Sabado and the family gets together. Cesar arrived from Caracas, and he tried showing me a lot of places too.

He arranged a new teacher for me, and I canceled the school, which was expensive. This teacher is coming to the house.

Met Henry a friend, who will show me some of the Mountains. We left early by Bus and then a downhill walk to the Chama River and a two hour climb to the funicular La Montana Station. We started at the 5332feet Station and went up 2442meter. It is very hard on my lungs going so sudden up. I am just out of shape. Too many Arepas.

At night I hunt Mosquitos. They love me and are always waiting for me.

The family here is Rafael Quintero, father. Elsa de Quintero, mother.

Maria Elsa 22 y. old. Studies Architecture. Juan Carlos, 24 years old. Rafael Antonio 21 y. old. Both study Ing. Technic. Dona Wency (Abuela) The maid Theresa.

The Hacienda is called Qra. "El Consuela"
Today I had my first lesson, so much to concentrate.

A visit to Jerry my friend up in the Hills at 6000 feet. Beautiful house, great view. But for me it was bad. Many "no see ems" attacked me. Everything is biting me. My legs look like I have the measles. And now it is raining and hard.

Teacher Roland Flores gave me my 2nd lesson. I am starting to get it. I even went alone afterwards on a Por Puesta and arrived where I wanted to go.

Today on my visit to the city I got into a student uprising. The police had their Gasmask on. It was not good to be around because of the foul air; I turned and went home fast.

Last night not much sleep now the neighbor's dog barked all night. Maybe it is the brown squirrels but they are all over climbing night and day through the old trees.

I watch them too and it distracts from having my lesson.

The War is over, it says so on the news. What war? I have not seen the news at all. Must be desert war.

Up again 5:30am for the vegetable market. Have to get the freshest produce.

8:30 Spanish lesson. 11am swimming. And the day is so busy. A fantastic Dinner again. And more Relatives as company.

And up early again for another tour to the Paramore. A long drive almost to St. Domingo on the highest paved Road in Venezuela. This is a plateau high in the Mountain with fog and moors. Many hiking trails.

We have really great weather here. Went to visit friends who have a farm. We tasted lots of new foods and I liked especially the Zapotas.

Afternoon we spend driving with Rafael and Elsa into town to get ice-cream.

In the evening, we all were invited to General Pardo who has one of the oldest and beautiful Hacienda. It is really like a museum so full of Antiques in private hands. Our dinner was something rolled in Banana leaves and a Guavas Dessert with clotted cream. Coffee afterwards in the little cups people favor. We were made so welcome.

And another day of learning. Have a lot of homework.

Rafael 50' Birthday today.

I gave him two Tapes of Venezuelan llano music. For two days already has been a busy kitchen. Cooking for the Fiesta.

Went today to Jaji, a very old town. Every old home there is redone and painted in different colors. It looks like in the 16th century style. No signs or wires are aloud everything is underground.

I cooked tonight: Lasagna. But had to use noodles since I could not find lasagna noodles. But everybody liked my pasta dish.

March 6th

Went up the teleferico to the top and walked down to the 2nd station. Needed the exercise. Lot of snow on top of the mountains.

The weather is changing and always is a cloud over the Mountains now. But by 10am it is usually clear again. The rainy season starts in April.

March 9th

Today a trip to Los Nevados, a Village deep in the Mountains. Went by Teleferico up, with entertainment by musicians playing 2 Quatros. A Qatro is a small guitar. Arrived on top in heavy snowfall. No choice, from Radonda Station we walked 7 hours in either snow or heavy rain. The Posada was very nice but primitive. No heat, very cold. My feet hurt like…Our cloth were wet. We ate and went to bed but no sleep, outside the dogs barked. But it was all interesting and different to see how people lived like this so removed from civilization.

In the morning, we were provided with Mules and I had a Horse to get back to the teleferico. They animals did not want to leave and only screaming and shouting got them moving. It rained all the way to the station. We got soaked again. So cold, Hot chocolate in the station saved my temper. But we all were frozen through.

Down in Merida, where it was nice and warm, I took all my layers of cloth off. I do not like cold weather.

Celebrated my farewell tonight at the Belansante Hotel with Elsa and Rafael.

Trying to fly today to Caracas. It is raining and fog and no planes would come in this fog. I had already said goodbye to everybody. There was a big group seeing me off. But then a plane came in and off it went.

In Caracas I stayed in the Avila Hotel with a beautiful park full of Birds. And very good Rum punch. Cesar and I had our last Dinner together I had to go back to USA. Venezuela is a small country but has the most beautiful places to visit.

Prince Edward Island, Autumn 1991

A bicycling trip with my weekly biking friends to see a different place.

Six women, Judy as our driver and food supplier when biking, Nancy, Patty, Bobbie, Susan and I expecting good weather and fun. And we did have fun.

Our long drive already till Bangor Maine in one day and arriving late and finding no Motel room for us. One room was found finally and all of us had to get a space for that night maybe in bed or on the floor.

In Brunswick Canada we crossed by ferry, the 8-mile-long Bridge was built in 1997, now cars can cross to Prince Edward Island.

Our sights were of large Potato fields, it is true that is the biggest export for the Islanders. But Mussels is second.

In Charlottetown our first stop we settled for the night and next day rented our bicycles for our week long trip.

We biked the whole Island from Tignish to Elmira. And always there is that red earth. Even the Beaches were red. Found out it is from high iron content. That is why potatoes grow here so good.

Many stops were made especially at bakery's. The fresh rhubarb pie I cannot forget. Our overnight stays were fine except it was very hot, unusual, and we had to get used to sleeping without Air-condition and locked windows in many places. Most of the windows were painted closed.

Our most memorable stop was at Green Gables. Lucy Maud

Montgomery wrote the story on Anne Shirley living there.

And we saw the show of Anne of Green Gables as a final evening in Charlottetown.

Sometimes we could bike on closed train tracks converted into bicycle trails, we were told when finished it would be the Confederation Trail, 449km long. Now one of the most beautiful bike trails.

Costa Rica, January 12, 1992

A trip to Costa Rica with 4 changes in planes! My suitcase came on a different flight but at the Airport later.

A taxi to San Jose to my "Family stay"

The Delgados family: Turid and Alfredo, a young Alfredo, Michel, Carlos and Lisbeth. Abig family to feed.

Temperature are nice, but did take my feather sleeping bag.

I am trying to brush up my Spanish again but this time in Costa Rica. School was a long walk to a Bus, about a mile and half. Downtown to morning classes with cultural tours in the afternoon.

Food is cheap in the stores. Coffee almost free.

My first dinner was rice and beans and Bratwurst with Squash.

Missed the earthquake at 4am. The dogs barked

School is as always hard for me, learning the verbs!!!

In the afternoon we went to the Irazu Vulcano by bus. The steep Road goes all the way to the top at 10 000feet. It is desolate on top. A tame Cotamundi came up to us to beg for food.

Having a school trip is fun since the teacher is explaining everything. We stopped for hot chocolate. Which I needed badly.

Mornings I get to take the dog for walk I love it, good exercise. And then off to school for more learning.

Afternoon we all went to Braulio Carrillo rain Forest. A muddy trail and lots of rain and fog. It is a real Rain Forest.

I finally found out what makes me wake up at 5:30. Turid doing her Aerobics.

In school we celebrated the Teacher Milagros birthday with a big cake. And then we went to the Natl. Museum, very interesting. And then to the suburb of Santa Anna. Beautiful area of San Jose.

Our dinner was cooked by Michel, it was again very good but then no water came out of faucets.

Off today on a trip further away with all the students finally at 2pm. It was a hard drive. Most Roads are just dirt and potholes. The last 35km took us 2 hours. A very dangerous Mountain Road. Our Hotel Sapo Dorado is beautiful. Great food. My favorite salad is served: Palmitto and cheese. And Mora berries. A type of Raspberry and Blackberry. We did have all the fireplaces going because it was cold up here.

Monteverde finally today, read about it so much. But it is cold, and the wind is blowing. And then a 4-hour walk, to learn about all the plants and some wildlife.

Not many tourists were there. We went to the Hummingbird station. The birds have no fear and sit on my finger. Then to the Butterfly reserve. Most Butterflies were asleep.

Then we left to see Arenal Vulcano. Bad roads again and rain and we got lost. I did ask at a gas station for direction we had to turn around, and then our Bus got stuck, a wild trip. Finally, after many hours found our Hotel Don Carlos.

Our rooms had a lot of spiders and Roaches running around and had to clean up first. And no sheets were provided. That comes also with a dirt cheap trip.

Many Bats in the roof. But I slept good.

The usual Beans and Rice, toast and eggs. But lots of Coffee.

One could hear a strange sound which turned out Vulcano Arenal spitting fire and rocks. Great to look at night.

The Roads are very bad and no signs showing the way. But it is a scenic country. Sometimes cold and then hot again.

Stopped in Zarcero which is known for their topiary in the town square.

At the house San Jose again, Puckie, the dog was waiting for me. Nobody takes the dog for a walk. And then school again.

In the afternoon went to San Jose to walk around. There are many hippies still here especially in the Plaza Cultural.

Jan. 21, school again and afternoon to Alajuela and Sarebi. Beautiful drive again.

At the house the dinner was bad. Mostly now Rice and Beans. I have to buy fruit myself. So many vegetables are for sale. Maybe my family is out of money? My stomach is complaining no more Beans please. I will never eat Beans again.

School and trip to Cartago, Mirador and Orosi Valley. There are no bad looking areas, no slums. Most people have vegetable gardens.

In Orosi we went to the Rio Macho across to the Hotel Rio Palermo. Hope to go there one day with Kevin to stay.

Tonights Dinner was good again and we even ate from the good dishes.

School and off to Cerro la Muerte. Another beautiful place with lots of woods. Hoped to see a Quetzal there but none.

Driving along the Pan American Highway today. Always thought of it as a big Road. No, it is almost all washed out and just sometimes room for one car and always up or down and many curves. It is not maintained at all.

Tonight went to a play "Taxi" at the Angel Theater. It was very good. With a Dinner of Empenadas and queso.

My school time is finished. We had to study today all the fruits which the teacher brought and we tasted them all.

Celebrated afterwards at the Nacionale café.

Walked today all over town again to check out my next Hotel stay, Hotel Dorado looks good. I need to be closer to town.

I will miss looking at the sloth in the tree by Delgados which I did every day.

My next adventure is ahead. Met an American couple a few days before, who inquired if I could housesit their farm up in the Mountains so they could go for a short vacation. Fine, and was told I would find the key for the Gate so and so. All this without knowing me?

After I got up by Bus to El Rodeo at 2:30pm there was no key. And nobody was around. I climbed over the wall, but had a surprise when a big German shepherd greeted me on the other side. Max, he was friendly, lucky me. I made myself at home and when the couple came home days later I hated to leave.

The farm is interesting. Lots of things grow there. As I walked, I stepped on the biggest frog I have ever seen. 10 inches at least. He slapped me on my legs and I was told they can be poisonous. Picked enormous blackberries and cooked Dinner.

Max is now my shadow, he liked me.

Walking around I could see finally what was grown here. Much coffee in the hills, Avocado trees, Banana, Grapefruit and Orange trees. Lemon, Peaches, apples.

Chayote, blackberry's, onions, garlic. That is all the stuff I could recognize. There is a very magnificent view from the house. Not a good Birding area, very shy.

Walking up to the Cerro la Cruz, 2 hours up and total wilderness. And I am hiking alone. This is great.

Saw a lot of Hummingbirds, Butterfly's and Lizard's.

Some Abuela came in the afternoon and invited me for coffee. Everything was served on the best dishes, a plate full of Yucca and cake. It was so sweet and nice. And we had to sit in the good room. The men in the village are all having a macho look. Not my type.

Went hiking to the cloud forest again, it is just beautiful.

At the farm it is nice to eat Apples and Peaches of the trees. And then went to the Abuela to give her some fruit and postcards of Maryland. She was very happy.

Feb. 2 going back to San Jose, I will miss Max. Hope he gets fed.

I enrolled in another school again and like it. Only 2 students to a teacher.

Saturday I will go to Manuel Antonio and hope to stay there a few days. But first a few more days of school. I use a lot of Taxis. They are cheap.

Went to Moravia, an old town, for a few hours. Too many tourists there.

Early morning, I had to get to the Coca Cola Terminal at 5am. The first Express Bus for a 4-hour ride. On the Bus had to stop a kid behind me playing his Radio to loud. I am on my way to Manuel Antonio.

What a surprise is Manuel Antonio. All the Hotels hang on the hills and going to the Beach is either up or down.

The water is so warm I did not want to get out of it. And a lot of little coves were one could swim undisturbed.

Evening is very hot and no Aircondion. Even the rain did not help.

Feb. 9 and it is still raining. Sounded good on the roof. Hitched a ride down to the Beach at 7:30am with some very helpful drivers who already had a Beer in their hands and offered me one. A little too early!

On my todays walk in the park, I saw a great Anteater. Many Agouti's with Baby's. And then the usual Monkey's and Bird's. A green snake crossed my path and then a yellow snake. Wonder if they were poisoned.

Met finally a person who could watch my cloth when I was swimming. One has to watch always because the Monkey's steal everything They sit in the trees and only wait for that moment to come down and gone is your stuff. And if not monkey, it is people. Too bad there is crime in such a beautiful place.

Went to Dinner to a place called El Salto, high on top of a Mountain.

Having trouble now getting on a Bus back to San Jose but if I would have known it, I would have spent the waiting time in the water. Was told it was raining on the other side of the Mountains and cold.

Busses did not run then. But I finally made it back to San Jose.

That night it was Cocina a la Gladys, my Landlords cooking. She mothers me.

Had to extend my visa and had luck. And went to a very good play at Teatro Melico Salazar for folk music and dance. The best show and learned to dance the Salsa.

Today's early trip to a Coffee plantation and factory.

And a lunch treat at the national theater coffee shop. The National Theater is on a historical list. It is a beautiful place all the furniture is over 100 years old and classical music in the background.

Visited the Jade museum and found a place for cocktails with free food called le Ambience.

And walked again for many miles to work off the calories.

Panama, April 4th

I am flying today to Panama for a few days for my first time. The plane did not arrive for a few hours and then it was a quick flight to Panama City and to the Hotel Granada.

A taxi driver I arranged for took me to see the city. He was interested into showing me everything. Saw the old town Veijo. Never read about it before and was surprised about the history there.

Panama City is not for a woman alone to walk around. Even if it all looks very modern.

Had a very relaxing time at the pool then I met a group of people from the environmental protection agency. It turned out they were here watching a Japanese ship full of illegal caught Dolphins, caught in floating nets. It was interesting to me to hear about it.

Today the exciting trip to the Canal! For 70 years the Panama Canal has been working, and one can watch most of the action. The little ship took me to the Miraflores Lake. It all is so amazing watching the "mules"(motorized little tractors) work. And it is a hot day.

At the Casino that night I lost $60, which is a lot since I usually play only $20.

There is not much to do except enjoy the pool. Food is excellent. And I have a good rest.

Costa Rica

Returning to Costa Rica. Surprisingly the plane left on time. Staying with Gladys again. It is like a home for me, we play puzzles and she cooks great.

Feb. 19, a Jungle trip today. First by Bus to San Miguele, Ouarto Viejo and Lunch there and to the Rio Sarapiqui on a boat. Till we came to the rio San Juan which leads us right into Nicaragua and then to the Rio Colorado.

Then swimming on the Beach but waves were very big and could only go to the knees it was dangerous. We are in the wilderness. No Roads all traffic by boat.

Our Huts had no electric so it was early to bed. But food is always good. Along the Tortuguero Canals by boat with lots of fascinating wildlife. We are now 112 km from Barra del Colorado.

Fresh caught fish for Lunch. Delicious.

Nights are very noisy, animal sounds and people talking and no walls just tents.

A delay now since the steering on the Boat is broken. But it happened right in front of the Oro verde Lodge. There we got a new Boat and new driver.

This was wilderness and I am glad I did this trip.

I said goodbye to my "Tica Mother Gladys" and checked into a Hotel for Kevin's arrival. He needs Air-condition.

Kevin and I went to see a performance of Panama Dancers and to El Pueblo. But all the music there was Disco, too loud.

Sharing my room with a snoring Husband is hard. Very bad time for sleeping.

We rented a car and took off to the Braulio Carillo Park, a long drive. Went to Limon all on unpaved Roads and many potholes.

The Hotels in this areas have been disappointing. So we looked along the Beach and found the beautiful Villa Caribe. It is like a dream place. Had nice Calypso music to listen to. And the waves from the open Sea.

Leaving was hard but I have to show more of Costa Rica to Kevin and all the beautiful places.

Arenal. We booked at Arenal Lodge, but it was dirty and hot. To get our money back we had to wait till they rented the room out first. I do not like to make reservations I rather gamble on sleeping at night.

There are many Hotels, and we found Fortuna Hotel Las Cobinas, great. Saw from there the action on the Vulcano Arenal very clear. And the rumbling went on all night.

Driving to Monteverde was again beautiful except the Road! Distances take much longer because of it.

Stopped at Sapo Dorado to go hiking the Baja tigre Trail. Many different plants to see but no animals. Maybe tomorrow.

Monteverde, February 26th

Here we saw two Quetzals finally. A very green bird and very elusive, with red feathers underneath the wings.

Driving now to the Beaches on the Pacific. Crossing very dry countryside. And again, very rough Roads to get there.

Found a very nice Hotel and it is good sleeping tonight.

Miles of Beach to walk and rocks to sit on to watch the waves and sunset but not very safe for swimming.

The Dinner was again fresh Fish, excellent.

Our drive now to Manuel Antonio in very hot weather and very dry countryside. Had to cross by ferry one River but it was full when we arrived and had to wait 1 hour longer. Baking in the sun in the meantime.

Our Hotel El Salto was very hot without Air-condition on arrival, even swimming did not help, the pool was hot and we stayed hot. Kevin does not feel good in heat, but I love it.

We hiked early next day through the park and drove on to Dominical along the Ocean Road. Managed to get up to Tabanti Lodge at 10 000 feet. I froze, now Kevin loved it. I used every blanket that night.

Morning was cold air and fog! Then rain. Iracu was rained in. So we crossed the Mountains to San Jose and checked into Garden City Hotel.

Drove to Heredia, and Alejuelo both very beautiful old towns. Took Kevin today to the Airport got rid of the car and tomorrow is my departure day from a very beautiful country.

Hasta luego Costa Rico.

India and Nepal, October 19, 1992

This is my first time to India. I have an invitation to stay with friends of my sister Petra in New Delhi. I will get to know India through the family much better.

The plane was almost full of Indians, everybody was going home. The Food served on the plane was Indian dishes great tasting.

A middle of the night arrival in New Delhi, but Rakesh Mathur my new friend was waiting. Driving through New Delhi at night and no traffic except some cows sleeping in the road! In the middle of the night it was still very hot. I wondered how hot it would be in the daytime.

The home had Air-condition, great, but Mosquitoes since there are no screens used anywhere. They Mosquitos have been waiting for me. Had to kill many first. It became a joke because nobody got stung except me.

Their house is big with many rooms. One can get lost in all the little hallways.

Today I am meeting the family.

It is a big family with children and grandparents. It will take a while till I get to know who belongs to whom.

Had to go to the Bank at Conought Square, Conought Square is really a circle, really 3 circles. And each circle is full of business and small stores and banks.

To me the women look like Butterfly's with their colorful Sari's. Each Sari is a different color.

The food is Vegetarian. Lots of Yoghurt, which I love, then fresh fried bread, Nan. Outside is the Tandori oven and a person is making the fresh bread as needed.

Watched from window the night action outside. Cows walking by. Cars do stop for cows but not for people. One has to jump fast out of the way for traffic.

Early up for a tour to Agra. The Taj Mahal! A hired driver picked me up, he looked like out of a movie, all white outfit and I met the other people on the tour with a big Bus. We did stop at a Karis Restaurant for breakfast and it was very good. I watch the life from the Bus. There are many beggars on the streets and many little children running all around.

They look so beautiful with their hunted Eyes. It is a coal pencil using for painting around the eyes and are very hungry looking. It is not a good life for them. They are born on the street and that is their home never school. It is a big class system.

Camels, Elephants, Horses, Water Buffalo and all are pulling heavy loads. Much too heavy and all of the animals are skinny.

Passing now sugarcane fields. And Rice-fields. It is a very flat country to Agra.

Then in sight the Agra fort! So big. And next the Taj Mahal, a white marble masterpiece. I have read about it and now here to see. I was told 10 000 people come every day to visit.

I will have to come back to spend more time at this incredible Monument.

Our Bus driver on the return was driving crazy. He was in a hurry and used the Horn all the time. Nobody could rest, we all expected to crash anytime.

New Delhi's sidewalks are like mini cities. With tarpaulins across, people live there. It is just like the movie or book "City of Joy" Each family has about 10x6 feet space, and it is kept very clean. I still wondered where are the toilets.

We all made it home safely that night. Dinner at 10pm, found out almost every night it is so late. And I am getting attacked by the almost lonely Mosquito, so the hunt begins.

Today I was waiting for the tour bus for 2 hours. Not very punctual. It was a city tour and had the worst tour guide, he could hardly speak English and I need to understand something.

We stopped at all the places: Lakshmi Narayan Temple, Humayun's Tomb, India Gate, qutab Minor. All places are being restored to the old splendor. New Delhi is big but almost all the streets are in circles, it all was built by the English. Why in circles?

Jama Masfid Mosque, Red fort, Chandri chouk market, Rajghat, Ghandis Memorial.

Then the guide told us we need to shop, that is when I bailed out and went home by taxi.

This afternoon was a birthday party for one of the children. 30 other little guest. They all were so nice.

Met today Rakesh Aunt Prem (70), she was the first woman Pilot in India. The family is in the airplane business now.

October 23

Today a lazy day. Shopping, eating. I am surprised how much gold people buy. In bracelets, necklaces. Saturday is a big holiday, the festival of lights. People buy each other many presents for that day. It is like Christmas. Many stores have little lights on and houses are very festive. The big dinner was lamb rolled in pastry and the usual very good yoghurt with it.

Nepal, October 24, 1992

Having bad luck at the Airport with my ticket but my friends straightened it out. I am flying to Kathmandu.

The flight over the Himalayas!

Once we crossed the mountains there was Nepal. From the air very green. One can see that the villages are always on the ridges or on top of a mountain. Kathmandu is in a low valley surrounded by Mountains.

I was welcomed by my Nepales familie Uttam Banya at the airport with yellow flower garlands and I was transported up to his Father's village in the Mountains where young Uttam built a small Inn one hour from Kathmandu.

What a view from here!

Lantang on my left and endless tips of snow mountains.

In the evening Uttam and his friends entertained with a drum and singing. Since there is no electricity, one looks for other things at night.

Candlelight is all. Toilet was a little too far away and I had to be careful not to fall over chairs and not hit my head on the low ceilings.

Blankets are layers of sheepskin and wool pressed flat. Very warm and needed since there is no heat.

I am in Dulikhel, the name of the village. One can see all the different Mountains and I was to know the names after a while.

Uttam and I took off on his motorcycle in the direction of the Tibet border. The Roads were totally washed out and we were lucky not to get killed when our bike suddenly fell in the mud.

The towns or villages we passed were busy. It is the day of the cow, so all cows are painted and have garlands woven on their heads of flowers.

There are rice paddies on the ridges and water has to be brought from far away.

As we came to the Friendship Bridge, we met some nice border guards who let us come into Tibet territory. We looked around in the

Chinese stores. I bought there a bottle of German Riesling wine! Made my knapsack very heavy. 200km now to return by motorcycle. It took us 8 hours and I could hardly walk after this trip.

Tonight, all the girls are singing for Devali. A Tihar festival. One boy dressed in a Sari and dancing for us. Then he gets a basket with rice and the girls start singing. And the men keep putting money into the basket too.

It will be a 5-day festival I am told.

Why do Dogs bark at night? I cannot sleep. Told Uttam to get rid of the dogs. No tourist will come to visit.

(By the way Uttam installed by now real flush toilets.)

After I have rested and still felt all my bones in order we took off again by motorbike to Rhanapur. Ate in the old Pagoda Restaurant all the way on top. Such an old city with so many historical buildings.

We went to the circus! Have not seen a Circus like that in 30 years. Very old fashioned. 2 ½ hours and never stopped the action and all for 50 cents. A bear riding a Motorcycle, a tiger riding a bike with 3 wheels. It was amazing. The tiger and Lion show was very good, but the animals are treated more rough then I liked. The Horses were very skinny and the Elephants too. I just hoped my 50cents went for fodder to the skinny animals.

By now it got pretty cold and a warm chocolate was warming me.

Tonight, we are invited to Uttams Fathers home. On the motorcycle to the Mountain Farm and a walk down a hill and a great welcome from everybody.

I am glad I had my presents for everybody. Mother had dinner but somehow I could not eat the food. I had Rice with Buffalo milk. Some tea and we all watched a little TV powered by Batteries, because it was a Holiday.

At night I could hear many voices singing but only men sang.

Breakfast is outside on the lawn in the warming sun.

Now it is time to go to the family compound again. Today is the big day of the Divali Festival. Everybody got oiled and scrubbed. Our hair got braided. It is a big ritual. Then brown paint was smeared on the floor. The paint is fresh cow dung mixed with milk. It dried very fast. And the same hands were cooking the food. No washing hands. The floor is now a holy ground.

Then the 5 boys had to get their blessing from the father. All sins are this way absolved. Then the 4 sisters had their turn.

Since Uttams father never had a sister and always missed out being blessed he asked me to be his sister. What an honor. I did not make a mistake and even did the 3 times around with fresh spring water and then 3 times with oil. Then I washed his hands and gave him fruit and spread yellow flowers on his head and rice on his shoulders.

Then I did the paint on his forehead, one big yellow streak covered with 5 colors and I gave him yoghurt and a garland around his neck. Finally a tray with nuts, fruits, candies, coconut, breads and many spices. All this is for good luck in the future.

As of today 2017, Father is still in great health. I must have done it right.

And then it was my turn to be bestowed. I even got some money in my basket. So I would never run out of money hopefully.

By now my Hair was turning a strange color from the oil so I hastily went home to wash it. If I would use the oil my hair would have eventual turned black.

Today I am going to Kathmandu and will stay there for a while. The city is very dirty. No garbage collection at all. The pollution is so bad the eyes hurt.

The streets are very small and too much traffic. I am still with Uttam on the Motorbike and we had a flat right in the city. With the mess lying around no wonder.

Did some shopping and eating Roti bread and Tandori chicken.

My camera is breaking down and what to do?

I signed up on a bicycle tour and will meet my other 2 members this afternoon. Two young American girls. Nancy, a lab worker and Rosanne a Bartender. The guide Sonam is a Gurkha, and very tough looking.

We met at Mike's for Breakfast. A place everybody goes to. Food is excellent and it taste good outside in the garden.

Biked today 38km, tough because so much up and down. From Temple to Temple, and all the sights between. Stopped at the Temple for burning the dead. Many pyres were going. It is very primitive seeing the bodies dumped on the floor till they are ready for burning. Kathmandu is crowded and biking here is difficult. So much foot traffic and other things to watch out. Animals, cars.

At some weaving places we peeked inside, and one could see very small children working on the weaving of carpets. The little hands can make the knots smaller. And the carpets bring more money. It is another sad affair. Families have more children so they can weave. And the children are almost sold to the factory. It is slavery.

Oct. 30 through the countryside to Bhaktapur.

What wonderful place to see (Most everything got destroyed in the May 2015 Earthquake) 1000 year old Buildings.

But we had to go on to Nagakot.

Now that was mountain biking. Up and Up and the most beautiful countryside to look at. The mustard plant was blooming, Acelia's and trees it could not be more beautiful anywhere else. So I stopped a few times and got my rest.

Then 4 miles downhill to the Farmhouse were we stopped for the night. Arriving just before getting dark.

There was the famous Himalayan Mountain Range in the evening sunset like pink candy.

That night the showers felt good, all by solar. Food was Tibet style, Choco cake for dessert.

Waking in the morning, watching the Mountain range from my

window, beautiful. But I did not want to get up because it was freezing cold.

Sonam convinced me of getting up for the next bike ride. We used Novega bikes.

Breakfast with fresh Roti bread and lots of coffee and all the energy for more downhill biking. Even that is hard on the hands. All potholes, washboard roads.

There is only a problem with little children. They love to run next to the bikes and scream like hell. Right now about 20 of them.

At the River we made camp which was set up by our hired helpers. But it is cold at night. And the children are sitting and watching us. All have runny noses.

The River made a great noise at night and I slept so good. The campfire was going at 5:30am, a little early but was told we have a long way to go.

The help brought warm water to the tent and a cup of tea. Very good. And the children are still watching. Do they go to school? Difficult to eat when so many hungry faces are watching. I was told they got rice but it does not fill them up.

Along the trail now we watched people, especially women carry heavy loads and they women are so small. I guess 4-foot tall.

We biked up to the Damanpass, 12km steep. I always wonder how these Roads are built, in the two hours only two trucks came by. Traffic is not heavy on this Road.

Our next camp was near the fire tower, and we climbed it, a great view to the Himalayans again. I am sticky and salty and dirty. But no chance of washing up. Not in that cold water.

But a very good Chinese dinner with potato dumplings filled with vegetables. I do not like the meat.

But fresh flan for dessert. We have a real good cook. He drives ahead, with live chickens tied to the chairs on the Van. When needed chop, chop.

There was no sleeping, too many dogs barking outside and I am getting a cold.

We stopped now in a village called Daman, for food. A very dirty town. Nobody cleans and I could not eat anything in that place. Many people have camped there and left fecal matters and garbage. It is the last camp for climbing the Annapurna trek.

No hygiene here. I am on a diet now. Even the tea was dirty.

We bike in a different direction, south, all downhill for 46km. Over 2 hours with stops. One does have to watch for potholes especially when there is so much to see. I clocked myself going once 35km an hour. And then after a bad curve I slowed down.

We are stopping at a River spot with a school next door for lunch. All the children left the classroom and are watching us. I found out the population is 45% under 15years. And the average family has 9 children. Not much grows on the stone ground to feed so large families.

35km more to Heruda and then to the Terai. It is getting hot now, and very tropical. Coming in one day from 8000 feet to sea level by bike is strange. But I like it warm.

We are camping by the River with warm water! Great. Finally, a good wash. Dunking in the River with many children again watching.

All the sewage from everywhere goes in it too.

Passed Bhainse a small village.

In Heruda now. It is a village full of people. Mostly Rickshaws. Very few cars.

Our campground is ok. We had Dinner by candlelight. Macaroni and cheese with Cauliflower curry. I guess no more live chickens.

I love camps near a River. I sleep pretty good. But the 6am Rooster!

Fresh tea, a warm bowl of water for my face and I am good as new. What must the helpers think; here we are in their eyes like rich American women catered to.

6 guys! Then our guide Sonam. And there is a very big class system with the guys. Each is assigned a different job.

Now we are in the Terai for 63km in the boiling sun. Loved it. Many people are greeting with "Hello" or Good buy. That is the English everybody knows.

A shady spot for lunch and again children surrounding us. They have not seen bikers ever coming by.

6km more to the River Lodge and camp. Showers and toilets!!!.

I figured my nose is running because of all the black smoke from the exhaust of cars which are going to India on the same road.

And a good night, only trouble is at night, going to the "toilet". Which is a dugout with a tent around. The natives just go anywhere. We are close to the Indian border and a lot of Indians are around us now.

34km through very beautiful countryside. Hot but different. There is much produce growing. But nasty children throwing stones at us.

We finally came to dirt roads again. A few miles over grassland and camping till afternoon near the big River to Chitwan. I am very congested.

Late that afternoon a boat came finally to pick us up to go to Chitwan across the River.

A short walk to camp.

Told to be ready by 2:30pm for the Elephants swim. That was fun for us and the Elephants.

Next day we rode the Elephant through the jungle. I call it a 15foot tall grass jungle. Love the way the Elephants move. Encountered a rhino. I do not like how the Mahouts made the Elephants corner the rhino. It scared the Rhino and one could not watch with a good feeling. The Mahouts were macho and trying to show off.

Our tents here are awful. There are three beds in each and for $140 a night! How can they charge so much? And no luxury!

I had been on Safari in Africa and had it a lot better.

But Dinner was very good.

I still think we should get our money back from that camp.

They call it the Jungle Island Resort!

Wake up 6am to go ride our Elephants. This time we came to a Rhino who did not like us and my Elephant was not happy either, bad morning. So the Mahout hit my Elephant over the head with his sharp hook to control. It made a bleeding spot. I complained to him, and he stopped, but what about the next time?

Now off on a canoe trip but we had to walk for 45 minutes to get to the canoes. Lucky no tiger was on a prowl. The boat looked flimsy, but it was sturdy not to sink. Saw Alligators and a Chilkal or crocodile sunning on the Banks. Mirga, a barking deer, spotted deer, chital, hog deer, Jaghuna langur and red Monkeys.

At 2:30 we had to take the Elephants to wash in the River again. I think that was my highlight of my trip. I did not have to hit my Elephant he was very willing to listen to me.

To have such a close connection to such a large animal is difficult to describe.

It showed the big Brain this Animal had when one of the women slid over the head of the Elephant going downhill into the pass of the next Elephant. The Elephant stopped so fast and lifted the foot for her to climb up again. She could have been squashed!

Next day again at 6am for the last ride. It was a crazy way of riding. The Mahouts decided to go off the path and my body got hit by every limb hanging low.

Met Richard Ewerts from Lonely Planet books on the other Elephant. He seemed to be very bored with everything. He told me he was revising the book on Nepal again.

And then by boat back to the other side of the river. Our crew was waiting for us with the bikes. Pedaled till the Lama Hotel and then decided to enjoy a van trip to Nharanganghat.

A big day for celebration there. A good pick nick now and will bike to Mugling. Now a beautiful Road, after every curve another pretty view. And once a while I could see the River on my right and the Mountains on my left. The Road was built by the Chinese.

At Mugling I saw a very nice Annapurna Hotel and decided to rent a room and leave the others to their camp. Was a great idea. A clean bed is sometimes very nice.

Today it was the last Chicken killed but it tasted very good. Fresh food it is the same with fish. It does not get cooked if the cook did not see it alive. As usual children surrounded us. I used my only Nepalese word Namaste and all of them smiled.

The Hotel Annapurna is first class, the pillows are so good, and I had my best sleep yet.

I am watching the Boats coming down the River from Annapurna and most of the people in it look very wet and cold.

We have our last Breakfast together because the help is leaving for Kathmandu and we are going north again. We will be staying in Hotels from now on.

So we are taking a Bus to Pokhara. A very bad Road and the Bus is old.

Pokhara is a tourist town. Even all the Nepalese love it. It is very scenic and has a pretty lake with a Hotel in the middle.

Walked by the campground which is the starting point for the Annapurna circle trek too. Everybody has left the garbage again and nobody cleans up. It stank and was the pits. I am turned off by trekkers who are so dirty.

There is a shopping street just for tourist to buy Equipment and junk. And one can exchange used equipment.

Our evening we spend in a Restaurant listening to music but so many people in it made us sweat and it smelled!

I like the Hotel, and Sonam and I are enjoying it. The other two women are only in a bad mood. They are in their tent.

There is only electric from 5-7pm in Pokhara.

Pokhara, November 8

Hotel Trabogan is good. We biked today for 24km around the area. To some old Temple Busin Buddha and to some caves which I did not go inside and just relaxed outside.

Biked to a Tibetan Refugee Camp which had a nice monastery and a new Temple.

The main attraction is the Carpet factory. They dye, spin and weave beautiful carpets. Bought two little yak carpets.

Biking now the old Road was fun. Since the Chinese built a new Road we had no traffic at all.

In the evening, I found a very good Pizza place.

Saw some busses go buy. Fresh painted on the side Deluxe and have no windows. The mechanics must be very good to keep them going.

Another thing, never tell jokes to a Nepalese. They do not understand it and get insulted.

Hotel Trabogan Pokhara, November 9

A Bugle woke me up this morning. Never found out who was playing.

Watching the Annapurna Mountain range in the pink morning light and very clear sky so close. Here I was in an exciting place. Many porters are already walking on the path uphill with heavy loads. November is the best month for trekking I was told. But nights get very cold one has to have a very good sleeping bag.

Today to Begnas hiking now with a very good packed lunch from the Hotel. It was a good tasting. Problem, no toilets anywhere, so I started to hold it. I was not going to squat down in front of people. No trees either on this trek.

Later to Devi Falls which are underground in a cave.

One cannot see the Falls only the mist and the sound or roar of the falls.

Stopped at another Tibet Refugee Camp, which was built in 1984 and is a very busy place. Even the Nepalese have come to the Camp to get jobs there. Beautiful Carpets are made but very expensive.

Later went to the Fishtail Lodge to see the National Dancers of Nepal. Met a few tourist there and we exchanged our views on Nepal.

The view to the Machuperi Mountain, (Fishtail), is very holy to the Nepalese and cannot be climbed by anybody.

Lots of Mountain people have come into town to shop. They almost look like animals. Very dirty, unwashed. Water is for them luxury.

We are leaving at 5am for Sargakot. I still have my runny nose. It is a walking trek. Beautiful so early. We passed Rice paddies and then up the Mountain. It was hard and very steep. Almost 3 hours of up and up.

This time we have a pack of wild dogs following us. I try to keep away from them. They constantly kept fighting with each other and some of them got pretty bloody.

So many Mountains around me. Which is which?

We passed a lot of Trekkies who were going for week trips. Many supportive porters around them. Some porters carried even deckchairs. It is the only income for the porters.

That evening we had Indian Dinner, it was too spicy for me. My mouth kept burning all night.

We are trying to go back to Kathmandu by plane. But no plane is at the Airport. Then a plane arrived and if one only knew how it works, to get on the plane one had to run fast. We did not and had to wait for another plane. There was a cow wandering around in the waiting area. And that is called an Airport.

Arriving in Kathmandu our guide was not there, and we had to take a taxi to the Hotel. Our rooms were full with other guest and our luggage was stored. It was not a good ending and a lot of argument because we all paid quite a lot for accommodations. No farewell Dinner!

Met a nice person who helped me get my ticket for New Delhi because I am trying to leave earlier.

Went to a Chinese dinner at night but the food smelled bad, and I could not eat it.

The last night was very noisy in the Hotel. Too many tourist are here. All of them are sloppy and look like the last hippies from the 60's. Went in the day touring again and stopped at a Hindu burial.

Nepal is a very beautiful country, but a little depressing. Time stood still there. With no birth control and so many children! No schools for them so they run on the streets.

And the dogs! Too many, scrawny because there is no food for them. All the animals are routing in the garbage. Which is lying around everywhere.

It is good if one knows a family like I do and gets to see the beautiful side of Nepal.

And that is where I am going now. Up to Dhulikel. Spend the time with Uttams parents and gave them some items as a remembrance. Honey was given to me, but I wonder if I can take it to the USA.

When going back to Kathmandu I could feel the difference and see how dirty the air is in the city. Right away my cough and runny nose started again.

Found an old Antique scale set that I still have.

Next morning at the Airport a big mess. All planes are canceled. Now all this is still before cell phone or e-mail. And if a phone worked it was unusual. So one never knew ahead what is next. 2 breakfast have been served and now even lunch. 6 hour wait.

Again one has to run onto the plane, there are seat assignments, but the natives do not accept it. Poor stewardess could not make people put the seatbelt on. It was funny to watch. Constantly somebody got up and so the plane would not leave till everybody buckled down.

Had excellent view of the Himalayans, and are circling New Delhi and one wonders why are we not landing?

New Delhi

Well we made it, and I ended up at my friend's house again and had the deepest sleep. I guess I was exhausted.

Run into a cow today. Was not looking. They are all over. We went shopping for cloth and jewelry. Life for a well to do Indian is good here.

There are so many gold stores. Never have I seen so much. And all the women buy more of it.

I have now some very leisure time with my friends. Tea in the afternoon.

There is a caste system in our house. One man comes daily just to clean the bathrooms and floors. One person only for the toilets.

Dinner was tonight at 10pm again. It was delicious but I was falling asleep.

Traffic is choking in the city. There are Camels pulling many wagons, donkeys, mules, horses and the ever loose cows in any place. Rickshaws, Motor taxis, people, dogs, cars, buses, children. And nobody is getting run over or I did not see it.

New Delhi, November 16, 1992

This morning found a tick on my chest. And Mosquitos were waiting for me. So the hunt was on.

And we are off into the countryside to my friend's little estate. It is Hot here! And this is winter.

Next door the farmer had a camel and a Buffalo. I love Camels.

Went to get my ticket to go to Jaipur by Bus. Was told it would be a luxury Bus.

Next morning arriving at the Bus station, and right away I saw it would be another adventure. A very decrepit Bus was waiting there. I wonder what a regular Bus would be like. I paid $3 for a 250km trip. I guess I cannot complain. Had a very nice seatmate who explained to me many things and then he fell asleep.

We passed so many Camels.

Through the first Gate of Jaipur. It was so impressive. The city is surrounded by Mountains like a fortress. And the inner city looks so pink. Very crowded and many weddings are going on. Lots of Elephants and Horses are used as ceremonial mounts for the grooms.

My reserved Hotel Gauanir was very dirty and unfriendly help and I walked to my Rickshaw again to find another Hotel. I know a little commission the driver will get but he found a very nice place Hotel Nirma. I hired a Guide Salim and he is very knowledgeable. We went to the City Palace, Janto Martar Observatory, Rambagh Palace, Gaitor

Matris memorials.

Everybody has something for sale. Are these real Diamonds in the store? Beautiful Carpets.

One has to keep the windows closed because there are many Monkeys trying to get in, some of them look real mean. I guess living here I would get a dog to keep them away.

Next day was not good for me. Whatever I have is hurting me all over. Had to stop at an Imat Clinic where I got some pills who made me very sleepy. So now I cannot walk and are switching to a car, because the bouncing of the Rickshaw hurt.

I did get two carpets with the Horse design I wanted. It is a shopper's delight here. But there is always a bad view like a very skinny Horse or dead Camel just lying there. And many dead dogs.

Next, I took the Camel ride up to the Amber Fort, very impressive.

Now I upgraded to another Hotel Ashok needed Air-condition.

S For the Wedding Horses are used, the Groom uses a beautiful decked out mare. It is symbolic for a man to switch from Horse to woman. Yuck.

November 19

Now all the medicine has kept me awake, and the bedroom is so beautiful. But my legs are still hurting like heavy weights. Why?

By moto rickshaw now to the city to see the city Palace. The Maharaja is still living there in a secluded section. No entry for me.

But there was so much to see, so many treasures.

And then to the Old Muslim section, there everybody is a Gemstone polisher. Outside raw sewage is flowing but it is almost all over Jaipur, shit and sewage flowing. Just going to an outside toilet is tough since there are no walls and men stand right next to me.

Back at the H. Ashok I tried opening a glass bottle of water with a knife. Very stupid. Cut my hand between thumb and forefinger very deep. One of the waiters rushed me on his motorbike to Dr. Sogam, were I had been before. She was surprised seeing me again. She did a great job of stitching my hand.

As I was waiting in the waiting room I looked around and saw a lot of blood on furniture and on her Apron. Not much hygiene. But I came out of it very good.

Had my Hands Henna painted today, it is a tradition for a wedding I was invited to.

The Henna painters are professional and just go around and do the Henna painting.

At the wedding I found out the women do their own entertainment. The sing and dance and the men are in a separate area and drink hard liquor.

Dinner did not start till 10:30pm. And I had to kill Mosquitos who selected me all evening for their dinner.

Now back to New Delhi with a fresh dressing on my hand from Dr. Sogam.

By Bus on the "Deluxe" and having a very thin seatmate was good. Slept almost all the way. And took the Auto rickshaw back to my "home".

I am ready for my return trip. A late departure to the airport and off with a fully loaded plane to the USA.

Venezuela, 1992

A return to the Llanos-Bad stuff can happen.

With great anticipation I began my return trip to the Llanos, in Venezuela. It is a vast isolated plains area. It is cattle country and a big bird sanctuary and it is either flooded or baking in the sun.

My flight from Caracas seemed to be taking longer than before and the plane landed further south, near the amazon.

The pilot decided to go to a different airport.

So now back by plane and on arriving at my destination in San Fernando and stayed there the night. Locking my door with some of the furniture since no key was in the door. Most of the populace appeared to have spent the weekend imbibing.

Next morning by bus to Elorza, a 6-hour trip. The Bus was packed. The seats were tiny, the music excruciatingly loud and continuous. And when a young man tried to get into my knapsack, I had it. I turned around and caught his arm still in the bag and broke his arm. The Bus driver opened the door and out the would be thief went.

Even stuffing Kleenex into my ears did not help. Because the bus was an "express" service, no rest stop was provided, and no toilet on board. I wondered whether nature's need was as discomforting to the other passengers as it was to me.

On arriving in Elorza I found a "taxi", a piece of unrecognizable junk of unknown vintage, it had no doors and only one forward gear. The fare was still $1 for what turned out to be a two-block trip.

Next, I had to slide down a muddy embankment to get into a small boat. Below the boat was a very fast river, floating carcasses of Cows, trees and underneath piranha, large crocodiles, anacondas, electric eels, and other nasty critters. A long 2 hours by boat and that in the open sun there was no roof.

Arriving at the Dona Barbara Hato, climbing up the muddy embankment I looked pretty dirty.

The stay at the Hato, (Ranch), was very good but on the day, I was to return, no boatman showed up and I tried for 3 days to hail any boat going by on the River, no luck. So it was decided to go back overland by jeep. It was a bad choice, but I had to decide what to do.

We had so many problems it would take pages to fill. We got stuck so many times and only Horse-power, we had to get, got us out again. 8 Hours in blistering heat without any water, I was so happy when we finally arrived in Mantecal for my Bus back to Merida and later home.

Honduras, November 1993

My interest going to Spanish speaking places is to get more fluent in the language.

But first the fun thing. Going to Roatan Island and swim and dive. Stayed at the Fantasy Island Resort which was very beautiful. Lots of Birds and many parrots. The coral reef of the Caribbean is the largest in the western hemisphere.

Flying to San Pedro Sula and visiting Chiquita Banana plantation. I was surprised that the daily income of workers was $3 a day.

Much of the countryside is farming.

But I have never been as hot as in Honduras. The Capital Tegucigalpa was the hottest. Houses had tin roofs and the heat made everything boil under the tin roof. My mattress was like a hot cookie sheet at night.

Finally left for Copan on a long bus ride and I enrolled in classes. Copan is a very sleepy town. Roads are sandy not paved. Copan Ruinas was a new dig from the Mayan civilization and about 5 miles out of town. I spend every afternoon watching the unearthing of Copan Ruinas. I rented a Horse most every day for my transportation. Since school was only 4 hours in the morning my afternoons were free to explore.

Room and board was with a local family. Made trips to the warm springs which were plenty in the countryside. Warm Water comes right out of the earth and one just builts a stone fence at the river and has a private hot tub.

But all that had to end eventually.

Hong Kong, Singapore, Indonesia, February 8th, 1994

Going to Indonesia the cheap way by Garuda airlines.

"May all of your memories be of good times and good friends."
(Fondly by Kienasts Family) January 1980 written in one of my travel notebooks books. It was always my outlook.

Hong Kong

In Hong Kong with Kevin for a short trip.

Hong Kong was great again. Love this city. It is so full of life. And having Kevin this time with me was even more fun. We stayed at the Omni Prince Hotel but to me the YMCA on Salisbury Rd. is my favorite and convenient to all places. All the rooms there have a view of the Harbor. It was full.

We walked, we shopped, and we ate strange food. Great bakeries everywhere. And we arrived at the Luna Festivities. Everybody was in a happy mood.

The transportation system is so excellent.

Went for a day to Guengshou, very interesting. Stanley market is still good but bigger than ever.

To Hotel Excelsior is great for drinks and food and the view from the top! It is supposed to be the longest Escalator in the world to get up there.

We did not go up to Victoria Peak it was always in fog.

And then came New Year's night, the rain stopped and the fireworks started.

The peach blossoms were blooming and Kumquat trees. They were used for decoration for the New Year. And brought in pots as presents to friend and family.

Our last day we spend in Lantau, I had good memories from a visit before. It is still a beautiful Island to hike or do nothing. There is the largest Buddha Statue in the world. About 3000 feet above sea level.

A few more markets to visit and our time is over too soon.

Dropped Kevin off for his flight back to USA and I took the next flight to Singapore.

Singapore, February 13, 1994

And here again it was the biggest festival, New Years!

It is big and beautiful, celebrated with flowers everywhere.

I have to say the rules in the airport how to behave in Singapore cannot be missed:

Fines for Cigarette butts, not flushing the toilet, picking flowers, importing chewing gum, smoking under 18years, and I could not get the rule about filling the car before leaving Singapore to Malaysia. The gas was very cheap in Malaysia but a $1000 fine there.

Went to Sentosa Island because of the old prison history from the Japanese invasion. I was the only tourist there at the time. There was a movie "Guest of the Emperor" which had a lot of that tragic time and the suffering of the women prisoners. So now there is a park with signs of the happenings from that invasion time.

Had to go to the Jurong Bird Park. The Raptors there are unbelievable smart.

The Quay has changed since my first time there. It is now cleaned up and all of it are Restaurants, no more smoking dens anymore. It has become a high class housing area.

Did a night tour on a junk to Kusu and 2 other Islands.

And a quick trip to Malaysia. Johore Bahru is the closest city. Gave me a little idea about the country. Very much still the old style of women dressed in their traditional cloth.

Indonesia, February 14th, 1994

This is now an adventure since I have had very little information on this country. But I do have my "Lonely Travel " book.

Jakarta, getting there! bargaining with drivers from the Airport to the city. Congestion! Blue smog! My eyes started to drain, and I am wheezing.

Many people are walking around with face masks.

Booked into the Yanni Hotel. Except I forgot the Minaret was next door, the screaming of the caller at the most ungodly hours. 4am!! That is why it was so cheap. 5 times a day.

I arrived at Ramadan. Most everybody is fasting. It is a 90% Muslim country. Many people have 4 wives I am told. So I am in a very different world. Have mostly traveled in Christian countries. My driver today started out very happy, by noon he could hardly stay awake. His energy was gone. Not even water is aloud.

The old Harbor is exciting. Ships from all over the world are anchored or tied up by the docks. The old sailing fleet of wooden boats are being loaded. Men carrying loads of 150 pounds on their shoulders for the ships. What I could hear from the stevedores, they make about $1 a day.

It is incredible filthy, and the water looks like sewage.

Wednesday, 17, 1994

My appetite has left me. Maybe I will lose some pounds.

I noticed that the children all know: Hello and where are you going, what's your name, where do you come from? It is what I will hear for the next 6 weeks.

Mau ke mana- seapa nama anda- dari mara. In indonesien.

Have to leave this crowded City and on to other places. I need to find the train Station to go to Bandung. I do have to really try hard to understand and find out the right places. Not much English is spoken. But people are very helpful and I seem to attract a crowd right away wanting to help. I was told American's do not laugh enough and take life to seriously. Questions forever.

I was asked how I liked McDonald? It is a very special place to go out for Dinner here.

The Train is rolling at 11:30am

So now I am sitting in business class for $1.50 for a 3 ½ hour trip. With fans circling on top. First class would have been air-condition for $11. This is big money here.

My view from the window is rice plantations after the next for a while. Service comes constantly through the train. And the music is all USA. Right now, "Make believe that you still love me….Had Kentucky chicken except it was a neck and a wing. Still it did taste good. Now pillows are brought- for rent. The plastic on the seats make me stick to it. It is at least 90 degrees now and 100%humidity. The train does stop quite a lot.

Train arrives at 3:15pm in Bandung!

But it was a beautiful scenery, tea plantations, and the mountains mostly.

At Bandung I found a ride to the Hotel. No Air-condition here. But was told don't need it here at 4000 feet. I just wanted the sound of it so I could sleep better. There are Mosquitoes all over and I know they will keep me awake.

The street I am staying on is called Jean Street. Any Jeans can be made for $10. Store after store of Jeans.

There are many colonial Dutch Homes in beautiful settings. Most of them are empty and for sale. The Dutch used to live here but left after the war and the rich Javanese have taken over.

There is a street full of Clock stores. Many are old (Junghans German made).

Hotels are not good. I will stick more with Hostels. I always know what I get there.

For $5 a night at the Losmen Hostel.

Met Sutandi who took me all over and we climbed up to the crater. It is fascinating to watch the cauldron from the top, all smells like

Sulphur. Then we went swimming in the pool of water of 104 degrees nearby.

There are many tea plantations and in the middle of it is always a Dutch type-built house. It was 1950 when the Dutch had to leave but some are trying to come back again.

I was told that all the money from their produce went out of the country. It did not help the country. Native Children were not allowed to go to school, just had to work for the Dutch. It was as usual, all profits went to the old Country.

But that is over, and it is all settled.

Tonight, I will go to an Anklung Concert. What a surprise. Never heard that kind of music before. It was beautiful and all played on bamboo instruments. There were little children who played Tchaikovsky, the most romantic sound.

When I order food I try not to get the "hot" food. It is making me cough right away, will I get used to it?

Sunday, February 20, 1994

Van service to Panganderan. 7am departure and got there by 2pm. My "Express Bus was not express at all just the driver drove fast. I was in front and his attendant was hanging out the door screaming for more passengers, 20 and finally full. I luckily had the only window which could be opened. The Countryside is very green and again so many flowers everywhere. The green Terraced rice fields are always good to look at.

Pangandaran-arrival. No automobile can go into town only rickshaws. I had to rent two, one rickshaw for my bag and one for me. We certainly made a showy entrance.

My room is great, there is a swimming pool, and the dinner was excellent. All fresh food from the sea.

I have enjoyed the Beach and the pool, then rented a bike to see my surroundings. It is a strange town. Everybody has rooms for rent, good to primitive. But never saw any tourist. It was difficult getting here, there had to be many Mountain passes and it was always up and down. Even we lost our oil pan and had to replace it in the next town. I guess the tourists cannot afford to come.

There is a German bakery Adams. Had a very good cake.

The next day I went alone hiking in the Natl. Park. My guide did not show up and I was tired of waiting. I was told people have been lost there since nothing is marked but I trusted my sense of direction. A lot of up and downs and stumbling over roots. Saw a wild Oxen and many Butterfly's. Very big ones!

And then I saw my first Rafflesia flower. I was told I could smell it long before I see the flower but it all smelled old and muffi in the jungle.

The flower is enormous and the biggest in the world.

Came to a waterfall and a giant cave full of Foxbat's.

These are the bats who fly at night over the town. By now I have walked 4 hours.

A poisoned snake fell right in front of me from a tree limb. It is a jungle all around and the trails are small riverbeds. I am getting used to having wet feet.

When trying to swim in a waterhole many monkeys came right out of the trees and it was a race between them and my pile of stuff. One cannot relax with these little thieves.

Made it back in time for the German bakery and a very good Cappuccino.

I have now met some tourists, but none from USA. Mostly Surinam, Australia and New Zealand.

Hotel Sandaan on my next stop. Nice but 2:30 bellowing from the Mosque. Then at 3:30 again, then at 4:30 again. I finally fell asleep. My rest time is over and I am on my way to Yogyakarta.

Yogyakarta, February 22

With some other people we hired a van and guide at 8am. We stopped at places I could have never found alone. Saw how Tofu is made. At a Kuta Cracker Factory stop. Crackers are an Indonesian staple, they are made out of fish meal. I did not like the taste. Workers are so young, it is slave labor. Learned a lot on this trip. Tasted candy made out of Palm juice, ate coca seeds, great for refreshment.

There are sheep kept in cages on stilts, very strange. And many pigeons, which are kept for gambling. And always lots of fighting roosters tied to their cages.

My tonight stay was at a home were the woman kept an Owl, Harrier Hawk and many different chickens. I loved it. No electricity but the rooms looked so nice.

The Beach was not inviting with the undertow.

The Pancakes filled with tropical fruits and chocolate sauce on top for breakfast. A walk through the coconut plantation helped digest all this good food.

6am by Bus leaving, we are stuffed like Sardines in a Mini Van. Luggage is on the Roof. Transferred all of us onto a very unstable, across a River, but the Captain told me we are "very good". Except we are just sitting on the river dock and are not leaving. Was told the other Ferry is broken and we would wait for more people. Waiting now in the heat, no roof, so walking outside and watching all the little Sellers hawk their ware. But now we are called to get on the Boat again and fighting to get a place on Deck. The Boat was double "Full" of natives and Tourists. One always reads about the Ferries turning over and I was thinking about it and was ready to jump.

We went along the River with many stops; many fishing nets had to be avoided by the ship.

Finally getting off at Lili cap, it is an oil refining area and was told no photos.

A big pink Bus was awaiting everybody. And off in the direction to Yogyakarta. 3 hours' drive a lunch stop, then 3 hours again on the bus.

I slept most of the time even with an interesting countryside.

At the Ankun Hotel which the Bus Company owned. Great room with Air condtion. And breakfast included and a pool. But looking out the window there was the Mosque with 3 loudspeakers facing me. Yes, I know what is awaiting me.

From 5pm to 6pm all people are reading the Koran

Went to the show at the Ramayana Epic Fragment at the Salem Pujckusuman. 3 hours of Java Ballet. But never again. Very slow and I could not understand it. No Melody, the performers are very good and it was beautiful but...

Ankun Hotel, February 24, 1994

4am, the wailing started and no sleep after that. Sightseeing all day. The Sultan Palace. The old Water castle with the dirtiest greenest water full with children swimming in it.

The Bird market was full of suffering animals. From Monkeys to flying Foxes, very sad. The stench!! But one has to see it. There is no compassion for the animals from anybody. They are food. The Muslim religion is not understandable that it directs animals are dirty and not to be touched. Especially dogs.

It is not very clean here either, all the garbage gets thrown on the ground. And the toilets are very wet from all the water splashing. Standing over the open hole and I worry not to slip. There is no toilet paper since one has to use water only for cleaning.

Have tried today the Anklong. Trying to learn to play it. It is difficult.

Horse-carriage to Mariboro Road. It is a known Market of many Stalls for things to buy. One has to bargain for everything at least to 50% less.

The Horses have to work very hard because the carriages are overloaded. But all human have to work hard here too.

Cats look like skin and bones and if there is a loose dog it is hiding or half dead.

And so another Morning of prayer calls. I have had no sleep!!

Left today at 5:20am for Borobudur hoping to arrive at sunrise but a cloudy morning stopped that. The Vulcan Mercati was puffing away which contributed to the clouds.

Still was unbelievable. The Building is so big and in such geometric way it is difficult to describe. And then heat.

Prambanan to see the Shiva Hindu Temple, very impressive too.

The Mendut and Pawon Temple next. And to Gede Kota the silver craftsmen town.

At the Ankong Hotel refreshments and to a French café for chicken baguette.

Saturday less wailing from the Mosque? 10pm till 4am peace. I do not like the "devoted" men walking out of the Mosque. They have a very nasty calculating roving eye.

Fumigating trucks came around today with black smoke, wonder what it was maybe for mosquitos.

Was told to stay at Delta Homestays if I see them. Supposed to be the best Backpacker place.

Went to the Vredenburg Museum which told all about the Dutch and Japanese occupation. The Indonesians still talk about it. It is very hot and humid but I have a pool and Air-condition to cool off.

Many people keep fighting Roosters in the yard, very pretty ones too. I was told in Bali they use big knife spurs on the Roosters.

A lot of cages hang from Doorways and yards too, filled with songbirds. Each cage is full of Birds and a lot of suffering for them.

Finally, I am getting the Bus to Bali at 3pm.

An 18-hour trip.

Sunday, February 27, 1994

The Bus was full and the Driver never stopped smoking. But how did he keep awake? He never changed he must have been smoking something to keep him awake. My seat partner was a nice young man from Lombock who even spoke English. Got a lot of information from him for my future visit there.

We stopped at some Restaurants. The food I ate was totally unknown to me and it tasted alright but certain parts in my plate I did not like to look at.

On the Bus we had a phorn movie and 2 Chinese movies, I fell asleep. Not the young men on the Bus they watched.

Had reclining seats with blankets and pillows. And all of that for $20.

We arrived at the Ferry port in darkness. The Ferry was beached in the Sand and the Bus drove right on it. The crossing was one hour and we arrived just as the sun was coming up.

All Roads in Bali are winding and up and down. A very beautiful Island with many flowers all over. There are little temples on every corner. Different from Java. It is a Hindu country not muslim.

In Sanur I found a Losmen Agency Homestay for $15 a night and very pretty. Right at the Beach. Heavenly warm water for swimming. On walking around I met a very nice family who had an empty house for me to stay. I will move in there tomorrow.

So hot here!

Went shipwreck diving, fish are so beautiful. Very big and tame. Did two dives and it was great. The best thing, one has to do nothing, except go dive. No carrying the heavy stuff. It was my first dive in Bali, just floating along with the drift.

On my way to the Dive place saw a lot of Balinese women walking with their offerings to the little shrines. It is done every day.

At night windows close at all the houses. There are 3000 gods living in the Hindu religion and all of them are here in Bali too.

There are dogs here, either happy ones or scruffy ones. Feeding an animal is just not done. But at least they do not get kicked around in Bali.

Tuesday, March 1

I found out Balinese are afraid of the sea, there are Gods there. So a lot of offerings are brought to the Beach every morning. A cremation was held on a small Beach nearby.

Up this morning to see the sunrise, beautiful.

To take a Bemo,(transport cycle) to a travel Agency's to arrange trip to the Komodo Island. Everything was too expensive, tourist season prices right now.

So I bought a jet boat ticket to Lombock. With a Bemo to get my luggage.

For a day I went to Kuta. Heard it was an interesting place to visit.

It is not a nice place. But one has to visit to see. It is all Bars and disco and shops. And very Expensive Hotels for tourists. Swimming is not good because of the strong current there.

A sign in Kuta got my attention: cheap flight to Komodo and I bought now an Airline ticket for $75. Let's hope I did the right thing.

Now I can relax and go swimming at my Beach. I love my new home in Sanur. It is surrounded by a big wall and a moat on the inside with big koi. In the Bathhouse is a very big Gecko. He is good to have, loves spiders or any insect.

Outside men walk around with their Roosters under their arms. The Roosters are bestowed with lots of love. It is unreal. Roosters get massage, stroking, anything to make them feel good. Lots of money is involved in winning a fight.

Walking along the Beach is not fun. Many people try to sell anything. This is their living and if one does not buy from them it was explained no food for the family.

Flying from Denpasar to Bima.

Plane left early and lucky for me I was early. Stopped in Merpati, Mataran, Lombock and then to Bima Sumbawa.

On arrival not all passengers needed a Taxi except me. So the taxi drivers were arguing about what to charge me. It was too high for me and I told them all go, to hell. And hitched a ride with a young man who showed me how to take public transportation.

This is not for the faint hearted, first of all it is hot, very hot. The vans are small and always full and no open windows.

In Bima I stopped to shop for food. Lots of Bananas and bread and then by Bema to the Bus Terminal. They are always way out of town.

My Bus to Sape. Full too. Many animals under the seats or tied anywhere. Lots of fruit on top of the Bus and whatever likely in bags. Sometimes I wondered if my bag was still there. The Road wound around many Mountains and was very winding. Beautiful Scenery. The Driver was very good and took his time downhill.

At arrival I changed to a Horse cart for the next 5 miles. It really was a skinny pony. The carts are called Benhur. Then from the pier onto a Ferry with my cart.

At the Losman, I had my little Veranda and all the swimming in the sea around me. If only it would not be so filthy, all garbage goes out to sea.

Tonight, I ate only rice, yesterday's Nasi Goreng had a bad taste and left my stomach unhappy.

Near the pier the children just caught a monster eel. Could be a snake too, 9 feet long. I am not getting close.

By darkness many fishing boats are leaving with the lamps hanging on the side. Maybe a hundred boats?

Is there any fish in the sea left tomorrow?

March 3

There is no Ferry today and I will have to stay longer in this beautiful little place. Water sounds good all night, very good sleeping.

Too bad it is the rainy season. Showers come every day. I have taken my Malaria pills every day. I am prepared for everything. I think I will fly back to Bali on my return trip from Komodo. Too many days at sea and too many Ferry's.

The men in this area do not look very happy. Disturbing looks and the men have very crude features and when I see a good-looking man he is usual a transvestite or gay. All have beautiful long black hair. The women are a sorry lot; all of them carry babies on their back, and many little ones around them. Everybody again throws all the garbage into the sea and hopes the tide will clean up; all the houses are built on stilts for the water to come at high tide to take the garbage away.

On the bus to Sape I could see the most primitive people and looking at their living condition was very bad. But it is always warm, no fires are needed.

Going again on a boat, took my seasick pills. So far the sea is still, no waves, only the music is so loud.

Then the weather changed and the waves were pretty high. The Boat finally arrived at Komodo Island after 6hours. This was not a tourist boat it was a connecting Ferry going from Island to Island. There are never toilets on the ferries so one can imagine the hygiene.

It is raining again hard. But I am glad I am on land after 6 hours on the Boat. There was a moment of hair raising when I thought the Ferry would capsize. The waves came suddenly over the side and through us all over.

From the big Boat I was transported into a little Boat, squashed again with other people for 30 minutes under deck. I do not like going under deck. Especially when the ferry owner collected the money right away.

Komodo Island is owned by the Park Service and they have little houses with places to sleep. One is now totally away from civilization. No phones or any way to get off again till another ferry comes along. The entertainment is finding a Komodo Dragon. No Problem, one was sleeping right next to the pier when getting on land. It looked unreal. That huge size!

Around the Park the police compound is surrounded by a small wall. Wild Deer and wild Pigs have hidden under the Buildings so the big Dragon cannot get to them. Dragons will eat anything when hungry even smaller Dragons.

100 years ago the Island was a prison Island. But since 1900 a Natl. Park. Very big hills and all in grass. No trees. There are some bushes.

At night the kitchen cafeteria served very good food. Rice, and rice, noodles, egg and Beer.

In the morning the park Ranger collected us few people for the feeding of the Dragons. A smaller version of the Dragon was sleeping on the roof. It was trying not to get eaten by his parents. We first had to learn how to protect us, which was funny especially when about 20 of the Dragons came charging at us. We quickly had to go into a cage like pen were we stayed safe till the Ranger chased the Dragons with a long stick.

There was a lot of hissing and flicking of their tongues. Very strange unreal animals. Then we went on a safe hike and saw all from a more distance. Saw beautiful Birds, Cookados and many butterflies.

Went swimming with a group of people by the pier when one of the backpacker, Viking his name, came up screaming with a dislocated shoulder.

We finally pulled him onto the pier, and me, the expert put his arm back into the right position again. He fainted when I was doing it. I have a little experience from my Hockey player days.

Our dinner was lots of Rice today and rice. Our choices are small. No Electric to keep food and nothing grows on the Island one has to eat what is given.

But there was always lots of coffee and Beer.

March 5

Today is a bad and a good day. Bad for the young goat we all chipped in to buy and good for the Komodo dragon. It was feeding time. It is a barbaric thing to do. The Ranger carried the beautiful little goat in front of us, which was bleating like crazy. For 3 km we walked and many Dragons already were waiting for us. We did not know which direction to run, I stayed frozen. The Ranger threw the goat into the pile of Dragons and we watched how they ate it in 10 minutes. Somehow the Dragons are very happy and will leave us alone because this feeding has been going on for a long time.

I rather enjoyed watching the big dragons walking along the Beach or just doing their thing.

Flores was my next place to visit. And again many Ferries to get there. I took the next day the little shuttle to a Ferry back waiting in the sea. 6 hours with beautiful weather to Sape and then to Bima at a Losman Lila Galan.

Sumbava seeing it once is enough.

Next morning in the dark trying to find the Big Bus to Mataram. Everybody was pointing in different direction, I gave up and went back to the Hotel and there it was waiting for me.

A long drive now and from the window many beautiful Beaches but no places to stay or Hotels on this Island, so on I went.

Arriving late 9pm again was a hassle. Finding a Bemo to take me to a losman and all were full and the driver kept asking for more money. Everybody is trying to get more and more.

At the Shanti Puri I got a room and breakfast but sleeping was useless. The room was full of bed bugs crawling over me. By now I looked again like the measles. Nobody else had it so bad.

The greetings from everybody is always where are you from and where are you going.

It is the polite Indonesian way but sounds insulting to my ears.

I traveling now with a very nice couple who have talked me into getting around faster. By Motorcycle!!

Going shopping now for toilet paper which is difficult to find but as needed and looking at Yamaha's. For $5 a day I can rent one. A few minutes of lessons and leaving my passport with the young owner for security and off we went.

Now the rains are coming down. Never have I seen so many deep puddles and one had to go through them. From Cakranegara to Landangh Nangka. This is all Lombock.

By now I have found out what all the bugs were. Bed Bugs!!!!

The rain felt good and soothing on my itching body.

And I am covered like I have the measles and itching like crazy. I do have Benadryl and I am getting more in the drugstore.

Since it is Ramadan we can only get Vegetarian food. I am afraid to go to sleep because now I find out there are many places here with bedbugs and they wait for certain people to show up in the Hotel room. And I am somehow they like. My friends have not one bite.

Driving my Yamaha is fun. I am using the Horn like everybody; so many Horse carts are in my way. Hate to run over anything.

And I am itching. Again last night they got me. I need cortisone shots now. Found a Doctor but she was only a Dentist and directed me to a real Doctor in the Village. There I got my shot but I am so swollen up now. I am highly allergic.

And I notice I am not a vegetarian I need real food soon or my strength is leaving me. 6 days now. Ramadan or the bed bugs are killing me.

March 9

I dread going to sleep at night. We have cleaned the room and sprayed with very poisonous spray.

I slept last night at least. Had great fried Bananas and fruit plate. And no attack of bugs.

Driving now along the countryside. Nice to be able to stop when one wants to.

Kata over Selong. In Selong I got more good medicine, it is a nice town.

Village after village in the old style. All Buildings are on stilts, but the women did not look happy. The work so hard with big loads on their shoulders. The men are always in the Mosque doing nothing.

In Kata I had a flat tire right next to a wonderful Beach. Swimming helped my itching. Had fresh Barracuda for a feast. Fruit salad and Coffee and a milkshake.

Tonight at a B&B it is very quiet even with a Mosque next door. Electricity is out and the Mosque needed electric for their loudspeakers!! We sit by candlelight and enjoy the peace.

March 10

At Kuta Bungalow we did not like the Owners attitude, he wanted more money than arranged before the next night.

It was built on stilts and all animals were living underneath. Fighting dogs, crying puppies, neighbors who were very noisy, cats screaming. What a commotion. The Mosque never shut up, since electric came on again the Crier had to make up from the night before. It was impossible to sleep.

I finally checked out in the middle of the night and went across to the Yellow Flower Hotel. Much nicer people.

Drove today through the countryside and found good Beaches and good fish lunches. A young boy cut up a pineapple on the Beach for me, it was very refreshing.

Finally I found the perfect snorkel Beach. Clear Water, no garbage. Very strange fish I never saw before.

March 11

The bed bugs got me badly again. Now I am really sick, I am allergic now to the bite marks. And I itch!

I have so many pills and different creams but nothing really works because I am always getting new attacks.

But I am still on my motorbike seeing the country, there is just so much to see still. I am back at one of my favorite Losman and hope to get a good sleep here.

Went shopping for cheap cloth and shoes. Since it rained a lot, my outfits have worn out fast.

Will Take the 7:30am Ferry to Gili Trawangan. It is a little Island. Here my friends are leaving me and I hope to find new friends to travel with.

Ramadan is over and tonight is a big feasting. Lombock is very Muslim and so many Muslims have come to celebrate here.

I have returned my motorbike and taking now a Bus over the Mountains along the coast to another Ferry to direction to Bali again. The Ferry did make it difficult to get on and we all had to wade through the water.

It was pouring, getting wet was ok. And the waves came on top of us. Landed again on a Beach and a Horse cart picked me up. All the Losman are full but I got a room at Hamlin. A very nice Bungalow, but had to share it with a noisy group next door.

Great snorkeling and again different fish and strange water creatures.

Lunch was fried fish and I loved it.

I found out that Indonesia is one of the best friends of Hussein of Iraq. (1994) guns are fabricated here and send to Iraq.

There is the big difference between Bali (Hindu) and all the other Islands are Muslim.

I wish it would stop raining. It is warm but brings on more bugs. And now the electric is out, somebody brought me a smoke lamp. No water is running without the electric.

Trying to get some food is hard. Everybody just closed up.

Made it to Gili Trabagan MawarII, a little Island. Very lovely and quiet. The only noise is the reef. And the wind is blowing through my little Bungalow like a great breeze.

The owner gave me a plate of cooked peanuts, it was delicious.

Right outside is my beach, great snorkeling again. With colorful fish.

Climbed the hill for a good hike with a view of Bali and Lombock.

My place is very idyllic but I will have to move on.

The free range chickens and Roosters have all gone to be cooked for the Dinners tonight. Even the few Goats I saw are butchered.

Every time I see one Horse cart go by I feel sorry for the Horses. Very skinny and I have seen a few fall down. The drivers get off and just starting to hit them till the Horse gets up again.

In Trabagan I have again bad luck, bed bugs again. My body is attracting them. Nobody else has the problem.

I hope to be back in Bali in my clean house by tomorrow. Had my fresh Goat roast today not so bad. After so many weeks without meat anything would taste good.

I try to swim all the time. It does sooth my body from itching. Mawar is nice, a big golf course is planned, shame, it will ruin the countryside.

Tomorrow off by Boat, Bus, boat, bus to Sanur Bali.

It was not easy. Got pretty wet on the Ferry and on arrival missed the other Ferry connection to Denpasar. So now a 5 hour wait. My money change was running out and had a big hassle getting money small enough to buy food from peddlers.

Finally at 6pm we left. All on the Ferry started to get sick. The Ferries are not big, just converted fishing vessels. And every place is filled with passengers. I took my seasick pill and felt very good. A little high, wonder what was in it? On passing the Padang Bay there was the cruise ship Maxim Gorky anchored. I am sure the passengers did not get roughed up like us in the wild sea.

Arriving in Sanur, Bali late at night and no key for my Gate. The guard for the house had locked the gate and left for the night. The high wall around the house was not possible to climb.

Trying to find a bed somewhere, walking around with my bag in the dark was not a good feeling. Every Hotel or Losman was full.

There seemed to be nothing else I could do, but settle in on the beach and wait for morning. Although no one was in sight, the prospect of spending the night there was rather frightening.

I decided that I would remain near a lighted storefront on the beach. I was just settling in the sand on the Beach as a woman came out to inquire about my plight. When she learned what had happened, she invited me to sleep in her house which was located behind the store. I just wanted to hug her, I was so happy, what a relief. She told me she had a baby if that would bother me? No I would have slept with 10 babies just to get inside.

There was a big room with a traditionally large platform bed. On it was a Husband sleeping and two children. She woke her husband and explained what had happened to me. He immediately took a sheet and went into the store leaving his place in the bed for me.

So there I was safely tucked in with the young woman, her five year old boy and an infant who, from time- to- time, suckled from his mother. Woke up only one time to relief myself. Since I did not know where the toilet was I used outside the garden. Hope I did not kill any flowers.

Putry, the woman awakened me with a cup of tea in the morning. What a great family. What a wonderful feeling that was.

I made a lot of photos of the family and promised to bring them back when I develop them.

The thoughtfulness and hospitality of that family is something that I never shall forget. They refused to accept any money.

Finally, I could get into my house and cleaned first of all up and then took the film to a Photoshop, confirmed my flights, ate lunch and took the photos to my "new" family. That is the only way I could say thank you for helping me in the late night.

Sukade, the owner of my house took me now to meet his family in Denpasar. I got to know how a wealthy family lives. They have Kampungs. Everybody lives there and usually from Baby to the oldest family member. The Kampung is almost a walled small city. And each Kampung is more lavish done. There is always a very fancy Entrance Gate in a temple style. And constantly somebody is sweeping or cleaning floors. But out the door goes the dirt.

There are little tables with offerings outside in the garden and on the Road. The style of offering has not changed and it is only done so in Bali. The women wear a very interesting style of dresses. And always carry something on top of their heads.

There are temples full of monkeys and they will grab anything like glasses or wallets of you. So hopefully all the offerings keep them happy.

In Denpasar I went to a great Restaurant for Dinner and had my eyeglasses fixed. Which keep falling apart.

March17 at Sanur

Off on the motorcycle with Sukade to Ubud. Ubud is the Artist Colony and I booked into Ubud Hideaway in a Princess Room. Gorgeous!

Ubud is a town to walk. Temples, shrines, people, farms all fascinating to look at. Sukade was a very good guide and explained and took me to places I would have never found.

Ate Lunch on top of Lake Batur in the Lakeview Restaurant, expensive but very good food.

Bought a hand painted Blanket and wind chimes. Very good things were for sale. The Blanket was painted by some young girls with a Koi fish design.

I think every person in Bali is an Artist. I just have never seen so many things I would have liked.

In the evening I went to the Gabor Dance in the palace. It was a fast moving theatre show with Gamelon music. A little to high notes for my ears.

My room looked good but outside are dogs barking and are not stopping. So I am awake.

I had my first hot shower in 4 weeks! Usually showers are big containers and one stands next to them and pours water over the body scooping it out of the big container.

I moved again because the dogs kept me to much awake.

Rented a bicycle and biked many miles till it got to hot. Then a good swim in the pool to wait till it got cooler.

On my way back stopped at the Monkey Forest Temple where a

big Rooster fight was in action. I counted about 500 men. No women. But was invited to join, what an education for me. The Roosters were preened and massaged and then 2 against each other let loose. Usually in 2 minutes it was over. The head usually got severed by the 3 inch spurs of the other Rooster. The finest metal blades are used. Much money betting.

If a Rooster did not want to fight I noticed, his legs got cut off before he was dead. Very sadistic and I had to leave.

The evening entertainment was better. A Legong dance. That was action and colorful.

A stop by a beautiful River and I choose the last Hostel. But on closer look very dirty water in the River. There was a veranda for eating but no pool.

My breakfast here was good. Egg omelets' with Onions, toast and Jam and Butter. A bowl of papaya, pineapple, bananas and covered with thick canned sweet milk. And coffee. My kind of food.

The Bus to Lovina was hairy. Over the mountains and then Mt. Baktur for a 2 hour stop. Nice cool air up here. And then down again into the heat. And pouring rain. What can I say it is the rainy season I am told.

Many Hostels are here now and I staying at Permatia Hotel right on the sea. Went snorkeling right away but felt I was getting stung. Then I was told the corral was spawning and the little eggs bite.

Great sunset and a peaceful Beach.

Again some bug got me. I sprayed but still itching. Had one bite still from Ubud which is giving me trouble and got from a Doctor more Benadryl and some other medicine.

The Mosquito problem with all the rain is bad.

But the food is great and I have not lost an ounce.

Today to an Island Menjangan to Scuba dive. Very clear water and lots of fish. The Equipment was very good and new. We used a fishing boat but very flimsy and looked like it would fall apart.

Rented a bike again and covered a few hills and miles and ended up at the Dutch Monument with a very good view of the valley.

Then on to a hot spring which had a lot of Sulphur. It helped my itchy body. I spend 3 hours in the water.

Diving again today but the water is not as clear today.

Spend $25 for 3 nights, 2 dinners, lunch and lots of fruit. I cannot believe how much I can do for my $. Hotel Permatia was good.

On a Bus again, squashed into a seat till Alampuran, there I had to change a Bus again to Candidasa.

Another Bus to Kilapa Mas Hotel, right next to the beach with a beautiful tropical Garden. Except every room or Bungalow is made out of Bamboo. One can hear all.

But it turned into a very quiet place and I slept almost perfect, finally.

The waves woke me up.

Went to another Legong Dance it was very good. Especially when a rat jumped out of the Lions head. Everybody started laughing.

One more swim now and snorkeling. I have to get ready to leave. My first Bus is at 11am. Squashed into a tiny minibus till Padangbay. From there squashed into a bigger Bus passing Ubud and Sanur.

And now back at my little house. Made a trip today with Sukade to Nusa Dua. That is the wealthy part of Bali. Beautiful Hotels and everything is very expensive.

Signed up for one more dive to Amed Island. First of all the place is very beautiful. The Dive master Sirgha was also very good. He did a drift dive with me which was very different. We passed so many fish! It was my first time.

Lunch and then dive 2. Even better. By now I have learned how to follow and even use #2 pounds less. Just floating along no need to work. And now surrounded by fish and the biggest and most colorful anemones. White ferns tall as Palm trees covered with little black ferns. I felt like I was in an underwater Garden. Did not want to leave this place. And when finished with the dive we just came up and there was the boat. It followed us by our air bubbles.

At home Sukade surprised me with a Birthday party. A T-shirt and sandals were given to me. And a big bowl filled with fruit and my favorite Tamarin Juice. In the background music is playing Happy Birthday in Indonesian.

I have noticed that the Bank buildings are very beautiful which I found out why. In the 70's the government pushed for people to use savings. The more beautiful the building was, it appealed to the people and started to deposit their money there.

Sukade had today again a very nice breakfast ready for me. I am being spoiled and will have to get used that this will end soon. By bike we went to Klungkung to see the old Court and the mother temple Berhesha. And then the rain came again which took away the splendor of the biggest Hindu temple in Indonesia.

Staying the last night near the airport at the Sativa cottage Hotel. But it has no Beach but a great pool. I loved Bali the Island of the Gods.

Singapore

Singapore 27 March. Nice flight. Staying at the Allison Hotel. Taking a walk to the Raffles Hotel it is all renovated again. Then to the Night market at Bugis. Many food stalls are open all night but I did not try anything.

Having only 5 hours in my beautiful room because by 5:30 it was back to the Airport. And now it is raining here too.

Taipei, Taiwan, March 1994

Flight with Taipei Air to Taipei, a great airline.

Chao Lee, one of my Christmas Students, was at the Airport and was my guide for the next week. Had a great Hotel which was a youth Center.

Right away I found out about the carved marble statues of the Lions. I always wanted to know why only one had a rolling ball in the mouth of the pairs. Only the male Lion has the rolling ball in his mouth. Why? That question was not answered.

One does not hear what Taiwan has to offer and here was so much to discover. Taroko Gorge was the first big surprise. The Gorge is pure marble. It is all naturally beautiful. It is a land of green forest, soaring mountains, flowering rivers and meandering streams. And many Temples and shrines, palaces and pagodas.

There is even furniture carved out of marble.

Just visiting the Grand Hotel in Taipei is an experience. It is splendor. The color red is everywhere in the Grand Hotel.

There are trains going all around the country. Buses who run on time. The best Chinese food. My few days were not enough. Have to return for a longer visit.

Bonaire, May 1994

It is time for another diving trip and this time the Caribbean. Bonaire! Capt. Dan's place would have the perfect dive center I was told. And it was the clearest water I have ever seen. And the fish! Since there is no fishing for about 25 miles around Bonaire the fish are not afraid of people.

And my first night diving on the docks. It was strange, because some fish followed us and they knew they would get a snack when our flashlight was shining on a sleeping fish. It was snapped up fast by "our" big Groupers.

Sun Sand Sea what else is needed?

Venezuela, June 1994

A quick visit to my good friends in Venezuela. Went sightseeing in Caracas this time. We went to Hatillo, a very old town nearby.

To Merida for a bike tour again with my friend Cesar. Many steep hills to go up and down. Going down my brakes gave out. Lucky I could stop my bike on time. It was too steep. Then to Los Frailes. One of my favorite places for relaxing and Horse riding.

A visit to Simon Diaz, one of my favorite Venezuelan musician, to his Hacienda. A big Barbecue was held. Most everybody was there with a Quatro and beautiful Music was heard. And then back to USA again.

Poland, November 1994

Now was the time to return to Poland to show Kevin my birthplace showing him what we left behind. We crossed East Germany by car which was now better looking than a few years ago.

Went to Mistroje (Mistroy) first up north on the Baltic Sea. That is where our family used to spend summers before the bad times. A great aunt (Blandina),had been Mother Superior in the Convent which was owned by my family.

Meeting again Schwester Majella, now is 80 years old. She was our nurse as a young woman. Mother Superior now is S. Blanca. Had a lot of fun with all the nuns since some spoke English or German or only polish. So a lot of translating was done.

With tears and a teary goodbye leave and going south.

A long drive across Poland to my birthplace Glucholazy which was once called Bad-Ziegenhals. It is right on the border of the Czech Republic, then Tschechoslavika.

The town still has not changed, There is not much money in Poland so only the front of buildings get redone. In the town square is a big statue of a goat which is the namesake of the town.

Driving up the Hills to our house and visiting the polish people who are living in "our" house now. We have made friends on my trip before and are always invited to come again. Walking around always gives back old memories from long ago.

A drive to Cracow (Krakau) one needs days to see the town. It never got bombed and it is a treasure to see such old places kept up.

St. Mary's Church with two different spires of different heights from the 12th century and so much more to see.

The Wawel Castle!

And all the historical places too many to describe.

Driving now back to Dresden in Germany. Another beautiful town to see. That town was totally destroyed in the 2nd world war and now is being rebuilt. It accidentally got bombed after the second WW and totally destroyed. Nobody knows how many people were killed. It was supposed to be a safe city since no Factories had been there.

Chile and Argentina, January 6, 1995

A different trip now to discover the south of Chile and Argentina.

Santiago, Chile a short visit at my friends, and a quick visit to Valparaiso again. To the Beach since it is summer but it is very crowded. The water is to cold for me.

Then by Horse into the mountains for a barbecue. All of it carried by Horses.

I booked an express Bus going south to Valdivia. It is all first-class. It took 11 hours and I slept pretty good. In Valdivia I was surprised how much was in German. The street names, the food, the Beer and found out a lot of German's settled here about 1940. Chile's Lake District is known as the country's adventure capital. Rising above Lake Villaricca is the 9,341 foot snowcapped Villarrica Vulcano.

Now a Bus to Bariloche Argentina.

That was the most exiting trip over the Andes. That stretch of trip is called Lagos Andinos.

First by Bus, then by ship, in Puella I stayed overnight, great Hotel, on a Bus again, then by ship and then by Bus to San Carlos. San Carlos was full of backpackers and I felt right at home. Then a return again over the mountains the same tour back to Valdiva.

A trip now to the Island Chiloe. It is known for fresh fish especially sea bass. The buildings and church are all built from wood from around the Island. Fishermen fishing Sea Urchins and it is cold and foggy

By Bus to Tierra del Fuego hopefully.

Crossing from Chile to Argentina and back again a few times since both country's share the area with Borders not very much marked.

Stopped in Punta Arenas. A beautiful town. Loved the old buildings.

And to the Magellanic Penguin or Jackass colony now. There are Rhea or Nandu's running around and skunks!

In Punta Arenas on a Sunday morning awakened with marching music. Outside a big band was playing. Just for fun.

Stayed in the Hotel Jose Nogueira for one night. And then again to backpacker places. Sometimes it is nice to upgrade a night.

Calafate, the most colorful city I have ever seen next. A very antique looking town. Even my Hotel was filled with antiques.

I am running out of roads and by plane now to Ushuaia. The Pilot announced that he can only land if the clouds will open for him to see the landing strip. Kaiken Lineas was the airline. What a name. All of us kept looking for that little hole in the clouds and hoping.

Well we landed. Ushuaia must be the loneliest town in the world. 1868 it was built as a prison camp first. All buildings are built in the Balloon frame. Means corrugated iron roof, outer cover of overlapped boards, or corrugated iron.

There is even a ski center. Wonder who comes here to ski? The Natl. Park Tierra del Fuego is 140 000 acres and mostly forest with many beautiful hiking trails.

A boat trip on the Beagle Channel to Pt. Williams. That is the last town going south. So much wildlife on every rock. Every place was taken by Penguins or Cormorants or seals.

I was reading a book about the "Land of Fire" and wanted to see more of it.

It is called the "uttermost place on the earth".

It is the land of fire" because of the bonfires which had been lit by the natives before the white man came. I read the book about it written by Lucas Bridges who lived on the point of the Beagle Chanel in Haberton Bay. The Book fascinated me and I had to visit the Hacienda Haberton. Founded in 1886.

By boat was the only way I was told and on arrival I was welcomed by a Thomas Bridges who had a wonderful story to tell.

Then I met his wife, Natalie Goodall, who was from Ohio USA and still cooked the American style. We had good food and chocolate chip cookies. 40 years ago she arrived as a backpacker at the Estancia and fell in love with Thomas Bridges. And never left. (Natalie died in 2015)

Going back later by jeep 90km on a sandy road to Ushuaia. In Ushuaia I took a trip up the ski lift just to see some more wilderness. My view was the Martial glacier and the Beagle Channel.

Going now north in the windiest place I have ever been. Every tree is bent over. And all on unpaved Roads. Old rusty Busses now. The front of the Busses and cars are covered by heavy cardboard and only a little hole is cut into the windshield so one can see out. All so no stone can penetrate the Glass.

Reaching the Rio Grande through Chile, then Argentina. One only knew because of border guards checking our passports. It is a lonely place, crossing rivers and arriving in Puerto Natales. There was seldom a home or Hacienda in sight.

Booked a trip on the "Alberto de Agostini. A very nice ship Going along the River first and saw many beautiful sights again. I had very beautiful weather but was warned it might be very cold.

We stopped at little piers were people were waiting for us to give them mail. That was the only contact with many homes when the ship came by.

The boat sailed into Parque Nacional Monte Balmaceda. There the Mountain is 6000feet high with a Glacier called Serrano which used to be at sea-level but is shrinking. Awesome scenery all around.

Back in Puerto Natales walking around and discovering different things like the monster hand near the water and the wind is blowing. And going on by boat is iffy since all shipping is halted till the wind lets down.

So now by Bus to Argentina for 7 hours through absolute emptiness to El Calafate. Not a tree in sight, wind is blowing now 85 miles an hour. Staying on a Hacienda overnight. Everything is worked by Horse and dogs.

Getting to Parque Glacier Moreno now. Here is no melting of ice. 133m high wall of ice. And it is growing every year more.

Stayed in a backpacker place called Buenos Aires of the Familia Ribas. Out in nowhere. Very good food, fresh baked bread. Always wonder how little people need and are happy with it.

Crossing into Chile again by Bus to a Milodan Cave , discovered in 1895 with prehistoric remains.

Then into Parque Nacional: Torres Del Paine!

Foxes running around and Guanaco, a kind of Camel family only smaller. Crossing the Rio Gray, but all had to get out of the Bus and walk across the Bridge. I guess if the Bus broke through the wooden bridge we are safer outside of it.

Staying in the park in a backpacker home. Fantastic! Posada Rio Serrano.

It was once a big Hacienda but now just used for overnighters or Horse-riding. Which I did the next day. Not a fence in sight and just open plains to ride. Our saddles were cushioned by heavy sheepskins. The wind was bothersome.

I noticed every car or Bus here too had metal screens over the windows. One stone can do so much damage and no place to repair a windshield.

And arriving now by Bus in Punta Arenas for my flight to USA.

Puerto Rico, March 1995

Gone to warmer climate with friend Judy. We both needed a good vacation. Right away we took off to the Corillera Central. It runs from East to West on a panoramic route. We stayed in Paradores away from the tourist trail. There are many coffee plantations. And we saw how the coffee Beans are dried as they are spread into the middle of the Road.

Driving over them takes off the first hull or dry chaff. Chickens picking for bugs in the coffee beans. Not a clean affair. One could see a cow standing on top too.

Ponce and a Beach called Isabel and great sunsets.

El Yunque was our next place to go. A beautiful forest, we got to taste very good native food there.

Back to the Old Town San Juan! It is old and full of history. 500 years old. Towering El Morro, the castle. Built by the Spaniards, It is a maze of Tunnels and very impressive.

I then flew on to Vieques which then was still mostly occupied by the US Navy. But a great place for biking since it is flat.

A short trip to Culebra Island. With a most beautiful Beach called Flamenco Beach. 2 miles long. Passion Fruit was growing all over the Island like a weed. One of my favorite fruits now. Culebra is very laid back. There is only a very small town, Dewey, with a store which was seldom open. To stay there one had to find a family to rent a room, and I got to know everybody on Culebra this way.

Italy, late March 25, 1995

A quick trip to Italy with my Brother to his house on the Island Albarella. It is situated in the old Salt Lakes south of Venice. Salt produce has stopped and so the many lakes have become wildlife attractions.

A day trip to Padua was very interesting. Again there is so much to see there.

And it is my Birthday. It is so cold. We celebrate with going to Chioggia. I have fallen in love with Chioggia and it now one of my favorite towns to visit. It is very busy with Italians and no tourists.

By Bus to Venice another day, which involved first a Ferry, then change to a Bus, then again to a Ferry. Sounds complicated, but one only had to follow all the other people, then from the Lido with a Vaporetto into Venice.

Venice! It is beautiful! But on nice days, it is so crowded one can hardly move in the little streets. Tourist crowd the small alley's and bump into each other.

There was the Grand Canal, the Gritty Palace Hotel, San Marcus, The Bridge of whisper or sighs. The Bridge was usually the last sight a prisoner saw before being executed or thrown into jail, Rialto Bridge; the Gondolier's standing on their little Persian rug and entertaining his passengers.

Since it was my Birthday I decided to hire a Gondolier. First the bargaining for the price which ended up $80. Outrageous!

Very nice trip into small areas without the motorboats. But he would not sing. He did not feel like it.

More sights to see and back to Albarella again.

Driving north to Adria and to Lunch to Giovanni. Oh was that good. Just special cooked for us.

My quick trip is over and a return to USA.

Belize, September 1995

Another trip to warmer waters. Ambergris Caye Island) was my choice since it is known for very laidback. It is a Palm fringed place with Beaches and tropical jungle. One bikes or walks everywhere. There are some golf carts for luggage. But nothing is paved, no cars are aloud. The Bird life is renowned. To find many Birds one only has to go to the mangrove bays sit still and they will come.

Saturday nights in the town square is the weekly get together. A game called chicken poop is played with live chickens. That was fun:

There are painted numbers on the ground and one puts down money on the number and then hopes the Chicken will poop there. Sometimes it is a long wait, but one gets the whole pot of money!

Diving on Goff's Caye, and swimming with Manatees. It was so sad leaving the Manatee. It was a huge male who followed me around and when I went into the boat he put his head on the steps of the boat and it looked like he was crying.

South Africa, January 23, 1997

With Kevin this time to visit South Africa. It is always so great to show him places I have been to. He enjoyed every moment.

With our rental car we drove in direction to Kruger Park. Our first night we stopped next to President Kruger's house at Wayside Inn. Already there at the Inn many wild animals running around. It looked like they were waiting for us.

And then into the famous Park. There was a great evening scene at our Lodge with a Hyena mother and baby's visiting us.

Driving near the big Oliphant River. Beneath the high road could see many Elephants bathing. Every time we stopped Baboons checking us out. Kruger Park has so many animals especially Giraffe's and Zebra's.

Once a while one could find a big pile of Elephant manure in the road which was worked by the dung Beetle into balls and carried away. It is interesting just to stop and watch them.

The Lions took their time crossing the road and many times just lay down in front of us. By the way, one cannot get off the Roads in Kruger Park. So it is either waiting it out or turn around.

To the Drakensberge to Truckers Town. There we rented a beautiful roundel.

Passing "God's Window by car now. A great view over the Lowveld. Stopped at the Mac Mac Pools and Falls. Crystal clear pools are perfect for swimming.

A wonderful stay at Mount Sheba Hotel situated in a nature Reserve. Again thick woods and ravines with birdlife and flora.

Our rooms had fireplaces and private patio for total relaxation.

Bridal Veil Falls are reached by the Sabie River and a walk through dense woods.

Then to Old Joe's Kaia for an overnight stay. The Gardens are beautiful and reflect the splendor of the Lowveld. Birds!

Driving now to the Witzenberg to visit my friends in Tulbagh.

This is a big Valley surrounded by Mountains. I have visited here before and we have been invited again. Mont Rouge is a big Fruit growing Farm for dried fruit for export.

What fun it was for Kevin to just eat so much fruit. The fruit dries on big pallets in the sun. Apricots were right in season. Many people are employed on Mont Rouge. Every kind of fruit and wine is growing here.

Watched one day a filmmakers arrive to make a commercial near the farm. He brought his own 7 Elephants for the scenes. I was allowed to play with the Elephants, it was so wonderful to be so close and interact with them.

A trip to Langebaan Lagoon near the Atlantic. Many deserted fishing villages are there. Only St. Helena Bay is still active in fishing.

This is where I met "my" Bushman. He was on a walk to nowhere. But he was hungry for our fruit and took all we had when we offered.

We stayed at the Steenberg's Cove Hotel and had a great picnic.

The next day a big fish fry on the Beach and to Lamberts Bay to visit the colonies of Penguins, Cormorant's, Gannett's.

Stopped at friends from Du Plessis in ClanWilliam. Another big fruit farm.

Then Kevin and I took to the Road again to Avalon Springs Hotel. I had been there before too and loved the thermal waters. There was a Canyon with wildlife, many Rockdassie's.

At the evening bath, barefoot, on my way back to the room I stepped on a scorpion. Never thought I would have so much trouble from it. Did not pay any attention to it since it only was itching a little.

We are driving now to Oudtshoorn through the Karoo. Kevin wanted to ride an Ostrich, which he did but it hurt. And it is pretty dangerous because the Ostrich is not very tame. In the last second the hood is pulled of his head and off he goes. I was more interested in the little baby Ostrich. Touching, found out the feathers of the babies were like steel.

Now again to the Beach in Wilderness. Relax a day. Next to Mosselbay. There is a Museum with Bartolomeu Dias Voyage ship from 1488. When found one wall of the Museum was left open and the ship was dismantled to bring it inside on greased sleepers along a road and then pulled inside by a hydraulic system.

Nearby is the famous Bridge of Bungee Jumping. Wonder how many people get hurt doing it.

A stop in Swellendam, another old town and beautiful. Then to Bontebok Natl. Park. There are very different Zebra's, called Mountain Zebra.

Staying overnight in Struisbaai, summerhouse from du Plessis. And we are walking to the most southerly point in Africa. Cape L'Agulhas. It is known as the graveyard of ships.

Cape of Good Hope is next to see. With a stop at Groot Constantia, a Winery, and Hotel Nelson for high Tea. What a luxury!

And back in Tulbagh for a last visit at Mont Rouge. Tulbagh was almost destroyed in an earthquake but all the old buildings did not collapse . The Oude Kerk Volksmuseum is the oldest church in South Africa. The Old Drostdy is a beautiful example of architect Louis Thibault's work.

A day trip to Gordon's Bay. More different wildlife.

Last days in Tulbagh. Fun with the fruit harvest. Visiting Del Monte factory. My foot is giving me problems now. Very itching. Went to a doctor who prescribed a cream! I never saw a doctor only a nurse.

Kevin has gone back to USA and I am flying to Comoros Islands to go Diving.

Comoros

Situated between the Eastern African Coastline and the Island of Madagascar. There are 4 Island altogether. The scented breezes blowing from them earn them the name "The perfumed Isles".

Ylang-Ylang (cinnamon) from which is extracted the base essence of the world's best perfumes. And many of Gardens with the Cinnamon. Every spice growing it is from the Comoro's.

Moorish architecture is the look of these Islamic Islands.

World class diving is here. The azure waters provide everything from reefs to wrecks. But one has to take Malaria precautions. Warning signs all over telling that medical help is inadequate and having a good insurance for repatriation is very important. Never thought it would apply to me soon.

Toured a Vanilla growing farm. Interesting plant.

Diving was very good except my Scorpion foot started to swell up. It is now very infected. Still had one more good dive when I encountered 2 white sharks but they must have been not hungry. They did not even glance at me.

I am now pretty sick and I am on a emergency flight back to Johannesburg by Emirates. I need a Doctor, my leg is big, it was stupid of me to wait so long. In Johannesburg I had choice of having my leg amputated or fly to the USA right away, I was airlifted to the USA by South Africa air.

The flight stopped in Cape Verde at night and I begged the Flight Attendant to take me down the stairs but it was refused. So I only got to see it from the open plane door.

Arriving at the Hospital in USA, a very good Doctor took care of my leg without amputation. But it took 3 month of bedrest to heal.

Vietnam, February 5, 1998

A big snowstorm almost delayed my flight and to New York first. I thought the airplane would crash.

On my way now with Korea Air, 15 hour flight to Seoul. What a great airline. So clean and the nicest Crew. Changing in Soul for another flight again 5 hours more to Vietnam.

Saturday 7th, Saigon!

A noisy, full of life, City. It is called now Ho Chi Minh City but everybody said Saigon. It is still the "Pearl of the far East". Having watched always the Vietnam War on the news, itwas so interesting for me to be in person here. The welcome was great. And I right away fell in love with the food. The fresh bread in the morning! The great soup called pho and eaten anytime of the day. It was good every place but the best from the little street stalls. One could see how busy and good a place is when finding stems from the Basil which is served in the soup on the floor and Lime rinds.

First a trip to the Mekong Delta near Ben Tre.

By car first and then by boat to the first Island. Many Fruit farms, and all connected by little canals. Coconut Island or Turtle Island next. At lunch the fish was still alive before cooking.

Then by boat again to Tand C Island across the Mekong river. Very interesting to see a Bee farm. The tea there was so good with fresh honey. Even the Bees were nice and one could touch them, as they were swarming all around us.

Back to Saigon which is not called by the people Ho Chi Minh.

There is so much activity in this City. Everybody has a job and is or working on something.

Walking around seeing elaborate Buildings almost like Paris. The Post office was wonderful to look at it. Try crossing a street. One has to be almost smart about it. It is an endless stream of Motorbikes bicycles and Pedi cabs. If I would wait to open up as I would in America to make it across, I would wait till the sun goes down and only every Vietnamese will just go around you.

No I just took my nerves and started walking and never stopped.

In the evening I spend time in the Rex Hotel on the top floor. Knowing it from the News reel from the Vietnam War it is still the place to meet.

My friend Mai took me on her motorbike to a real Vietnamese place for Dinner. The Rice is cooked in clay pots which get smashed when it is done and out pops this delicious rice. It is a show to watch it, but one can only see it, if you know where to go.

Today I moved to the 6th floor to have a better view of the Saigon River.

Got a Motorbike to see more of Saigon, because Saigon is very busy on the Road and bicycles are not good here. There are no traffic rules. People just march right into traffic and hope all goes well. Went to the Post office, Reunification Palace, History Museum, Jade Pagoda and then Lunch. Not to miss the Saigon Hotel. A beauty and great afternoon tea.

Then to Gia Lam Pagoda, Thien Hau and Cho lon.

In the Palace one can see and touch many things. Especially from the WAR. The war room was made out of concrete and steel. There are m any secret passages. Outside one could buy live swallows for release. I bought two and it is supposed to bring luck. Hoping nobody catches my released swallows again.

Evening at the Rex Café for cappuccino and Dinner at café 13.

Monday 9th trip to Cu Chi tunnels. Roads are full of walking people. There was no Bus service. So people do a lot of walking. Even the animals know to stay on the side of the road.

Cu Chi was strange, on arrival a big US Tank sitting there as a reminder of American Troops. 5 km away from the tunnel entrance was US headquarters. It is amazing that all this happened underneath the Americans soldiers.

7000 Vietnamese lived there and they had 200 km Tunnels consisting of many layers with living quarters. I tried a short stretch of crawling, it was scary. I weigh two times as much as a Vietcong and had a hard time in the Tunnels and I could not fit in any opening except the one made for big tourists now.

There was underneath a big city. Kitchens, rooms, even a medical clinic. And the airshafts went right up to the US headquarters. Foreign visitors are now welcomed but have to understand the hard struggle of the Vietnamese people. And now they desire for peace, independence and happiness. The guides all had been North Vietnamese.

On to the Cambodian Border to see a big Cao Dai Temple. The eye is the most important symbol there. All religions are combined in it and whose saints include Joan of Arc and Victor Hugo. Watching the high mass was interesting.

I wish only our Bus would have had shock absorbers, roads are washed out and fixed but not smooth.

Gas is very expensive as I see I guess that is why there are so many motor scooters used.

Food is very good and lots of fruit. Our group of 6 got on a boat to Cholon. The Saigon River is pure sewage. It is a black oozing, bubbling fluid for 5km. Right and left all houses discharge into the River everything. We saw only the back of the houses from the boat. The StreetSide is beautiful.

Visited the Rex Hotel again for a good swim and got a sunburn.

Driving to Bon Thai and Bien Hoa today. Rt. 1 is the only road north and the traffic is heavy. One can see many Factories and 2 Golf clubs. It is very industrial.

A lot of US equipment is being used and since there are no new parts, clever ideas have changed the equipment.

No Radiator, no problem just a big tank on top with a hose

connected to the front takes care.

Many Catholic Churches are seen in the countryside. Grain is left in the road to dry, rice peppers, peanuts, tapioca. And everybody is careful not driving on top of it.

We are crossing a low Mountain range of 2000 feet called Bao Loc Pass.

Stopped at Dambri Falls, very pretty and we climbed it to the top. Looked like someplace in Costa Rica.

There are coffee and tea plantations. Many Mulberry plantation for the silk worm farms. Our Bus is again without schocks and we all feel drowsy or sick. Hoping we get to Dalat soon.

Dalat!

A winding road to there and what a surprise. At 4000 feet elevation, it was suddenly like Switzerland or France. Situated by the small Camly River. Dalat was founded in 1917 by the French. Many European fruits and vegetables are planted here. It was a holiday place.

The City is built in the French style with a Sacre Coeur look alike, same steps. A small version of the Eifel tower lit at night. And cool air.

So we walked around and could not believe this city just almost empty with the most beautiful French Villas and empty too.

After a night of killing Mosquitos I finally slept. Breakfast was not so good. We drove to Lat villages. They are very ethnic people, different language. And look like Mayan of S.A. Met an old 101 year man. He played music for us and invited us into his log house. There he served us a very potent fruit drink.

Then we hired Motorbikes and a driver to show us around, that was great and we saw a lot of back roads and places like the Pagoda with the famous monk, the presidential palace, flower Gardens and again some of the French Villas which are all empty but somebody keeps up the Gardens at each Villa. Lots of Art Deco on the Villas built around in 1933.

At the A dong Hotel. Walked to the Palace Hotel for drinks, so beautiful and not one guest.

High tea was served which I ordered right away. A piano player showed up just for me, the bathroom was worth just going in there to look at.

Prices are different in all places. Beer can be had for 75 cent and dinner for $2. And Spring rolls are so delicious with a fresh baguette.

On to Hai-yen

Another breakfast so so. But lots of papaya. I am always happy with fruit. We stopped at the Chicken Village. There is a statue of a chicken made out of cement in the center. It was requested by the people instead of a monument to Ho chi Min, they wanted a Rooster. At least 40 feet high.

Crossed the Ngon Muc Pass and had to stop in Po Klong Cham Gapal for a technical pit stop.

Riding this Bus is hard, it rattles like crazy. And the Road is like a washboard. But outside is so much to see and I have to fight with myself not to fall asleep.

Stopped for a quick look at the Cam ran Airport. It looks very deserted. And how busy it once was.

Nha Trang

Hotel Hai-Yen is very nice, rooms overlook the sea. And a beautiful Beach with very warm water. Ate many Mangos and Dragon Fruit in my free time. Had to bargain but that is fun.

Today some Scuba diving to Ebony Island Hon mon, and Swallow Island. On a very nice Boat. Many Australians are here. It is so beautiful for a vacation.

A cook is cooking for us in the back of the ship. When served 15 different plates of dishes came. All of them very good except I do not eat snails. Fed them to the fish secrectly.

And always a table full of Fruit for us to eat.

On the way back stopped at a village were women picked us up in round basket boats. You have to know how to handle them or one goes in circles. When we tried to paddle them we got a big laugh out of the ladies.

Tonight will be some dancing by a Vietnamese group.

I do think one has to have guides all over Vietnam; it would be difficult doing it on one own.

On we drive. Again the Roads are used as drying for shrimp now. The Bus has a very hard time driving between them.

There are no Birds flying around. They get caught very fast. And eaten. Even Egret are on the menu.

Bullocks teams for transportation are now on the Road, they have very heavy loads.

Qui N Hon Seagull Hotel

At a Beach Restaurant had the best Breakfast, the yoghurt is fantastic. And crepes filled with Bananas is a specialty

Driving along the north Coast, so many Beaches. We are all longingly looking out. No Hotels have been built yet. But I guess that will happen soon with so beautiful sandy Beaches.

We finally stopped at Dai Lanh Beach and rented a beach chair and all got to enjoy it for a few hours.

And then off again and always looking out of the Bus window to take it all in.

Another stop and met a lot of young men who wanted to practice their English on us. They told us life is better since the Embargo was lifted.

February 16th to Hoi An an Unesco Heritage Site

Another bone rattling trip by Bus. Tylenol is not helping much.

Stopped at SA Huynh Beach for a refresher. Again the little ponies are working here hard. And our Bus is full. Everything goes on it. We are on the north, route 1. It is really the only road. The traffic is heavy now and we had to stop for another technical stop.

Hoi An

Hotel Hoi An is nice and has a pool. Showers are always in the middle of the bathroom and when showering everything gets wet.

Rented a bike and did 10 km to the Beach Rd. Hoi An is very old many buildings are over 500 years old. The town is a living museum with its old Bridges and wooden houses. The town has been well preserved. It was once a major port in the 17th and 19th century.

The best Dinner again. The dumplings! And Pina Coladas. Maybe all for $3. Then off to a Bar to meet the Aussies and drink Beer.

A very good sleep last night why not always? It is my biggest problem not able to sleep.

We are touring Hoi An. I was told there are 800 historic homes. Small streets and winding around and lots of flowers. All houses are wooden and carved entrances of different design. By 10am it was hot, sweat is pouring of me. Needed my coffee and to the pool for a rest.

Will rent a bike in the afternoon again so I can see more of the surroundings. Right now I am trying again to look inside the old houses. Many Orchids are hanging in the courtyards. Blue is a favorite color of houses.

I noticed on my bike trip, there are no goats or animals loose to eat the produce growing next to the highway. No Garbage. Many Schoolchildren are around and I am told all will go to higher Education. Who will work the land?

Had a great Duck dinner tonight and Cau soup(Fish). Special water for the soup is from Hoi an.

Next to Danang and Hue.

Great views from the Bus, but still an old Bus. Coming to the Marble Mountains. Always remember from the Viet war as a big point for the planes. But it is different now, there are many stonemasons carving. The big statues are so real and can be shipped to USA for $1000 or less with bargaining.

Now at China Beach, endless Sand and not a tourist in sight. "Mash" was supposed to have been here. But the water is cold tried to swim.

To Danang. We drove right through the old Military grounds. Lots of it is still standing like awaiting maybe a plane? It was the biggest airbase in Asia at the wartime.

Over the Hai Van Pass to Hue (Pass of the Ocean clouds). This dramatic stretch of road has the best views of the sea far below. At the nice stops many Vietnamese trying to sell trinkets. I did not need one more because I bought my statue near Saigon already and it was heavy enough for me.

Hue

Hue located at the Perfume River and was once the ancient capital of the Royal dynasty. Despite many wars, Hue still attracts tourists because of the rich architecture and famous for the temples and the Citadel. Hue did suffer from fires in 1945 and war bombardments in 1968.

Hue is very French looking. We are staying in a very old Hotel Hung Vuong.

But next door is the new Marin Hotel, very elegant and has everything one can wish for. There are many rich Vietnamese Tourists. Even at the Tennis court everybody looked a little heavier than the average Vietnamese.

Overall, everybody is pretty slim and slender. Especially the young women. And they are all dressed in the national Bao-Dai dress. Very proudly worn. It is long and has tails so it can be worn on the bike too, looks very graceful.

Biked a day trip to different places around Hue. Saw the King Minh Mang's Tomb. It was one of the hottest days.

Waiter tried to cheat me today, have to watch out that not extras have been added.

Dinner today was shrimp and noodles, spring rolls, vegetables and fruit juice.

All very fresh and all for $1.25.

February 19th, Hue by train to Hanoi!

Mosquitos did not let me sleep last night and I had such a beautiful room. The group has all upset stomachs. Not me. I take my daily Pepto bismol. It is hot and humid all in the 100s.

Saw the walled citadel which contains the Imperial Palace

The perfume River is very clean and we took a boat to Charlie Hill. We saw many of Pagodas, every 1/2km is one. It was the style of the Khmer building.

I biked 10km in the boiling sun.

But went next door to swim and to feel good. Drinks by the pool, even towels and shampoo was provided.

At 9pm we sat at the station to take the Reunification Express for our overnight trip to Hanoi but every mosquito must have been following me. Even the smoke from cigarettes did not help. We got settled in the train by midnight and I went right to sleep. The cluckety of the train was a great sound. One could hear the Engine, it was a noisy one. Our windows were made out of Metal and we had been told to lock ourselves in. I had a dog chain wrapped around the handle and lock from the inside.

The other compartment with the group did not listen and they lost their shoes that night.

I did spray my bed before just to make sure no bedbugs would reach out for me.

We arrived at 2pm, 18 hours later. On the train we could not walk to the dining car. The locals had so much stuff in the walkway and hammocks hanging across. Every space was used. We could get to the toilets if one calls them that. The usual hole and a bucket of water.

Hanoi

I have read about it and have been anxious to see the city. It has such a long history. A very cosmopolitan looking city, so French. Most of the buildings had been built by the French. Lots of trees and lakes. Little Cafes with very good Cappuccinos. And the best chocolate cake. Apple pie with cream, vanille ice-cream on top. A different feeling from Saigon. More sophisticated.

We are going to see the Water puppet show. Was that fun. The actors are standing in water up to their waist and have puppets in their hands. It was funny and sold out.

By the way every street has a name by a manufacturer. So our Hotel was on Coffin Street. There is anything to be had for a funeral and all is made there.

I did find 2 egg cups.

Saw the Hoa Lo Prison (Hanoi Hilton) and did a cycle tour. Vinh Quang Hotel is old and rickety but very convenient. And it has Air-condition. Did see a lot of Hanoi today all with a guide. I am surprised of the Architecture and how beautiful many places are here. Even the new buildings are built in the old French style. Many people speak

French especially the older men. They have the Bibi hat on, cigarette holder like little French men. In school English is taught as the first foreign language, and people are trying it on me all the time.

Toured the Ho Chi Minh's Mausoleum. Very dramatic built. He was called Uncle Ho in his lifetime. Nearby was his house where he lived and worked. It is built on stilts and is now a cultural relic.

Besides the city is very serene, shaded Boulevards and many parks.

Seeing the Hanoi Hilton or what is left over gave me a reminding how bad it was for the American soldiers.

Fascinated by the Opera house.

Trekking to Mai Chau, February 22

We got a new Bus! Good springs and another guide I can understand. It took a long time to get out of Hanoi. Traffic was bad and I have now a cold. We are going to meet the hill tribes.

We have been walking after the driver dropped us off. Too many hours on the bus, and have settled in a Long House of the Hmong people. It is very long and big. Lots of room. Even a shower and a flush toilet are there, but only cold water. And a difficult walk to get there. The Long house sits on stilts about 80 feet long. And 50 feet wide. There is a TV blaring, and I am not sure how it works. Was told by a generator with running water.

Lunch was in a little town on the road, all food has been good because I have not gotten sick.

The dogs are the ugliest I have ever seen and mean, but I guess they are raised for dinner like pigs and have nothing to lose.

I never know now what is served; it is excellent tasting but when asking what it is? I know the rice.

In the middle of the night a phone is ringing! And we all tasted the rice schnapps, very potent. But it stinks like poop.

Since it was an opensided house I could hear the snoring, all the noises. The rooster started underneath at 3:30am and then all the roosters in the village answered him.

Village life!

Grandma was 79y. And is drinking and chewing only Beetlenut. They had been married 58 years and no children. So they adopted 3 girls. 2 of them were helping. We entertained Grandma. She had one tooth left and showing it proudly to us.

Our guide Duong is a good guide. He loves his job and explains everything.

Breakfast was coffee, cheese, bread, banana. And now 1 hour by Bus into the high Mountains and walk back downhill.

Lots of children tried to follow us. We learned about how the water gets to the fields and how the energy is produced by a very small motor and water. I still did not understand the system.

Dinner was great tasting and I slept very good this night. Going to the bathroom was difficult. The floorboards made so much noise everybody woke up and somebody would start giggling.

There was a Bullock tied to the stairs on the bottom and one had to say nice things to him to pass. It was the only way to the Bathroom.

Now we are trekking to Nanh Binh staying at the Hoa Lu Hotel.

Started hiking at the Tai village, the women are quite beautiful and the costumes on the guys look very good. But water is scarce in the village and food is scarce too. But there are lots of Peach trees. In old times everybody produced poppies but now there is a 10 year prison fine for doing it.

Many potbelly pigs running around and then we watched the slaughtering of a yellow dog which was sad. It was like killing a pig. The dog knew ahead.

Many people are now in the fields working, planting something and the roads are full of children going or coming from school.

Our Hotel is good, has all the comfort we need. Warm Water.

Taking cold showers it not fun.

From Hoa Binh to Hanoi

We have seen a lot of Vietnam, the ancient capital. The river tour on the Da River in a very small boat lasted 3 hours. The Boats were paddled by 2 women, who still besides it are busy trying to sell us anything in their bags.

A beautiful countryside. We hiked 3 hours and many people invited us to come in.

The school was out and all the children hung onto us like pied the piper. Nice cool weather up here and no rain.

After so many sights a long drive back to Hanoi and falling asleep on the Bus.

In Hanoi I went shopping, lots of bargaining but Saigon had better stuff. A Dinner at the Mocha Cafe was very good, especially the curry's and vegetables in Oyster sauce.

Dessert: crepes with lemon and cheese. And a Mango Lassie as my drink love it.

Halong Bay

Adventure on Halong Bay. Again a long 5 hour, 180 km Bus trip to Halong Bay.

Beautiful roads but full of people, driving fast is not possible.

And again many potholes.

Arriving at a very beautiful Hotel with a view of Halong Bay. Halong Bay means "Where the Dragon Descends into the Sea". Which is the Bay of Tonkin. There are 3000 limestone Islands and all are interesting and beautiful, many have caves but I have no interest in caves. Staying on the Boat was good but lots of little boats stop and want to sell stuff. Like Coral and other endangered stuff.

Right now people live for today and do not worry about over fishing or destroying the coral.

Every family can have 2 children which is perfect. And there is no planning for the future yet.

Taking a Bus to a Ferry again and then a 5km walk to a Market.

Rented a motorbike and I got fleeced at a traffic light. My Camera was on a string and it hung out of my pocket and was grabbed very fast.

That person was faster than me he was on a bigger motorbike. How embarrassing.

But I am sad too because all my photos are gone too.

Found some china I was looking for.

Our group Dinner was at the Indochina Restaurant in Hanoi. It was very good and the most expensive dish on the menu was $7. I had Prawns in coconut milk, the best.

Hanoi is cold and one can feel it is still winter.

VinhQuang Hotel Hanoi, February 28th

I am in a Restaurant were one has to choose meat. It is hanging from the hooks. Goat, calf, pork, chicken, muskrat, something like a Mtn. Rabbit and small Deer. But there are so many flies my appetite is gone.

Off we went on a last hike with rain and slippery ground, 4km up the Mountain to the Huong Pagoda. Thousands of stone steps had to be done. Once up people were burning money for good wishes. And all this is done only in the spring. But coming down was more dangerous, the stairs were slippery.

And that was Vietnam. To the airport now, cool and grey sky. Flying to Bangkok with a 10 hour delay there, very nasty place if one does not know the Airport.

Venezuela, April 1, 1998

I am looking for another Hato to experience a different place. Hato's are the big Ranches of Venezuela. With a group of friends from Venezuela we went to Hato Callejas.

But getting there was trouble. The Road was long with many stops to see some of the countryside again. Places like Laguna Muchuchi way up in the Andes. In Barainas our Lunch was waiting and as usual excellent. Never have I had bad food in Venezuela.

Filling our Gas tanks now and going to S. Vinvanto, there are no Gas stations anymore and had to get Rum and Beer.

We got on a Boat in San Vicente. Saw a lot of river Dolphins on the River Apure. And one very big Anaconda resting on a sandbar.

In the evening we stopped at an Island and hung our Hammocks. The Hammocks had even mosquito screen covers. Only problem for me I could hear all the snoring. And then a Tamandua started to climb down from a tree to inspect us, kind of wild cat or Anteater. It was very exciting to watch it. And the sunrise over the River was magnificent.

We left early because we did not have enough food so back to S. Vicente for refills. There are too many hungry mouth in our group.

Went upriver now, with many Dolphins following us. Anacondas lying again on sandbars.

Lots of wildlife is around us. And the big Morpho butterfly is flying around our heads.

We made it to Hato Callejas on the Rio Caimana. Both sides of the River are owned by the Hato.

By jeep for 1 hour to a most beautiful Jungle spot. So many animals! The trees are full with strange birds. We did not get to see a jaguar but he left tracks in the sand.

Then the big surprise. Don Ramon had Buffalos. And to cross the River one needed to ride one or by boat. I choose the Buffalo Diamante. Even western Saddles were provided. Now that was something new to me. Riding a Buffalo in a western Saddle! Crossing, we submerged completely. Did not know Buffalo swim so good.

We hung Hammocks and then prepared Lunch. I took a walk and loved all the different Butterflies again. Hammocks are always carried like luggage. One does not go anywhere without them. There is always a place to hang them even between two cars.

Going back I was the only one who wanted to go by Buffalo back to the Hato. It took almost 3 hours. By car it was 1 hour. But it was the softest ride and silent. Horses make noise. Cars make noise. This animal was great. I had only a string through his nose as a bridle.

Don Ramon is a great cook and I watched and learned a lot from him.

He has built many little canals with levees and has kept the Hato very green because of it. And it was the dry season. Many Capybaras are running around. The Hato has 5000 Buffalos.

My Hammock is to short it is made for South Americans not my length.

Went today Piranha fishing. That fish is very tasty except it has many bones.

At S. Vicente and to Cubati and back to Barinas on the S. Christobal Road. Up in the Mountain everybody went swimming, not me, too cold the water.

At night it was difficult to sleep, maybe the Altitude?

At 7am we all got Horses. Not very good looking but tough. I picked a very ugly one but he looked very smart. For 5 miles we rode through the mountains and then stopped at a River to get into tubes to float down the River for 2 hours.

There our Horses were waiting and we took off again for another great Ride.

And then back to Merida by car.

I am a Buffalo Rider.!!

Poland, November 1998

To Poland to see more of my birth land with Kevin again. Renting a car in Germany and then driving east, staying one night in the Wartburg. A castle Martin Luther wrote the new testament there. Johann Wolfgang von Goethe visited here too.

Then to Dresden, again so much to see but so little time to stay. Driving along the Elbe River into Poland.

It is cold! We are in my hometown and trying to visit many places I had missed the last time.

One can see more now of the Goat head signs. Glucholazy! People are proud of that name. I have not found out were the name came from.

Then a quick drive to Krakow. No tourists at this time of year. This time we visited the Wawel Castle.

We decided since it is winter, we should drive to Zakopane in the Tatra range. A traditional skiing center and resort town. Skiing should be great, we did not try it but we watchted. Our car had no snow broom or anything to help for the heavy snowfall and we had lots of snow to clean off constantly.

Soon we went back west to warmer weather and arrived in Germany again. But it is snowing here too.

Morocco, Sahara, January 1999

This was a trip from hell.

I saw an ad for a trip called "A silent and sacred walk in the Sahara" and I signed on, since women are having a hard time alone traveling in Morocco. I had images of walking through the desert by camel, actually a dromedary. Camels live in Mongolia. The silent should have been a giveaway.

Air Morocco was very good, the service was excellent the Airline had lost my luggage I found out on arrival (which didn't reach me until three days later), so I was dependent on the kindness of the group who lent me clothing to supplement necessities.

Changing planes in Casablanca to Marrakech and no suitcase on arrival there.

I had a strange feeling when meeting the group at the Airport. I was an outsider right away, they all knew each other. On the drive to the desert no words were spoken. Why? With the new "friends" to Quarzazate, our first stop after a 6-hour drive. Crossed mountain passes high in the Atlas. The biggest pass was tizi n Tichka Pass, very cold. Our car was breaking down, radiator trouble and we all had to get out to give the car a rest we were told. And snow was falling. At least I had my coat.

There are Kasbahs on the hills but no people in it, it is just too cold to live here in the winter. In the fields one can see men plowing with little donkeys in the snow. I would not call them fields. Maybe little paddocks cleared of stone.

Finally arrived at our Hotel Belevesis. It was now at lower levels of the Atlas Mountains again with a very beautiful pool but ice cold water. Wondered who would go swimming.

There are many movie people in town for productions which are being filmed here all the time.

The set from Cleopatra, the English Patient, and all Harrison Ford Movies.

Somebody went to Airport to check if my suitcase arrived, nothing.

And here is the surprise for me. I am in the middle of a strange group called "Rolfers". First I thought they meant weightlifters and was corrected by the so called Boss, they are the New Wave People. Our so called leader dampened my spirits when he announced that for the rest of the week, 7 days, absolute silence would be observed.

This came as a shock to me, because my understanding was "silence" would come from the desert's solitude. I had no idea that I had just spend a considerable amount of money so as to get in touch with my inner self. Most of the group apparently knew and understood the nature of the trip.

It is very cold today as we left the Hotel, I should have stayed. At least my room had heat. Found a bike rental and got to see a little of the side streets.

We drove to the desert I tried to make a stop a few times to get some socks and warm cloth and finally in Zagora I bought slippers and a pullover. And a pair of panty's. It was funny the panties were hanging in a little hole store on the wall shop. But I am still freezing. I need more warm clothing.

The scenery is beautiful and I try to enjoy it. Made the driver stop at a crossroad with signs to Timbuctoo. Had to make a photo. We passed Mountains and Oasis's. And now are in the Sahara.

Tents were set up, and I took the farthest away from everybody. My tent is very cold. The wind is blowing right through it! Our toilet was a hole with a plastic sheet wound around some posts.

At Dinner came the announcement: Silence from now on.

From 9pm to 10pm would be discussion period.

Wow I was stunned.

What was to be discussed?

I was sold a trip by a travel Agent in USA with a crazy group of outcasts and weird acting.

No talking to each other or anything!

I am still trying to see about my suitcase but who is going to get it if it ever arrives in the Airport since I am having nobody to talk to?

And today of all the bad things it is raining in the desert! It has not rained in years here.

I have found the Berber handler of the Camels and can communicate with him. The Bedouins keep far apart from the group but are doing all the cooking and serve food.

I decided to make friends with Bedouins and get to ride the Dromedary when all the others walked, about 16 miles. That is what I Like. I have seen quite a lot of wild Dromedary and ours do not like the wild ones. They start grunting and groaning like crazy. I have found one Dromedary who likes to snuggle like a cat.

Sand is in everything, they wind is always blowing and it gets into the food, sleeping bag. My shoes are always full of sand. My cloth have become smelly. Me too.

Not much water anyway, one cup in the morning for brushing the teeth. But always lots of hot tea.

Since nobody will talk to me I talk to myself and have gotten the leader very mad. But what can he do? He is not allowed to talk. It really is a funny situation.

My unwillingness to become monastic was a disruption to their leader. After 2 days I decided to travel with my camel and driver alone. I camped with the Berbers and was able to learn much about them and their land.

I spend my time more and more with the Bedouins. There is a dog who loves me and I have now a friend I can really talk to. I have gotten a very good massage from my new friends. We are camped now between the Dunes, keeps the wind down.

Dinner is good but always the same. Dates, figs, soup, stew, oranges, apples tea and coffee.

I do sleep good in my tent. Roll myself in my sleeping bag, which I had carried with me. My tent is far apart from the group now. All of them are snorers anyway.

Today a sunny morning and it is getting warmer. I can hardly wait to get on my Camel again for our 6 hour ride. The Camels are so sure and never stumble just going along fine.

Our lunch stop was not in a nice Oasis like yesterday, the terrain is very rocky now, the wind has blown the sand into dunes here. It does not look like the Sahara one sees in the movies, never would I think of rocky ground but now we are camped in a sand dune again. The weather forecast is bad. It is raining and the sand is everywhere.

And my Bag has arrived. The zipper is broken and my red coat is gone.

I returned sweatpants to Jim sun lotion to Michael, socks to David t-shirt and socks to Jawad, pullover to Abdullah.

There is the Meditation moment when the "Cult People" fall down to pray. They all seem to have problems, what?

Last night silence was broken by the Leader, because some of the people talked to me. He kept reminding them of a vow and all went very quiet. He even used the F…. word, disgusting.

I can see how people follow a leader, benevolent? I am a thorn in his eye.

I tried to cover my tent for the night to keep out sand and rain. And did it rain. Maybe I should stand out there to wash but so much sand and it is cold. Everything is wet in the tent.

At least on other trips there had been a river or something to wash in.

The Dromedary are always gurgling, grumbling, snoring but never spit. Old tale.

Have seen 1 hare, birds and Lizards.

Linda is ready to follow me. She cannot take it anymore. Our tents are broken and leak. We have to set them up every night ourselves. So we all race to the pile of tents to get the best one. And the best foam mattress. I take 2 blankets and that leaves somebody every night without a blanket. I feel like a warrior with my possession.

The Bedouins do not look like the ever get paid. When I am in their camp I see nothing of value. Who is getting the money for this trip?

The food is good but plain. And lots of Beans are served every day.

This morning it is very cold 38 F.

Today it was a talking day. The Rolfers were allowed to talk. One told a drawn out story what happened out in the Desert, he saw the Divine light!

One guy saw the blue lights in his head leading him the way. Far out! My god how can people be like this.

What is the saying: Get a life and move on.

The scenery today is beautiful with a blue sky but cold.

Mohamed and Jawad and I left alone. Hallelujah. I rode the Dromedar and they walked and explained a lot to me about life here and especially about the seashells we found. Mohamed likes to sing and he was happy to do it. Our talk about the silence group left us shaking our heads.

We passed a military post. All Buildings painted in pink colors.

At the Oasis I saw a stork, donkeys and goats. And many Birds and Hawks. We have our tents here tonight. Outside my tent are donkeys fighting for the kitchen scrap.

My tent is now with the Bedouin's and I have nothing to do with the group anymore. I like the nomads. My little French, their little English and my book helped in having a conversation.

Mohamed was preparing Lunch for me and he could not eat because it was Ramadan. He was the only Muslim in the group. Sorry for him.

Boiled egg on a beautiful salad with Sardines on top. And always Olives. Tea and water. All served on a beautiful carpet.

I am told the manners of the group is horrible. The do fart and burp and never say excuse me or please. They are worse than the Dromedars.

The Bedouins are: Hatik our server
Fatima the cook
Mohamed Camel driver
Duammene Camel driver
Ali?

When I got to the next camp my tent was already set up by the Bedouins, a good feeling. No more racing to the pile.

I watched Fatima making bread and ate some of it. So good. We laughed a lot and I tried to get her recipe.

When I went for a walk in the Dunes, there was the Leader with his girlfriend talking up a storm. What a Hypocrite. Cheating.

Linda has come to ask if she can join me. She is not a believer anymore, so she says.

Had to put rocks on the tent corners to hold the tent down from the wind. But by evening it was calm and only cool. The Oasis has the clearest water coming up in a little hole. When I saw one of the women going with shampoo to wash her hair I just stopped her before she soiled the water. She is from Chicago and does not know anything how to behave in the desert.

Our lunch Oasis was just a Gully in the sand dunes. No tree or bush, nothing. There was that silence! Beautiful.

We had to leave by 2pm because a big sandstorm was coming. It was difficult finding our night camp again, I trusted the Bedouins.

Linda is very sore and has many blisters on her feet. Elliott joined her in the walk and they talked. That makes now 2 disciples less.

I did enjoy it alone better but cannot have it all.

Linda now with stomach problems. Fatima tooth infection. And no Medicine.

Leader is sick. Serves him right.

Jawad is sick.

There is no sanitation and it is no wonder everybody is getting sick. Dishwashing is never done. No towel or cloth gets washed just shook out. And the same big towel which was used for rolling out the bread is at night a blanket for Fatima.

Last night was freezing. I wear all of my warm cloth at night and still not enough.

Rode the Camel today again and Linda walked. Today it is warmer and I am told next month would be 100degree and there is no shade.

In the afternoon at camp I had my nap and then climbed the Dunes. Evening are always very cold. And the "crazy group" is out in the desert now without any tent just to prove the can do it. For 24 hours and no food.

At night the cold dampens everything and the blankets are like big weights, only very wet. Only one more night in the desert and then hopefully a Hotel. I am eating now a lot of Pepto Bismol hoping to prevent what all the others have.

Alik and Halid are eating, Ramadan or no Ramadan, they are hungry. Today we all went by Land rovers over the roughest Roads to Oasis Hamid. It was a horrible place. Very busy and dirty. Garbage is everywhere. The land is covered by it. Mostly plastic bags.

Everything is grey. Except the women have very colorful covered dresses on. Lots and lots of children. I guess the only entertainment is sex. Seems to be they all have money but nothing to do with it. Why are they living there? It is nowhere.

Going back to camp a very good lunch was awaiting. And the Bedouins told me of dancing later on.

The silence has been broken now. All of them are talking again. We sit around a fire.

Sunday 17

To Marrakech next.

But difficult since our transportation did not arrive. We finally got 3 jeeps going with all the drivers having arguments which one they get to drive. At 10am ready to go but Ali, one driver while loading fell off the roof of the car and injured his chin. Trying to stem the bleeding he is driving now. At the first crossing the two front cars got stuck in the sand and had to be towed by our Ali out of the deep sand.

At a Hamid we filled with Gas and got on a paved Road but 5 minutes later our car had a blowout.

We drove over very rough terrain before and nothing happens. And now this. There was only one spare tire for 3 cars and so it came to a big argument again till it was decided who could change the tire.

Going on, saw a bag fall off the roof. It was not mine and did not say anything.

Finally reaching the Atlas Mountain range. Snow, sleet, rain, fog anything to make driving treacherous. Again the drivers are very stupid trying to pass each other. I finally complained that I will vomit in the next second, that stopped our driver a little.

Zagora was a lunch stop. Ok.

Then off again and driving too fast and lucky a policeman arrived behind us. The fine was $20, reduced because foreigners in the car. The Leader wanted money from me to help pay. I laughed in his face and told him to go…

Arriving at the Hotel Alon was good. Washing again and again, after 8 days of no shower and always the same cloth.

Today is the end of Ramadan and everybody will be partying and a noisy night in Marrakesh.

I did not sleep good anyway. Just looking at my bed made me so happy.

Walking today around the city to Bahia to look at carpets. I did buy a Kilim carpet, did not need one, but this one had all animals on it.

From my Hotel window I have a beautiful view of the famous Koutoubia Mosque and behind the Atlas Mountains.

Went to a natural health Pharmacy, but no Myrrh for sale and then to the big Medina. It is also called Djemaa el Fna square. That is a teaming central plaza with the unending medieval circus. There is so much going on. There are clowns, Acrobats, fortune tellers and snake charmers plying their trade. Anything in the world is on exhibition. And pickpockets! And the air is filled with the smoke and sizzle of grilled kebabs. I sat upstairs in the Arguna Café watching it like a ringside seat and had mint tea. Save from the pickpockets up there.

Then took a Horse carriage ride back to the Hotel Alon.

Did not get to the see the promised "Dazzling horse fantasia" The agent who was supposed to take me there never showed up.

I am ready to see more alone, Casablanca first. Have dreamed about going there. Have always read about Ricks café and wondered if it is really there. It is.

Flying to Casablanca, Linda who wanted to see Morocco too joined me.

Jamad, my arranged driver was waiting at the arrival and took us sightseeing. Stops were made solely at my insistence. Even then, I learned little from the guide except how tired he was from having spent the past month working with tourists! I could not understand what he was telling me anyway. Not a very good English.

Rabat was important to go. Had to visit the Mausoleum, supposed to be the biggest in the world?

Then came Meknes, it used to be the imperial city of Morocco. Meknes had a lot of old Ramparts with old Gates to the City. Up in my view on a hill was the snow-white old city of Moulay-Idress but closed to non-believers.

The countryside has been very green with many farms. Grapes, wheat are planted in this fertile ground. Nice little hills and all are covered by Olive trees. And Cork trees are growing here.

Volubilis is next, an old Roman town with the best preserved ruins in Morocco.

We finally arrived in Fes. Again a walled old city. Checked into Nuyoa Hotel, not so good. It is really the pits, dirty. Had to change rooms already. Nothing seems to be working. The elevator does not work, going up it will reverse and one sits there till it decides again to go up or down.

The feeling here is very medieval, almost 16th century, time stood still.

Our Dinner was good. Pea soup, beef and vegetables. And rice.

My night was busy with phone calls from men checking if I am available, what a country.

Today a tour of Fes. Walking along the winding lanes, there are no roads, just wide enough for a donkey to pass. There are many Artisans in Fes. As usual we had to stop at a Carpet shop. Tea is always brought very fast so one has to linger and look. In the meantime the carpet man is showing carpet after carpet in front of me. Jawad is not getting a commission since we are not buying. He is mad. We stop at a Pharmacy, again the same try, and again no commission. Pretty stupid way of trying to get money of the tourist like me. At least I had some good tea to drink.

It is a problem finding a good tour guide especially one interested in showing more of the history but this guy just wants to make money.

Jawad invited us for Dinner at his house tonight. It turned out a very strange evening.

A nice house.

We are taking our places in the Dining-living room. I ask were his wife was, she is cooking I am told. He told me she is an English teaching professor at the University. So I did expect to have her join us. But no, Jawad brought the food from the kitchen and we ate very good food, but still no wife. So I ask where she is. In the Kitchen! That is where she belongs, I was told.

Linda and I are getting fed up with his answers and do not feel good about this. So I ask why can she not eat with us?

His answer was suddenly a big argument "that our wives are just as good as you and so on and then proceeded to insult us "You American women want to change everything but not here!".

We got up to go and on my way out I opened the kitchen door and the wife was sitting on the floor eating from a metal plate like a dog, leftovers. Jawad grabbed me and slammed the door.

The life of women in Morocco is hard. Women are treated as inferior under Morocco's Koranic law. They are legal minors, inherit only half share, need permission from a male relative to marry and can be simply divorced by their husbands. But a woman who has a child out of wedlock is treated with even more disdain. Even if they are raped, because it will bring dishonor to the family. Many times they will get killed by a relative like a brother. There are no services or help from the Government. This is one of the dark sides of Islam.

Getting back to the Hotel was the best thing for us. I consider myself a veteran traveler having visited about 140 countries and mostly on my own. So it was a great surprise and disappointment to me that I could be misled about a tour which seemed so much to offer.

Ireland, June 1999

It is time to go to ancient Ireland to visit with Kevin Joyce, my husband and Judy Kienast a girlfriend. We are on our quest to find Kevin's family or what is left.

First thing to see, the Cliffs of Moher in County Claire.

Walking along the dramatic Cliffs and looking out over the Atlantic.

Then to the Burren, a lunar like area of petrified limestone. We are driving on very small back lanes.

Dunguaire Castle in Galway next stop. Kylemore Abbey, the Lakelands next. Ashford Castle, the home of the Guinness family but now a luxury Hotel.

Saying here is: a forty shades of green.

Eating mostly in Pubs and staying in B&B's, going out to the Pubs in the evening for good conversation and marvelous musical sessions.

Arriving at the Rock of Cashel, an impressive pre-Christian settlement. It dominates the flat countryside for miles around.

We are staying in Irish homes in the countryside or in towns and villages and live the Irish life.

Stopping in Cork, Killarney the departure point for many of Ireland's emigrants and the last stop for the Titanic.

Kevin knocking on doors, he had addresses trying to find lost relatives. Not much luck.

Driving now the Ring of Beara. Stopping at some little towns, all are colorful painted.

Then to the Ring of Kerry along very steep Roads along mountains and a winding Coastline.

If one stops for direction a conversation is bound to begin. The Irish love to talk.

Arriving now at Adare Manor. It is very beautiful. Ireland's prettiest village. It dates from the Norman Conquest. Thatched cottages line its broad street.

Food in Ireland is a welcome surprise. Salmon, trout, lobster and shrimp, as are beef, lamb, and game.

Traveling now along the coast past rugged and windswept cliffs north. Crossing Carrick-a-Rede with a rope bridge swinging over a 80 foot chasm.

There is the Giant's Causeway, hexagonal columns which were formed over 60 million years ago. Then again it is said that it is the work of Finn McCool, he lived most happy and content obeyed no law and paid no rent.

Bush mill Distillery to see now. Making Whiskey and we are enjoying a sip. It is the oldest distillery in the world. 1608.

Dunluce Castle. It was like a dream in the fog.

There is Carrick with the highest sea cliffs in Europe. Very windy one had to watch not to get blown over the rim.

Stopped at a cemetery with W. Yeats grave. The city of Knock nearby and Donegal.

Mayo is a county with astonishing variety of scenery.

And we finally found relatives, dead and buried. The Gibbons. And we found a live one! Annie Gibbons, 100 years old. (1999) We had many questions and she could answer many to Kevin. It was a treasure to have Annie tell us so much.

Dublin now for last. Visiting the Guinness brewery, and a statue of Molly Malone. Which we now had to read up on, she has a long history.

Poland, June 1999

Driving to the celebration of the 100 years Celebration of the convent in Miedzyzdroje.(Misdroy) with my sister Petra and friend Ursel. Many people had been invited and we beautified the place with flowers and food. It was a great party and lots of Vodka was used for the celebration.

Many nuns came from the motherhouse in Breslau (Wroclaw) to take part and after the party we all went to the Beach to watch the sun go down. It was one of the beautiful moments in my lifetime when all nuns suddenly started to sing. Such a peaceful moment.

The next day we all did go swimming in the Baltic Sea. It is nice warm water with great Beaches.

At night we all drunk quite a lot of Eierliquer. It is made from eggs with spirits. It even gave us the Wurst dance by Sr. Raymunda. Nuns have fun too.

In the hallway was still the Guestbook from 1900 on and I copied a few pages of my family when visiting over the years.

My grandmother Helene Glatzel: die schoenen Tage der Erholung und fuer alle Liebe und Guete den lb. Schwestern ein herzliches "Gott vergellt".

Misdroy 26.9.1938

Helene Glatzel

We felt like writing the same too.

Another story by my aunt Margot Glatzel: Zwei kleine Oberschlesier und ihre Mutti danken allen den Schwestern besonders der lb. Oberin, Sr. Blandina, dieser Tante, fuer die schoenen Tage die sie im Hause verleben duerfen und alle Liebe, die sie hier gefunden haben.

Sie hoffen auf ein Wiedersehen! Christine, Wolfram und Tante Margot Thieman.

Misdroy, August 1, 1942

Another by my Uncle Schorschel: Man trifft sich ueberall Bekannte, ich traf hier sogar meine Tante.

Recht herzlichen Dank dem ganzen Haus "Stella Matutina" fuer die Liebevolle Aufnahme

29.8-31.8 1938

Georg Glatzel Beuthen o/b Onkel Schorshel.

Above the Guest Book hangs a clock which got my attention because it was in perfect condition. Built 1900. The Sr. Sister felt it should go home with me and is hanging now in my house in America. Naturally it was smuggled out of Poland hidden under the seats of my rental car. No Antiques from before 1945 can be taken out of the country.

Czech Republic

Driving across the Czech Republic, and stopped at the Schiffshebewerk, Boat lift, Niederfinow. It lies on the Oder-Havel Canal in Brandenburg, to watch how Boats get lifted from one canal to another, of 36 meters up or down, built in 1914 one in Germany.

We are taking now a train to Prague. It is a beautiful city! It is impossible to imagine missing Prague. I had been there before and I never had enough. Music everywhere. Many classic musicians' playing in the street's. At the Prague Castle are concerts: Beethoven, Dvorak, Preludes.

Outside the Prague Castle is the changing of the guards every full hour and at noon with a solemn fanfare.

There is the Charles Bridge. A Museum on its own. It was built in 1357 and 30 baroque statues are lining the Bridge.

The Old-Town Hall with the Astronomical Clock since the 15th century is ringing every hour with a procession of the 12 Apostles.

There is the Ghetto in Old Town. It was once the biggest settlement of Jew's.

Prague is a medieval wonder. But one has to watch and be aware of cabdrivers and petty crimes.

Cuba, November 15th, 1999

A trip again with a lot of flight changes. It is so close but had to go over Canada to enter Cuba.

Landing in Varadero, Cuba at 6pm, and from there by car 2 hours to Havana. I am here for a bicycle vacation. It will be special because bikes are outnumbering cars or carriages. One gets to meet by bicycle the Cuban people easier. It is a big Island country. Immigration was no problem just the Officer wanted to know about all the countries I had been before. He has heard of them but never has been out of Cuba.

Staying in the Pan Am games Village. Which were in 1991, and is now a reasonable place to stay.

My friend Christine McCoyd was there and prepared me for my tour.

I had a very good bicycles imported from Canada.

Lots of food is served in Havana, very healthy and fresh. Mostly vegetarian.

The roads are great for biking and kept in very good shape. There is no traffic. We stopped and had snacks and a Cubra Libre. What a place to bike now. There are the old cars but they have to stay near the cities. Because potholes are not good for them.

It was funny when a man came by and had a big pig on a leash. Looked like he was just handling it like a dog.

Had Lunch at Don Giovani in Havana. What an experience. Pizza, the best I ever had.

Then we biked through the city and got to know all the little side streets and I noticed a lot of rebuilding of the Old Buildings. No tearing down. I know 2 years from now it will be a showpiece.

There are so many old Mansions and many are decaying, money is short for building supply.

Many Oil-Riggs are out there. Who gets the money from the Oil?

Had a very good massage tonight, Dave, a Cuban, he looked like Michel Jordan. Charge for one hour $10. not allowed to charge more. And we have to pay in $ Dollars. US currency is used all over, which is strange.

Had a very different dinner tonight. In Havana, in the old Mansions, people can have small private Dinners for "Guests". The house was called "La Grigera" and it was very elegant.

Slept very good last night and ready for another day of Bicycling. Breakfast tastes good, it is plain, but it is lots of fresh food.

We biked to the west of Cuba, Sonora, a biosphere with the steepest ups and down and so much beautiful scenery. Bicycle touring is fun, but if the wind only would stop. The terrain was hilly and we have an extra challenge of distances of 50km.

Stopped at a commune and talked with the people there. There is really no food except what they grow in the gardens. Not anything for us either to buy to get for Lunch. I had enough cookies to sustain me but the others in the bike group gave up biking and joined the support Van. I knew we had to go downhill eventual and there was a 6 mile downhill!

Not much wildlife to see but a lot of Forest and glorious big trees. And some cattle ranches.

Here is now our Resort Soroa, very tropical. I have a little house on a hill with lots of birds outside.

Made it to a hike to the Castillo los Nubes in the skies. It was once a private residence and now a Restaurant. Passed a waterfall and I thought it was a tough hike.

Signed up for a quite different kind of massage. Needed one. I was told I would have Peter nr. 2.

As I walked to the old Building in the jungle, I heard music from a cave and walked through lots of flowers in there. Then I saw the big roman bath in front of me filled with mineral water which came right out of the wall of the hill.

But it was cold water! I skipped it, to a sad face of the masseur who tried to tell me the cold water was important before. But I still had the best massage for a $10fee.

The Dinner was great, Schnitzel and fresh lettuce. Flan! Nice place to stay longer. But no, we left the next morning.

First by Van to Vinales which was a long drive. And finally by bike through the countryside. It is more farming now by independent people. No communes anymore. But still the Children I noticed were housed separated like chickens, and all had to pick coffee. It looks like everybody has a job or has to work. No sitting around. I always wondered what the people were thinking when we pedaled by? There is not much guiding now but only one road anyway. And they are empty, traffic zero. Horses, Oxen, dogs and us bikes.

I had my first flat. As much as I bike I will leave that to the bike leader. And it happened near our Van. What luck.

Arrived at our beautiful La Ermita Hotel. The Pool is freezing. A big frog is caught in my door and got squashed. So sad. There are dogs running around, very skinny. But my view is first class.

I have switched from Cuba Libre to Mojitos now. They are much better.

Restaurant food is very good. Had a lot of Papayas. I eat too much. And a very good Band was playing.

We are on our way to a small farm. We have been invited to join the family for a few hours. A very gracious family. Again, more food was awaiting us. Jams and fried platanos. And turkey meat. There are many turkeys strutting around.

I gave the host a big bottle of Aspirin, which I brought on purpose, and it was accepted as best for them. Aspirin is unavailable for them and too expensive.

The host saw me admiring his Brahma bull called Jardinero and asked me if I would like to ride him. Never would I say no. And off I went, the bull was trained neck reigned with a nose ring. What fun this was. I can scratch this off now from my bucket list.

I am learning how nice and overjoyed the Cuban people are when the find out I am from USA.

They do not understand that their life would change drastic if the embargo will be lifted. (1999).

So far the roads are wonderful for me for biking, seldom is there a car. Stopped at a Ranch in Vincentes which had a spa and I had another treatment in the mineral pool. It can only improve my looks.

On the way back to Hotel we stopped at a farm with two women owners. They told us their father 50 years ago planted many fruit-trees and a botanical garden. It was very interesting walking through it.

We had a good dinner with Cuban music. I am eaten alive by the small mosquitos, looks like I have the measles.

It does not bother the children they are happy playing out by the pool.

From Vinales to Cayo Levy.

We are all suffering now from a small biting fly called Hehanes, not a mosquito like I thought. My body is swelling in many places. I am allergic to its bite. But again, it does not stop us from biking.

Left early for a 55km trip. Another flat. What is it? Why me. Had to wait for the Van and we had a deadline for a ferry at 11 am. And headwind and stopped 3 miles before, did not know I was so close I could walk with my bike. Passed mostly through Banana plantations.

Got on the Ferry to the Island. It is private and only for guest of Horizontes, very beautiful. Sand so white and fine.

And fresh fish for Lunch and then 3 hours on the Beach just doing nothing. The water was very cold but I did go swimming.

At La Hermita a very good Dinner and talk with many Cubans about anything. My chamber maid even wrote me a note: wishes Sweet Dreams, from your chambermaid Teresa.

Today to Pino del Rio. Mostly downhill by bike then up again. The countryside is so beautiful. No towns, no people, just good roads.

Back to Havana. There is so much to see on this big 4 lane highway without heavy traffic. Autobuses pulled by Horses. Old cars. But all in a slow traffic pattern.

This evening, I walked to Hemingway's Terrace Restaurant. He wrote the book "The man and the sea" here. A very nice older impersonator gentleman was sitting by an old typewriter with a Mojito. Upon talking with him he wrote me a poem which I still have.

On my way I saw the oldest fire truck going on call. I could not believe it still worked.

On my walk in Havana I stopped at an old Antique store. Lots of silver and jewelry for sale. I found out it is like a pawn shop too. If no money, people will look for anything they can sell to buy more food or something they need. In old times lots of money was here. One can see it on all the Old Mansions and most of them are filled with squatters.

There is a beautiful National Hotel; it is a treasure of the state. Kept in perfect condition. And the shiny old cars!

There is the Memorial for the "Maine". It had an eagle on top but was toppled in the revolution. One can still see how prosperous all of it was. Now it needs all paint and Mortar to fix. Or it will crumble. Still it is clean no garbage.

That evening we did get to see Varadero some of the touristy areas of Cuba. Horrible, one expensive Hotel after the next built on the peninsular. Far away from Havana. The daily flights from Europe land there and mostly these tourists just go to the Beach and are not interested in the Cuban history.

Crete, Greece, May 2000

A quick visit to Greece with Hapag-Lloyd airlines. Crete first at the Amalthia Hotel with my sister Petra few miles west of Chania. Very dry but beautiful area. Chania is mostly a waterfront with little fish Restaurants along the Harbor.

But driving the next day we discovered in the countryside many little sleepy villages. And we stopped at many and tasted the food or the wine and the typical dishes.

The highlight of Crete is the Samaria Gorge near the highest mountain of Crete. One walks it slow at a distance of 42km all downhill. The start is at 8000 feet in a very cool spot. All the way down to the coast at Ayia Roumeli.

A lot of climbing over rocks. Balance is very important since there is not a regular path.

Some Mules were stationed on the trail. And after asking why they were there I was told if one gets injured only way out is by Mule. It was a beautiful hard walk of almost 8 hours. We had water and food. One place was so tight in the Gorge, only 9-foot-wide and the walls were straight up to 2000 feet. Could almost get claustrophobic. In WW.2 Crete was occupied by the German Army.

The Gorge plaid a big role in it since it was a hiding place for partisans and Allied undercover units.

At the bottom of the trail a Ship awaited us to return to Chora Sfakion. There are quite a few little villages along the Coast, but all can be only visited either walking or by ship.

Another day for Mountain biking. Went by Van to the top of the Hills unloaded the Bicycles again it was mostly downhill.

2000 July 2nd - By train from Beijing to St. Petersburg, Russia

July 2nd, 2000 arriving in Beijing after a 13 hour flight from USA on United. Food was served by a very grumpy crew.

Immigration was smooth and driving now to Beijing. A beautiful new highway with many trees newly planted. I was told every year china is planting 5 million trees.

Staying at a very luxury Hotel Ukraina. Piano music is still played at 10pm.

Our tour group had a late Dinner, with one of the travelers celebrating her 82nd birthday. Big time change for us.

My roommate is a 30year old Vietnam Veteran soldier. He told me he had been very depressed since the war and thought this trip would make him feel better. I noticed right away that he was a little deranged because his suitcase was chained to the iron heater in the room. Was I going to run off with it, I ask? He always chained all his stuff every night. He did bring the Chains from home, so he was prepared to do it. What was in store for me? One does a lot of things to save on the single supplement.

After a particularly good breakfast touring Beijing. Since I have been here, 1988, it has changed very much. Many new Buildings, and the beautiful Chinese downtown Beijing is gone. There are only a few old houses left. Right away I missed the Hutongs. Hutongs were one story family compounds in Beijing. They could not be 2 story because of the throne of the Emperor who had to have the highest floor. It is cleaner now and no more is the toilet wagon coming by to clean the night pots every morning.

There are now toilets everywhere. And the spitting has stopped.

Saw the Forbidden City one more time and then to lunch, which was fabulous.

We are driving into the country in the worst rainstorm through Mountains. Stopped at a Bee farm and we learned a lot of bee farming. Many hives had guards watching them. Would people steal the honey? Nobody gave me an answer.

Planted in the fields are Soybeans, Corn and peaches. Many roadside stands are having produce for sale. The orchards are miles long and some of the trees I could not identify.

We are trying to get to an area where it is less touristy on the Chinese Wall.

There we took a ski lift to the top and the rain started again.

I huddled against the wall and tried to stay a little dry, hopeless. At least it was warm. By the time I got back to our meeting point I was soaked and wanted only a coffee. The rain never stopped even on the drive back.

Today I met my Chinese friends the Wang family again. Wen was living with us in the States and prepared her family for my visit. Her father Luis and grandson Pesis took me out for lunch to eat Jauzers. Pesis spoke fairly good English and translated for his father. I got to interact with the family and learned some of their customs. There is not much privacy in their apartment and little less personal space. The kitchen was shared with quite a lot of families and it was so small. And such good food came out of that little kitchen.

I have met the grandmother who was for me interesting, since she had still the bound feet.

The Greatest Rail adventure in the World is coming up.

This trip is a must for every fan of Railways. It is the poor men's train, cheap.

The train is leaving at 6am. So early but could not sleep anyway. The train station is all new and very organized. There was a waiting room just for Foreigner's, us.

We settled into our compartments. With all the luggage there was not much room left for us 4 people in a compartment, leaving it outside by the rack, our luggage was going to be stolen maybe. Watching the countryside going by. Always north. Many tunnels washed out roads, lots of damage because the rain has not stopped yet.

There are many rice fields.

Our lunch was alright, but the kitchen is very small on the train and it takes a long time for the food to get ready. Rice, shredded cabbage and beef. It will repeat the menu from now on, almost every day it was on the menu. Something with Cabbage anyway. Next to the kitchen was an enormous mountain of cabbage which had to be used by arrival in Russia.

I do look out the window all the time. The view is changing constantly. This trip north is unknown places for me.

Each coach has a Samovar and one can get tea or coffee any time.

Dinner at 6:30pm. Shredded cabbage and chicken.

There are not many Chinese who can speak English on the train. But a lot of Mongolian and Russians are passengers too. They all try to talk to me and test their English. This is fun. At every Train stop we jumped out to exercise and trying to buy food from the local vendors.

Last night was interesting. We stopped at a very small town around midnight, which is on the border from china to Mongolia. The train track is different width, so all the undercarriages changed, all wheels come off. All this is done in a small carriage house and every wagon has to go in there. It is very noisy job. One has a choice: sleep or watch.

Standing outside was interesting too. Electricity was not used, and one could see the Milky Way so close. The Coachman let us look inside to watch the changing of wheels when our wagon got his turn. All goes with a lot of rattling and banging. We could proceed now on a wider-gauge track through Mongolia and Russia. I was told the rails had different sizes so Russia could not invade China by train. Or vice versa.

Then immigration started. Fill in papers, more papers, stamps and again more papers and more stamps and finally the ok. All this from 8:30pm to 2:30am.

And then train started to move again. And everybody fell asleep.

Trans Mongolian Railway operates some 1110km inside Mongolia. Dating back to 1938. Continuing across Mongolia, the scenery does indeed have an uncluttered beauty. One can see sometimes Yurts, animal skulls, bones bleached by the sun and an occasional Horseman riding full tilt next to the passing train and laughing as the Horse rears.

Breakfast was a long wait, but it was delicious. The cooks overslept. In the meantime, watching from the moving train. It is a very dry. And a lot of raptors sitting on the telephone lines. Since there are no trees their only advantage is from the powerlines.

Beautiful Cranes. Lots of camels and many Horses and cattle roaming. All without fences.

Deer herds and big groundhogs.

And it is so dry.

Finally, breakfast, which was Omelet and very thin pancakes with Lingonberries. So good.

Mongolia

Not a tree for hours. And we are suddenly arriving in Ulaanbaatar. Mongolia is a rich cultural country with religious tradition.

Many Gers or yurts around the city. The train stopped right downtown. The city is almost all new buildings since independence from Communist rule. Still the Soviet influence one can see.

One third of the population of Mongolia lives in the Capital. This is the year 2000. The carcass-laden Horse or car in the city streets are still common sight. Fresh meat transported to the stores.

Getting of the train it started to rain again, it had not rained in such a long time here I was told, rain is following me from china. The people love the rain.

Ulaanbaatar Hotel was nice, a quick cleanup and an excellent lunch: soup, salad, noodles which I love.

July 7th

A trip to the History Museum. Much of Mongolia's involvement with Horses was explained which was of my interest.

Dinner was at a French Restaurant! I had 2 duck legs which were very good but too much fat stuff on it.

Ulaanbaatar is surrounded by an unending steppe. The Capital has traditional Gers and Buddhist monasteries. And modern high-rises.

Filled up with a very good breakfast of Blinis. When the train arrives in Ulaanbaatar it brings fresh supply to the kitchens of everybody. There are no gardens, and all food is imported from Russia or China.

Driving in the countryside by jeep. Roads are sandy lanes or rocky areas all with enormous potholes. No speeding possible. We covered 300km in 9 hours. No paved Roads at all.

In a Mongolian "Motel" overnight. Gerts, for 3 people. It is a round house made from animal skins and inside decorated in the most beautiful colors. Red is the favorite.

We are here for the Naadam Horse Race trials. About 80 children on their Horses racing for about 15 km. Only children are used for Jockeys. Maybe 5 or 6 years old. We followed them along in the jeep. You can see the thrill on the young jockeys faces.

Some Horses had already lost their jockey and still were racing along with the herd.

One child was lifted into a kind of Ambulance, I guess he was hurt. Each child jockey was dressed in a beautiful national dress.

Some Horses were already sluggish but the lead Horse was going strong, cantering ahead and not letting any Horse pass.

It was very exciting.

Ger Camp

The Ger is beautiful. Gers include wooden framed beds and dressers, and a wood-burning stove.

Bathing and toilet facilities are located in a separate building and we have a good cook.

The scenery is amazing with lots of long rolling hills. A perfect sunset. Had to learn how to close the Ger for the night. Especially the top. Looks all difficult but managed it. One must leave a hole for the chimney so that the rain cannot get in. The mattress is made of Horsehair and the pillow too. I guess the tail of Horses are used for that. Very heavy. My body feels like lead too. Hope to sleep tonight better.

We stopped at the Preswalzky Horse Reserve called "Khustain" National Park. 100 or more Horses are there now and are doing great. The first ones were imported from the Netherlands, which flew 16 Horses to Mongolia in 1994. Sometimes they are called Takhi horses, the Mongolia name.

Michael hopefully does not wake me again with his snoring and sure enough he wakes me at 4am again. Why? And starts opening and closing his zippered bag making the usual noise. He had bad experiences in the Vietnam War and has not gotten over it. There is something strange about him.

Food is good. Very good bread and fried donuts.

A 3-hour drive to Karakorum, the ancient Capital of Mongolia. Visiting there the Erdene Zuu Monastery. 108 stupas are still there. The number 108 corresponds with the 108 worry beads that the monks carry. It is still impressive what one can see. A lot was destroyed by the Communists. But all is under restoration again.

Today's camp is by a river. Something like hon...river.

I am moving tonight into the other yurt. Arlene and Fran have an extra bed. I have had enough of Michael. Snoring is the worst.

Driving with the jeep through the deserted desert I needed to relief myself badly. There was no bush or tree in sight for miles, nothing. We stopped and I made sure that no traffic was coming. Mind you it was a little hilly and went off the road 10 feet.

As I was squatting, a big bus came roaring along and stopped next to the jeep. Out jumped about 20 women who joined me. Men went onto the other side of the road. I love company but this was a little much. All the women tried to have conversation with me but I had a language problem, their smiles told me it was a successful stop.

We went again this afternoon to Karakorum to walk the turtle boundary. There are fertility stones on all four corners. It was a big city once. The home of Genghis Khan. And nomadic remains is still a way of life in modern Mongolia.

We are now visiting a family in a Ger unannounced. This is the real thing. Mongolians greet you with a handshake. The Ger is round and can be packed up in a very fast time.

Inside is again the beautiful furniture and one has to squat or kneel or sometimes there was a little stool. We were offered Mare's milk (airag) served in bowls and we had to hold them with both hands and sample other foods.

Afterwards I was offered a Horse to ride and took advantage real fast. Had been waiting for that moment. Then went riding over the Grasslands. No fence and the Horse just loved it.

I rode many miles and arrived with the evening sun at camp again were the friendly owner took the Horse home. But I did stop at another farm where the family was shearing the sheep with a big scissor. A woman was milking the sheep.

At dinner to much beef. One cow was slaughtered on our arrival and the skin was hanging to dry. Much blood still dripping, I lost my taste for meat that evening. To much red beef slabs lying around. The beef was served even for breakfast. And cabbage salad.

I slept finally peacefully.

Back to Ulaanbaatar, 375km a long way on the primitive roads.

We are 4 jeeps and there is again a lot of racing. My head hurts and my back. No springs in the old cars. Many broken down cars lying beside the Road. Was told when a car breaks down one cannot leave the car alone the owner needs to wait for help. So, they people sleep till help arrives in the cars. People prefer older trucks because they can fix them.

Stopped at a monastery which was left by the Communist as a show peace. Beautiful music sung by the Monks.

Japanese Mongolian Restaurant for dinner. Outstanding food.

Today to Gorkhi-Terelj Natl. Park. Very different looking. Many beautiful trees and the Ger camp looked like a mirage it was so beautiful. I went out looking for a Horse. I was told only ask the owner seen traveling along and a good Horse was given to me to ride for hours. It was a tough little Horse, up the Mountain and down no problem. No sweating. The Horses are so in shape to work.

Later on we sat all together on our porch by the camp and had lunch. I wish not to see beef again.

Went to a big Ger supposed to be the biggest in Mongolia for Dinner and throat singing.

There was a contortionist I do not like, I do not like that kind of stuff. I loved the throat singing.

Dinner was beef and shredded cabbage. But added this time was carrot salad, mixed with garlic and cream, very good.

And the stuffed dumplings!

I am being stuffed too. Some of the people said the food is bad and was like puke. O well. I liked it.

Then some Mozart Music: Eine kleine Nachtmusik and that in Mongolia.

Here comes now the Naadam Festival. The festival originated many centuries ago. It now celebrates the independence from China. All the training of the Horses and the wrestling, and Archery, all in competition now.

The first race is 30km and the Horses go in full Gallop.

I waited 2 miles before the finish line and saw 300 horses coming across the plains. One Horse died right in front of me.

Was told it happens a lot. There are no checkpoints and some Horses just cannot make it.

There was the Elite of Mongolia; it looked like a fancy Horse race all over the world. People dressed in the finest and so elegant.

At the Archery competion everybody was dressed in the tradional outfit.

And so many Horses milling around. Many people got run over by the Horses, there was no order, no direction or police. It was all very exciting for everybody.

And now onto the Mongolian Train again.

This time a very ugly primitive train. "The Trans Mongolian" with very stinky toilets leaving Ulaanbaatar. At 5am we woke up at the Siberian border. There we had to walk a short way to the Mongolian Checkpoint no toilets at the station. But then we found toilets we could use for 10cent by a bar. It was a hole in the ground but clean.

We are waiting. And waiting. No train lockomotive has arrived. It had to be a Russian Locomotive for the new track.

Have eaten whatever we could find. And then the border guards arrived, and we are all filling out papers again. And this is for Mongolia still. We must repeat everything for the Russian side again.

But everybody is smiling and very patient and I am too. 2 hours of paperwork!

And the toilets are closed on the new Russian train! I finally begged the wagon lady of my situation.

Yes, the Mongolian trains were the pits, but the Sleeping arrangement was great.

It took 12 hours to reach the Russian border.

Thi is called here now the Buryatia country.

I met a lady on the train who explained a little of the people I will meet in Ulan Ude. They are called Buryats and still speak in a different language and dress old style.

Ulan Ude the 12th

On arrival in an unnamed stop we got off the train and went by Van in a driving rainstorm for 2 hours to a Buddhist monastery and then to a Village of Kharlun, the residents of mixed Mongolian and Russians. Under communist rule Buddhism was practiced here secretly. The big Boss of the village was awaiting us to show us the Museum first. Then the children of the school presented us with a welcome drink and performed for us with singing and dancing.

Then a big feast was awaiting us. That was the best food yet.

First, for good luck we had to throw some vodka over our shoulder, I liked that custom.

Cucumber salad, beet salad, green salad, poseys with pork, tomato salad, sausage, deep fried hotdogs.

Waffles and cake with blueberry jam, fresh currants, raspberries. Bread and sliced oranges and lots of sugar powder to coat all the desserts.

Hard liquor and wine flowed freely, and a balsam liqueur.

And everything is made right in the village, not from stores.

We had to rest at the Geser Hotel after the feast. Did not get to the Hotel till 12:30 at night. The Hotel is ok, it is old, but everything here is old. This is the farthest away from any store and so people have to do with what they have. It is Siberia after all. I did change my room to a larger one. $18 added is a very good price.

Breakfast was horrible. White wieners! They looked bad. Barley was served and I put sugar on mine, and it was edible. Just like food for me in 1950.

Arrival in Ulan Ude. Interesting with lots of old architecture. It was once a Cossack garrison on the Selenga river and prospered as a trading post between China and Irkutsk. The Buryats make visiting Ulan Ude a rich experience.

Saw some Siberian animals in the Zoo. Horrible place.

And then to a Russian Restaurant for lunch which was fantastic. Soup! Chicken and potatoes, crepes filled with pine nuts and ice-cream.

Need to walk after this.

We crossed the bridge to go to the "Believers". The Old Believers were a group who disagreed with the changes made to Orthodox worship. In 1653 they broke away from the church and did it the "old Way" speaking Russian, crossing themselves with two fingers instead of one, keeping their beards because it was outlawed by Peter the great. Then exiled to Lake Baikal in the 17th century, and many descendent of the members are still active in this area.

Five "Believers" were waiting for us by their village. And we have listened to their live story, never knew about them and loved to hear the old history. Then they sung to us a few of the centuries-old songs. Noticed some were in German.

Walked down to the village and met a lot of people and was able to take photos. An old Lady invited me to see her garden with good vegetables and she was raising Rabbits for meat.

Then to Galena's parents' house. Galena was our tour guide in Ulan Ude. (Ludmilla and Alexander parents name)

Again, we had to eat, starting with Pizza. A big fish caught in Lake Baikal and homemade Vodka, it tasted exceptionally smooth. It feels like we are eating all the time. And everybody wants us to taste their food.

I picked a lot of Raspberries and currants, my favorite Berries along the hedgerows.

In Ulan Ude we got ready for the next tour to Lake Baikal.

Breakfast consisted this morning of this:

Waiter!

I wave, nothing, he waves back, ok.

3 slices of bread please, cheese please, coffee please.

Waiting.

Me, can I have some toast please, 3 pieces please- yes they are coming.

Eventually I got buckwheat in a bowl for breakfast.

Now we are driving to Lake Baikal. Left the Hotel at 8:30am for a 3-hour trip but it turned into a long many hour trip. We stopped for fresh smoked fish. Which was sold from the back of cars. Berries and Honey, mushrooms. Our snacks. We ate it all.

Along the road one sees only countryside and a lot of Birch trees. It is very green. And we are 5,771km from Moscow.

Mika city (Slyud Yanka) is the station for us to get the local train to Lake Baikal.

It is so strange to see this big Station out in nowhere.

The station is like a shopping center for all people. This is where one buys and sells. People come from all over the countryside to make deals in this place. Somehow most people here are wearing expensive sweat suits. The expensive sweat suits were brought on the train from China and sold here.

We finally left on the local train for our Pine guest house.

What a surprise this train was. It was the Circum-Baikal old railway. It was luxury. It took us on the old railway around 86km and passes through 39 tunnels. Considered then to be the most complicated built railway in the world. Permafrost, frozen earth, and breaking the ice. There is still a train down in the cold Lake water when it broke through the ice. It was a nightmare for the engineering. We settled in our Dacha and had Dinner and lots of Vodka. The guesthouse is next to the old train track and has again lots of history when it was built.

At 11 pm the Orient Express came by. A luxury train. Just looking into the windows of the passing train was fantastic. One could see the chandeliers in the compartments. The Orient Express slows for the curves on this stretch.

And here I am on the slowest cheapest train and having the greatest time too. Toilets are way in the trees, washing place is a sink, with cold water under the trees. To cold and forget about washing. Brushing quickly teeth but that is all.

Next day by boat across Lake Baikal to Irkutsk. 2 hours across. Used to be the train was shipped across but too many accidents happened and now one goes by ship only. Knowing it is the deepest Lake in the world. Baikal contains one fifth of the earth's fresh water. The lake is 1 mile deep and has 1500 species of marine life.

Then by bus to lunch in Listvyanka at a guesthouse. Great food. And a little bear kept begging from us, he was found in the woods and is now a pet.

Now to Andorra Hotel by Horse wagon to Irkutsk.

Irkutsk is Siberia's Capital and most colorful city. The ancient wooden houses are typical of old Siberia.

Hand carved and almost every piece out of wood. The doors are very low, over time the Roads have been paved and it is hard getting into the front door.

The big market is full of food. I got snacks. There is no shortage except no rubles but $ were welcome. For me everything was so cheap. But here the average person makes $50 a month.

There are very rich people in Irkutsk. I saw big houses, new developments, and many Land rovers. The Hotel even had a casino.

Went for Dinner to Restaurant Riviera with excellent Russian food. I have to watch more what gets served, there was squid on my salad. Yuck.

The women on average have horrible Hair. Many colors are used and it looks like they need conditioner.

Sunday 16th

As I was walking out the front of my Hotel, I thought I knew the Nun walking in front of me. Sure, enough it was Sr. Daniella from my hometown in Poland. What a coincidence?

As she told me, she has walked for the opening of the first Catholic Church in Siberia 700 miles with a group of young Christians. They had a truck following them. It was like meeting old friends. Each person had used up 3 pair of shoes already. I was invited to meet the Bishop. It was very exciting to be around them. Never saw so many people in church. Standing room only. I guess the communist could not keep religion down.

I am in my room with a good coffee. Every floor in the Hotel has a beautiful woman in charge of a little kitchen. She sits at the desk and watches what goes on, on her floor. She even makes cappuccino. She inquired if I needed company at night, anything goes.

Trans-Siberian Express to Moscow

Our train is leaving at 2am going east. The good news, we all got first class. What luxury. We have a conductress who speaks English and is sweet. But this is still not the Orient Express.

Most everybody has somewhere business or visiting somebody. This is serious train travel. The train is full of Chinese, Russians and from many other countries. They all have lots of luggage and are hoping to sell most of it on the train.

The most legendary train route in the world, the Trans-Siberian Railroad snakes its 9289km way across two continents and eight time zones.

From the train one can see lots of trees. Very few openings in the trees. Under Stalin all along the track trees had to be planted so one could not see out of the train.

Then one could see a small town maybe with fields and some animals. Meadows with flowers. Many Delphiniums.

Getting now lots of sleep. The train has that sound clickety clack, it is soothing.

Breakfast was very good. 3 eggs with parsley and dill, chives and the best bread. Ham and cheese with coffee.

Last night's Dinner was excellent. It is a small kitchen with a big pile of Cabbage again. At least 100 head.

On such a long trip we will eat them all I guess.

The dining car is almost empty. It is too expensive for most passengers on the train. We supplemented our food with fresh bought chickens at the train stops. There are always some babushkas selling food. And it is always homemade. One has to jump fast out of the train and buy or it is gone since they have so little to sell. I try to buy from the very old Mama's.

The cooks were willing to cook it and got some out of it I am sure.

The train is 35 wagons long and I have not seen a Russian order any food. Just us foreigners.

Have tried my Russian. "Dobraye Utra" (welcome) we hear a lot. Very beautiful young girls work on the train. Our is a mother, daughter team. They are the boss. Mother comes by to inquire and check on us if we like the food on the train.

Spacibo-thank you.

I look out the window, sleep, eat, reading. Michael is still the noisy man. We all would like to tie him down. He cannot sit still, he did bring a lot of Balloons and is blowing them up for every child coming by.

For every wagon are 2 hostesses. One is asleep, one is on duty. They are always cleaning. And are very polite. There is a samovar on the end of the hallway which is kept always full of hot water by them. Our problem is stopping the hostess not to close our curtains all the time we open them again. For us it is like a game. There is Air-condition on the train.

In old times one was not allowed to look out the window and the habit is still there of keeping everything closed.

I have to stop eating ice-cream. It is so good. No diet cream!

At a train stop I bought from an old Babushka 2# of Raspberries for $50c.

Some currants too. One of my favorite fruits.

All stations are full of old women who are trying to sell anything. They are not getting any retirement and are left to themselves. Many are starving.

It has been raining now for a few days. But it is fun to travel in first class. 9pm and the sun is still shining in the evening. We have to reset our watches constantly.

Another morning and rain. Russia seems to flood away. And it is always the same scenery for the last 1000 miles.

Lots of haymaking by hand outside. In the rain. How can it dry?

KM 2012

Some South Korean TV crew just filmed us. I tried my Japanese, but they did not like it.

The highlight now is for us all is food. The good food is less every day. Our group buys from the train stations when we stop, food to supplement. We do need fruit which is berries.

It is getting hot outside. Glad we have Air-condition. There is a smell of body odors, cooked food, not good, on our train.

For lunch we had fish soup. Was not good and did not eat it. We had borscht, again one can only eat so much of it. And we do not get any exercise except going to the food wagon or toilet.

We crossed the Asian -Europe line. KM 1777-1778 at 3:30pm local time. Hoped the train would slow down but no, at least it was announced.

Ekaterinburg is next. So much history here. Our stop was not long enough. It does have memories of my school learning about the murder of the Romanov Family. Must go back one day.

Dry countryside now, no rain for a long time.

Set clock back again, then Dinner. Buying Raspberries and trying to sleep.

Wednesday 19th

Again, Michael decided to make noise. We all cannot sleep with that man. There are 4 beds in our compartment, and he is the only man but what a disgusting person. He never thinks of anybody else.

Had coffee and cheese and reading a lot, breakfast is not till 8am. The train is running on schedule.

Hostess is still smiling and always cleaning, her name is Christine and she told us she is employed by the state for 3 months. She studies in Irkutsk law.

Quena is single but I do not know what she does besides working on the train. She is a cleaning nut.

The scenery is still beautiful with lots of wildflowers. The houses one sees from the train are all made from wood.

Had Blinis today and they were very good.

Noticed the train is going extremely fast today, trying to catch up time? Could hardly walk in the walkway with all the swinging of the Wagons. The trees are flying by.

We are in Jaroslav and crossed the Volga River. What memories that brings to me. The music, the stories, when the River was running red in the revolution. All this comes to mind. Having read so many books of the History of Russia.

I see passenger ships on the River. And the town is kept beautiful. So many churches and shining roofs in the sunlight.

One more lunch with soup, salad, Steak and potatoes. Chocolate, ice-cream.

70 more miles to Moscow and arrived there at 4pm at Yaroslavl station. Very impressive and again beautiful with lots of art in the Building.

There are 9 train stations around Moscow. I am glad our guide was waiting for us. We are driving along beautiful old historical Buildings. Looks like Moscow is being rebuilt. It is very clean. The new Russian flag is flying more. It changed in 1991.

After Dinner we went to the Metro. One should visit all of the stops because they are all very classic and with lots of Art. I never saw something like it. The Barrock, the elegance of the statues, every station more beautiful. "Dante's Inferno" was my favorite.

Finally, Red Square! After reading all the spy stories about this place to see it now alive in front of me! The Kremlin is a masterpiece. St. Basil's Cathedral is by far the most recognizable symbol of Russia.

Only disturbing for me was seeing a lot of drunken Russians. Lying, sleeping it off on Benches or behind bushes. It did not disturb anybody.

Our hotel Ukraine is big, 11th floor is my room. A great view with 15 feet ceilings and beautiful parquet floor. Antique furniture and my mattress too was antique. Fluffy big feather pillows.

For breakfast we had Eclairs, cheesecake, cheese of all kinds and blinis. And real Torte. The Dining room is gorgeous with big ceiling and chandeliers.

Going to see the Lenin Tomb today, changing of the guard and much more.

Then to the Museum of art.

By boat to the Czars Nickolas and family gravesite.

St. Basil Square.

The Bells are chiming 6pm and off to Dinner at a private home.

But it is raining now again with lightning and thunder.

Dinner was great, our host family overdid themselves serving from Caviar to poppy seed cake. Then Vodka, Wine, Jagaden berry wine.

The best poppy seedcake, like my mother always made.

Today we all said goodbye to each other. We had been a long time together. 4 weeks in very crowded spaces!

I am going alone on to St. Petersburg by train which is not leaving till midnight.

I walked through Moscow for 9 hours, looked at the Kremlin again. Lines were long to get in. Saw the Armory but so much more to see there. 10 years ago, nobody could get into this place now it is open to the public. Perestroika did a lot. It is a wonderful city I predict it will be one day the most beautiful.

Many churches to look at.

In front of the Hotel Babushkas and lots of people were selling produce from the country. Pfifferling! (Mushrooms), Raspberries, currants, Jagadinos, a small Vegetable. The growing season is short in Russia and people are stocking up.

Moscow to St. Petersburg, 22nd

My hired driver delivered me to my compartment on the train. Train Nr. 3. I would have not been able to find it since all is in Russian. The train is smooth like an airplane. A four bedroom just for two today. Sharing it with a young Russian man who is into high tech. Found out he makes about $5000 a month (2000y) when the average is $52. He is happy with the Economy. He has a math degree from the Sorbonne.

I slept good for 4 hours. Looking out, it is raining again. There is no village along the track or any towns. The train is called the Red Arrow.

Reminds me of Dr. Zhivago. My fantasy.

Arriving in St. Petersburg in the rain. Lucky I am staying close to the station in a private Apt. House.

My Hostess is a Russian lady, Nina. She lives alone and takes travelers in to make a living.

Making breakfast for me, spending too much money on food supplies. I told her I do not need so much food.

To get in or out of her Apartment is very hard. I have to open and close about 10 locks. What is going to happen in an emergency? I am not happy living with all the locks but I am told to many burglars in town.

St. Petersburg was founded by Peter the Great in 1703. 1924 it was changed to Leningrad, 1991 changed again to St. Petersburg.

Walked to see the city. A great walking city. St. Petersburg is a little more crumbling. But a lot of Buildings are being renovated.

I am impressed by the Hermitage. It is so much bigger than I thought. So much to see and do! One needs many days for it.

I walked a lot of the streets met the natives and went to Peter Fort. A lot of history was made there.

The graves of the Romanovs are there now since 1998.

It is easy to walk and find historic places in the city. I love the canals and the little Restaurants.

But Nina makes a beautiful arrangement of food. Everything is very elegant and served with particularly good silver and porcelain. She comes from a very Old Russian family. She does have health problems, which could be cured in the USA quite easy, there is no medicine here. She needs Hormones and has no Doctor services for her. And going to a Hospital, she explained, is like a death wish.

I have not slept as good as last night. Only woke up once at 2am and it was daylight. It is called the white nights of Russia.

For Breakfast homemade rice cereal by Nina. Very good. She wants to please me so bad. I told her I would skip Dinner she wrung her hands because it was so out of routine. She already bought again food.

I had other plans. I left and went straight to the Alexander Theatre. The Kirov ballet was performing there Swan Lake. By a Russian I was told how to get a ticket not tourist price. It was only $15, right in the middle of the Orchestra. And it was an experience to. One could drink and eat in the performance. At intermission, the elegance of the Foyer! Champagne and little sandwiches were for sale.

Went again to the Hermitage, I can never finish there. It is indescribable. So many of paintings I have heard or seen on photos are exhibited here. The Dutch Masters are still my favorites. Monet and Manet paintings.

The entrance fee is only $6. I spend again 5 hours there.

Then I took a boat trip on the River just to rest my legs. Too bad I could not understand the commentary on the boat from a tour guide.

The great evening now to Swan Lake. There were signs not to take photos, everybody did it anyway. The red Caviar sandwiches and a glass of champagne cost me 5rubbles. Where in the world can I get something so good so cheap? And it was allowed to take that to the seat and get more refills.

The Ballet was beautiful, the dancers were like porcelain dolls. And I think I heard the sweetest violin in my life. It gave me goosebumps. By the way a regular ticket to Swan Lake cost $100.

Afterwards I went for a coffee and a drink, the sun was still shining at midnight.

My next seatmates at the Restaurant were Hong Kong tourists who told me that they did not like Russia. They had been stopped by the police 3 times a day for passport checkup.

When I saw police, I usually did not make eye contact or went in another direction. Maybe my blond hair did not call for it. But Chinese immigrants are not wanted in Russia.

Today I forgot my passport in the room and could not change $ into rubbles. So, I held my $20 bill in my hand and sure enough somebody came and changed it very fast. $ are needed and wanted.

The Church of Spilled Blood was magnificent.

The average price of a bottle of water was 5 rubbles, a coffee 5 rubbles 40 rubles for a sandwich. $14 got me 30 rubles in exchange. This is the year 2000. One does not drink regular water. It is unhealthy and needs to be boiled for everything.

There is a heat wave and having no windows open at night is hard to sleep. Many Mosquitos I was told and there are no screens.

The journey is complete, an unforgettable experience along one of the world's greatest rail journeys.

Copenhagen, Stockholm, Sweden

A final big breakfast and to the Airport to Copenhagen and were I will meet friends from Sweden.

It was a very good flight. But nobody is picking me up? A long wait but then there was Ulla, Filippa and Johanna. And by train to Helsingor. An interesting train trip passing forts and castles. Then by a ferry, to Sweden. A drive through the beautiful countryside to Filippas family farm.

Horses, Beef cattle and brother Hendrick the farmer.

Spend a few days there and learned about the farms there. Sleeping with an open door is good but many Mosquitos again and finally had to cream myself with lotion which worked.

They do sleep late here. Drove around, ate cherries and Berries. Then back to the ferry for the 1 1/2hour trip to Denmark to get the Train back.

I booked a Hotel in Denmark accidental in the red light district. Was interesting. I had a beautiful room.

At night I walked over to Tivoli Park. Tivoli Park was built in 1843. And was the first amusement park. It was on my list to visit. Very noisy and lots of lights, food, friendly people. It never shuts down.

A wonderful trip altogether.

Nicaragua, 2000

I go to Central America to talk and practice my Spanish. Heard of a particularly good school in Granada, Nicaragua.

I prefer homestays to integrate with the natives. It is living mostly primitive without air-condition. And food is very good but simple.

A very full flight, I must have been the only Gringo on the plane. My immersion started right on the plane. Almost everybody near my seat wanted to talk to me why I choose Nicaragua. There were still political problems.

My driver was waiting for me and we finally found my luggage, which was broken open and a few things missing.

Driving through the countryside to Granada, very dry but interesting. Many Cowboys on their Horses riding along the road. I was surprised how many Horses I could see in the fields.

Granada is an elegant colonial city on Lake Cocibolca, the largest lake in Central America. At the city's center is the tree-lined Parque Central, dominated by the magnificent yellow Cathedral of Granada, built in 1583.

At my new home I met papa Ernesto Diaz who drove me around to get my bearing. And introduced me to people of the school.

Mama Iliana, my house mother, fed me a very good lunch.

I am a little worried about sleeping tonight. It is very hot. I do have 2 fans in my room, but it is hot air being pushed around.

There are chickens running around and a few dogs in the backyard.

I found a bike to use and went for a 2-hour trip. Again, I met a lot of people. Everybody is very friendly.

I was told not many Gringo women come to Granada and not on bikes.

Found a nice little cafe and had a coffee and watched people for a while. The weather has been building up to a big storm and I made it just home before the rains came down. I thought the roof would collapse. The Roof is only metal sheets.

Later on, as we drove to the grandmothers house, we could see a lot of wind damage. Abuela Nicolas had a big farm with lots of fruit trees. I was in heaven. Mangos, and ripe for eating!

Dinner was fried Platanus, rice, ceso blanko, fresh tomatoes, all delicious.

Driving through the countryside one can see poor hovels. But all is clean, no garbage on the Road or at the homes. People must work hard to get the food and cannot afford much.

Then again there are expensive cars on the Road. I was told a lot of Sandieestas are still around and the like to have big cars. The Sandieestas have big houses. It is the red painted color what gives away their homes and the red flag flown.

The night was noisy. Dogs barking. A little baby nearby crying a lot. TV's blaring. And at 2 at night the neighbor started to have a party with very loud music.

Little mice running around too. It is a little too much.

Then at 6am a Guinea hen started making noise and that is loud next to my room and a dog kept jumping at the fence trying to get at the hen. I am thinking of moving to a Hotel.

Left at 9am for a trip to San Juan del Sur. I was told it would be a 2-hour drive and lots to see. And again, so many Horses!

The Beach was totally empty except our family. It is black sand, but the water temperature was just right. Nice and warm. I did forget to bring my swimsuit but found a shack which sold me a nice bikini.

Then we had lunch on the Beach, fresh caught fish and Lobster tails. Very good Beer and coffee.

Tonight, maybe I can sleep? But a lot of firecrackers are going off for the big fiesta tomorrow.

David Ortigo is running for President and will visit tomorrow.

Today a Sunday and it is hot in the morning. 105 degrees already.

For the party 1000 Horses are supposed to show up. So, I took the bicycle and went into town to the meeting place. I met a lot of Horse people and their Andalusian Horses. Somebody offered me his house for rent. I am going to look into it soon. I do always meet people when I am walking or biking.

Coming back to the home, my room is like a stove, even the mattress is hot.

The house has a metal roof and so the heat just boils down on us.

Back at the Horse parade now. Found out that almost all the Horses are stallions. The men do not like to ride mares or geldings. It is not Macho, sitting on a mare or Gelding. Loud music on all the floats with loudspeakers shouting into the public.

Drinking is done and showing off their costumes people wear. The parade was over 3 hours long and all in this heat.

In the evening, we sat at home to rest. But the neighbors started to fight. 2 Brothers trying to kill each other. One was throwing stones at each other and one was holding a big wrench. A few stones came flying over our fence. It was a wild evening. Finally, both parties fell asleep. I kept thinking that this fight will come into our house.

I never slept that night, hate to leave; I liked my "family". I need a more peaceful place. It will be very disappointing for them if I move, since they depend on the money I pay. I will miss the good cooking.

Everything turned out quite different for me. My first day at school was interrupted in the first hour. I was told my daughter Kara was trying to reach me.

She needed me to come home right away. She told me my husband Kevin was injured playing Ice hockey and was going to die. His head was split like a watermelon from a hockey-puck.

A race to the Airport to Managua. No plane and all seats sold out for future flight. I begged a young man to change for another day and I got his ticket and made it to Baltimore at 2am that night. I could not believe my Kevin's injury. He was in a coma. But he fought for his life.

It all worked itself out fine over the month, but it was a very difficult healing process for Kevin.

So, Nicaragua was a short trip.

Paris, France, March 21, 2001

A weeklong trip to France was fun and an adventure. Traveling with my friend Judy again. Lots of rain in Paris and almost everything was flooded. We walked many miles through Paris, visited the Samaratine Store for lunch. The top floor has the best view of Paris.

Sometimes a little blue sky would show but very seldom. We saw the Montmartre Church which is unbelievably beautiful.

A day trip to Mont-Saint-Michel in Normandy.

Surrounded by dangerous moving sand and now called by some "Marvel of the Occident". The Abby built on a rocky islet was a center for pilgrimage in the middle ages. Naturally all this was done by us in pouring rain too.

Walking many miles again in Paris, passing the Louvre, and lucky nobody in line, and finally ending up at Sacre Coeur, for me a most beautiful place. And a very imposing view from the church tower. Outside I had to use the Carrousel for one spin. Paris has many Carrousels, all old. I am collecting wooden Carrousel Horses, and my joy is sitting on them with the music playing.

At our Hotel California Saint-German, we spend little time, there was too much to see. Meeting a friend one evening for a concert: Ave Maria with chants. In the oldest church in Paris Eglise Saint-Julien-le-Pauvre.

Since it does not rain today, we are going to the Village of Barbizon. There was a Hotel while Louis Stevenson lived there and wrote his "forest notes". The town is an artistic center because of the landscape, Millet, Corot and Daubigny lived here too.

Then to Chateau Fontainebleau in the French forest which was the residence of the Kings of France and Napoleon.

On the last morning looking out of our Hotel window a very blue sky and no rain! But Paris is flooded! The Seine is covering all the sidewalks.

As we departed, I had to write a little story of our Hotel experience:

A friend and I traveled to Paris, staying at a nice hotel in a spacious room with a large walk-in closet.

During our first night I was repeatedly awakened by my friend's snoring. I finally moved my mattress into the closet, which was big, closed the door and was able to sleep.

When I told my friend about her snoring in the morning, she

denied it. I guess she thought I was an eccentric who enjoyed sleeping in closets.

When we returned from sightseeing, I saw that my bed in the closet had been neatly made. Each day for four days the same thing occurred.

I often wonder what the chambermaid must have thought about someone who apparently preferred being alone in a closet rather than awakening to a beautiful view of Paris available from the bedroom window.

The story was published a few times in travel magazines.

Malaysia, Borneo, 2002

A stop in Los Angeles to break the long flight and did a 35-mile-long bike trip to Will Rogers Beach.

A 14-hour flight to Taipei and then 5 more hours to Kuala Lumpur and then again 2 more hours to Kuching, Borneo. A lot of changing planes and no rest.

On the last flight I met all my new travel companions.

By now I had my third chicken dinner, getting tired of flying and Airplane food. All flights had the same dessert: Sago pudding, tasted like tapioca.

There are many "Bills" in the group and almost everybody looks grumpy, must be the long flights.

In Kuala Lumpur we all went to the wrong gate and had to walk a long way back to the new gate. But good exercise to stretch our legs.

There is one Lady in our group so full of jewelry I think she has a hard time moving with all the weight. She is attracting everybody's looks.

Arrival in Kuching, we were given a lecture with slides which was stupid because as I looked around everybody was nodding off. We all needed a short rest.

The dinner was so spiced that I could not eat much and stuck to the desserts.

Noticed in the Hilton Hotel store a lot of face creams were for sale. But all had ingredients for whitening the skin.

My Hilton Hotel room view is beautiful. The River views! I can see the Fort Margherita named after Charles Brooke's wife explanation follows, the Hotel is the most elegant place.

Today we met at 9am for our walk but first breakfast. Lots of yoghurt and Donuts! Donuts seem to be a national food. I am getting used to living in 5star Hotels, it is a big luxury.

It is raining, no it pours. That is the reason why it is so green here. I always read about the Kalimantan mold in houses and how it destroys things fast. With so much water around and rain!

The bus ride to the Cultural Center was interesting. Many big houses, they are Palaces!

As the guide told us most of them belonged to somebody related to the President. In 1841 an English man James Booke was the ruler of Sarawak and that is why so much influence of English architecture is there. His Palace the Astana was across the Hilton for my view, it was built in 1870 as a bridal gift for his wife Margaret.

The streets are very clean, and a sign said no drinking or doping, a death sentence.

At the Cultural center one got to see every tribe in longhouses. A lot of dried up heads, (shrunken)? and a warm welcome.

Evening dinner was noodle soup for me. Too much chili is used in all the other food. But good Beer.

February 26th

Today to Baku Natl. Park by boat. It is a one-hour drive in pouring rain. Baku is one of the best places in Sarawak to see wildlife in natural surroundings. And when we got there the tide was so low all boats were stuck. Waited 3 hours for the tide to come up.

I did not like the boat ride. It is an open sea voyage, but it was our only choice to Baku. The waves were high and a very rough sea.

But on arrival it was worth it. The bizarre long nosed proboscis monkey's, Lizards and some interesting birds. Tropical mangrove and swamp vegetation. Watched Macaques Monkeys digging for clams. There was time to hike and swim before returning to Kuching. And did I sweat.

Back at the Hotel for cleaning up and Dinner. It is a very sedate group of tourists. Nobody is into Adventure when I try to suggest of doing something exciting.

Going to Batang Ai Longhouse Resort. We stopped in Serian and I bought Bananas and tried to sleep on the Bus.

What a beautiful country. We arrived at a big Dam in Iban country with a beautiful lake. There we had to catch another Ferry which took us to the Longhouse Resort. It is enormous. So big and secluded in the trees. It was built in 1995.

There are no tourists except us. This great Longhouse is almost empty. The Resort is built on 20foot high stilts. I enjoyed the warm pool and a beautiful Buffet Dinner. Always a long walk inside to get anywhere. And one could always feel the swaying of the building.

A beautiful sunset.

At the community center we had to see a movie about Orang Utans. As we watched the lights kept getting switched on and off. Then I saw a hand of an Orang Utan playing with the switch. It was a funny moment for all of us. And then to bed because our morning walk starts at 6:15am.

To see sunrise and listen to the Birds. We are in the middle of a jungle. And the employees are the "old" headhunters of Borneo.

Then we went to visit an Iban Longhouse village. First into a very slim boat and it poured rain again, and then climb up a slimy hill to a school. There are 7 Longhouses in the village with 106 children. Each Longhouse contains about 40 people and has one chief. Longhouses are built high on stilts about 50 feet high. Very rickety feeling since the buildings do sway and one can hear and feel every move. Looking for a toilet was fun. It is about 30 feet up in the building. A little room with a board and a hole and one could look down. Pigs were looking up. Waiting for our dump.

There was no furniture at all in the Longhouse. I had difficulties to sit on the floor. Never know what to do with my legs.

But the children must stay in the School longhouse and get to go home only on weekends. I gave every child a pen which I acquired from my Post office. All behaved so good. Clean. No runny noses and healthy looking. When the teacher asked them in front of us what their ambition was: 8 out of 10 wanted to join the police force. English is mandatory even in the jungle.

So what will you do with such educated children? Not one wanted to be a farmer or hunter or fisherman or even work in the Hotel.

On our Nature walk I got to know of plants and trees used into medicines. Climbing along trails and shaky bridges made of hemlock way up in trees.

Back to the Hotel. A pool to relax and Ibanfood for Dinner.

Did not like leaving for Kuching because this Resort we are staying is so peaceful and beautiful. Wonder if tourists will come again, they need tourist to keep up the Resort. I was told it is all about September 11.

This is an Islam country mostly. But in the city the natives are Christians and other small religion.

Stopped for Lunch in Lachau. I have a very sore throat and bought some pills called strepsils. They helped but now in Kuching I have awfully bad pains in my Stomach. Wonder what brought that on? Since I avoided all sharp food. And no beans. Anyway 2 Pepto Bismol and Gaviscon helped a little. 1 Prelosix now and still paining.

Am I going to die? All these thoughts go through my mind. Could it be a hernia? A bad night for me, so much pain. I took all the medicines

I had. Cepacol, Naproxin, Mylanta. Still not much better.

Today from Kuching to Kota Kinabala. It is very hot here now and it looks like everybody has stomach trouble.

Everybody is visiting the Pharmacia.

One day to see the city. Walking up to Signal Hill for a panoramic view. Visit some Toh Tze Chinese Temple.

I am eating a little, but we have to get on another flight to Sandakan.

Sandakan

At the Renaissance Hotel. An incredibly beautiful place built into the hillside in the jungle.

Tried to swim but so many men are sitting around the pool and staring.

But I could eat some of the barbecue.

Bill from N.Y had to have a doctor and now feels better. Got a lot of medicine. 50% of our tour members are sick.

My room is beautiful.

A very good sleep but a runny nose now. Outside it is a real jungle. Wonder how they keep the mold away. There is a little creek running along next to our Hotel, but it is full with plastic bags! Even the Beach a little further is full of plastic bags.

Sepilok Orangutan Rehabilitation Centre is next. What a place. It is all worth just getting here.

There are Orang Utans walking around or in trees. We cannot touch them but they are allowed to touch us, they just walk by and quickly touch us. They are just as nosy to meet us as we are. Very smart animals as I could see.

Then we fed the Orang Utans in the woods with sugarcane and Bananas. All of them are free to go and some are released long time ago but still come for a good snack.

These large apes-man's closest relative is gentle and highly intelligent. Called "Wild Man of Borneo too". To avoid spreading disease, touching the animals is not permitted. However, one can meet some of mature ones hanging around the Registration center because they are fond of human company.

All the trees have some Orang Utans climbing around and are happy because of the feeding stations provided. There was one Macaque between getting his fill too.

Back at the Hotel I enjoyed the pool and a good lunch. Our city tour to Kampang was interesting. It sits over the water on stilts.

Nearby is an Australian Memorial from the second World War. Out of 3000 prisoners only 6 survived in this camp.

We have had quite a few accidents of people falling. Now Bill fell and does not look good.

Still all of us are again at dinner which was very good. Shrimps with lots of coconut jelly.

Flying now to Kota Kinabala 40min. Flight.

We are moving from places fast and it is very well organized. By Bus now to the Center of the skulls! Old Skulls!

The people here believe in spirits, everything evolves around it. So after the bodies have dried up at the cemetery, the skulls are collected to have the ancestors nearby.

And it is hot.

The Hotel Sutera is the finest yet. So big and elaborate built. Many pools and a wonderful Beach. But Sea nettles are out there, too bad. So, I canceled my snorkeling tour. I know I will get stung by them. I will vegetate by the pools.

There are 16 Restaurants. What a choice.

Today instead of sitting by the pool it is off by Ferry to Sapi Island. A very beautiful spot. But again, no swimming in the Ocean, sea nettles. They are huge and look mean. Wish I would have known that they do not touch humans. Nobody told us anything about them.

Walked around the Island and saw Monkeys who tried to steal my pack. When I shooed them, some showed me their teeth.

This afternoon we all tried parasailing. Talked Lina to be my partner in the tandem.

Going up was exiting, upon looking down and seeing the mass of huge jellyfish we prayed that our tandem would not fall into the sea.

Then Pete went up and to our horror his boat engine stalled and he landed in the sea. No pain from jellyfish and I was told now they do not sting.

The Air-condition is very high one cannot set it warmer and I am glad having a Balcony to get the fresh air.

Went again to a Kampung(town) on stilts for a fish Restaurant. All fish are still alive till the last moment before cooking. The food is very bland, no spices had been used.

I liked the cooking in Coconut milk and will use it now more often. Nee goring: fried noodles, bean sprouts, eggs, prawns, shrimp, chicken, garlic, sautéed all, add onion.

Now to Kuala Lumpur 6

Our group has been good. Lots of fun. I noticed no cattle or Beef in the store for sale. Mostly chicken.

I love Kuala Lumpur, it is a beautiful easy walking city. 3 million people and 2 million of them are foreign workers keeping this place beautiful. Supposed to be no unemployment here.

Women have no worries being assaulted. There is a strong death penalty for that.

60% is middle class so no real poor people. No slums, no squatters.

Went walking all over and ended up in Chinatown. Bought 2 egg cups there, old. $2 each.

Visited the Kuala Towers, so impressive and a quite different style of building. Floor after floor is shopping and food courts. The sky bridge is 58.4m wide. 170m up. And that is scary so high.

Malaysians love to shop. And I had a great duck soup Thai style. On my way home a car went out of control and jumped the sidewalk. Missed me by inches.

Today a surprise at breakfast. Leberkaese! Real German. It was delicious and with fantastic bread I loved it. There was even ice-cream for breakfast. Many choices in Buffet style.

Trip to Selagong Pewter Factory. I have been collecting their eggcups for years and found it interesting to see it all done right there. $14 each. More then what I paid in the USA.

Toured a batik factory. Expensive to buy.

And now to the Batu Caves. Instead down it is up. 272 steps great exercise. Inside are many Hindu Temples and lots of Monkeys. It is an exceedingly popular tourist attraction.

Another stop at a rubber farm. Was interesting how so much rubber juice comes out of a tree and seeing the processing.

Always keeping my eyes out for fresh coconuts to drink. Its jelly like flesh, its sweet and cool and is one of my favorites.

Stopped at the greatest Bird park. 5000 Birds are living there. It is like a jungle in the middle of the City. Everything is very well taken care off. It is 3 acres and covered by a mesh roof so no Bird gets eaten. Almost all Birds are free and can fly anywhere. Had a fresh Coconut for a snack again. Love the milk and white jelly.

My Taxi driver wanted to hear all about Sept. 11. It was fresh on everybody's minds. He was explaining that there is a difference in Muslim and the Arab Muslims. He tried to explain to me the fanatic style of the Arabs.

The Iraqi Embassy in K.L. is next door to the USA Embassy, strange. Why?

Went to a Dinner Restaurant which used to be the Parliament Building. Then the Ministry residence and now a cultural Center and Restaurant.

Walking around tonight by the Hotel, it gave me more insight how clean and safe the country is. The Hotel is all black marble, Chrystal chandeliers and flowers.

The country is doing well especially with the cleanliness.

Singapore is first in cleanness Brisbane second, and Kuala Lumpur 3rd.

I noticed all over K.L. little arrows on walls or posts. After asking I found out this is the sign to Mecca. And when it is time to pray it is helpful to the people.

Walking back alone at night to the Hotel was very romantic. All the trees and streets transform into a veritable wonderland of lights at night. Earning its name "Garden City of lights" and the towers are lit beautiful. Arriving at 10pm in the Hotel and finding a string Quartet playing beautiful classical music.

Never did I see a cow or pig or Horse either tied up or free. Usually all are by the Longhouses on the Islands.

Lucky me today. On arriving at the Airport, I was not in the computer. A lot of arguing and getting personal together what to do with me. Got a better seat this way, before I had in Economy and now in Business class.

But we are delayed already 2 hours. Mechanical problems. Fixed it finally. No Air-condition on the plane.

But we made it home.

Scandinavia, September 15th, 2002
Finland, Denmark, Sweden, Norway and Russia,
St. Petersburg

Kevin and I are flying now to Scandinavia first. Leaving the Farm in August is very hard it is harvest time, much to do, haying is the most important time now, but far lands are calling, and we are read.

So far, our Air-plane is a disaster. It broke down before we even left the airport, unloaded everything and had to rebook from BWI to Dulles Airport in Virginia. Taking a Taxi at rush hour! The Driver tried very hard to get us there. The Taxi was paid by the Airline.

A rude person from British Air told us all planes are full as we arrived in Dulles. Standby now. Got on but this plane had a broken air-condition. Mechanics now are at work trying to fix it. We still have patience.

Finally, a long flight and we arrived in London and since we are delayed, we missed connections to Helsinki.

Maybe we will get to Helsinki eventuel.

Well, we made it!! We are in Helsinki!

Our group is together, 44 people. It is scary so many, but Gate-1, the Tour organizer is particularly good.

It is very hot here, unusual. Not any places with Air-condition, we are sweating a lot. So, we walked and stayed outdoors. Helsinki is beautiful and full of flowers. Long days and nights with light in the sky. It is different in the winter it is 20 below zero.

Many drunks are sitting around the parks and streets, and they leave a lot of garbage lying. I do like the cobblestone streets. Saw the Temppeliaukio Church which was carved out of solid Rock.

The beautiful Scandia Grand Marina Hotel used to be a warehouse from the 17th century. Old beams in our room, naturally I knocked my head last night.

Copenhagen, Denmark, Saturday 17th

It is hot here too and this late at night. And again, Air-condition in a few places only.

Went right away to the fabled Tivoli Gardens. It is the world's oldest theme park which had inspired Walt Disney to create Disney world. It is open since 1843. Delicious street food, amusement rides and all over the twinkling lights. A wonderful old-world setting. Since it was Saturday everybody was out drinking. And it was Gay pride day too. Watched the midnight fireworks.

Admiral Hotel is hot. Sleeping is difficult, no fan no air.

But a very good breakfast and off to see the sights of Copenhagen. We do enjoy the group.

Kevin and I went to visit friends in Sweden, which was taking a 550 Bus, then the train, then the Ferry to Sweden.

Our friends picked us up to go to their country home. A big Farm with lots of Farm Animals. We could do some hiking since the sun never goes down at that time of year.

And return trip to Copenhagen.

Sightseeing and visiting the Rosenborg Palace which holds the danish Crown Jewels. To see Hans Christian Anderson famous Little Mermaid, Christiansborg Palace-seat of Parliament.

But first we took a canal boat trip and stopped at Amalienburg Castle for the changing of the Guard.

One of the Lady's on our tour fell and she looks pretty bad since she hit her face. And I again hit my head on the beams in our room.

People use for transportation mostly bikes. There are very few cars.

Evening leave on the BIG Ferry to Oslo Norway.

The big "Pearl of Scandinavia" was awaiting us. 11 stories high Ferry. We got an outside Cabin finally I had to change very nice. I need a window even if it is all night.

Great Food on Board I only ate desserts. Love them.

Kevin got a bottle of Champagne and we celebrated "Our first Cruise". This Ferry is big!

There are 10 Restaurants, 4 Bars, 2 Discos, 1 Nightclub on board. And a big supermarket which was packed.

We did not spend much time in our Cabin. Only 3 hours! And I looked out a lot because of the full moon.

Morning looking now at the Long Fjord near Oslo. The weather is great.

Oslo

By Bus through Oslo to the Rica Grand Hotel except our luggage was forgotten at the pier. Luckily it was found later on.

Taking a Ferry to the Viking Island, lots of History there. There are Viking ships preserved in perfect shape. They were buried in the mud and are exhibited now in an air-controlled room.

Stopped at a Horse store but all was nice to look at, too expensive.

We are told every Restaurant is good. Yes, and expensive. The living standard here is very high.

Traveled to Vigeland Sculpture Park, a strange place. City Hall, the Waterfront, to the top of Holmenkollen Ski Jump which was an Olympic site and again lots to see there.

It is another beautiful town, and the suburbs have many wooden villas, which are painted white and surrounded by fruit trees.

In the market vegetables are scarce not as important but lots of fish is eaten.

Today to Balestrand. A long drive through beautiful Norway's Fjord countryside with some of the most breathtaking scenery. Left at 8am and arrived at 5pm. We stopped a lot. The Bus went along many small Roads, tunnels, onto a Ferry at Fordness, off the Ferry and again on the north side on Norway's longest Fjord. Sognefjord. Then winding Roads again. Saw one moose. Maybe a Reindeer herd? And we ate a lot of good food.

Balestrand

In Balestrand we are in a 100-year-old Kvikne Hotel, most beautiful. Balestrand is an art village. With many Galleries. To get some exercise Kevin and I went rowing for one hour on the lake. And a big smorgasbord for Dinner. There goes the exercise. But since it was still daylight at 10pm again a nice long hike helped.

Kaiser Wilhelm of Germany had his ship "Scharenhorst" docked here. There is a big Statue of Fridjof. It was given by Kaiser Wilhelm. Who is Fridjof? Balestrand was Kaiser Wilhelms favorite Vacation place.

Now from Balestrand to Jostedalsbreen. Starting out by Ferry through the Fjord country, getting then on our Bus again through Mundal, a pretty little town. Walter Mondale's Ancestors home. Passing through the Stalheim Canyon to Gudvangen.

The Glacier Museum was next and a climb onto the Glacier too. Shrinking 6 feet a day, very sad looking. In a few years there will be no water for the lake.

Another long drive through more beautiful country. With stops for Lunch, food is very good. Had Norway porridge soup: Yoghurt, Butter and other ingredients all good.

Everything is very expensive, so we used most of our money on food. One Beer was average $6 or $7 a small glass.

Sandwich, soup, coffee or juice $20!

Going by Boat, Ferry, train, slow train, Bus to Flam Mt. Railway. Ferry stopped in Vangsnes were we got on the Bus and then by Boat for 2 hours, landing in Flam. There we hiked and ate again.

Then by the famous Flam Mountain Railway for an unforgettable ride descending 2.600 feet and passing waterfalls and Mountains. It was a spectacular trip. The train must climb the steepest tracks. It was a major challenge to build the track with so many tunnels and steep slopes and round sharp bends.

In Myrdal we changed to an express train to Voss and then by Bus to Bergen.

It all sounds complicated, but it was all fun and we had the best time.

On arrival in Bergen found out our Hotel Admiral had broken water pipes and were told not to bathe...what?????

As sweaty we all were.

Bergen is beautiful and very hot. Our room was small and as usual no air or fan. Not much sleep this night.

Understaffed Hotel and food was bad. Even the coffee machine was broken!!! And irritated tourists.

It does not bother me, things happen. We went to the Market and had good food there. It is an old town 900 years old, so maybe the pipes are that old too.

It had a big fish market too. Saw for the first time a Monkfish for sale. Disgusting looking fish. Flat and big eyes with an Antenna hanging off its head. It is to lure fish into his mouth.

There was Whale meat for sale. Norway is one of the country's not stopping to kill Whales.

The city is old and big and old Germanic Buildings, all of them are restored.

Trip with the Funicular to the top of a mountain and to our surprise big trolls, statues, awaited us. Since it was so hot, we decided to walk down.

Stockholm

A very late arrival. Hoping for some air-condition in the Scandic Park Hotel. None and no fan and it is very warm. Windows do not open. Found a fan and plucked it in hoping to get relief. It was a heater. Hotel is full and we are having another bad night.

Today we got another room with air-condition. The staff is very sourly.

Stockholm is built on 14 Islands and is from the 13th century.

A nice city tour, especially the City house which was so elaborate built in 1920. That is the place for presentation of the Nobel price every year.

Had to see the Pippi Langstrumpf Museum. Parked in front, many baby strollers. Looked so funny. After talking to some Mother, we were told that is the place to come with children. I grew up reading her stories and of her dreams. How she painted her old white Horse with black dots to have a Knappstrupp Horse. A Knappstrupp is an old breed. I have a replica in my house now. Made of wood. 200years old.

Then there was the Vaser Museum to see the Viking ship which sank on its maiden voyage in 1628. Interesting. We rented bicycles and toured quite a few miles.

Our farewell Dinner was ok. Had met a few couples and made a few friends.

Stockholm to Helsinki, 25th

Onto another ferry "Symphony". About 3:30pm we left for Helsinki. We slept good on the ship Silja Line. Kevin snored and that is bad for me. Makes me cranky. It was again a big ship! 2600 passengers but only 1600 were on board. We upgraded for $50 to a big room with window. There is a 6 story Atrium and Movie house, Disco and supermarket and again full of shoppers.

Rented bikes in Helsinki and biked to Summer Island. It was warm here too. And then walked to the old town (Stamla), to listen to good music performed by the soldiers Band. Police was in force on their Horses.

Great Breakfast, Good bread!

Outside our Hotel a lot of Gypsy Women mingling around. They come from Russia to Finland and get social money care and food. And then go back wherever they came from.

St. Petersburg, Russia

A luxury Bus to St. Petersburg. 2 Drivers and a Russian guide Natascha.

Our first stop is Vyborg for lunch. A dead town. There is nobody walking around. It is all falling apart. The buildings look terrible. I wonder were the food came from for our lunch.

St. Petersburg, 28th. The Venice of the North

It was my third visit to St. Petersburg, and I felt a little like coming home. We arrived late at night and our Pribaltiskaya Hotel was a Monster Hotel built just for tourist and way out in the country. At that time tourists had to stay there with tour groups. We took a taxi that late to see some of the nightlife in St. Petersburg.

I had on my last trip a nice Dinner on a Barge Boat. Tied on the

Canal. So that is where we went and had again great food. Salad 2 Kielbasa 1 Coffee and bread 1 wine and beer and all for $14.

St. Petersburg is great city. It was founded in 1703 by Peter the Great.

Our windows at the Hotel did not open except one inch and it is hot. We just have not had much luck with our rooms. But then again, the Breakfast was very good and we left on our first tour very early.

There are many Churches to see, again the Hermitage! St. Isaac Cathedral. The Churches at that time are slowly opened again for services. We have a particularly good tour guide too. Her name is Valery.

Walking around we met a nice young Russian couple who just got married and invited us to celebrate with them. Pure Vodka we drunk, and it is only morning.

And for the evening we went to see "Swan Lake". It was beautiful and the costumes and the Dancers, all excellent. I did miss the Violin I loved a few years ago; it was a special solo. I really enjoyed showing Kevin all the places I had been too.

Anyway, our Hotel is so huge that one needs a map. I finally found the pizza place I was told, on the fourth floor and had a late supper at midnight there.

Our beds are not comfortable. Sheets are rough like sandpaper and the pillows are like Rocks. A sleeping pill was needed.

Today is a walking day. All the way to the old Bridge but it was closed and so back to the Hermitage Bridge. On the way there we stopped at the Market by the Church "Of the spilled blood" and bought my favorite Romanov Dishes. A set for 6 persons. And onto Kevin's back in the Knapsack. He carried it all day.

A walk now to Peter and Paul's Fortress. Met an Old Army man, who spoke good English and was telling us very proudly his life story; we spend many hours there and took a taxi to the Hotel back. By now the weight of the dishes felt like 100 pounds to Kevin.

At 7pm we went to a Folklore show, which was beautiful, in the Alexander Palace.

The palace is still beautiful one can see the splendor of the 1900s. 1917 was the Revolution and many of the buildings just sat empty for many years.

To Dinner to a Restaurant called 1913 with live music and very good food.

Chicken Kiev, salad, dessert: 2 baked apples filled with nuts and Raisins.

Coffee and tea all at 10:30pm.

Then a quick ride to the "Church of the painters and Artists". Bought an oil painting with my favorite scene. A troika Scene, 3 Horses pulling the sled.

Again, it is 12pm. We never get to bed early it is just too much to see.

Today to the town Pushkin to visit the impressive Catherine Palace. It is so large and so long and one room almost connects with the other room like a mirror image.

The Palace is full of art masterpieces. The Amber room was just half completed. There is a story about the German's taking all the Amber of the walls and transported it to Germany. But it was never found. (It was replaced to its splendor again).

It is still hot and smoky, somewhere are fires burning and difficult to breathe.

Pushkin town was long time ago Ocaristown. In 1917 it changed to the city of children. 1936 to Pushkin after the poet who lived there. It is beautiful and fully restored. The German Army burned it in the 2nd war. But it was rebuilt again to its old looks.

The old Imperial Train Station is now a Restaurant, we ate. Salad, Beef stroganoff, Blini pancakes and coffee.

Catching a flight to St. Petersburg for a return home.

Helsinki

There was a light rain but not enough for the parched country. Many trees are drying up and flowers are dying. Nobody is watering anything with so much water around why not?

Staying in the Scandic Hotel for the last night.

A full flight back to USA. The security in N.Y. is horrible. Nobody speaks English at the Airport I guess we have to learn Spanish, and personal are very rude.

Galapagos, Ecuador, November 2002

Petra, my daughter, and I are traveling to a faraway place we have dreamed about: The Galapagos Islands.

But first we have to fly south and change many airplanes again. From Miami flying to Quito, Ecuador.

Quito is at a very high Altitude of 7000 feet and I can feel it, my ears hurt, my head hurts. I drink Chamomile tea, drank Matte tea and taking every pill to relieve my head. I just feel lousy.

The Hotel Dann Carlton is beautiful we have something like a condo, but I am lying awake. Petra sleeps.

A new day and a good Breakfast and we are going to see it all. Went by long taxi to the Equator line, interesting. It is called the middle of the world monument. Stand astride of the Equator, with one foot on each hemisphere. History there. The Valley is very dry and was told it never rains here only the fog catches water. So many active Volcanos all around. One blew up 2 weeks ago and the ashes are still on plants and in the air.

Quito is quite unlike any other city in the world. Spanish colonial architecture and art, narrow cobblestone street, red tiled roofs.

And the Old town. Never saw a cleaner city in South America. Many street cleaners are around picking up any stray garbage. Saw the Government Palace with lots of Guards around. The Cathedral, the convento of San Diego and we stopped at many other 16th and 17th century Churches.

Then we went up to the Panecillo (Hill) with the Virgin of Quito and there it rained.

At dinner I finally got so tired that I fell asleep at the table. It was again the Altitude.

Quito is in a frenzy of Celebration for two weeks. Music one can hear and very loud. Never found out why.

Chiva trucks drive around fully loaded with happy people. I guess it was the visit of Chavez from Peru and Fidel Castro and Petra and me.

Saturday, and it is raining hard. Still there are parties in the park.

We are going to Otavalo, the Indian Market, it is a 3-hour drive. It is one of the most popular destinations in Ecuador, a magical land of lakes, mountains and terraced farmlands. We stopped at a few places. It is a very green country I guess with so much rain.

Otavalo was surprising. The market dates to pre-Inca times and is famous for its textiles. Many sellers and a lot of good things are for sale. The ladies wore the native dress and looked beautiful. They are small people. Maybe that is why Women wear the Bowler hats to make them taller. Sometimes 2 hats were worn.

Today we leave for the Galapagos Islands at 5am. First to Guadequil on an awfully bad flight. My ears felt like they would explode. Many people complained on the Plane and the Stewardess went to the Pilots and somehow it was better afterwards.

Changing planes to Baltra. Baltras landing strip was built by American servicemen in World War II. It is now an Ecuadorian naval base. A very dry Island and then by small Boat to the big ship "Ambassador ". With 65 passengers on board. It felt like a smaller version of a Cruise liner. 75 crew members.

Lunch was excellent but we got the second worst room on the ship. Small. We got rid of all the furniture except our beds and we could finally turn around in our room. The ship was full, and no change expected. Air condition was broken, and windows did not open. The ship was built in 1958 and needs an overhaul.

And then the fire alarm went off to test us for emergency, naturally

Petra was in the bathroom.

Then we were off.

We had a rough landing onto the Island Leon Dormido by small boat but still it is unbelievable to see the animals so tame. One has to watch out because in the sand the seals are resting one almost steps on them. Or the big masked boobies and frigate birds they do not move.

Walked four hours and it was tiring because the ground is not all sand, many rocks and big boulders to climb over.

The return to the ship was again very rough. The sea became rough with big waves.

A quick stop at North Seymour Island. We are fascinated by the red crabs called "Sally light foot". They are all over the Island and not scared at all.

Had my gin and tonic and try to relax for Dinner.

Our toilet got fixed but still no air condition. Somehow our beds are made up neatly in this tight space. One wonders how the maids do it.

Dinner was excellent. Forgot our Towels for the next day's Beach tour. Did we need them! It was so cold. The water is ice cold.

Waking up early for breakfast is very good. And at 8am to a wet landing on Cerro Brujo to swim with the sea lions. This time I was dressed warm.

I wish the waves would stop. I am trying to snorkel, but the water is so cold. It does not stop Petra. In the water the seals are waiting and lots of fish. They hope to have playmates and enjoy swimming with humans. I did not like it when one of the big bull seals came remarkably close. But he only was looking into my eyes. None of the animals are afraid; we are like landscape to them.

A quick shower on board to get warm again and breakfast for a second time today.

Anker's aweigh and another Island to be seen. Kicker Rock was passed. Not for landing. But it is a strange looking Rock.

A great lunch and a nice nap for me.

Isla Espanola was quite different. So many animals! And it looked pretty crowded they were all bickering for space.

The trails we walked on, are very rocky and dangerous to walk. Very uneven terrain throughout the Galapagos. Sure enough a few injured legs. People kept slipping off the rocks. The seals were lying in the few places were was sand and one could not disturb them but had to find a way around them.

On board that evening was dancing and a very good Dinner. Spinach soup, salad, only my steak was like roadkill. But I did not come to eat steak.

Next stop at Santa Cruz Island to visit the Darwin Research Station. To see the Giant tortoises and one called Lonesome George who is supposed to be 100 years old or older. Time spent there was too short. We hoped to stay and see more. There is a small town called Puerto Ayora which was nice to walk through.

The next spot to see is Cerro Dragon which means Dragon Hill. Many Endemic land Iguanas are there. Orange yellow with large spines along their backs. On this Island the arid landscape of gigantic prickly pear cacti, up to forty feet tall. The Islands cliffs are excellent for viewing the swallowtails and red-billed tropic birds. It should have longer, so much to see.

Then it was back to Quito and USA.

Thailand, Cambodia and Laos, October 2003

A tour trip now again with Kevin. Not backpacking but in 5star Hotels.

Trying to read direction in their language is not possible but somebody will always reach out and with a big smile help.

It is my second time in Bangkok, and it is very different now. Much more cosmopolitan and very vibrant. It is a tourist dream and a shoppers paradise.

Visiting now the Grand Palace complex home of the Royal family, the legendary Emerald Buddha in Wat Phra Keo and the enormous Reclining Buddha in Wat Po near the Chao Phraya River.

Taking a long-tail boat ride on the canals of Bangkok, eating fruit from vendors and drinking fresh coconut juice.

Entertainment at the Hotel in the evening was good.

Today we are going to experience the "The Trans-River Kwai Death Railway ". Everybody has seen the Movie or read the books. It is a sad place to see from World War II. Work was started in 1942 by the Prisoners of War, 250 miles in one year! Most of it through dense jungle. 16 000 Prisoners died and many other laborers of different countries.

The famous Bridge on the River Kwai is fascinating. I can see in my dreams all the action there. It was good to have read and seen the Movie before.

And we are sitting now in the train with first class service. Afternoon tea. By the end of the line we took an Elephant further up to the mountain Station.

To visit now Ayutthaya, the fabled ancient capital of Siam. Magnificent ruins of temples, palaces and crumbling fortresses provide testimony.

In the town of Lop Buri a short stop. There are so many Monkeys all over and everybody has the windows barricaded. Monkeys are trying to get into everything. A reverse, they try anything to get into the houses.

Another stop in Phitsanulok to see Thailands most beautiful Buddha image. The Statue was cast in 1357.

In the evening we took a Tuk-Tuk, a 3-wheeled open air-taxi within the city and stopped at the night market. Kevin had this great idea to eat anything offered. Worms! Deep-fried Grasshoppers! Scorpion's, Roaches. He tested them all.

He did not get sick. Why not, his stomach is delicate.

The next day we rented bicycles and had a guide to show us more and came to Sukhothai. Again, many stone temples. Watching farmers threshing rice. Stopped at a pineapple farm and tasted pineapples and papayas. A visit to a Lepra Village was new to us. Still segregated from other people.

We are now at the Golden Triangle. It means where the borders of Thailand, Laos and Myanmar meet. Lampang is in the middle, it is known for the Burmese style of temples. And a young Elephant training School.

The surrounding mountains and forests are home to the many colorful mountain tribes of the north such as Lisu, Lahu, Yao and Karen.

Laos

A boat trip on the River to Laos. The people we saw from the River looked extremely poor. It is not a prospering country. Our boat trip was too short to get any ideas about Laos really, but at a short stop for a cold drink I noticed there was not much for sale and no cold drinks anyway. There was no electric.

Back in Thailand again and more to see.

In Chiang Rai which is bordered by Burma is the gateway to meet hill tribes. A side trip to the Burmese border was interesting. The Border was very open, and we recrossed, many Burmese people were begging for food. One could buy Burmese Jewelry and I did find a beautiful Ruby ring.

Staying at the Rimkok Resort Hotel was luxury!

Next day our transportation was waiting to go to the Karen tribe. Known for their women. It was a shock to see the old ladies with the betelnut juice running down their faces. They are very addicted to it.

And then meeting the young Karen women with the golden bangles around their necks! I wondered how they all had such long necks. It is not that. The weight of all the metal pulls down the shoulders and makes the neck longer. Horrible. A very primitive life. And still all had smiling faces.

So many villages to visit and all had different dialects and costumes.

Stopped at the village of Wiang Pa Pao Chiangrai. The Restaurant was called Cabbages and Condoms. The owner is pushing condoms and distributes them for free. His motto at the Restaurant is "Our food is guaranteed not to cause pregnancy".

We have arrived at Chiang Mai the principal city in the north. Some call it the "Rose of the north". Known for its handicrafts it is again a shopper's paradise. For silk, laureate, silver and the famous hand painted umbrellas.

Trying to do a traditional Khantoke dinner sitting on the floor with cushions and watching the graceful Thai dancers perform their dance. I had to switch to a chair.

Next day we went to an Orchid farm to learn more about How to grow them and keep them alive.

Today to the Elephant training center at Ta Yaak Village. For many hours we watched the training.

The young Elephants learn to paint which keeps them occupied. Was interesting how "our" painting was done.

Then we rode up the Mountain on a large Elephant. Room for us three. He sure was sure footed because the trail was very slick.

Almost every place like Buildings or Restaurant had a sign: No Durian. It is a very good tasting fruit. But it stinks like something very dead.

We rented bicycles with a very good guide again. We passed by a group of Musicians in the park who either were blind or lost a part of their body. All had stepped on mines in Laos.

A flight now to Cambodia, November 4, 2003

Checking into our Princess Angkor Hotel in Siem Reap.

Getting our passports done for entry tickets to see all the sights. The Temples of Angkor. The Khmer Empire which was abandoned in 1431 following by the Thai kingdom.

There is so much to see and too long to describe all of it. Every Temple or building is a treasure. Miles of archaeological Buildings and then Angkor Wat!!!! It would take too long to describe it.

We took an Elephant to some of the sights. And walked right by a "Terrace of the Elephants" from the late 12th century. Carved Elephants and giant garudas adorn the wall.

At night we went to a Restaurant which served great food and a beautiful Cambodian traditional show. Curries are the special and lots of Rice.

The next day we went to an organized concert by a group of talented people who lost their limbs in the war or on mines. Which still happens to this day. But not at Angkor Wat, they have been cleared there. But beware of mines if you decide to go off the beaten tracks.

There are Mosquitos which represent danger, and one is warned to wear long sleeves, dengue fever is easy to get from them.

Visiting the Ta Prohm monastic complex, it is very overgrown. Intentionally left unrestored, massive fig and silk-cotton trees grow from the towers and corridors. Flocks of noisy parrots' flit from tree to tree adding to the jungle atmosphere. And many movies have been made here too.

And again, a small group of men playing music, except none had legs or some lost hands too.

For a sunset view we climbed Phom Bakeng. From the top, views over the jungle and Angkor Wat towers are unequalled.

Our next trip to Tonle Sap and a stop at a market that was not our kind of food. Mountains of snakes for sale. That's for dinner.

Tonle Sap called the Great Lake, is one of the largest freshwater lakes in the world. Floating fishing villages dot the semi-submerged forest. When the water recedes in the dry season people tow their houseboats further out.

Dominican Republic, October 2003

Another trip with Petra for a good rest we both need it. At the Sunscape Casa Del Mar we enjoyed our time. It was beautiful, pristine Beaches. Food was very good, and we feasted on all the fruit.

I went diving to Isla Catalina. And we did visit Casa de Campo. The most exclusive residential area in the Dominican Republic.

Our room had the most beautiful view too. We had many choices of Restaurants and each served fantastic food.

One could walk off many calories on the trail to the little village down the road called Bayahibe.

The economy has been built on agriculture, sugar, coffee, tobacco and cacao. Mining is especially important too. There is a big gold mine Pueblo Viejo in the Cibao valley, it is the world's largest open pit gold mine.

Papua New Guinea, August 2, 2004

With a stop in Brisbane, Australia.

I will never forget this trip. A trip to the unknown. It was exceedingly difficult to arrange this trip. Very few people go to P.N.G.

Over the internet I found a person living in Port Moresby and advertising Budget Tours. Benjamin was his name. They go by first name only. He was very convincing in arranging everything and I sent my money to his Bank.

Itinerary was sent to me, it looked just what I wanted to do. But I went on the most dangerous and exiting trip I ever had.

Brisbane, Australia

First, I flew to Australia since only one flight goes to P.N.G. from Cairns once a day. There is no other connection to Papua New Guinea.

Delays happened and I was worried my luggage would not make it. Then once on the plane were I had a reserved seat, had to get rid of a man sitting in my seat already, he refused to move ahh...

From Dallas USA to Auckland? New Zealand. Why was that not on the schedule? Never found out why we flew to New Zealand first.

Brisbane, Australia next.

There my good friends Lola and Timocy awaited me for a short visit.

Their homestead was an old Queens land Style Farmhouse. Over

100 years old. It was surrounded by big old trees full of very beautiful Birds. But it is winter here and cold. Needed quite a few blankets at night. Weather is like Arizona. Sun gets very warm by noon.

Lola is cooking the best food. And even a trifle for Dinner.

Outside passion fruit is climbing like a weed all over the trees.

Went to Brisbane today and it is an old beautiful downtown full of Queensland houses. There is even a subway, we took the Bus to the Lone Pine Koala Sanctuary. 130 Koalas are there. One can carry them but then they like to pee in your lap.

There was an exhibition of heelers (dogs) working with sheep.

Stopped for fresh juice, internet and got my flight changed at Quanta's. This is still time without cell phone and very few internet places.

Friday the 6th. Slept very good, Ambien helped.

We went on a tour of the biggest Cannery in Australia. Golden Circle Factory was fun, I even got to dress like a worker there. Queensland first pineapple farm was located right downtown Brisbane.

I never knew what all was involved in such a big factory. Over 1000 employees and quite a lot of computers are used. Even the containers are manufactured here.

Visiting Redcliff, which has much history. It was the first settlement in Queensland.

Found a great diner there, Pam's Café on Nudgee Beach with a buffet lunch where I ate too much. And we needed to walk it but went shopping.

A cold morning again 40degrees. But I decided to walk today and went to Bondall Preserve and Midgee Beach. And the birds are just so beautiful. It is a very hilly part of Australia, so I got good exercise.

Every morning a big Kookaburra Bird sat outside my window. What a noisy bird but fun to watch.

Saturday 8th took the Bus to downtown Brisbane, the countryside is very dry since it has not rained for a long time.

There is Roma Park, A few years ago it was a dump and now is a beautiful place. Full of flowers and lots of strange plants.

Went on the Queen shopping street with 1200 stores. Noticed

Opals were expensive. I have many from my other trips but did compare the price and looks.

Coffee in the Café was $2.80, Beer was much cheaper. A tea $2.80!

But we had Dinner at Nudge Beach tonight again. Which was fresh fish and all for $27.00 for 3 people.

Saying goodbye to my good friends is hard. We all knew I cannot come this far maybe ever again. A tearing farewell at the Airport.

Cairns

Flying now to Cairns where I will catch my plane to P.N.G. But again I have a break for a few days. The Airplane is delayed. Staying in a very good Backpacker place. And it is warm, needed heat, great feeling. Walked the city and started to sweat fast. Cairns has changed to a tourist city. A lot of the old places I knew have gone and new Hotels have been built. The prices have gone up too. Just a takeaway dinner was $10.

The Bohemia Hotel is still nice for $60 a night.

I booked a trip to Green Island.

But breakfast was Wheaton Bix cereal. Awful but filling. It tied me over for a few hours.

Getting to Green Island was by flying Cat "Prince". Lucky, I took precaution for sickness. On arrival I rented a chair and Umbrella for $20. My money is not lasting long because things are so much more expensive.

The Glass bottom boat trip was not good since the reef is just recuperating from an assault by acid. Still big fish surrounded us all over. Big Clamshells one could see and was told they weigh about 200 pounds. Big Anemones with nemo fish! But I could not go into the water it was too cold for me.

On my way home bought a steak dinner for $7 which ones has to cook themselves on an open Barbie.("Grill" in austral Liengo. It was fun and included salad and bread.

Today I am off after I had my Wheeta Bix to ride a Horse. But noticed I had bites on my legs. Bedbugs oh no. but it turned out sand fleas from Green Island. I still think I have bedbugs. They had come out at night and attacked me.

And now my face is swollen and they bite are all over my body. Good cream is helping some. I am so allergic to the bedbugs.

My Horse ride was still good even as I itched like crazy. Saw Wallabies and a big Lizard.

Went to the steak place again to repeat my day before dinner since it was so good.

When telling people, I was going to P.N.G. I heard only negative remarks. I was told horror stories of what happened to people. Wonder what is wrong there?

Thursday 12th

Air Nuigini - what a name. At Airport check in trouble already. Very unfriendly workers.

I had reserved a seat in front and was told all booked out and they tried putting me in the last row. A lot of pleas from me and the head steward changed my seat to the front again and spoiled me with champagne.

Port Moresby

I could hardly believe I made it to Port Moresby. Two assistants of Benjamin awaited me. No Benjamin. Pankus and Lynard. Nice gentlemen. PNG is a land of contrast and surprises. There are 700 different languages. And everything is told by mouth from the old to the young. There is no written language in PGN. 30 years ago, one could not even go to visit here.

On my flight I met a woman Alix and she seemed to be going in the same direction. So, we stayed together and checked into the "Weigh Inn Hotel". To our standards very primitive. But for here, first class. Clean and big rooms with air condition.

Outside are guards walking around the Hotel. We are surrounded by a 15-foot-tall fence covered with barbed wire and I feel like in prison. But was told it was necessary.

We went for quite some miles of sightseeing in the afternoon with my Guides I had. It is a poor country, no economy, no export. And rain has not fallen which made all the surrounding fields dry. Nobody is working them. Jobs are scarce. Cannot take photos, everybody wants money for doing it.

The Restaurant at the Hotel had a nice Dinner. Prawns in Garlic sauce. And fresh fruit salad as dessert.

Friday 13th. I could not sleep very well since the bedbug bites still were very itchy. Why always me?

A good breakfast, Omelet, and lots of coffee.

Alix and I with our guides, drove around and went to cash some money and went to a Museum. It had lots of live animals outside too. Never were we alone. We always had our bodyguards next to us.

Then in the afternoon Paulos took us to the airport for our flight to Mt. Hagen. When asking where Ben was never got a good answer.

So far, all people have been friendly it is hard getting used to their faces. Their eyes are very deep-set most makes them look mad.

Mt. Hagen

Finally, in Mount Hagen at the Airport Hotel hoping to see the big festival, which is held once a year. It is called the Mount Hagen Festival. It is the biggest in P.N.G.

Many people in their native dresses walking around. Everybody from all over comes to it. The city is full of people, and some are very primitive looking. I found out of their lifestyle later. So many miles they had walked just to come to this festival to meet and greet and shop. They come by foot, by Bus if there is a road. There are no Roads in P.N.G. and one has to fly but not many people can afford it and will not enter the little planes which are used for traveling, they are scarred.

So far Alix and I are the only white folks and are getting a lot of stares. They ones who have cameras beg to have a photo taken with us. I hired a bodyguard who is like my shadow now. He is big and we feel safe.

There is a big Market, and it is a photographer's delight. Everything is sold here. Furniture to food. Most fruits and vegetable grow here. Chicken cannot be fresher since they are alive till a buyer buys it. The weather is perfect. Even Tobacco is for sale.

The women all have a Bilum on their heads. It is a crochet handmade bag and very practical worn like a headband.

Big ropes are for sale which were made from plastic bags, everything gets used. Beautiful colorful dresses are for sale all made in the villages.

But almost everybody is chewing Betel nut. Disgusting, since it turns the teeth so brown. And it is a proposed law not to allow it anymore.

The women have tattoos on their faces. They do all the hard labor. That is tradition I am told.

P.N.G is the most second country in the world with violence against women. Pakistan is first. It is a land of diversity. It is exotic looking. But it is the most expensive, least luxurious and the least efficient place in the world.

Roads are frequented by armed bandits. Many Airfields are broken up. Fares are high, schedules non-existent.

And why do tourist still come? Because it is the last place on earth to experience something so different.

To see the land of the Headhunters and Cannibals.

Still the transition from stone age and tribal warfare to the computer age will take a while.

The big currency here is a pig. A small pig is about $300 and then up.

And now I found out I will not be able to go to Tari after Mount Hagen because the tribe there decided to ask for more money for the use of the runway. So, there is a war on and no flights, all this is called a tribal dispute. Travel here is a special adventure and part of this trip is that the country is unspoiled by mass tourism and computers.

I am waiting in the double fenced Hotel compound for Ben, my guide. He did not show up. And he is not going to show up either I find out. Nobody could leave the Compound without a bodyguard. What a wasted day again.

Well at least the Dinner was good. Barramundi-fish. And Crepes with ice-cream.

And we waited. Never did anybody come or call.

Saturday 14th

A cold morning. It is like in the Andes South America at 6000 feet up. Everything was in the fog. Got ready for my festival trip at 7:30am. Names like Huliman Wigman and Asaro mudman are in my head having read stories about them. Still no guide. I am getting very worried.

By eight still nothing, no phones worked and who would I have called? I am getting mad because I was afraid, I would miss the show.

The Hotel finally arranged a ride for me on a truck. The best part I was told would be watching all the people painting their faces and I missed a lot of it.

The sound of the Kundu drums and the singsong practice gave me already the Goosebumps on arrival. Such proud people, 70 tribes have come together this week. There are 800 tribes in P.N.G.

This festival was invented by the Government to bring all the tribes together and show off in front of the Governor what they can do and pretend they are on the warpath. It is to let off steam once a year. In old times it could not happened such a get together.

Each tribe is trying to outdo each other. With painting their bodies and their outfits. The outfits are so colorful. The headdresses are made from bird feathers and what artist they are! Many months of work is involved. Knick-knacks to create mosaic of bones, insect shells, sunglasses, mottled blue snakeskin, fur scraps, cigarette foil paper, vivid feathers, bottle tops, dog teeth, crucifixes, pig tails anything.

The women have Kauri shells around their necks to show how wealthy they are. The more and the bigger and proudly showing all the finery off. Weapons can be brought but not to use. There are spears, very strange looking ones and are used in warfare mostly. And then the Axes! Some are incredibly old, and Arrows.

To watch there must have been at least 50 000 natives and a few tourists. As I said it is difficult to get here and as a tourist one has to use the little planes and there are not many.

Everybody was polite and I could make photos without any problem, just saying thank you which brought a smile to the fiercest face, tenkuy-thank you.

I wondered if it rains what would all the paint do. And all the oiled bodies how great they looked. By the way cooking oil is used for the bodies. The people have body painting and decoration, face painting and human hair wigs decorated with feathers, flowers and moss. There were dancers alive with green shrubbery, dancers in towering white head-dresses, dancers in blue skirts and red faces, their beards painted white.

Instruments include bamboo flutes and pottery whistles and harps.

And then there were the Mudmen. They make themselves fierce looking with covering their bodies with grey mud. Then create drama with strange headdresses.

There was all the relentless rhythmic dancing, shuffling, chanting and stamping with earth shaking feet. Old men wearing bone daggers and face paint, near naked kids. All this went on for hours in the boiling sun.

Then the big speech from the Governor with a lot of bla....

Funny to me but not to the people. An argument broke out on who had the right of way to march first when marching to the grandstand. Weapons were held up fast.

I was told the recipe for beetle nut and how much it would cost. One takes one wormy looking plant 1. Inch long, 2. ounce crushed lime, 1 nut. Mix and all for 80 cents. It gives a small high.

There was a market and all homemade stuff for sale, Not made in China. The Keena is about 35 cent in US money. So, I could buy a double dip ice-cream for 20 cents. For me ridiculously cheap but the natives who still use seashells for money it was high. Many have no cash at all.

Back at the Hotel that night a good Hamburger and lots of fruit.

Sunday 15th

Driving today to Wabang over a 9000foot pass. Very cold, lots of fog. Took us 3 hours. We stopped at the highest point for some warm soup. There was a shooting Gallery, and I tried my luck. Yes, there was shooting Gallery, just an old shack but it was a good break in the driving because the Potholes are as big as the car. And the driver was crazy driver, I tried to make him drive slower. To no avail.

In Wabang was another singsong. As we got closer to Wabang the driver pointed out a few villages that are burned out or still smoking from a war last month. 160 people got killed. A few years ago, the same Valley had fights and lost 300 people. The fighting can erupt from the smallest argument to deadly warfare.

This singsong today was not for tourist, I was the only white person. But everybody was friendly, and I felt good. People came up to look into my eyes. That is important to the people.

I saw real old people who must have worn the same outfit all their lives. Old is 60 years.

This was the real thing I could feel the tension in the air. There was even a tent like structure called the dating spot. Very erotic.

It was very noisy, and it got worse, it is all to let off steam. The dancers wore more yellow face makeup, fresh "ass grass" on their rumps, hornbill beaks strung around their necks and dangling down their backs.

This area is still ruled by who has the most pigs, and villagers hold grudges for generations.

Here the Huli are the largest ethnic group and the men are famous for their striking decorative wigs made from human hair. Wives and children are required to donate their hair for the men's elaborate wigs. It is a male dominated society and for that reason a lot of warfare. It is not unusual to find villages only a few kilometers apart unable to communicate. Pidgin English provides now a new means.

A long drive back and a stop at the Kulum Lodge. A birders

paradise. Willie Wagtail was one bird I enjoyed watching. And plumed Bird of Paradise walking around.

So far, I have not heard from my Guide Ben who was to take charge of me. Wonder where he is?

Dinner that evening was Vegetable salad, green salad with tomatoes, leg of pork, mashed potatoes, more vegetables, chicken curry and beef. Fried Bananas with ice-cream for dessert.

Nothing from Benjamin, looks like he run off or what?

Went walking with my bodyguard into the village. The houses are like stone age. Inside is nothing. No furniture at all. But the gardens around every little house are wonderful. People digging for KauKau, sweet potatoes. The Earth is very black! All grows.

The old Lady I was invited to talk to, is happy. She owned one pot, a few bowls, no furniture and was smiling. She has grandchildren running around and they shoot every bird and so provide meat.

There is no cattle or any other hoofed animal in PNG, if there is beef it is imported from Australia.

Had lunch in Poronan Lodge, a most beautiful place.

Then I am traveling now to Benjamins village in the Wahgi Valley, but no Ben only a guide is taking me. I have to find him; he has all my money.

Have not seen Ben yet. Wonder what he did with my money because I seem to be only getting little for it.

A rough ride through the mountains.

Drove through burned out areas again and after asking found out tribal fight against another. Again 100 or so died. 80 on the other side and all a few month ago. But now nobody will move there for a while.

The tribe from Ben is about 1000 people and all are expecting me. I must have shaken 100 hands, everybody is affectionate. At least they were expecting me.

Mother and Father Nelson greeted us happily and welcomed me with a handmade Bilum bag. A bilum bag is usually woven from grass at the coast. In the Mountains it is crochet. It will be treasure forever. It takes month to make one. By now all the neighbors have seen what is in my luggage. Everything was taken out and inspected with a lot of grunts and sounds. The custom here is, one shares everything. Well I needed most of it still and had to collect everything again.

We all walked through gardens and high Elephant grass and went to a funeral. There was a lot of chanting and it was explained to me the father who died was 103 years old and fought in two world wars.

At the funeral we all had to cry. It is a tradition, so I just thought of the two chickens being killed for dinner and had no problem.

A story was told to me: When the first white man came it was thought they were the spirits.

But somebody saw the man poop and went over and smelled it and proclaimed the spirits have the same shit.

I thought that was a good story.

Fog is now all over and it is cold in the evening. So, we sit in the big Hut which is very smoky from the cooking fire. I am sitting on the big oil can which is used for me as a chair. Hope to eat the food and not get sick. I see only one plate now and one pot. There are 8 people in the Hut. Just watching Mrs. Nelson cook such a good dinner in one pot. And we all had plates! But eat with fingers.

There is a hut just for me, newly built. But a long walk to a toilet. I wore all my cloth to stay warm. Sprayed myself with all the poisons I had and hoped no bugs tonight.

I am thinking how interesting we had a conversation for about 5 hours. A constant translation was going on, since people outside the hut wanted to know what I was telling inside. So there were 5 languages translated because so many people do not speak the same language. I could understand some of it if it were spoken in the piksen English.

The Dinner was good, but I could not eat the fresh killed chicken. The sweet potatoes from the open fire were delicious. Everything was cooked on that open only fire. I did have to go outside a few times, the smoke was just too much, and my eyes started to hurt.

My friends from the Mt. Hagen sing song belonged to this family too and looked different with no scary faces. But some of the men still wore big earrings and had bones drawn through their nose.

I went that night 2 times to the outhouse it was scary for me. No lights at all. Just my flashlight and the Batteries are low. I could never see anybody else visiting the outhouse. Very strange.

It is very cold this morning, all the women followed me and watched me brushing my teeth I wondered what they were thinking. I found out that one shares everything one owns and so the ladies tried a few things of my cloth but after a while gave it back.

Then I pulled out my photos from USA and that was a hit. Especially of my family in the snow.

Then the question came up what I was thinking about my new friends. Them. One could not lie because everybody came close and looked into my eyes. Then all the women hugged me and all saying goodbye to me.

By car now to the biggest Coffee and tea plantation in PNG. It is interesting how the tea gets cut with an enormous chainsaw. Bushnell nr.1 tea. Labor is cheap $60 every 2 weeks. The payroll at the plantation is done by Helicopter every Friday. Because of Ambush on the roads.

So, I am back at the Poroman Lodge and getting cleaned up. It was an experience for me. I have a beautiful room with a porch, clean body and my laundry is done by the help.

Still no sighting of Ben. He has my money for the future trips.

The Hotel had entertainment with a young group of boys and girls from a Christian Mission. Then dignitaries from Australia for finance arrived. That gave me people to talk to.

It looks like my Ben took off with my money and other several people I am meeting. Lucky, I have always cash on me. Still my money with Ben is gone.

I found a new bodyguard, but he cannot drive. He used to be a "Rascal". Was in prison and is reformed now. Big! We finally found a car and a driver and went to an old Australian plantation which is now run by the natives. Except they do not know what to do and are ruining it all. There is no supervision, and the "blacks" are cutting down the beautiful Alleys of trees for firewood.

And as I saw everybody was chewing Beetle nut which keeps people from working. PNG natives are not workers. They eat when they feel hungry and the same with work. Then they spit all over with red slimy juice. Even the little children do it.

The recipe for Beetle nut chew is 1 bag of calk, 10 cents.

1 stick baka, 5 cents.

1 nut 50 cent. Mix it.

So that is where all the money goes.

I have not much money, but I have tickets for all the flights. Still had to pay $30 for extra weight. That was my bodyweight included. One reason to eat less. Would be interesting if all Airlines go by bodyweight.

Now I will have to get rid of more things because I have more flights.

A beautiful flight over very steep Valleys and Mountains, very scary looking down there. They are saying here "it flies on a wing and a prayer" It is total wilderness and I was remembering of flights having been lost here and never found again. The Aussie pilot seemed unfazed by the wee landing strip or the clouds that rose from the overheated land. Then we dropped about 6 feet which was not much assuring.

Nobody at the Airport to pick me up in Madang. After trying to get a ride for two hours, I hailed again a truck ride into town. The only Hotel Coast Watcher is very nice, and I paid extra so I would have Ocean view. It looks here like everyone's dream of a Pacific Island resort. There is no tipping at all.

A big storm tonight and met up with Alix again. We had a very good dinner together and some good Beer. Spring rolls, prawns with peanut sauce, banana slices and capers. Very good.

Thursday 19th

The Coastwatcher Hotel is great. All open walls and fresh air blowing. With good Ambien I slept very well.

Went to pig Island to snorkel, but the sea was rough, still the water was clear since it is very protected, and it had a beautiful reef with many fish. There were no people on the Island, and it felt scary looking at the jungle in it. I did not venture from the Beach. It is known for snakes.

There are many Foxbat's which are the biggest. My tree by the Hotel is full of them. And they are always trying to fight with each other for a better spot on a limb.

The Hotel boy climbed the tree for me to get some fresh coconuts, what a treat. The milk in it is very fresh.

And all the people are friendly and are happy to see us.

Abinon-good afternoon.
Learning to speak the pikson fast.

A good pizza. A quite different recipe: Banana, shredded chicken, green spring onion, cheese.

Need to sleep early for the flight to Wewak. Wewak is the furthest one can go in PNG from civilization. And I am anxious to get there.......
5:15am ready, breakfast and off. Temp. 80 degree

Now an Airport in PNG is usually a hut, a big scale, a runway. And that is that.

It is now 7:15am and I am told the plane is broken somewhere.

9:15am still no plane. I got weighed again and had to pay extra. This people are bandits. How did I gain more?

2pm still no plane. I am getting very hungry. There are no toilets. Went behind the Hut. No water, nothing. I saw a woman walking around with a sandwich and offered to buy it from her, she gave it to me, nothing has ever tasted so good. White bread with spaghetti topped with peanut butter and a fried egg.

9 hours of waiting and finally a little plane arrived and we took off for Wewak.

Again, nobody at the Airport awaiting us in Wewak. Alix and I hoped somebody would come. In the meantime, everybody went home and we looked at each other: now what? Both of our money never was paid but we have not figured that out yet.

An old truck came by and the owner let us sit on the back and took us to town. The Floor of the truck was rusted away, tires very bald but the driver drove so slow we could have walked to town. Except it was dark and we did not know where the Hotel was.

Now the real adventure starts. Our good guide Ben never paid for our Hotel and has now gone away......he is not reachable. What to do?

The Windjammer Hotel did not expect us at all. But everybody tried helping us. I am glad I carry always extra $. Met some Australian Soldiers on vacation on the plane coming to PNG and they gave me 2 addresses in emergency.

Well this is the first emergency and I need to use it. Sue and Richard Baker who have been living here for a long time and are Art Dealers in the Sepik area and collect Artifacts.

They arranged quite a few things for me which I could have never done. After that we felt better and had our beers.

The rooms are expensive and no water to wash except a few hours in the middle of the night. Who wants to wash then?

My next trip was to go to the Sepik River. One of the world's last wild places, it is remote and utterly secluded.

These jungle fringed waterways are a taste for adventure. Travel there is by dugout canoe. (Or the fancy Sepik ship)

Finally found a car with a driver but took at least 2 hours to solve the Hotel bill. Nobody could quite understand about my reservation trouble.

Then driving 100 miles over the toughest dirt roads filled with potholes and stones in the middle of it. Rocks! Up and down, many fires in the fields and woods. We did lose the bumper and just drove on. Wonder what else fell off.

On reaching the River at Angoram, again it took a long time to get a canoe. A lot of talking, that done, and my driver-translator and I are on a boat. We are boating on an arm called the Keram River first to Chimondo Village. Watching people wash in the river, living on their little primitive boats. One even had a pig on board. The rivers are the ancient highways for the people of the western Provinces. Now and then we would pass a family in a canoe, or fishermen tending to nets on the mud-banked shore. Villages came and went, collections of thatched huts built on stilts to protect them from floods.

A short stop at a village before, to talk to the headman there about something I never understood what. Just felt bad when we left, and I had an uneasy feeling. My guide did not like the Head chief he explained. Children did not look good, needed food. The Chief had 4 wives, which is average.

Crossing the River to the Chimondo Village a big welcome for us. Head chief Adam gave me flowers, and everybody stood at attention. Again, I never could follow what was arranged. The Chief gave me a coconut as a welcome drink. I needed badly.

My guide James who could talk some English told me to go into the haus tambaram (Spirit House). It was about 15 feet above ground, and I had to climb a chicken ladder up. Not very safe but I had no choice. It was full of the most beautiful carvings. The large carvings tell the story of the village and are called storyboards. They are priced for their antiquity all over the world. There is no other writing, and this is like a book and everything is expressed on it.

The longhouse is completely built without nails. All rope bindings. Traditionally men's longhouses are the center of each village, culturally important for the storing of weapons, ceremonials artifacts, and the skulls of enemies. Cannibalism was a way of life for the people until the arrival of Christianity.

I set up my sleeping bag and Mosquito tent. James got all the food out. Watching James taking his shirt off was a big surprise. It was very hot! But he had 1000 or more skin tattoos. He told me he was called a Lizard man in his hometown. The skin was raised like on a lizard skin. What pain he must have gone through! We were surrounded by all men of the Village; no women are allowed in the Tamboran. Except I was in it.

Sue Baker packed my supplies and thought of everything. Even salt and pepper. Soup, tea, coffee. Sheets and a pillow. I am glad I did not have to eat the Village food.

After James cooked by the stairs, he brought me the food wrapped in a big banana leaf. He mentioned not to eat all of it and to offer the rest to the Chief Adam.

Extra food James cooked for him, Sago Cakes and dried fish. Horrible smell and I tried it but tasted like an old shoe. Chief Adam invited certain people to finish it all what I had. A Chief rises to be a leader because of their skills, leadership and wealth and generosity in gift giving.

Chief Adam got again a coconut for me and then showed me the "toilet" in the bush. It was a long way to walk and everybody followed.

I watched the village life below me. The children did not wear any cloth, staring at me as much as possible. The women were aloof I think they did not like that I was living in the Spirit house.

At night I saw a few natives lying near my stairs and sleeping. By the River a big fire was burning and surrounded by men and a lot of talking. By 6pm drums started to come on from across the River.

The village is made from reeds and bamboo. Gleaned Sago palms and fish from the river. Not much choice what food.

A fire was lit right underneath me to keep the Mosquitos away. So, I was told.

Two times I had to go to the Outhouse in the dark, it was an experience. All the men followed me again. I had to switch the flashlight off to relax.

Across the River the long Bamboo drums were drumming. Had I known what they were saying I would have not slept at all. All night boom…

At 4am the Roosters started right underneath me.

An early breakfast was Ramen noodles and coffee.

And then James told me what had happened. The village on the first stop thought I would stay there but James liked Chimondo better. Except nobody understood why we left when we crossed the River.

To ward off a big fire what the drums from across promised and burn me with the spirit house inside, all the men had to watch out for me that night. It was a lousy $5 what it cost me. And it would have been especially important for the poor village across the River. I gained an insight into this society still governed by sorcery and ancestral spirits in its daily lives.

I was ready to leave fast. We packed and we left at 9am by our wooden canoe to Angoram where we started out. No sunroof on the boat it was hot.

At our arrival in Angoram there was a strange silence. Everything was closed, were before it was teeming with people.

I wanted an ice-cream so badly. There is not much electric except everything is done by Generator or solar power.

Anyway, there was shooting before we arrived. The Brother in law of James got drunk and killed somebody. Since it was a relative of James the Victims' relatives burned our car. No transportation now! So now we are waiting for the Police from Wewak which could take maybe days to arrive. And when they come, I could go back with them in the back seat with the Murderer and in the trunk would be then the body. None of it appealed to me.

There was another English couple in the same predicament. They had almost the same experience of village life.

We walked over to the Angoram Hotel, which was a dump and tried to phone to Wewak. The Owner of the Hotel had a car, but she was not going to share it with us and even drove off.

Sue Baker, the Angel, arrives at 4pm!! She took care of me right away. I already saw myself in this dump for a long time. No water either.

I was dying of thirst.

Coming back to Wewak I found my luggage was moved from the Windjammer to the Airport Hotel down the Road.

It was the worst place. The people hoped at the Windjammer Hotel I would never come back again and just tried to get rid of my bag. Never got explained what happened there.

So now it is 9pm and I have a room. But it is so filthy and no water. Had to go to the Manager Margaret who took care of me and gave me a good Dinner.

It took me a while to clean up and getting ready for my 4am flight to PortMoresby.

In the morning naturally no plane at the runway and went back to the Hotel to have breakfast with Margaret.

It finally came and no room on board. Somebody got off or whatever, but I had suddenly a seat. These planes only take 6 or 8 people.

Plane had to stop in Madang for Fuel. How did fuel get there? By boat?

Port Moresby, Paulus? was there. I complained about my "organized" trip and that nothing was paid. Yes, I was told Benjamin run off with the money and nobody has been paid.

Had some fruit Pizza. Incredibly good too.

Thin crust, sour cream, cut up fruit on top and short baking and then ice cream on top.

Stayed one night in the Weigh Inn and now for my vacation to the Loloata Island. Which is my second address to go to in needed.

Monday 23rd

Loloata Island is a dream.

But now I discovered my credit card which was in my bag fell out or was stolen when my luggage was moved. I guess somebody went through all my stuff. And since nobody could use a credit card if found somebody found and deposited in the safe in Wewak and Owners there had forgotten to give it to me. I am feeling a heart attack coming on.

I must forget this and look at this beautiful 5-star resort. I have not ever stayed in such luxury. My room is beautiful and overlooking the sea. Heaven!

The Owner Dick Knight is immensely helpful but could do very little to get my credit card back. Called the USA to cancel it.

The snorkeling is a dream. No need to dive.

My neighbor at Dinner suddenly stopped breathing and keeled over. I thought he died. His wife slapped him in the face, and he woke up. Something was wrong with him.

Since I have medicine for heart attack and breathing problems, I offered to get it from my room.

It is dark outside by now, but I could not miss the big snake lying across the walkway. Black and white stripes. A dangerous water snake. In my hurry I just jumped right over it. And on my way back did the same again.

I got the medicine into the man and made some sugar solution and chamomile tea. He was fine the next day.

Next morning the drumming sound of the blue pigeon woke me. Sounded almost like the drums from the Kinda in the mountains.

Took a long walk to the end of the Island. Pretty birdlife around, nobody can kill or hurt any animal on this Island. A lot of Wallaby's and blue pigeons. They are almost the size of a turkey. Even a white pigeon is around. They are very elusive.

All these birds would have been trophy birds for the natives for their finery.

Went snorkeling over to the Lion Island by canoe saw a very big lionfish.

Further out the sea is rough, and I cannot go far by 12 noon. Storms come fast.

Lunch was excellent always a lot of fruit.

In the evening today a lot of snakes are in the sand. I am told they are poisonous. At night, a very strange animal visits, called Cus Cus. Maybe a Goodfellow's tree kangaroo.

Wednesday 25th

Kayaking around the Island. Early in the morning is best, the sea is very still. Beautiful corral underneath, from the darkest blue to red. It all looks like a painting.

Lunch today was a smoked chicken with fish in coconut sauce. I walked again around the Island; food is good. I hate to see my time getting shorter. I love this place.

Have not found out much about my departure anyway but somebody will let me know.

I called the travel office and was told my money never got there. Then how come some of my tickets were paid? And now more money is wanted from me. I just gave them hell on the phone and hope my life will not be unhappy after this experience.

From Loloato I had to go to Port Moresby and stay overnight in town. I wish I could have gone straight to the Airport. There is no way one can just walk around. Even in town, the Hotel has 10-foot fences with spikes on top.

The Dining room had some nice people and we had good conversation.

In the morning, the Hotel wanted money from me, and I told them call Benjamins office. I am out of here at 5am. I am lucky not more has happened to me. I have heard horror stories how people have been robbed of everything. Even got hurt or killed. Papua New Guinea was one of the most exhilarating trips of my life. If friends, ask was it worth taking? YES! It just is not trip for the fainthearted.

Happy to be in the plane and off to Cairns.

Maybe in 100 years people will have it better organized, they natives do not comprehend our world. And they think they are the center of the earth.

As a follow up.

All travel Agencies have had trouble with PNG Holidays, (Ben Nelson) and some have gotten the police involved.

I got mail Inquiry from the police:

This was the report from the police: If anybody knows the where about of Benjamin Nelson, we would very much appreciate you contacting Mr. Ormsby or 6-mile police station ABO number 306.

I guess I was lucky that not worse things happened to me.

Mt. Kilimanjaro, Tanzania, January-February 2005

Photo album with great photos.

I am on my way to climb Kilimanjaro!

I have a broken toe, wonder how that will play out. Have been many weeks working out in the Gym climbing steps and should be in exceptionally good shape.

Flying again now with Kenia Air and have not been able to sleep on the plane. But the food is good. There was a lot of turbulence too. Movies are so bad. I always wonder who decides for the movies.

Checked into the Holiday club in the London Airport lounge for $18 a day great place. There are floors of Bars. I chose the quiet section. And all the food and drinks one wants. Fresh baked cookies too! Relaxing, this is good. Halfway now to Tanzania.

My next flight is. again 10 hours. Nairobi, Kenya next. Changing planes to Dar es Salam, and changing planes in Dar es Salam to a very small plane. The Pilot of this flight told me to sit on the left, Mt. Kilimanjaro best view. Hopefully, I will be on top of it soon.

The small plane from Dar es Salam had only 2 passengers and when the pilot found out from the Stewardess that I was going to climb the Mountain he made a special circle flying around Kilimanjaro, with me sitting next to the pilot in the cockpit. I felt so privileged.

On landing in Arusha, Tanzania, my luck was bad again. Nobody was there to pick me up. Could not call the Hotel since phone lines were down.

Finally, I hailed a taxi, but we broke down shortly and had to wait for help again. What is it? I look for trouble.

Met a few Masai's with their big herds of cows who were walking by. Nothing has changed since my last visit 20 years ago. But there is overgrazing of the land now. The Masai still wear their colorful red frocks. Naked as usual underneath. We tried to have conversation till a tow truck came.

At the Protea Aishin Machame Hotel.

Very Luxuries with a beautiful Garden. Went to Dinner and to sleep early.

Slept like a Rock. Lost two nights flying and it is catching up. My toe feels better in the warm air.

A big blue sky and a view of Kilimanjaro from my window, I could see in the sun the glitter of the snowcap, the square top of Kilimanjaro. Some people in the Hotel are celebrating their downhill climb already and I hope to do that in a week too.

In the Garden a big Hornbill is preening his feathers and blue monkeys are after the Mango's. Mango season now and hardly anybody is picking them. I am eating Mango's all the time drinking Mango juice. The pool looks good, but I will not use it because of my toe. Do not want an infection.

Talked to people who already climbed the Mountain and got some advice. All said Pole-pole. Walk slow.

Arusha is at 5100feet and surrounded by fertile lands that nurture Coffee plantation, bananas and horticulture by private farmers. Mostly

Roses are grown. Arusha is a bustling town. Streets are filled with 4x4 game viewing vehicles. It is known the safari capital of East Africa.

Driving today to Mt. Meru Natl. Park. A beautiful park. No poachers are there so lots of wildlife. Saw already 150 Giraffe's. All of them look healthy and Colobus Monkey's a first for me. Wart hogs everywhere. Buffalo and Zebra. And all types of Deer.

At my request we stopped at Momella Lodge. Many memories from times before. The road to it was all washed out and it did not look good. The Lodge has been in Movie's like Hatari" with John Wayne and Hardy Krueger. I had been here in the 70' and then it was a beautiful place. Now it is very rundown and no guests. Who wants to stay in a place like that? The pool was just a hole in the ground now. So sad but I but good memories.

On the way back I saw a Gas Station it was called "House of Lubrication". Good name.

Today is the start for my climb to Machame Gate. At the Gate we had to fill out so much paperwork. Our carriers could only carry so many pounds. I think 40pounds was the limit and so one is told to bring as little as needed.

We walked the Machame route straight up. First through high Elephant grass which got shorter the higher we went. Still I thought a Lion could be hiding in there. There has been no rain, so the trail was dry but difficult. I am using Diamox 2x a day. We started at 1490m and I noticed I am very hungry. I guess that is why we had 3 times a day noodles to satisfy my hunger.

Machame Camp

At 5:30pm we stopped and made camp. 2980m now.

We have an incredibly good group of porters and cooks. The guide I am not so sure. He looks like it is his first time. It is freezing and I had to beg for another sleeping bag from the guide. He had extras. I had to share my tent with a middle-aged miner from Pittsburg. He was I think afraid of me because he put his luggage right between us. We all have tents for 2 to share. And one tent is there for eating. We sit close to each other to keep warm.

Difficult to go and pee. In the dark it was difficult to find the toilet shack. There was no toilets hack. Bushes! And my thoughts always are on Lions.

Shira Camp

Next day arriving at 3pm at 3840m. It was steep and extremely hard.

Our breakfast consisted of scrambled eggs, sausage, cucumbers, Toast, jam, peanut butter, honey and porridge.

Tea and coffee and always hot chocolate.

Lunch: bread with good filling" 1 egg, bananas, cake and juice.

Dinner Noodles, potatoes or rice, vegetables, very good, chicken curry or beef curry always something different.

Avocados and watermelon.

One porter carried just Eggs on his head and some only carried chairs or a table. We did have all the luxuries.

To Barranco now

We climb up and down sometimes to 14500 feet. I am feeling good because the Diamox is helping. Ibuprofen 3x a day, Tylenol 4 times a day I am full of drugs!

I drink a lot of water and eat a lot of chocolate. The nice thing when we come to a good rest our porters have already started on the tea.

Zuwardi, the guide has been climbing for 15 years, so not his first time. He wants to please everybody but now I think we are moving too fast. By his suggestion we skipped a day of rest. It came to haunt me bad. One needs to acclimate one day for sure.

We have 20 porters for 5 tourists.

We are settled in a Valley with strange growing trees. Barranco is across the Glaciers and drops off into a steep ravine. It is surrounded by 10-foot cacti vegetation.

I can see the "Wall ahead" which will be tomorrows climb. To me that was the scariest climb.

I am wondering how I will do it. Today I have seen people who are coming down again. Some of them are extremely sick with Altitude sickness and some are just too cold and are freezing.

One woman was sick sitting on a rock and was wrapped in blankets and still shook very much. They never made it past the Wall.

So here we are in front of the Wall, I could not believe the steepness. How do the porters do it? It was scary for me, because one had to climb boulders which were bigger than me and had to use the help from the guide to get over them. I clawed my way up the Wall, sheer drops of 1000feet next to me. I wanted to close my eyes. It was challenging or more than that.

4700m or 14000feet is Karanga

Barufu at 15500feet now.

We arrived here at 1:30pm. We are all very dirty by now. The wind is fierce, and the black sand gets into Eyes and everything else. Wish I would not have worn a bra.

Our tents keep flying away and we all are trying to stake them out with stones around. There are enough stones for that. The toilet tent has blown over the cliff and it is gone. There is a wooden hut hanging over the side of the cliff and one can go there for toilet. But it is so dangerous hanging lopsided almost everybody stays outside of it. So, in this dry air nothing goes away except the toilet paper. Everything just dehydrates.

I am feeling great today and looking down from the Mountain and seeing the lights of the Rose Plantations way below.

In the meantime, the cook has somehow managed to make a very good meal. Even French bread! Dinner is early at 5pm and then we are told to go to sleep because wakeup call is at 11:30pm. The last climb to the top is made in the dark. I am glad because it is supposed to be extremely dangerous. And me looking at such a height straight down makes me sick. The wind is blowing 50miles now I was told. Many people in the camp are sick. Vomiting, diarrhea. Not us. The Altitude is getting to them. We have lost three members of our group. They will return with one of the porters. Too sick to continue.

Zuwabi kept saying Hacuma matata- no problem we will go on. I filled all my pockets with water and chocolate.

So only two climbers left. My tent companion and me. At 11:30 sharp we got going for the final attempt. Now I am told the wind is 80km an hour, same as 50 mile an hour.

At 17000feet my right eye went blind. I kept seeing only little red lights in it. The other man had bad diarrhea. We both did not look good. After talking we decided to climb on. It was the worst decision I ever made. My Brain was shutting down slowly and I just did not want to quit. I did not know what was happening to me, but my guide should have known and made us turn around. But no.

At Steller point my left eye was losing vision. It was almost a race to Uluru point now. Whatever I still could see was so unreal. By now the sun came up and the Glaciers were shining in the morning sun.

My camera was frozen and a little clicking I could hear but some photos did make it. When I look at the photo from the top I look like a Zombie.

By now Zuwabi was getting worried about me and decided to go down the shortest route on the Scree wall. That means one slides downhill and hoping not to hit a boulder. It was so fast I could not even say a prayer.

We reached Barufu and went to sleep for one hour and then 5 more hours of a slow walk downhill. My sight was coming back now, I was lucky. By 9000feet I could see with my left eye again. In Camp I took some medicine, Aspirin for blood clots, Plavix for the eyes and dexamethasone 4mg for swelling of the Brain two times. And then I was like new again.

That night we made camp at Mweka. I was better feeling and by morning my eyes were fine again.

It all was a scary experience, and I would never do it again.

It would maybe not happen like this if we would have had an extra day to acclimate at halfway. Most people do take that extra day. My head was going to have an aneurism because of the fast way climbing up.

In the Visitor lodge is a book which tells of how many people have died climbing Mt. Kilimanjaro. It is not a simple trip.

Serena Hotel

I am booked now into a very beautiful Hotel. Rested and walked around the property. And there in the Bushes was a sign:

Kiss of the Sun for pardon

The song of the Birds for mirth

One is nearer Gods heart in a Garden

Then anywhere else on Earth.

How appropriate for me.

With a guide I went to Arusha one more time. I love that city; it is very colorful. Still crime is big, and one has to have a guide. Maasai warriors in full regalia stroll the streets, mingling with tourists for photo opportunities.

Tanzania time pole-pole take your time and do not rush.

There was a story on me in the Arusha newspaper having an older Lady climb Mt. Kilimanjaro. I was called Bi-Bi, mother, in the story. (Rest in photo Album)

Austria to Hungary, Slovakia, Hungary, July, 2005

With Kevin on a bicycle trip along the Danube. (Wien-Vienna.) I had done the section between Passau and Wien by Bicycle the year before, which was beautiful. The name is like music. And it is a beautiful city. Our goal tonight is to hear a concert in the Schoenbrunn Castle. It is very hard to get tickets. Since it was hot and no air-condition in the Castle we could only suffer for a short time. But all the windows were open, and we enjoyed the music on the the Benches outside.

As we walked the streets of Vienna many musicians are performing with classical and new music.

Our bike trip was called Hungarian Rhapsody. We had rented great bikes and our luggage was transferred every day to the next Hotel stop. All along one could see fields of Sunflowers and they all were facing the sun.

Nice little cafes all along the Danube or Donau river. Had to push on sometimes because it was nice just sitting and watching the River Traffic.

Bratislava in Slovakia

Crossed the border on the bike trail Slovakia. Just a little sign telling us we are now Bratislava Slovakia. An interesting city. Many statues in town. Little ones, humanlike looking out of manholes. It was fun to discover the narrow streets and courtyards. I never knew I could lift a 1000-pound cow (photo).

The country is small, and we crossed into Hungary, again just a little sign on the trail to tell where we are.

Hungary

And more little villages. We are using the River-dam cycle pass and some country roads. Noticed many storks in their nests with very hungry baby's.

Reading any sign was impossible. The Hungarian language is so hard.

Our Hotel Panorama in Mosonmafyarovar we could only find with difficulty, since we did not know how to pronounce the name.

The Hotel had Goulash for Dinner, one of my favorites. Many foods are mixed with paprika which gives it a strong flavor.

We stopped at a farm were people were picking fresh Apricots. Kevin's favorite fruit. He made friends with the owner and we bought a big bag full of Apricots.

Getting through a very marshy region now to Gyor. We had to bike through a lot of water because of floods. There were some rolling hills which surprised Kevin since I promised him no hills or mountains.

Stopped at Babolina stud farm. It is the cradle of breeding Arab Horses since 1816. The current herd of Horses is over 400 horses.

Tata is our next overnight at Hotel Kristaly. Very strange Hotel, no food is served here. So, we are in the dark night trying to find food.

Today we traveled a very hilly and densely wooded hills range. Some uphill stretches are having wonderful descents.

Arriving in Esztergom finally and needing a rest. Many women were outside sitting on little stools crocheting. It has the largest church in Hungary. It was built in 1500's.

And now to the Countryside of the Danube Bend. Hotel Thermal Sturovo is our tonight place. We did enjoy the thermal bath that night in the Hotel.

From Sturovo now to Visegrad and crossing the Danube by Ferry. Across the Danube we could see a mediaeval Castle.

Again, a crossing with a different Ferry to Scentendre. The most visited unusual artist's village. Many old buildings.

And we are near Budapest. It is fun trying to find our Hotel Kulturinnov. Maybe not fun since we did not speak the language. How do you ask directions in Hungarian?

But in the meantime, we traveled along all the historical streets, we were not lost. We looked at it as sightseeing. Saw the Parliament, the funicular which has been running since 1870, old Bridges. There are 9 Bridges across the Danube. One of them we had to cross. Which one? We found "our" Bridge, but it was closed because of a runner festival. We made it somehow across.

Saw many sights of Budapest. There are many to describe. We did visit the Opera which was a treasure to see. A lot of gold as ornaments.

A trip to the south to the Puszta. Hoped to experience the Hungarian Cowboys. And did we!

In Lajosmizce we were welcomed to a great performance of the famous horsemen and a carriage ride through the Puszta, the big sky country of Hungary. These men can ride. And all without a saddles.

I got to ride a very beautiful Horse and with a saddle. Would have loved to take that Horse with me.

Kevin joined the whipping show. One must get a bottle from a post with a whip. Difficult, but Kevin did it and got his bottle of wine.

Later we stopped at a Restaurant Szamla which had great food. And we were entertained by a Gypsy czardas group. It is hard to sit still when that kind of music is playing. As I looked at the dishes I fell in love with the design. I asked the waiter if I could buy one plate, he said wait a minute.

And he came back with 6 plates wrapped up- "present from the owner" I was told. Every time I use my plates, I will remember how nice everybody was.

Egypt, January to February 2006

Having been to Egypt before but never on an Adventure trip there.

This was going to be good because a friend of mine was a tour leader. Doug Baum has made friends with Bedouins in Egypt and decided to bring travelers to them. Especially if they liked Camels. That his was priority.

My Lufthansa flight was on time and first-class service. Not that I flew in first class that will never happen.

Cairo impressed me right away. It is busy and big. All around is the color of grey. Since it seldom rains it was very dusty and the Air stagnant. It is teeming with cars. Just to many. And no traffic rules. To cross a street, I always watched for a woman in her flowing black dress and walked beside her.

Buildings are old and some of them are very beautiful.

Crossing the Nile over a long Bridge. Many Cruise boats are waiting for tourists underneath. The Sheraton, my Hotel, was on the River and a great view from there of Cairo old Town.

Met Elsie, one of the group, and we went to the light show at the Pyramids of Giza. I only needed Omar Sharif walking on to the light stage and I would have been happy. But it was only his voice telling the story of the ancient time with very old music, very fitting. The show was gripping history.

The Great Pyramids are impressive, and the gazing Sphinx is the watch dog. The Sphinx was not as big as I always thought.

Outside from the Sphinx area, a Pizza Hut and KFC are there. Hawkers trying to sell head scarves and rides on camels. It looked and felt all like a Circus.

Having Falafel afterwards and bargaining a taxi back to the Hotel. For everything one must bargain.

Noticed no heat in the rooms and it was very cold.

Today we all went to a racing stable of Racing Arabian Horses. Very athletic looking Horses. When the Horses retire from the track, they are given to anybody to pull carriages or anything. Sad ending because the Horses have to work hard now pulling wagons. All Horses are Stallions. I wonder where are the mares? Egyptians do not geld Horses; it is not manly I was told.

The men are very eye catching, many look like Omar Sharif and all are very polite and always a happy "Welcome" call.

Then we went to the Sakkara and Dahshur Pyramids. They are named after Sokker, the God of death. Not many tourists come here. It is out of the way. The lonely Guard at the Pyramid was happy to see us and rode fast to us on his camel to meet us. Strange looking saddlebag with his rifle sticking out of it. We did stop for flatbread on the way and shared it with him. It is only in the 40's. I did bring my warm coat.

Elsie in our group saw finally her favorite dog called Canaan dogs. They looked to me like Mongrels. She told me they cost about $1000 in the USA! The guard offered her 4 free dogs right away to take home.

In Dahshur one temple is open to the public. I did not go into when I saw the entrance. Straight down a slippery slide or chute. Not for me. That was dangerous looking.

All the Pyramids are in drifting sand. Either buried still or new ones are uncovered. There are places still to be discovered.

Near the Nile is very green lush land. Watered from the River. Vegetables are growing for miles. Hay is planted for the Animals. Many donkey carts, buffalo's and cows and Horses are plowing fields. People are working everywhere but no garbage disposal and so much of it is dumped anywhere. Even in the city it does look bad. So much garbage piled in big hills. Wonder if they are on strike? Stores are full of everything. And people are walking around with the phones glued to their ears.

In the evening we met Doug's Bedouin Family for Dinner. Adel is the name. A Muslim family. Adel has the camels for the Pyramids for tourists to rent.

There are no chairs in the house but a sofa, found a few pillows to sit on. Nobody ever sat on the sofa. I am never comfortable sitting on the floor. My legs are too long.

Food was plenty and very good. Rice and peas are the main, spinach salad and fried chicken, the usual strong Nescafe is served in small cups.

I was offered the Hookah pipe afterwards but declined. I was told by an Uncle that many people in Egypt have mouth cancer from it.

At the Hotel later there was a wedding reception, lots of noisy big band music, lots of clapping and dancing. The outfits were beautiful, lots of glitter. The bride looked to be about 15 years old.

Driving now to our camel adventure.

We are on our way to the Bedouin's in Nuweida. Quashed in a Jeep with 7 people. I am in the middle seat in front and on my right is a policeman with a Machine gun type on his lap. He is supposed to keep us from being what?

The government told us we have to have police protection when driving.

Stopped at a satellite city for food, fresh baked bread. Outside sand is all one sees. Garbage all along the road too.

Then the tunnel under the Suez Canal. Have always wanted to see it and begged for our Jeep to make a stop going to the top to see the Canal traffic. Boat after boat in line! So many ships, fascinating to watch it. The Canal is very small so traffic comes to a stop on it many times. And all this fighting because of this small Canal. But it does save a lot of time for ships once through instead of going around South Africa. Quite a lot of guards sitting around on top. All having machine guns sticking out of their little "caves" and watching us too.

Hours now of driving in the sand through the Sinai, crossed some

Mountains and arrived at the Red Sea.

Saw my first crusader Castle from the 12th century. It was just sitting there on Faraon island and known as Salah al-Din's fort. It is in a strategic position overlooking Aqaba Gulf. And it was still in perfect condition.

Looking down the cliff one could see the clear water of the Red Sea. I could see why people wanted to dive here in the Red Sea. For me, the water was to cold.

A few more hours of driving and finally arriving in Nuweiba on the Red Sea. It is supposed to be like a Riviera.

Famous for stunning sunrises and sunsets.

Our Hotel Habiba is a dump. But we have no choice, since most places are old, and the season is over and all of it looks dreary. The wind was blowing, and it did not feel like a Riviera.

Weather is cold. Went to meet some of the Bedouin family, friends of Doug, in the desert to say hi. I froze everywhere. But we were served sweet tea in all places which was supposed to keep us warm. All the Bedouins are welcoming Doug, he has a lot of friends here. We crowded all in one room and it felt at least warmer that way.

Our host Saleh bin Suleiman is going to be the guide and provides the camels too. Saleh's English is minimal, but one of the other guides speaks better English. The houses are quite simple, no furniture. Some have carpets. We sat around by an open fire on a concrete floor. I was uncomfortable. Water is scarce so things are not as clean, and I kept falling asleep. Maybe the smoke did it. But then food was brought on a big plate and we all ate from it. Rice, chicken, chickpeas, tomatoes, cucumbers, cheeses. The cucumbers are so good.

My observation of the family there was a few deaf children and mute. Some had clubfeet. Maybe a lot of inbreeding?

But all are loved the same.

Back at the Hotel I had to catch or kill all the Mosquitos first. The room was full of them. Did not sleep good my Pillow was bad. Sheets to short, blanket to short, Bed to short. I had to wear my heavy socks and pants to be warm. This is not complaining only observation.

Friday 27

A very cold morning, I am putting on all my clothing to keep warm. Breakfast was served near the Beach. Nice but this is winter! In the summer it would be good. The splashing of the sea was great. Lots of pillows are used here for seating.

Today we drive to the Mountains by jeep. Desolate countryside. Lots of Canyons but no sign of life. Saw some Military and Bedouins on their camels going by. The driving was over Rocks and over dunes of sand and then parked near a Canyon called Colored Canyon. It is one of the most impressive natural sights of Egypt. Going in was first beautiful but then it became very steep through Rocks. 3 hours of climbing.

Then a wonderful lunch. Fresh Bread baked over an open fire.

Later went to see a little of Nuweida. The town is mainly for Israeli and Russian tourists. Not now but in the season.

We had Pizza there.

Today we left to meet our Camels. I was given a very hungry Camel I called him the Geezer. He wanted to eat anything edible. It is a dry country to ride. Not like the Sahara. What here is called an Oasis is a lonely tree maybe. Around us it is all white sand. Not much growing food for camels.

So now our journey on top of the "ship of the desert" starts. We are going to travel through untouched wadis, canyons, oases, and at the same time into traditional Bedouin culture.

We have made a stop to meet some Ladies of Wadi Samghi village. The keep their faces totally covered.

Our cook is very good, but my stomach is not good. Hygiene has not been very important. I was given Berber tee for my stomach. It is made from the Baethran plant and then called Rabee tea. Very bitter like a Underberg(a german schnapps) It helped some.

Going to the toilet at night is a problem again. There are no toilets. One must go around the back of camp. Hoping nobody else is there already. There are 6 men and 3 women in our group. Slipping out of my sleeping bag is difficult too. Getting into it again is worse. All the sand follows inside. And anytime one uses the zipper everybody wakes up. Because we all are lying like rolled figures in line to keep warm.

Then I started to vomit again in the middle of the night.

All around us are the Camels lying on the ground sleeping. They do have hobbles so they cannot go too far. A strange noise camel make, sounds like burping. And the camel bulls are constantly complaining.

My Camel is a Bull too but quiet and stubborn. He has the strongest neck, and if he sees some green food he will reach for it. I am getting a good workout when on him trying to pull his head back.

Got to ride and hike to a different Canyon. A good lunch in a sunny place and we are riding to an Oasis. We will pay extra there to have shelter. It gets so cold when the sun goes down.

Tonight, the food is not good. Flatbread, tomatoes, good cucumbers. Lots of humus. But I can only eat so much of the bean stuff. It is not good for my stomach. Our dishwasher is usually a goat licking the plates clean.

Lunch is always canned Tuna. I am sticking now to the bread only.

We have reached a Valley with a beautiful inscripted white Rock called "Maktoub", the inscription Rock. Some of it is 3500 years old. Many people have come by here and it is like a post office to leave a message carved into the soft Rock.

Crusaders, pilgrims and tourists. All maybe on their way from or to St. Catherines.

Usual Tuna and flatbread and cheese still.

Some jeeps came by to visit and they took us all on a ride over the sand dunes.

Back at camp waiting for Dinner which took longer tonight. By 7pm finally a soup and a stew with rice.

The Sinai desert is bleak.

Everybody snored so loud tonight no way to sleep. Doug of all people who kept me warm but was the loudest snorer. I was in a killing mood by now. And the Moon was full, so it was like daylight. The reflection on the sand was like a light.

In the morning, the wind stopped at least. There were little animal tracks all over in the sand. Foxes, rats?

It is warmer and a few layers of cloth of mine are tied to the saddle. And I am in love with my Geezer Camel. He is like a Lincoln Car. Very dependable, but snitches food whenever he can. The minute I get off he uses that time for sleeping, eyes close. I have not quite hit his language about getting up or down, but I am learning. I am not here to train him he is teaching me about the life of Camels.

Beautiful blue sky today, as I sit on my Camel. My daydreams are interesting. And sometimes I fall sleep.

There has been only one waterhole in 3 days. It is amazing how the Camels last so long. At Oasis Ain Hudra we got chaff and some wild plants for the Camels. Besides it the Camels ate the same food we ate, all the leftovers were fed to them.

The Oasis we are stopped now is mentioned in the Bible as Hazeroth and still supports a few families.

Stopped at the Nowained Graves and a group of Bedouins were camped there too and tried to sell us Beadworks.

Everybody tries to sell something. It is the only income for the desert dwellers.

Lunch as usual. Tuna, salad, tahini, bread, cheese.

We are riding steep hills and I never knew Camels could climb like a Horse. But with so much weight on it, it would have been dangerous, and we got off at the steepest parts of the crossing. Some of the Camels did slip and fell and one refused to get up again. Not till we unloaded everything did it stand up again.

Breakfast had been always fresh bread called "lebe". It is baked right on the coals and the burned spots are scraped off. Many stops still and then a good buy to my Old Geezer. I wish we could have traveled longer on the camels.

It has been a great day of riding and I hate to see it end. But we are near St. Catherines and have to take a jeep the last stretch. We gave away most anything we did not need any more to our Bedouin friends. They are all friends of Doug and we had very good service because of him from them. He has supported them with Books and money so the children could get to school.

Driving now to St. Catherine's. At a check point stop we identified as Canadians. USA people must have a man with a gun in the car and we tried to avoid it. We left our gun toting man behind in Nuweida.

The Monastery of St. Catherine is 1600 years old. It is the oldest active monastery in the world and is at the base of Mt. Sinai. Inside is the location of the "burning bush". The Bible, Quran and the Torah refer to St. Katherine's. It has the world's second most valuable library, over 6,000 manuscripts of unique historic importance (behind the Vatican) located here.

The Guest house is beautiful. Here is the unbelievable Castle? Monastery? It looks like a fortress. But beautiful Gardens are in the walled place.

The shower felt so good, the rooms are basic but clean and a beautiful view from the window into the mountains. All around the Almond trees are blooming.

Dinner was in a big hall on long tables. I liked the food. Potatoes! Hot soup was particularly good. Beef and gravy with zucchini. Orange slices and cake pudding.

We had to get ready for our early rise 3am, to climb the Mountain.

But I had a bed and still could not sleep. I guess I was too excited.

Climbing Mt. Sinai is tough but worth it. It is usually a 3 hour climb along a footpath. One can do it slow or at any speed. There are camels for rent for $7 to bring you up almost to the top. It looked too dangerous on the Camels since they were driven up fast. And that in the dark.

One still must do the last Steps of Repentance to the top; it is not for the faint of heart.

At 3pm we started to the top of the Mountain for the sunrise. It was very cold, and I hated to leave my bed.

I got dressed and had on to much cloth, and got hot very fast going up, it was very straight up. To 2,624m.

My expensive flashlight died on me after a 15-minute use. Some young man gave me his cigarette lighter; at least I could see some of the rocks and not fall over them.

The Camels never stopped and walked right over you if somebody was in the way. And the trail was small.

At the top I started to freeze since it still was dark. Blankets were passed out by whom, I never found out?

Still I am cold. There is a chapel on top, but doors were closed.

And then I saw a tent and heard singing in there and entered it. I was welcomed by pilgrims from Korea who invited me and gave me warm soup. This are the moments I will never forget.

Finally, when the sun came over the Mountains it was a chilling moment too. Red like blood was the color. Most people started singing or praying. It is one of the holiest places to visit in the bible.

Mt. Moses, also known Mt. Horeb or Mt. Sinai and by its Arabic name Gebel Mussa. It is here Moses is supposed to have received the 10 commandments.

Coming down a few meters a Kiosk was set up with anything to drink and warm coffee or chocolate.

I am going down a different way. Mostly 3600 steps which were built by one monk Stephanos many years ago, maybe, which was leading us to the gate of Stephanos. Here he heard confession of the pilgrims and giving them absolution before letting them pass. The tourist does not come that way anymore. Doug found this out and uses it as his secret way.

The steep way down leads to beautiful views and the smell of herbal plants is everywhere.

At the Dining hall had a good breakfast. Then I tried to find an acquaintance, Father Justin. But was told he was gone; I could not believe it. So, I checked with another Monk who told me Father Justin is in the Library and awaiting us. But he had to leave in 30 minutes to go to USA. F. Justin is American but has lived many years in St. Catherine's and is rebuilding the Library into the Computer age.

There is a Bell tower which houses 9 bells of different sizes and an ancient wooden bell. The wooden bell is used daily. One more look at the Burning bush which is tended by the monks with water drawn from a well.

Leaving for Cairo again. But we had only a small jeep. All of us 6 persons pressed like sardines. I called it the torture truck.

And our policeman had to fit into it too. He was big and took the whole front seat. With his loaded Machinegun right there.

A long drive with a few stops and we are back at the Sheraton in Cairo by 11pm.

February 2nd

Today we are going to the camel market in Birqash, a Cairo suburb. There were about 800 Camels, all for slaughter like cattle. Two little babies were kept aside. The slaughter people had fallen in love with them and are keeping them alive.

Most of the Camels were driven from the Sudan and did not look very good. They are raised strictly for meat.

Outside the Market, a lot of dead Camels lying around. Nobody takes care of dead or dying ones. Stray Dogs are having dinner.

Driving along, many little stores with fresh Camel meat now, hanging from hooks, was for sale. The hump on the camel is expensive to buy. It is special for people. And always live Camel is tied up outside the store ready should they store run out of meat.

There are around 100 pyramids near Cairo, many much older than the famous ones in Giza.

Had Lunch and had to get the Camels ready for our ride to the Giza. Our Bedouin friends supplied the Camels, and we rode from the village to the Pyramids. Great Camel I had again. Very tall. This one I called my Rolls Royce. Very fast up and down. He listened.

Wild riders on Horses show off how they can ride their Horses and kept coming between us. Which made our Camels spooky and Julie fell of her Camel onto the hard ground.

We had to call a Taxi which transported her to the Hospital for x-rays. She had bone chips and bruises.

Dinner at Adels, Doug's Bedouin family, and a late trip back to the Hotel.

Today is a Holiday in Cairo and we went to the Egyptian Museum. There is so much to see it would take weeks and so we had to skip much and look only at King Tut's exhibition.

Then to the Citadel which was again a surprise. It was huge and in perfect shape. It is the biggest Mosque and had at that moment had 2000 worshipers for the Friday Service.

The wind came again, and we all got cold and went back to the Hotel because it started to rain too.

There we got the news that a Ferry leaving from Nuweiba capsized in the storm. 1400 people on board. Not many alive. They were on their way to Mecca.

There is a small Museum called Mr. And Mrs. Khalil Museum. What a treasure. It was a private collection, and I was the only person that day that came to visit. Van Gogh, Cézanne, Peter Rubens, Pizzarro, Mary Coro, Toulouse, Lautrec, Gauguin, Corot, Delacroix Paintings, Rodan statues. It was the finest collection I ever saw. There is no advertising, and I don't even remember how I found it.

Have to go on a diet soon, to many sweet things.

Moving now to a cheaper Windsor Hotel. It is old and historic. Over 100 years old and the Elevator too. It is stuck and I was told somebody will come and fix it. Time stood still here even the switchboard is still in the old style. Phones have to be plugged in when somebody calls. Love it. Like out of an old stories from Agatha Christy. I am on the 5ft floor and my room is filled with Antiques. Every time I walked by the switchboard, I had to think of Lily Tomlins telephone character.

The Hotel is full of men and I need to move to a more woman friendly place. All the cleaning people are men. There is still a caste system and the better educated ones do not labor like cleaning.

I walked all over Cairo today and got lost. Forgot where I was staying. Asking did not help since nobody heard of the Windsor Hotel before. Finally took a taxi. Never had so many stares of men, it is a rumor that foreign women are all cheap. That is why so many women cover up to get away from the sexism.

Stores have the sexiest outfits in the windows and all men stand in front of them looking at it. Stores stay open till 1pm every night.

Trying to sleep again is not possible, since I think my mattress is antique too. I did better in the desert on the Sand.

But I had heat and Air-condition to drown out all noises and the prayer call in the Mosque.

Walked in old town around today, went to the Christian Coptic section. Much to see there. And to the usual market Khan el-Khalili bazaar everybody is trying to sell so much gold. I stick out too much and feel extremely uncomfortable being hassled all the time to buy.

I have always known what Baksheesh is, but here it is important to know how to use it. It is an essential means of supplementing income. Everybody must use it. One must carry lots of small change and to keep it separate from bills. The women here just do not go out alone.

I changed to the Houras Hotel for my last night in Cairo.

I will leave for Luxor on the train. It will be 11 hours. Maybe I am lucky and will have a compartment alone.

At the train station nothing is written in English it is difficult to find out which is my train. Supposed to leave at 8:15pm but found out 4 trains leave at the same time. How can I make myself understand?

Found a lady, covered, only her eyes one could see, who spoke some English and she explained which train to take. Mine was the last to leave, and it was a scary feeling when one does not understand a word. And hoping I had the right train.

I ended up in a wonderful compartment alone. Clean and to my surprise a porter came and took my orders for Dinner. Now I was being spoiled. At 9pm a delicious Dinner of fish, chicken, noodles, rolls filled with Beef, salad, potatoes, bread, cheese, butter, cake. Then my bed was turned down how much better could it be?

At midnight I took a walk in the train and the crew invited me for midnight snack and I fell asleep soon after in my great bed.

I was awakened by the Porter at 5am for breakfast because Luxor arrival was at 6am. Still dark outside.

This is now for me my Agatha Christie time. I am going to look for all the places she wrote in her books about. And places of Lawrence of Arabia.

Luxor

Staying in Hotel Emilio, it is nice. Luxor is clean, a difference from Cairo.

At 8am I am already on the East bank of the Nile to see the Valley of the Kings. Burial site of pharaohs who ruled a thousand years. There are over 60 tombs in the beautiful Valley. I was content visiting just a few and especially Tutankhamun. It is amazing how vivid the sunken reliefs and the color of the murals have remained within these tombs even after 3000 years and countless tourists. So much to see, it is all fascinating to me to be here now and to see it all. The Tombs are big and new ones are discovered all the time. Little villages are on top of some of the tombs and only by accident are tombs discovered. So, the village gets moved.

A stop at Queen Hatshepsut's Temple (El Deir El Bahari). Very impressive. It is so large. And a stop at the newly unearthed Colossi of Memnon.

Luxor is the cruise ship Capital of Riverboats. 305 ships are anchored on the Nile. So many are docked and not any tourists.

Always is there the call from the Minaret for prayer, it is done by electronic so it will be all at the same time.

Luxor is the world 's greatest outdoor museum. Luxor Temple with its avenue of sphinxes. McDonald is on top of the "Street of the Lions". I guess nobody knew what was underneath. It served a very good McArabic burger.

Walking around at night was bad, to many tout's hassle for something. Everybody has something to sell and are grabbing, calling, and stepping right in front of me. It turns me off and I will not buy anything from them.

Made it to the Winter Palace Hotel, famous from Agatha Christi.

I buy great fruit to eat. And there are about 500 Horse-carriages in town. No cars. But must watch not to get run over. They all move in a fast gait. I call it speeding.

The women are not free to move around since it is very Islamic. Now many are wearing the black dress with a face veil.

Breakfast was very strange. A lot of beans.

Bought my ticket for the night show at Karnak the next day. I was told not to miss it.

Took my time walking through a few temples in Luxor and are surprised how many pillars are still standing.

Spend the afternoon relaxing at the pool which I have not been doing much. The view from the pool one can see the Nile and the Valley of the kings.

Left early for Karnack. The temples start with the Avenue of Rams. It is a huge complex, 100 acres, with many Pylons, Obelisks, temples, courtyards and a sacred lake. The Great Hypostyle Hall with its gigantic columns with carvings. Everything is big.

Here was "Death on the Nile" filmed by Agatha Christie. Karnak at night! It was great. And impressive. The biggest pillars and lit at night! One had to just look and feel the presence of many years ago when the "Old Egyptians" walked around. There was music and one was invited to use some imagination.

Rented a felucca, kind of sailboat with a motor. Had to slap a few times the owner on his grubby hand till he got the message not to bother me. He showed me the birds flying around. Large and small Kingfishers, egrets. There are 3 kinds of fish, good and easy to catch.

Went to see Karnak one more time in the daytime. Walking through history one more time, past the heads of gods and animals beneath pillars carved with lotus buds and papyrus.

And the Valley of the Kings again. Hatshepsut Temple, Colossi of Memnon. So much to see and not enough time.

Must meet my night train to Cairo again. Train left at 8:15pm. This time I shared a compartment with a woman from Algeria. Could not believe how fast she got our room messy. All over her cloth but she went to sleep right away and it is ok better this then a snorer.

The food again was unbelievably beautiful served and tasted very delicious.

Arrived at 5:30am in Cairo and took a taxi to the Horus House Hotel. By 6 am I was in bed and slept another 3 hours.

There is not much I can do in Cairo alone except renting a driver again.

It is cold outside but when the sun comes up it gets warm. I have been using the internet cafes to communicate, it is very cheap.

But a bottle of water is expensive, and one must bargain again.

I took a taxi again to Bat Zuwayla. It is an old section of Cairo. 1000 years old. Many stalls, all selling something. A lot of Jewelry. Turquoise galore. A nice pair of earrings $50. But I do not need anything.

Just eating something is good. There are many smokers. Only the men. Women either never smoke in the open or maybe at home?

I do remember the Bedouin women all smoked, but they did whatever they wanted.

So far, I have seen on the streets all different races and religious people. Copts, Christians, Muslims.

And I still eat a lot of Oranges and Tangerines. They do taste better here than anywhere else.

Finally got a room facing away from the Mosque. Prayers kept me awake, not a soothing sound.

Millions of cats are all over outside. Not much to eat for them and all are thin.

Spend some time in the Zoo today. For 25 Piaster entry. It looked like I was the attraction. Many people came close to inspect me. I am the only blond and foreign too. The women are staring, and the children have the scariest look in their eyes.

The Males all were teasing the animals and were throwing stones or anything into the pens to get their attention. Very cruel but all the animals were well fed. Would not visit again and fled back to the Hotel. I usually like to visit Zoos, but this was not a good experience.

My flight home is at 1am and I must get ready for the Airport.

Croatia, Bosnia, Montenegro, Herzegovina, Croatia, Venice, Italy, May 6, 2006

With Kevin into a new travel area.
Zagreb, Croatia.

Croatia is the furthest eastern edge of the Alps on the banks of the Danube in the east. Its central region is covered by the Dinara Mountains.

Interesting on our walk seeing the St. Mark's church roof in Zagreb with the multicolors from 1880. A trip to the huge Mirogof Cemetery with impressive architecture Mausoleums and tombs, it is among the finest of European cemeteries.

There are street musicians. Zagreb's picturesque markets and statues are beautiful.

The restaurant food was excellent. Zagorski, a kind of Strudel with cheese, my favorite. And I think the ice cream was the best ever.

Bosnia

Crossing the border to Bosnia and Herzegovina over small Mountain roads. Stopping at Jajce and the Pliva Lake region.

I was warned not to get off any trail because of landmines when walking around. 1 million mines are supposed to be still buried.

Jajce, which was very much bombed in the last war is being rebuilt but looks pretty bad with so many bomb craters and destroyed homes.

At the Restaurant we stopped a private kennel full of wolves. They were like Pets for the Owner. Fascinating Animals.

Sarajevo

Staying at the Hotel Grand. Our view out the window was of bombed out places.

But our tour to the supply Tunnel at a farmhouse to the Airport was interesting. It is now a Museum and we marched right through the family's house down some stairs into the Tunnel. It was then the only gateway to get out of Sarajevo during the Bosnian war. The house was still bullet pocked. Inside we watched a film that explained how the Tunnel was built. It took four months to dig, 2500 feet long. 15 feet below the ground and five feet high ceiling. We walked single file 75 feet, onto the other end I tried to image myself of the 4000 people who had passed through daily loaded with 100 pounds of food on their backs to feed the landlocked city. I was told 2 million trips had been made. This was for the 300 000 people in Sarajevo shut off from the world.

There are still graves in any available place.

Sarajevo is visited by tourists again. Bridges must be rebuilt.

We are now in Mostar. The photo of the famous Stari Grad Bridge was shown so much in the war and the destruction of it. It is now rebuilt which spans the Neretva River. And it means that life is slowly but surely returning to normal in what is most certainly the most beautiful city in Bosnia.

Dubrovnik

A trip in Dubrovnik is not complete if you do not walk the city walls. 1,940 meters long, it is one of the most beautiful fortification systems in Europe. At some places, the Wall is 25 meters high. Looking down, picturesque rooftops of the buildings are with unusual chimneys.

The baroque Cathedral was constructed on the foundations of a Romanesque sacral structure. The cathedral is furnished with valuable paintings of old masters, among Tizian's of the "Assumption of our Lady" above the great altar.

A nice sunset cruise took us around the coast and views of Dubrovnik. The wind came up and it turned into a very rocky cruise and we all were glad to be on land again.

Montenegro

Next day over the mountains again to Montenegro. Stopped in Budva referred to as St. Tropez of the Adriatic. With many seaside café's, is reflecting a faded Riviera ambience.

Cruising the Bay of Kotor and drinking Turkish coffee on board.

Kotor is unique; it has a wall built straight up the dramatic rocky mountain. Surrounded by Mountains. The markets selling locally made cheese and olive oil.

Bosnia

Pit stop in Bosnia again. I love all the little places where one can taste homemade foods.

Croatia

Going north along the Dalmatian coast with the most azure colored water to Split, Croatia.

A great place for overnight again. Lots of wine is produced here. Some of the best-known varieties of Croatian red wines.

Trogir our next stop. Another old town and is like a museum. Romanesque to modern interiors. Having lunch here and very good.

Next Zadar, Vodice and to Plitvice Lake. Or plitvicka jezera.

Plitvice is a National Park and full of interlinked lakes. It is divided into upper lakes and lower lakes. The highest is at 639 meters and one follows many different pass ways to the lower lakes. All is surrounded by forests and numerous waterfalls.

At some of the larger lakes we went by boat.

Afterwards we came to an area were heavy bombing left many buildings in burned out shape with warning signs of Landmines in the area of Kvarner Highlands.

Getting back to the coast again to Opatija, a warm and sunny place. We hired a little boat with a captain who puttered with us around for a few hours and suggested a Lunch place for us which turned into the most expensive 4 star, with very good food. The Lady's room had everything stocked one could ever need.

Slovenia

Now to Bled for overnight. My memories will be the highlight of this place. I loved the lake, and we did have very good weather. Our Hotel was first class and had rowing boats for use we took advantage off.

We rowed to Bled Castle, it is Slovenia's oldest and perches at the top of a steep cliff above Lake Bled.

Stopped at the little Island in the middle of the lake.

Food in our Hotel was fabulous, especially the desserts. We rented bicycles to do some more exercise into the countryside.

Ljubljana was the next stop, a city full of life. It is like a small town but then it is like a metropolis too. It is a city of culture, many theatres, museums and Galleries. It is a city of music and concerts.

The medieval town of Radovljica is our next stop at the country Inn "Lectar" in a 500-year-old public building. Serving food since 1822 and all the traditional Slovenian food. After dinner everybody started to sing, and Kevin found a Guitar and played beautiful blues music.

Next day a visit to one of the caves in the limestone mountains. Postojnska was not for me. I do not like caves.

Driving to our final stop, Venice, have been there many times and still love it. Even with all the tourists shoving one around. Chioggia for a quick visit it was better since not many tourists go there. Not the mass of people.

Our final day spend walking around Venice and in the morning by water taxi to the Airport. The Water taxi came right in front of the Hotel to pick us up and dropped us inside the Airport entrance.

Poland, January 5, 2007

To Poland this time with my friends Ursel and Werner Ott. We went to Trebnica (Trebnitz) to meet a few of my friends in the Motherhouse of the Barromaier nuns. The convent has many guestrooms which used to be the nun's rooms, I am always welcome there. There are still 200

Nuns at the convent. It was a Holiday in Poland and the nuns had good times, especially when one of the Nuns came in a Bear costume and started dancing for us.

Trebnice is close to Wroclaw (Breslau) and a daytrip to it with a nun was interesting since she could show us many places we would not have known. The town was totally bombed in the war but has been rebuilt exactly in the old style again.

Saying goodbye to Sr. Raymunda is always difficult one never knows if we see each other again.

We are calling this the nunnery trip since we are staying mostly at convents. Gliwice (Gleiwitz) now.

Tschenstochau to the Church of the black Madonna. Sr. Blanka was here our tour guide.

Arriving in Konigshutte and checking out my Grandfathers Building which we owned and was taken from us after the war. Wolnosci 50 is the house number.

Now on the way to Glucholasy (Ziegenhals). My birthplace. More restoration has been done since my last visit. Except behind the backs of the houses nothing gets done. There it all crumbles.

Driving up to our House on the Hill was as always, a total remembering of what happened here when I was a child. The street is called Chopin St. Ul. 5!!

And nothing has changed on the house since 1945.

Then to Nissa(Neisse) Still with a lot of war damage.

Driving on to Kamieniec Zabkovichi (Glatz). A small city. Many places are empty, and the big Castle on the Hill is like a ghost house. There were stray dogs sleeping in the stairwells.

We stayed in a smaller convent and only 8 nuns were there. All of the Convents have the best cooks.

In Karpacz(Krummhuebel) now, it is a ski place. There is the famous Schneekoppe, the highest mountain in Silesia. As children we used to come here and many stories have been told about Ruebezahl, the Giant who lives up there. Naturally there is always a man dressed like him walking in the streets.

The old Wang church made out of wood is still a draw for tourist, since it was brought here from Sweden 150 years ago.

Our home is this time a beautiful Convent called "Marta". Since it is so close to the ski area the nuns rent out all rooms in ski season.

Here I had my favorite polish food. Sr. Martha knew what I liked, stuffed Dumplings with plums. Cinnamon butter on top, heaven!

Azores, Spain, Monaco, Rome, Italy, Dubrovnik, San Marino, Venice, Italy, May 2007

Fort Lauderdale, Florida by ship across the Atlantic. With Holland America's "Veendam". Great ship. 21 days.

Kevin and I celebrated Easter on it. It was so beautiful and so much fun. Watched from our deckchairs the Atlantic for flying fish, Dolphins and clutter in the water.

We docked after 5 days in the Port of Ponta Delgada on Sao Miguel Acores. Such beautiful Island and cleanliness! The Green color of fields and forests almost hurt my eyes. There are 135 000 cows on this Island.

A drive to the Sete Cidades. There are 7 lakes, all beautiful. It is unmatched in beauty and charm. The water is sparkling clean and the Azores people are warm and friendly. Even here the Romans left ruins like the waterworks. Wherever one looks Calla Lilly's are sticking their heads up.

Almost all homes are traditional Portuguese and built elegant in baroque style. And that is where we are going to spend a few hours to visit friends. It is like paradise here.

The city gates are an artistic construction. Need many more days to come back here again.

Cadiz

Next stop in Cadiz, Spain. We are taking the tasting trip to a winery Tio Pepe. But not only Wine, many Horses are here too.

The Equestrian show was nice with Andalusian Horses.

Cadiz a typical Spanish town supposed to be the oldest in Spain. The streets are very narrow.

Barcelona

Gaudi's Barcelona next. Guell Park is unique of Gaudi's imagination and work.

La Pedrera also known as Casa Mila very crazy built. And then Sagrada Familia Church! Still not finished.

Again, one of the best Lunches from an open fire. We were warned lots of pickpockets in Barcelona and to watch out.

Monaco

Monaco is the world's most densely populated country. It is impressive to see such organization and everything runs smooth. The main attraction is the daily ceremony of the changing of the Guard. At precisely at 11:55am, the carabineers perform the elaborate ceremony.

Looking down from the Palace a wonderful view of the Grand Prix.

It always intrigues me how it could happen here. Streets get closed and nobody can go anywhere at the race time.

The Casino de Monte Carlo another dream for me to happen. The elegance! One feels so queenly inside. And I was lucky. After entering the gaming rooms, I was awe struck by the world's most illustrious place. It is legendary to me. I was looking for James Bond. I won with my first 5 cent bid - $100. Loved the sound of the clangy machine and we were invited by the Casino personal to the fancy betting room. No bets under $5000. I just watched.

Rome

The stop by ship is called Civitavecchia. A long way from Rome. 2 hours to drive. We tried to go to the Eternal City inside but so early already lines formed for miles. It meant a 3 hour wait. I got to talk to a Swiss Guard, which is a 90 strong army for the Vatican. The guards are recruited in Switzerland are tall and must remain unmarried during their tour of duty. The red, yellow and blue uniform was designed by Michelangelo.

The Pantheon is the grandest antiquity built by Hadrian in 1266AD. The Cupola made from bricks was the largest freestanding dome in the world till 1960.

Nearby is the Trevi Fountain. Rome's most famous fountain as it flows dramatically from a whole in the wall. Neptune is the central figure representing calm and stormy sea.

The tradition is to throw a coin into the fountain if you wish to return. And I did and I returned twice now but not giving any more money.

Now to the Spanish steps, it is the popular meeting place.

The Coliseum must be seen and many men dressed as Gladiators are running around trying to be guides.

One of my favorite places is the Piazza Marco Polo. It is grand!

On the ship again and a big dinner party tonight. We try to do Trivia every day and Kevin will play Guitar on the walking deck and entertain.

Dubrovnik

We are now in Dubrovnik by ship again. It is the second time in 11 months. It still is fascinating. And many of the roofs have been now repaired.

Italy

Leaving now for Venice Italy. We have been very lucky with the weather, for 21 days not wind or wave on the water. So our trip of leisure is over. A rental car will take us now around. The leaving of the ship was hard. Nice to have such good service.

Lucca, with the amazing high towers. Naturally, we had to climb all of them.

Trying now to find the entrance for our hike along the Cinque Terre. We started in Monterosso al Mare. It can be done on foot, train or ship. We did it by foot.

There are five Villages clinging to this most inaccessible bit of Italian Riviera coastline. Each is a variation. Like a gangly clump of Oysters, the houses grow on each other. There are no comfortable hotels in the area but rented rooms are the norm.

Depending on one's pace and how long one stops for a glass of wine, one could do it in one day. But we took our time and walked slow and averaged 3 hours every day.

Vernazza is next, lots of lemon trees here. Gardens are terraced and drop into the Mediterranean. Wine growers use monorails to ferry themselves up or down with the grapes and Olives.

Many heart stopping views of the coast and the romantic little villages. The well signposted goat trail we hiked along is easy to find.

When finally reaching Vernazza it looks like it could fall into the water.

Corniglia, different. Smaller and very narrow lanes. With many vineyards hanging on the cliffs.

Never understood why a wine was sold with Adolf Hitler on the label in every store.

One had to climb 300 steps of the trail into the village and out again.

The enchanting colored pastel houses of Manarola overlooking the turquoise sea. The whole town is built on black rock. One can walk the paved path called Via dell'Amore so named for romantic vistas.

Getting to Riomagiore, were we have rented a pensione right down by the water. In the morning Kevin running for fresh bread and having outside breakfast was very Italian.

Next day a boat trip to Porte Venero.

Our Apt. was good but plain. We could talk to everybody next door, or to the other people on their balcony's.

And now by car to Pisa. Everybody has to see Pisa. Did visit all the Buildings and the Duomo. All very impressive. Kevin was more interested in the Gelato.

We stopped at many Gelato places.

Sienna was for me to see. I wish the Palio would have been on. It was not the time of year. We did climb the tower.

Driving inland to Casa Bolsinia, a country house hotel. Kevin played his Guitar for the evening hours. It was beautiful to listen to it. Even the Farmer made it a point to come and listen. The Tuscan kitchen is highly recommended.

Going now to a castle San Leo with a view from the towers for miles.

San Marino

Reaching finally the Republic of San Marino. Is it the smallest country in the world? Hotel Titano was excellent and we had a beautiful sunset and with wine.

There are 3 castles in San Marino, and all can be visited.

Our trip is coming to an end we must go to Venice for our return to USA.

Costa Rica, May 11, 2007

South to Costa Rica with Petra. Hotel Aurola in San Jose was our first stop. We did a Day trip to Volcan Poas. Stopping at big green plants called Poor Man's Umbrella, then along the Suzio River to where it merged with the limpio River.

We took the Aerial Tram in Braulio Carrillo Park. Lots of wildlife can be seen there. Blue jeans frog- very poison. Found sugar cane Beetles, 10 inches big. They make great pets we were told.

A stop at a Banana Plantation run by Dole.

And into the tropical Rainforest in Tortuguero Park. Stayed at the Pachira Lodge. Did it rain! There I saw for the first time the strangest Lizard, like a green leaf. About 30 inches big.

Many howler Monkeys and lots of tropical birds. Not much sleep that night, the Monkeys made noise on top of our roof.

The Selva Verde Reserve was next. There walking across a 300-foot suspension Bridge over a jungle River.

Arenal Springs next. It is a new Hotel and right near the Volcano. It has his own Natural volcanic hot falls and pools.

Visiting Finca Julieta nearby which had a lot of tame birds. Our guide showed us what one could eat out in the forest and so many different flowers I encountered.

Now to Jaco to the Amapola Hotel on the Pacific. Relaxed a few days there.

A short stop at Manuel Antonio Park and then to Sarchi to look at the finest paintings on wooden furniture and Ox carts.

In Grecia we stopped at the metal temple. It was sent from Belgium to Limon on the seaport in 1892. From there all was transported via train to Alajuela and later to Grecia in carts and wagons pulled by Oxen.

Stopping at a coffee plantation where we had to taste different fresh coffees and learn about the history of the coffee bean.

Then we decided to go to a place very few tourists ever go.

To the Golfo Dulce.

Up early at 4am to catch the Bus. It was supposed to be the fast Bus. To Palma Norte 5 Hours. The Driver did stop a few times for a rest. It was very strange to go over snowcapped Mountain and a long pit stop on top. We needed it. At 11000 feet a nice Restaurant with a big fire to warm.

Many Hummingbirds sitting on the window frames inside and outside trying to get warm too. Then the Bus continued down to warmer climate again. Eventually arriving in Sierpe, the last big town in Costa Rica. The Road ends here and no more Bus service. The train from San Jose used to come here but stopped in 1968. The train is sitting there for many years.

Next to the train is one stone ball and it is guessed it is 5000years old. How was it formed so big and perfect?

We tried to connect with a small plane to our destination, but nobody wanted to fly in the upcoming storm. A fisherman offered to take us by boat. What a mistake! After this no need.

For me to go on a thrill ride ever. I thought we would drown. We were on the open Ocean! The waves came over us and we were totally drenched when arriving at Punta Rio Claro. The boat shot right over the rocks and sand onto the Beach. What a landing! There was no pier, and nobody expected us.

On top of the hill one could see the "Lodge" How to get up there in this rain and water flowing down the Hills? It felt like the sky's opened up.

We crawled in the mud up. Our cottage was a simple thatch roofed cabin sitting slanted on a hillside atop a high bluff. Yes, getting there was exiting. We discovered the plastic sheet on our roof did nothing to keep us dry. Our cloth, our bed, everything was wet. But it was warm climate and we decided to always wear our swimsuits now. There is no electric here only candles. We are surrounded by Rain forest with tropical Beaches. Almost all trees in the forest are huge mango trees. And full of Mangos, very ripe. The funny part was, the Monkeys. They thought we were intruders walking around and kept bombarding us with Mangos.

There was an open airy Restaurant and cooking was done just for us. No other tourist there. We did have to protect ourselves at night with Mosquito nets. But we always had to clean out the nets before using them, because Mosquitos, spiders, frogs, crawly bugs, everybody tried to hide in a dry place and that was our bed.

I would say if one wanted to go to "there and beyond and even beyond there" then this is the place.

We did walk and enjoyed some time but never saw the sun for 3 days and decided to go back to San Juan. Easy said but how? We did not take the boat back; we hired a man to carry our bags and walked for hours to Palmer Norte where I have reserved a small plane to bring us back to San Jose. No plane ever arrived and finally we took the bus for 7 hours back.

Tracopa Air is advertising as always on time. Not so.

Finally arriving at our Hotel Britanio in San Jose and just enjoying a hot shower and a good sleep.

Passage to India, November 13, 2007

A timely departure and a lot of room on the plane. Food was awful. This is Air France and I expected good food. Changing planes in Paris gave me time to eat good food in the Airport.

Now my flight to India is full. Seats have become smaller. Left at 10:30am and arrived in New Delhi again in the middle of the night, 12am. I haul myself bleary eyed through the crowded New Delhi airport.

Namaste: Welcome to India from my driver who was waiting and an hour drive to the city brought me to the Hotel Grand Godwin. Clean but too noisy. Never got to sleep and moved into another room in the morning.

Many years ago, in 1992, I backpacked through India and now I am staying in better Hotels, I have upgraded.

But now I find out on top of me is the sundeck and I hear deckchairs moved at 5am. Wonder how it will be at night? I did glue black plastic bags to the windows to keep the light out. I always carry duct tape and plastic bags with me.

Today toured some of New Delhi and was surprised how much cleaner the city is since I was here last time.

The cows are gone! No red spittle! But there is one cow looking in the garbage downstairs still.

The traffic is horrendous and grey smog is all over the city. Looks like dirty air. My eyes sting and itch from it.

I did go to see Humayun's Tomb and Sayan tomb. Much Indian history there.

Slept better with my sleeping pill.

Breakfast is so good. Love all the spices. There is always fresh bread and the pancakes. I have to stop eating.

Moved to the new Shervani Fort View Hotel. It is a small boutique Hotel in an expensive area. I think a little overpriced but clean. The room is small and has many buttons I have to figure out which ones to use for the lights especially.

Every Indian woman is wearing a Sari. In 1947 there was a day of burning western clothing for men and women. But the men have gone back to western outfits again. The women look beautiful, every Sari is different.

There is a sign: Walk Foot over Bridge. I think their English is different too.

Most of my money is spend on taxis. It is quicker, even if I try to walk a lot.

The policemen have beautiful Horses but there are a lot of Horses still pulling carriages and wagons. They are always loaded and the Horses to skinny. It is a sad sight.

A Van trip to Agra. Lots of traffic it is so bad one cannot describe it. The smog is still with us and it is hard to get air.

Agra

The Taj Mahal a monument of love built by the emperor Sha Jehan for his wife Mumtaz. It is the most photographed monument in the world. And now these days' men get away with giving flowers and chocolates to their wives only.

It took 20 000 workers and 1000 Elephants and 22 years to build the Taj Mahal. It is pure white marble with much inlaid stones.

It is impressive. I am walking around, I do not feel the love coming to me, as I was told. Guides always make up stories.

And guess who I run into- Jesse Jackson!!!He was doing some peace talking and made a stop to see the Taj Mahal. There are not many Negros here and he stuck out especially since he had a large entourage with him.

Staying today in the Hotel Howard Park Plaza. It is Grand with beautiful Gardens. Excellent Dinner and hopefully a good night. One more quick trip to the evening sunset at the Taj Mahal. Beautiful.

To Rajasthan. On my quest to see the Mawari Horses.

Jaipur

A long 200-mile drive to Jaipur. Roads are bad and full of traffic. Camel wagons, Donkey, Horse, Rickshaws and anything with wheels. Nobody follows the rules of traffic. Weaving in or out is the fun. I just close my eyes and hope for the best.

Stopped for Lunch at a Ghost city called Fatehpur Sikri. All historical shape. It was abandoned because of scarcity of water but it remains most complete of a Mughul city.

Jaipur our next destination, the colorful capital of the state of

Rajasthan. Traditionally dressed Raiput men wearing colorful turbans and sporting magnificent moustaches.

The General's Retreat is really a palace and converted for Guests as a Hotel. It is beautiful and again with many flowers everywhere.

My bedroom was so nice, and I slept very good makes me feel very happy in the morning. The Host is a Maharadsha family. Old Family's like that need money and have opened their homes as B&B's. Some have very beautiful Restaurants.

Underneath my window are the Croquet courts and in neat shape. It must be difficult to keep the steady dust out. Jaipur is so dirty. Many cows are walking around, and the usual camels and working Elephants mingle with the traffic. There are stray dogs all over. They do not belong to anyone. I do notice people are feeding constantly the animals.

Stopped at a Palace, it is the highest-ranking Maharajas living there. A splendid place. Just going inside, one is transported into a different world. Yes, the style of the Rich.

Took a bike Rickshaw ride through town. What a mess this town is. No rules on the Road at all, but one is safe even if it looks like a crash coming up.

Had Dinner at a 300-year-old Narain Niwas palace. Fantastic dinner. Watched how chapattis are made fresh for every table.

Chicken cooked in a Tandori Oven, Chicken Tikka, my favorite, it is marinated in cheese. Paneer and Roti filled with cheese and fried.

I slept so good and did not want to leave I felt like I was at home.

Pushkar

The Pushkar Fair was next. Something I have wanted to visit for a long time. It is always held at the high Moon once a year.

Drove a long way through the Rajasthan Desert now. It is a quite different landscape. Very dry and lots of Sand.

Up the Hills, through some valleys. And finally arriving in the Pushkar Valley.

What a place!

Pushkar is located in the Thar desert. It is considered a holy place and is situated adjacent to a lake which is off limit to foreigners except once a year.

Many holy men are walking around. And I was told nothing from animals can be eaten or used in this Valley. Total Vegetarian not even a leather belt can be used. There are 1000 temples in the city.

There is much to see in the city itself and one can find fine food, even prepared on the streets. I can hear drums and was told they go on for the whole festival.

All guests are housed in long rows of tents. It is highly organized. Clean and with many toilets. We sleep in rows and it looks like a Hospital.

Signs to read: "Attention for Tourists PLZ keep shoes 30 feet away from Lake. Woman should dress upwell in public. Drugs/non veg. Strictly prohibited in town. Respect the Hindu culture.

Do not embrace in public and dress up. Photography of bathing pilgrim's in holy lake is strictly prohibited".

Going out again after a short rest to see more of the Camels and Horses. They are everywhere. As far one can see, Animals and Fires surrounded by people. Maybe 100 000 Camels. I came to see the famous Mawari Horse. And I saw my dream Horse and was ready to buy her but too difficult to bring her home.

Went to the sunset Café to watch the sun go down over the Fair. And to top it off with a spectacular firework. For Dinner that night to the Rainbow Restaurant.

After this we had a 3 mile walk back to the tent camp.

Today is a lot of Horse performance.

It is exciting for me because now I will see the Marwari Horse in Action. Not all Animals brought to the fair are for sale. Many are there just to be seen and admired. Like a livestock exposition. Attendees come from all over the north of India.

The colors of women's Saris are like butterflies. Men wear more plain outfits, but each has a turban wrapped to perfection on his head. Turban colors identify different classes and tribes. The men of Rajasthan, where Pushkar is located, are known for their mustaches and competing for having the longest moustache.

I am learning a lot of "my" Mawari horse. Told there are 5 types. But I see little difference. It is a beautiful bred Horse and has an instinct for always finding home should anything happen to his rider. The breed population declined when the British came to India with their own Horses. However, thanks to the Rajput families and other horse lovers, the Mawari has emerged with a promise of a good future.

The distinctive feature of the Horse, which is amusing to observe. The Mawari can move independently his ears in different direction. The ears are called "lyre" or "scimitar" shaped ears. They curve towards one another so their tips almost touch. The body is like an Arab Horse except longer legs. I did finally ask how much I would have to pay for the one Horse I liked. $4000. But shipping was not possible.

And there are all the Camels. All of them are having different haircuts. With shavers many designs are made on the bodies of the Camels and many are painted to attract buyers.

It was all exciting and rented a camel cart for transportation to see more of the Countryside.

Ate Dinner at the Tent cafeteria, it was good and as usual vegetarian. The drums are not as loud tonight and hope to sleep more.

The nights are cold, and I was happy having a lot of blankets. The food is expensive in the camp, but I think since we are all tourists we can afford it.

Stopped today for a very good "Lassie" Yoghurt, cashews and cheese, mix it and drink it.

Driving through sand and mountains to our next stop. Seeing a lot of deserted crashed cars and busses by the side of the Road.

As we had lunch in a small place an Indian family was next to us eating. Close by sat a woman eating from a plate at their feet. All were in Saris and looked beautiful. But when I asked my guide why the one woman was sitting there, he explained she is the maid and she was not allowed to sit at the table, only on the floor. Disgusting to me.

Hotel Nimaj Heritage Palace. A Royal welcome for us. To live like a Raja, recreate the lives of the past and still have the latest modern offerings. There are many Royal retreats in the state of Rajasthan.

Our transportation here is an Oxcart. That is beautiful Luxury. The Oxen were the finest bred and festooned with garlands.

Some of the parts of the Hotel had not been redone yet and it was interesting to see the old sections. This is a place where the Movie "Passage to India" was filmed.

Big Gates invited us in and were closed in the evening. Afternoon tea with English sandwiches served by a turbaned young man.

My room is gorgeous. It is really a suite.

I walked a little through the village and had a following of 100 children just trying to see what I was doing. And all wanted to be photographed. There are seldom tourist so nobody was hassling or begging.

But the air is horrible. So much dust. We are all sniffing and coughing. Whatever it is, like burning tires. I was told it is the cooking fires of the village.

It is cold at night and daytime brings warm air.

This morning very acid smoke. We need gas mask. I closed the windows again.

There is no bottled water in the village to buy. So the Palace people are cooking water for us. It is like in an Oasis.

A flute player is calling for breakfast; he is standing in the courtyard for 30 minutes. It is a beautiful sound. I usually do not like Indian music. Especially the Sitar screeches. All adults and children play it. But this Flute was like in a dream sounding.

Walked again through the village. Everybody wants me to come in for a cup of tea. Lunch was Onion soup and Indian dishes.

After a good nap we all went by jeep through the countryside to a lake. Saw blue deer, a strange looking Antelope. Many beautiful birds and a great sundown.

Tea was served with biscuits.

Dinner that night on the Ramparts under a full Moon. My guide loves this, he is still thinking living is great with servants. He claims under the Maharajas care, everybody had a good life.

7am the flute player is at it again. I would love to pay him to go away. As much I love it I want to sleep in, I love my bed.

We are on our way to Jodhpur. A 3-hour drive through green areas, Alfalfa, cotton, Dill, potatoes, tomatoes, Reddish, Rice. And lots of cattle. The cattle are not for eating just work. Many peacocks, sheep and goats. Stopped at a pottery to watch water containers done. They were huge. They usually last 2 years if not dropped. Nearby a Gypsy fortune teller with his snake tried to tell us our fortune.

Jodhpur

Jodhpur is in the Thar Desert. We passed Battle scarred Forts. It is now the land of the Rajas. Jodhpur is blue. The big Fort is so impressive one can see it from far away already. Everything is in blue color. The Fort is really a palace and was the most feudal palace I have ever seen. Graceful inside. My visit was too short.

It is the Wedding Season and we saw a lot of preparations for this weekend parties. There will be lots of fireworks tonight.

Our home is the Ratan Vilas. A quiet colonial, family villa, fronted by a serene lawn area.

Went to Dinner to the Rock Café! Had chicken tikka. It is my favorite and gets better each time.

The Villa is beautiful. This family is into polo-playing. That is an expensive sport.

There is a 3-day holiday but I cannot figure out what it is with a big parade, looks religious.

Drove into the country again by jeep and saw a big herd of the blue Antelopes.

We have lunch in a very neat and clean place at Kulinda. I have watched all the time for cleanliness. One does not want to get "Delhi Belly."

I have coffee on the Veranda at our Villa; I like the lifestyle of the rich.

There are so many people needing jobs and one can get any help for cheap. Jodhpur has too many people without jobs. The Gardeners keep beautiful gardens with flowers and fruit trees.

For Dinner we went to a Havalu and sat on top of the Rampart with a view all over the city with very good food and service. Beer and Dinner $7! It would have been like $100 in the USA.

Stopped today a lot on our way to Udaipur. The land is getting greener leaving the dessert behind.

With a break at a Jain Temple. It is one of India's oldest religion. They believers wear a scarf in front of their face, so they do not swallow a fly. Never kill an animal!

Since we had to take shoes off, I stepped almost on a Wasp. Then I tried to kill it, I was prevented by a grab to my arm from the guard. No killing!

And driving through some very curving mountain roads. A hairy ride I must say. Drivers are so macho.

Udaipur

Our Hotel RamPratap Palace in Udaipur was again an old Palace next to the lake. Beautiful view from the window.

The lake is called Fateh Sagar. And in the middle of it is the most beautiful Palace in India. Now a Hotel Maharana Pratap. We had a tea ceremony there. The water is dirty, and it even stinks but nothing is more beautiful than the view.

The city is small and crowded. Many holy men are around. It does look like something out of a fairy tale. Lake Pichhola with the most beautiful Maharana Pratap Hotel looking like it is floating on top of the water.

My stay in Udaipur was to short, had lunch in the Royal Car collection Palace. And a little walking around and then to the Airport for my last leg of my trip to Jodhpur again.

This is a perfect country to travel as a woman alone. One only must hire a good English-speaking driver and stop at all the beautiful Heritage Hotels. There are always many servants who will look after one. I wonder sometimes what their salary is but it does cost less living here.

In Jodhpur I hired an Indian car with a turbaned driver to take me to Rohet Garh. Have read about this place as great riding and for a rest place. Was in touch with the owner Siddarth Singh and made my reservation to visit.

Rohet Garh is a Heritage Hotel in the Desert and I am going there to meet my private Mawari steed.

Rohet Garh has been for 12th direct descendent of its first ruler. It stands on a Lake shore and is an Oasis amid the sandy dryness of the surrounding Marwar country. The architecture is a blend of traditional Rajput and colonial. Few tourists come here. A little village is attached to the castle.

Arriving at the Gates which were enormous and painted with

beautiful murals. The Gate was high enough so Elephants could pass. On entering it was a quite different world. I felt like out of an Indian princess story.

Rohet Garh is the ancestral home of Thakur Dalput Singh. It was built in 1622 and has the appearance of a fort with a large courtyard. It is now a resort Hotel providing nearly every conceivable comfort.

I have an excessively big apt. on the Ramparts with a great view over the countryside. It is beautiful and one can get lost inside there. Still could not sleep. I had a room boy called Dedaran. He was always ready to do something for me. Wonder what all he could have done?

I finally fell asleep and woke to another sunny day. The weatherman on TV has it easy always sunny.

There is a lake down by the walls and many birds are attracted to it. Beneath the exterior walls is a section serving as stables.

Had to bargain with the management about my room rate. It suddenly was very high and got it down to my estimate again of $100 a night.

There is a pool and lounge tents. A sort of Cabana to read and rest which I am taking advantage off. I love being spoiled. Having coffee and tea served on the lawn, so English.

Rohet is surrounded by desert plains with no fences or roads. Sand is everywhere except for occasional irrigated grain fields, the stubble which feeds lots of wild animals, such as the blue Antelope.

Today at 7am I was on my first ride on a Mawari Horse into the desert, my cleaned and saddled Horse was presented to me. A 7-year-old mare. It was exhilarated at finally being on a Mawari. My guide Mr. Singh was on a black stallion. Very spirited Horse. And so light on their feet.

What surprised me was that they never sweated. It was extremely hot by 10am. Yet never did they falter although they moved very strongly. Apparently because their skin is so thin, they take thirst and heat in stride, and require very small feed rations or water.

Coming back a groom was waiting to take the Horse and I went to a late breakfast by the pool.

Oh, the lifestyle of the rich!

My nose is still running from the air in the city's. The silence here is strange after so much traffic noise and honking, barking and loudness.

Went on a 2 hour walk and saw many strange birds. Insects sounds, mongoose babies with a mother. A few cattle herders and goats.

The pool is cold today, so I had only sandwiches and a drink by the pool. A peacock just came by and ate the lizard that was eating my Sandwich crumbs.

Talking to some of the guest is interesting. There is music but not what I like. And for Dinner I had again the best chicken Tikka.

Leaving today for a ride into the Desert to a wilderness tent camp. A jeep took my travel bag ahead.

Today I am finding out how steady my Horse is in the heat. We stopped at a farm for rest. There was some shade. It was fun attempting to converse with the three women, who lived there, mostly by hand or sign language.

One embarrassing moment was when I needed to relieve myself. They motioned for me just to squat, but it was difficult for me to do so in public and in riding pants. The women took me by the hand and showed me a fence and then you squat right there I was motioned. They effort at modesty made me the joke of the day.

Finally, we left at the hottest time of the day. Horses did not like it and started bucking on leaving, so finally Dedaran had to ride each Horse in circles to tire them before I could get on again. And off we trotted, the Horse I was riding was 3 years old and I was not in the mood to train it. The sand is hot, and one can feel it on top of the Horse, heat is rising.

Crossing the desert one gets to see camels, goats, sheep and blue buck. All animals do not bother to run since there is no hunting.

Saw many foxes riding.

As the day's riding ended, I was the one needing water and was anxious to see the tent camp because by this time we had exhausted our water supply and I was ready for more fluids.

It was the most beautiful sight for me- the camp. And what a camp! Luxury. And I am drinking water to feel good again.

I was the only guest, and all the servants were spoiling me. I sat now in front of my tent cannot call it a tent. My Palace maybe. Flushing toilets, running water and accommodations fit for the rich and famous. (Madonna stayed here just a week after my visit.)

As the sun set, our horses could be seen standing next to a tree sleeping. It was totally peaceful for me to be the sole guest amongst the handful of the camp's staff and our Mawari. Riding 40 km and not having to do anything except relax!

It is almost like an African Safari except the waterhole here is dried out and not many animals are here. There is a pig with about 10 babies. And some partridges and geese. I am taking a quick nap after having a gin and tonic. Now awakened by a young man for tea and sandwiches at sundown, just beautiful.

Many candles were lit as it got dark.

Later my Dinner at 8pm was chicken Tikka by my request. There are many fires burning, and it makes this place magical but maybe to keep bugs away too.

My bed was just wonderful and still slept little. Just early in the morning I fell asleep again. But soon awakened at 6am with Chai tea. Yuck. Horrible forgot to tell them I hate it. But then an exceptionally good breakfast and off at 7am so it would be cooler to ride home. My Horse decided to buck again, and I decided to just walk and give up on riding faster with her.

We have a different way home much more trees. The sky is full of flying cranes. Love the sound.

Made it back to Rohet Garh and I will rest and read a book by the pool.

I have decided not to eat all this fattening food anymore. Lassie's, chicken tikka. One does not get much exercise since it is so beautiful to sit by the pool or up at the Ramparts.

I walked through the little village, but the children are very nasty here, trying to grab anything I have in my hands. Then I was offered Opium which I declined. It is illegal and deadly. 3 Villagers were so drugged lying there next to a wall.

Nice music in the evening.

Today we went on a ride with a new Horse called Bull bull but again young and my guide on a very young stallion. We had every excitement on our Horses. I wondered, how I did not come off. We had a bucking and a circling and then it is time for me to get off. I feel like I am here to train their Horses.

Found another good dish tonight called vegetable Florentine. Spinach and cheese on mushrooms then baked.

This morning I am on Bull bull again. She is behaving wonderful. The mornings are pretty cool, and it is good to ride out at that time. There are no flies.

December 2007

The Singh family invited me to go to one of the big Polo games put on by the Maharadja Baba Roja of Jodhpur.

Getting there I thought we would get killed. The driver never heard of careful driving and it did not seem to bother the family how he drove; we all could have been killed.

The Polo field is something. So clean and so many flowers everywhere. I was told by my Host Marvendra Singh Rohet to sit in the front row and wait for my seat neighbor. This turned out to be the Maharadja Gaj Singh of Jodhpur. It was like sitting next to the Queen of England.

I was impressed that I was a special guest. Felt very Royal. The M. arrived in a 1947 Studebaker car, such a shiny car! After introduction we both found out our love for Mawari Horses. He invited me to visit his stables, but I was short on time. That was the most stupid thing to decline I have ever done.

We retired to his tent after the game for coffee and cake.

All players got a little silver bowl as a present from the Maharaja.

I must go back to Rohet for my last night. I am closing my eyes on the return trip for the fear of crashing.

The last Dinner was potato soup, cauliflower, green onion with broccoli, chicken curry, lamb, Tandoori chicken with yoghurt.

Chocolate almond fudge with gold leaf decoration for dessert.

This morning a little walk again by the lake and then it was back to Jodhpur.

Jodhpur is hot hot and hot.

It was a great time in India, and I wish I would have rented from the beginning a driver with his car and then just toured India. Seems to be the best choice.

New Delhi Airport is a disaster. This is the old Airport still, must be a million people in the Airport. The plane was full and a delay as usual. And the seats are very cramped.

Paris is my new connection, waiting right now for the plane to USA.

Turkey, April 2008

Arrival in Istanbul, one of my City's I love. A trip again with Kevin, so it will be in nice Hotels overnight and not a backpacker trip. Our Hotel was perfect Germir Palas Hotel. Walking to everything. There is always something to see again. And the smell and the food! Love it. This time we went to a school and joined the class in some activities. And a visit to Hagia Sofia.

Naturally to the Cistern we went, which are now restored again. Mud has been taken out. And walkways for visitors are there now. The fish are still swimming around, and some are very big.

Still had to look for the Medusa Head forgot from my earlier visit where I would find it. Medusa, who had the head of a snake, had power to transform people into stones. The head is upside down.

The Grand Covered Bazaar is the biggest shopping center or souk in the world with 4000 shops.

A tour on the Bosporus was again interesting; it shows a lot of the life on the water. Huge Mansions line the River.

And today to Gallatasaray Kadinlar Hamami, a spa, built in 1863 or older. It is very hard to describe what it does to a body. One feels so good afterward and I can hardly wait for my next visit.

A description: Steamed like a Lobster, but I survived a Turkish Hamami.

Upon entering a large Building, I chose Nr. 4 from a menu of services: steaming, rubbing, and massage.

Everything came off and wrapped in a special bath towel, I was led to a cavernous and beautiful room. The ceiling was inlaid with colorful glass throwing a nice glow on everything. A large, raised marble platform, known as a goebeck tasi was in the middle of the room. 10 women could lie on it. It was heated from underneath in some fashion.

I was motioned to lie on the platform. The atmosphere in the room was steaming hot, and more heat was being directed onto my body from the platform. I felt like a roasted pig on a spit.

For 20 minutes I tried not to move, but from time to time I had to turn my body when I no longer could remain still. Then it was time for scrubbing. Cold water was poured over me, and a naked masseuse roughly rubbed me with a special glove to remove dead skin which came off in globs.

My body was completely scrubbed in this cleansing treatment.

The next step was a procedure called "tellak" in which soap was sprinkled slowly over my body and massaged into the skin. I felt now like a slab of meat being marinated for dinner.

Following the cool down after "tellak", I again was sent to the platform to lie down to rest. I just wanted to close my eyes and sleep, but my relaxation came to an end.

Surrounding the marble platform were about 20 sinks or basins. These were used in order to cool off between steps of treatment. Water continuously flowing into the basins and was scooped out by a bowl and poured over my body.

Following cool down after the "tellak", I again was sent to the marble platform to lie down and rest. By this time I was used to it and all I wanted to do was close my eyes and hope the treatment would last longer, but my relaxation came to an end again when an attendant motioned me to move to a sink again to have my hair washed. Once that was done, I was given a big towel and sent back to the changing room and from there to a room furnished with a bed and chairs and refreshments. Turkish tea and soft drinks were served before I left the "hamami. I enjoyed the experience so much that I went back for another session a week later.

I was told that in olden times one spends all day and there would be music and singing and dancing. Nevertheless, even without such entertainment, I thought the Hamami was great.

Ankara

Ankara a different city. More serious, we did go to the high court and it was a day for all Judges to assemble.

At the Ataturk Mausoleum a very impressive building. Many people stopped us and wanted to discuss politics.

A stop at one of the Underground towns. Kaymakli. They were built to provide refuge during recurring threat by invading Armies. Usually, 7 or 8 floors deep into the earth, it is made of corridors, storehouses, kitchens and even churches.

Cappadocia

Cappadocia is the most famous place in Turkey. Wind and water have sculptured the volcanic tuft of Cappadocia into a surreal wonderland of minarets, spires and rocky pinnacles. A breathtaking landscape with striking and bizarre rock formations. Many hollowed out places have been converted into Hotels. It is unique in the world and is natures wonder.

Goreme Oren Yeri is known for the "dark Church".

We were invited to one of the private homes, it gave us an idea how people are still living in there. Amazingly comfortable.

That evening a visit to an old Caravanserai to watch the "whirling Dervishes ". The Sema or sufi ritual is one of the greatest mystical performances. Live music with flutes, string and percussion in beautiful costumes, and always white.

There are still many Caravanserai, and all are rebuilt and in use. It was the stop for anybody to stay and eat.

Roads are very empty; the Gas is $11 a Gallon!

Antalya

In Antalya we get to see Hadrian's Gate constructed in the 2nd century. Hotel Marmara was directly on the sea.

Bakeries have fresh baked bread here 2 times a day. Turkish bread is delicious. The town has a lot of Pottery's.

Kevin and I rented a boat to have a leisure and restful cruise along the coast. Great Fun.

A visit to a carpet factory and watching the weaving, no little children, Adults did the weaving. I love Turkish carpets because of the glowing colors.

In Pamukkale we visited the spa and it is supposed to cure everything what is ailing. The water in the Terraces are the sediments of the springs with calcium, salts and other ingredients. Above the top is the ancient theatre of Hierapolis, and there the water is collected into a pool known as the "Sacred Pool" of ancient times.

Near the theatre is the temple of Apollo and remains of aqueducts, statues and columns.

Many poppy fields are in bloom all around.

Ephesus a very roman ancient place. Visiting the "House of the

Virgin Mary". supposed to be the last place of the Mother of Jesus Christ. The little church has been renovated by a Quatman Foundation from Ohio and attracts many visitors. In Ephesus one can feel how it was 2000 years ago. So much is still standing. In all its glory with many Roman ruins, it is better than Rome itself. One of the magnificent buildings of Ephesus is the Great Theater, which had a capacity of more the 25 000 people and is very well preserved. Many performances are still held here. The marble Road leads to the Celsus Library and the temple of Diana.

All streets were illuminated at night with oil lamps; it shows how rich the city was. The Avenue is 36 feet wide and 1970 feet long. All paved.

A short visit to Izmir.

Kevin had to buy Peaches. They were ripe! How delicious they can taste like that.

Pergamon, the Poppy place. Wherever one looked poppies are blooming. It is all built on top of a Mountain and not much room for our Bus to park. There the Acropolis was adorned with works of art and even the columns were beautiful.

Athena and Trojan temples, Temole of Zeus, Temple of Dionysos the god of wine and many other.

The Pergamon is the steepest theater in the world, has a capacity for 10 000 people. It made me dizzy looking down.

Needed a very good stop to eat. Learned how to make flatbread. I was told one can cook eggplants 43 ways.

Troy

Troy at last. Everybody knows Troy! One read it about as children and one always wondered where it is? The stories of Helen! King Priam, Hector, Paris. And the symbolic Trojan Horse. It is all there. 4000 years and it was the center of the Trojan War made immortal by Homer's poem the Iliad.

Canakkale is really the name for Troy.

Tonight, in Canakkale our Dinner was a lot of eggplant again and I was told here it is cooked 48 ways.

Nearby is a large wooden Horse. It is a leftover from a last Movie "Troy" filmed here.

A quick stop at Gallipoli. A famous place from the first World War, especially for Australian Soldiers. Visitors come to visit the nearby battlefields. There are many war memorials erected in honor of the soldiers who died there.

A message from Ataturk on one memorial:

There is no difference between the Johnnies and the Mehmets to us.

Where they lie side by side here in this country of ours, You, the mothers who sent their sons from faraway countries, wipe away your tears.

Your sons are now lying in our bosom and are in Peace after having lost their lives on this land.

They have become our sons as well.

Then we are crossing the Dardanelles, a narrow strait connecting the Aegean Sea and the Black Sea by Ferry.

Only one lifeboat was hanging on hooks. Interesting, what to do in Emergency?

In the lower deck even, Camels were transported.

Istanbul again after our roundtrip through Turkey. It is the only city in the world that spans two continents. Nightlife without stop. Music, food vendors, ice-cream sellers, and Gypsy is playing the finest music.

Topkapi is today's trip. Have been there many years before in Topkapi with friends, it has not changed. Still it is fascinating.

The big difference is the women. It is now much more Muslim and wearing covered faces on quite a lot of them. A shame since Ataturk, a president, did away with that.

Why would a woman go back to that?

Buying fresh pretzel from the street vendors was yummy.

We did get to enjoy a few hours at the pool at the 4 season Hotel with a fantastic view over the Bosporus.

Stopped at a pharmacy and found out Leeches are still used for healing and sold in bottles.

Israel, Jordan, Israel, November 2008

Again, to unknown places. I have been in Israel, but this will be different. My daughter Petra travels with me again.

Our trip is a visit to a friend in Israel and then Adventure in Jordan.

Starting out to the airport in the USA was an unbelievably bad experience. Saying goodbye to my husband Kevin and entering the Airport. I left my handbag in his car. It was close to departure when we finally got him, and our papers and passports returned. It was stressful.

Security is tight. Takes a lot longer this time, especially in Madrid.

On arrival in Tel Aviv, Rosalind picked us up and we got to go on the fast train going north for one hour. It was already night and we did not get to see the countryside.

A short trip by car to the Kibbutz Yizre'el near Afula. The Kibbutz was founded in 1948 and is very pretty. There are many little houses in a park like setting.

Then we met Pedro, the beloved house dog. We are staying in a kind of guesthouse. Our rooms have darkening windows, and we slept our 2 restless nights away.

A delicious breakfast awaited us. Such fresh food I have not tasted anywhere except on my own farm. Salads are eaten 3x a day and always is the food served cafeteria style.

I loved this recipe Spinach and Yoghurt
5 tabl. Oil
1 onion chopped
2 gloves garlic mashed

1 pack fresh spinach
500gram yoghurt
Salt and pepper

Heat oil, add onion, turn down, add garlic, for a minute heat again, cool it.

Boil spinach if fresh, squeeze out juice and chop it add yoghurt and all other, mix, eat.

Lunch was even better, so many choices, all fresh. So many different coffees and juices. The whole Kibbutz comes here together. Many people do not cook at home but can take food from the cafeteria home.

Everybody must help cleaning afterward and do dishes. It is interesting how everybody is doing something.

The retired older folks are even doing something. Many people want to live in this Kibbutz because of the beauty of the layout.

There is a housing shortage in Israel. And some houses are added but not many acres are left for it. The Kibbutz is enclosed all around by a tall fence and has a controlled Gate.

Walking around, I discovered how this place works. There are 340 milking cows. Love the smell. Cows eat sunflower silage. I wish I would like milk, must taste very good.

17000 chickens in long pens.

Many tanks with goldfish and Koi of any size.

A small factory manufacturing the well-known Dolphin swimming pool cleaner. It is exported to over 34 countries worldwide. All assembly is done in the kibbutz factory.

There are Beets and tomatoes in long greenhouses. Field crops in irrigated fields: cotton, tomatoes, wheat for silage, sunflowers, clover, corn and chickpeas.

Amaryllis bulbs are sent all over the world.

Then the big tanks with Carp fish, huge. All are raised for "gefillte Fish".

I find out each Kibbutz specializes in something.

Acres of Olive trees, Almonds, but the Olives bring more money. It used to be all Cotton in the fields, but the fruit trees are more profit.

The evening Shabbat was very beautiful with music and great food.

There is a Music Centre which has its own Orchestra.

There is even something like a nightclub for all. The band played very good songs in English and in Hebrew.

Now Petra is snoring bad. I cannot sleep. Finally, I moved her bed into the hallway.

Breakfast is always so good. And the sun shines every day.

Drove today to Mt. Bilboa, a wonderful drive over the mountains then to the Australia Park called Be-Shea-ma. And then to a Restaurant hanging on a hill, looked like it would slide anytime downwards. The food was excellent. I had mushroom lasagna topped with 3 different cheeses. Petra had lamb kebab, Rosalind a Hamburger. But service was slow and finally the bill shocked me: $70, expensive. I guess we paid for the view.

Shalom al Israel is said a lot. Peace.

Today we drove to the Golan heights on an interesting road trip. There is lots of Army activity. Saw quite a few beautiful Resorts around the sea of Gallileh. Stopped at the Golan Heights Winery in Katarin. Did not get to taste the Gewürztraminer because it sells for $40 a bottle.

El Amin, a little Art village was next, but most of it was closed. It is off season. Not many tourists are about.

Overall, the Golan Heights are very stony, and one wonders what all the fighting is about for such a dreary piece of land. But if any acre has had water it is transformed into beautiful places. Many wineries are here. And the wine is very good.

We saw a lot of signs saying no walking or trespassing because of mines.

At the Kibbutz we met quite a few people by now. A lot of American retirees have settled here.

I love the stories they tell.

Last night Petra snored to much must throw her out maybe.

Today, visited Afula to get some money and snoring medicine. And a great Lunch at the Kibbutz again. We took Pedro the dog to another Kibbutz in the mountains for grooming near Cesarea. They had the most beautiful Horses there. All Quarter Horses.

Have biked today too since I was given a bicycle to use. Need some exercise?

But there is so much to see in Israel, and we drove to the Lebanese border through Haifa a large modern City.

Went to the Grottos on the Border and had lunch at the Beach. No people. Bombs do come once a while from Lebanon. One has to watch out.

To a cable car Rosh hanikra, a short trip. Then to Nahariyya, a beautiful Beach town, walked and had coffee and ice-cream. There was a Politian selling his spiel and I got a very nice t-shirt from him. Nahariyya got almost destroyed by 800 Rockets in 2006 from Lebanon.

Tonight we are going to a concert in Beit She"an. A concert Hall made like a Bunker! It is 300 feet below sea level and no windows just small peepholes for air. The Acoustic was fantastic and listening to Beethoven No. 4 was perfect.

I did feel strange and felt pressure coming on and needed to get out soon. To me it was very claustrophobic.

The Hall can be used as a bombproof Building should it escalate to it.

Today one more time to the Golan Heights. It is fascinating what there is to see. And I can understand how it is loved by Israel. Many herds of Dairy cows and beef cattle in the Rocky Mountains. Anything flat is used for Agriculture.

Lunch stops are expensive and our bill for 3 was always over 300 scheckels, whatever it is in $. But it tastes is so good because all food is fresh.

For the evening, we ate in the Kibbutz for Dinner again and at Natalie for Cheesecake.

Jordan, Thursday 13th

Petra and I crossed into Jordan after my Israeli friend dropped us off at the border. It was like crossing into East Germany. Passes had to be shown in Israel, then on the Bus for 200 feet, off again, show visa. Guard could not read and told us we had no visa. Finally, the tourist Police came and stamped everything, and we went to immigration. There is more paperwork. All took over an hour. Then at custom, all our bags got opened. Our driver I hired through an Agency was outside and helped us getting out faster.

Abu, the driver had a good car. Driving is different here after Israel. It is very dirty in the streets and garbage lying around. Not many nice buildings so far. Bordertown!

As we drove into the highlands it started getting cleaner. If there was any flat place again it was used for growing food. Never saw so many greenhouses. Fresh fruits and vegetables are for sale everywhere. We could watch the harvest of Olives. And saw many Olive oil factories and all are busy pressing the oil. Pomegranates and small eggplants are displayed in roadside stands.

Jerash. A roman city and still very active in use. There was a Chariot Race announced in the Hippodrome and how could I miss that? Petra and I went there and met the Director. He offered me a chariot to drive after Petra mentioned I would like it.

Just seeing the crazy Horses tied in front of a 2-wheel wagon was not very safe looking. But a good driver and we were off. The young man stayed with me on the Chariot, which was lucky for me. Could I have handled the Horses alone? No way. I needed to hold with one hand and holding rains and the speed! I was only hoping not to fall out at the curves.

It was so good I almost cried. Everything after this experience was secondary.

We stopped at the temple of Zeus. The temple of Artenis and the Colonnades.

Driving to Amman and staying in the Hotel Geneva. We walked around since it was downtown. And many little stores around to look at.

Smoked my first Hookah pipe with Apple spice. Bubbling water in it gives a lot of smoke. I was told it is not narcotic and is good for the heart.

We shopped a little and ate some cake. The food is much cheaper than in Israel.

Friday, we toured Amman and found it very clean. In Amman, the Citadel is a good place to see. We had a stunning view of the city.

Then we drove to the "Castles" of the Crusaders fortifications. Most are built on top of old forts over 3000 years old.

Mt. Nebo were Moses is buried a holy site a stop.

Karak is an underground city. It was the ancient Capital of Moab. It is on the Kings Highway and Karak Castle dominates at 900 meters above sea level.

The majority of Jordan is desert. South of Karak the highway descents into steep valleys, called "Wadi's".

Then into the desert nothing is growing just brown earth and stones.

Many military Bases and miles of industrial Areas of Jordan we passed. Oil trucks coming from Iraq. We stopped in Taz with good Arab food. Kubbeh here my favorite food. Deep-fried balls made of a mixture of meat and cracked wheat stuffed with minced meat and onions. It was not a tourist place. The Owner was very apologizing for having only an Arab toilet. The famous hole in the ground.

Our long drive ended in Wadi Rum. We did stop a lot till we got there.

All along we drove next to a deserted railroad track which "Lawrence of Arabia" was involved in building it.

Arrived in the dark at Wadi Rum. There is so much history here. This is the place of "Lawrence of Arabia"

Our camp was 200 tents! I had to use earplugs, Petra's snores and so much other noises. But slept well.

At 5:30 am my Camel stood outside waiting for me. I went for a sunup ride. There was so much silence after we went around the mountain from the camp. Beautiful only me, my guide and my camel. It is a timeless place virtually untouched by humans.

At 9am Petra and I went on a jeep ride through the desert. We got very dusty with a lot of wind blowing sand on us. Met a few Bedouins. And invited us to drink tea. Can only drink so much but 3 cups is polite. It is difficult to resist their friendly invitation to share mint tea or cinnamon flavored coffee in their black tents.

Then we drove to "Petra" on the Kings highway. A beautiful scenic drive. Coming into the Valley of Petra it became more beautiful. With many trees flowering on each side of the Road. At Wadi Sun, the Hotels started, and I hoped my reservation was not here. All built for tourists.

Lucky us, we stayed right next to the entrance to "Petra".

I did the right choice. The Petra Resort is built right on top of the wall.

Petra and I refreshed first in the heated pool, and then started to walk into Petra which can be done by horse or carriage. The city is 2000 years old and was the Nabatean capital. It was lost to the world for over 1000 years but was rediscovered in 1812. By the way, Petra means Rock in Greek.

We walked 3km. One arrives at a place called Siq. You must pass through there; it is like a sliver of a canyon that protected the city from invaders. Half mile-long walking on cobblestones rutted by carts and chariots. The way is so narrow that it's almost completely cut off by the sun. The gorge is lined with ancient water channels and has beautiful bas-reliefs on the steep rock walls.

The most dazzling sight emerges suddenly when one comes face to face with Al-Khazneh, The Treasury.

It is a unique style, and one is almost dwarfed by its huge size of 43meters high or 140 foot high. It is breathtaking.

At the Treasury I left Petra to rest and went on my own to climb.

There are so many places to see. One can walk the Street of Facades with 40 tombs carved into the mountain, there the pavement is marble.

Climbing a mountain path, one reaches the Monastery, it is very grand. The main doorway is two stories high: doing it in the heat is already a feat. One can rent a donkey, but they do look very skinny.

By darkness we took the Horse carriage back which cost 20 Dinars. Made the driver drive slowly, usually it is all done very fast and cannot enjoy it.

Outside our Hotel is a tourist Blvd. With many little Restaurants which was built in the last 4 years, but our Hotel has many nice Restaurants too.

It is great living so close to this ancient town. Our room is right above the caves and we can overlook some of the ruins.

There is only one other place in the world like this: Macchu Piccu in Peru. Except this here is bigger.

From one end to the other end of the city it is 8km which I walked and climbed. There are donkeys and Horses and Camels to rent. Most of the Horses looked crazy and I liked going on foot.

Tonight is "Petra by night" it is a special celebration, and I had to go back to see that. First at the Treasury the concert with no electricity all by candlelight. 1800 candles were lit. The Bedouin music and the acoustic was perfect. Especially when only a flute or a guitar was playing. After that we sat there in silence.

The stars were shining and then the moon came right up over us it was giving me goosebumps.

Petra was invited by a group of 50 German women all named Petra. They came to Petra on an invitation by a German magazine contest. And when the ladies found out Petra was from USA, they invited her in all the celebration too.

The next day we visited "Little Petra" an area not many tourists know about. It is also called Beida and is older than Petra. Many tombs are there, and one can hike all over and see more buildings.

We tried to drive the old "Kings highway to Amman along the dead Sea. Very curvy road and finally we switched to the big superhighway.

In Amman we took a taxi to see some more of the city and stopped at a Horse supply store.

I was told by the taxi driver a rule woman sit in back of a taxi.

Ate some more interesting food on King Talal Street.

In the morning we met our driver for return trip to Israel. We made a big detour through the low sea level country. The fertile valley of Jordan with many Greenhouses again. We had been told all that was Desert till the Israelis showed Jordanians how to cultivate the land.

1-hour border crossing again. Lots of stamping of the passports.

It is nice to be in the Kibbutz again. So much good food and so fresh, we are lucky to have been invited here.

Afula, the little town nearby, has everything one needs. Malls and small stores. We looked around the shops a little. Paid for our bus tickets for next day trip to Jerusalem.

Biked today about 8 miles and had wonderful bread for dinner.

A luxury Bus to Jerusalem. The Tower Hotel is good and close to the old Walls. Food is expensive in the Restaurants. We stick to little street food places.

It is Shabbath and all the Hasidic Jews are in their finery at the Old Wall. Fury Hats and Coats. It is exciting to see so many nationalities in this place. The streets are so small, and many pilgrims are here.

Booked a trip to Masada and Ein Gedi. A little expensive but a must see. It is all my second time from 20 years ago.

Petra has not snored for the second night.

We did try a new electric plug on my noise machine, but the plug fried it right away.

Saturday 22nd and we are off after a strange breakfast. It is made mostly for Russian taste we are told. Fish and more fish…Eels!

To the Dead Sea, famous for being located at the lowest point on earth, lying some 400 meters below sea level were tried swimming which is fun because one floats only. It felt incredibly good.

Masada was again so impressive. It is very windy up there. We reached the top by lift. A guide explained the history which is interesting especially the way the only Road up was built.

A stop at Ein Gedi. A beautiful Oasis and it is a thriving Kibbutz community.

Jerusalem is colder now; we walked around again and visited some more places we had not seen.

Stopped at a small Restaurant but it was so filthy and expensive. Wanted $45 for two coffee and 2 sandwiches, had to argue about it.

Near the Damascus Gate we met a nice storekeeper and his son Tarek, who offered to take us by Bus to Bethlehem which is in Palestine. It is very hard getting there, and we hoped with a native it would be easier.

Next morning, we had a Russian breakfast again. Today 3 herrings on our plate!

Tarek awaited us at the Bus stop. From the Bus we had the view of the new Walls which are being built to separate the two countries. It was a feeling like going to the separate Germanys at the time.

By the border crossing, Tarek was pulled of the Bus by Israeli soldiers. My complaints fell on deaf ears. It was scary to see this especially for a young man. Tarek caught up with us at the Old Bethlehem and again was not allowed in most places. There are no tourist, and the shopkeepers are desperate to make money. We ate there and found better and cheaper food then in Jerusalem, fresh orange juice!

Going back was scary again because we had problems having a

Palestine boy with us who was catholic. It is very scary and does not feel good. Very much like a police state.

Back in Old Jerusalem we went to see the church of Sepulcher, which was full of pilgrims. The devotion is great. A lot of kissing of the stones.

Went up the David Tower and to the Museum. And had Falafel, but twice as expensive as in Palestine.

Mornings we have a very beautiful view of the Jaffa Gate. We decided to walk all the way to the Rock, there we hang onto a tour group and got inside just before closing to non-Muslims.

We did walk a lot and saw and met a lot of people in Jerusalem. Said goodbye to our friends and Tarek and his family.

Bahamas, November 2009

A weeklong trip into a sunny place does so good in the winter. Loved the blue water and meeting people with Kevin. Hours of snorkeling and sunbathing for me.

Lanzarote, Canary Island, February 2010

And I found another beautiful Island. Having my Brother Bernd and Sister in-law Klara living there was ideal. They knew the Island and especially all the Winery's. My interest was how a place is so beautiful with Volcanos going all the time. In certain places one could cook a hotdog over an open flame which came right out of the earth.

On the western side of the Island one could find beautiful light green stones which were washed by the sea and did not need to be polished. Made some beautiful Jewelry out of it.

The Island is famous for an Artist called Cesar Manrique. He was an Artist and Sculptor. He left his mark all over the Island. Even the great Museum was built by him right in the volcano pipes.

He built his house into the Lava tunnels, even with a nice swimming pool.

There are big white Camels on Lanzarote and had a great ride on them. Many hiking trails and so many wildflowers.

Ireland, April 2010

Our yearly trip to Ireland again and now with Ursula and Werner Ott. It is always different when one brings a new person to Ireland. We could show the Ott's places because by now we felt like we had been so many times here we knew Ireland. We stopped at many Pubs' for the evening music and a Beer. Pub food is particularly good.

Stopped at Kevin's relatives in Knock for a visit. One never knows when we will see them again.

On our last day leaving Ireland the Volcano in Iceland erupted. It delayed us all for 6 days because no planes could fly with ashes blackening the sky. We found luckily room at the Inn, but it was a scramble for it. Got to see a little of the natives that way.

I was worried about returning to the States because of missing my Departure for India. But I made with one day to spare for my flight to India.

India, Nepal, May 1, 2010

Having been in Nepal in 1992 and very good friends there it was time for a new visit.

Waiting in the airport and thinking and hoping all will go right. Had two root canals 1 week before. Then I hear there is a Maoist uprising in Kathmandu. Many problems. I was warned stomach ailment in Bhutan. What else can go wrong? And now I just heard yesterday Kevin has stomach problems too.

India

A bad stormy flight, but very good service on Continental too much turbulence. This time I arrived at New Delhi's new airport. And so many police around, why? It is midnight.

My driver was waiting for me and my room to. It was strange seeing in the middle of the night Elephants walking along the roads carrying big loads.

A night's sleep before my next day trip to Nepal, but the Airplane was delayed 6 hours. Too bad I could have slept longer and have had a nice slow breakfast.

I still have not figured out why so many soldiers and machine guns pointed at anything right now. There is trouble in Nepal.

Kathmandu, Nepal

A late arrival in Kathmandu and nobody is awaiting me. Where are my friends? A strange feeling but my friend Uttam showed up huffing and puffing and had to explain that there are no cars or bikes or taxis aloud to move. The Maoist will shoot at anything being wheeled. So, he had to walk.

A long walk! Only some tourist buses can unload at the Airport. We finally convinced a Bus driver to let us on for a short stretch to our destination.

It is sad to see this beautiful Country in a civil war. The country is coming to a standstill. It is in a current state of disrepair. In Kathmandu there is street fighting and one can see people walking with bandaged parts on their bodies.

Uttam and Shanti my friends, live on top of their building with a commanding view of the whole city of Kathmandu. Occasionally an Airplane still fly's over the city. We had a lot of plans but now only walking can be done. All the tourists are leaving, no trekking or anything like that is aloud. All schools are closed.

The Maoist do not want schools, maybe 2 days a week.

I go to some of the little stores in the neighborhood to buy food, but they will run out. There is no fresh supply coming into the city.

In the main streets lots of demonstrations are going on.

Shanti still cooks very well with the few things we have. I have to stop all the heavy spice and eat 3x a day Rice which calms my stomach.

My room is on top of the penthouse with a view to the Mountains, I love it. There is music playing someplace and all the sounds come up beautifully. Electric is out again we do have solar but must save it. It is strange to see the big city dark. The streets are grimy; it looks like a garbage dump. No Garbage has been picked up for a long time.

At 6am we eat oatmeal and tea, by 10 am a big breakfast like rice and vegetables repeated at 2pm and at 7pm.

On walking around, I am the only Caucasian and children cannot keep their eyes of me. We got a watermelon today, great, sweet and a big papaya.

The Onion smell is all over the neighborhood. It is used for everything. Since we live so high up, we get all the smells from different cooks.

Uttam built this house himself with 6 floors and we live on top. No elevator. Good exercise.

Walked with the Children Rajuv and Upama to Patan. What a long walk. We never saw a tourist. Patan is an incredibly old city with a lot of old Temples. Upama kept asking for street food which are only Bananas now. Expensive and soon more $.

The Garbage has piled up now and it is horrible. What will happen? Only drinking water trucks are allowed to move because they are needed. There is lots of fighting in downtown Kathmandu.

I am enjoying my little Apartment and wish there would be no fog in the morning. The weather has changed to rain land no hope for sun. And I am not getting anywhere. No plane is flying to Mt. Everest have tried to get to basecamp. Always fog there.

I found a place for calling to USA for 10cent for a 5-minute talk. And so clear connection. But again, it only works if the electric works.

We again walk and today to Pashupatinath. far. It has not changed in 20 years. Still the funeral pyres are going strong. The River is not clean anymore and stinks, it is really open sewage. There are many monkeys around picking up anything for eating. The Holy men trying to get some money, they are all very skinny.

This morning I noticed how everybody goes onto their balcony to pray around 6am. Little chimes announced the time.

As I look from my viewpoint, I can see the absolutions people do in the morning. Everybody is brushing their teeth.

Then they tend to the little flower gardens. Shanti is very devoted and touches all with holy blessing. There is a songbird who sings beautiful maybe called Treepie, sings like a canary.

Again, we walked a long way to the Zoo. It was not good. We should have stayed home. Saw to many injured people. The Maoist young men hit people with sticks right in front of us. There are dead dogs, dying dogs, garbage.

Many of the Marchers or protesters are brought into the city and paid with some food. They do not have jobs.

It is all very ugly.

Saturday 8th. Looks like the strike by the Maoists is over. We can use the car and are driving to Dhulikil.

There is a lot of damage on the Road and still with all the Garbage it is awful to look at. Suddenly everybody who has a car is using it and the acid from the car Exhaust is burning in the eyes. At least for a week we had no car fumes.

Driving and visiting Shantis brother at his house on top of a hill. Looks like a castle and has very beautiful gardens.

We left Rajiv and Upama at Shanties parents' house and drove up to the Mountain farm. Most of the Farm was in shambles and the Restaurant was with a lot of broken furniture. Uttam did not pay money to the Maoist Rebels and got punished by them in having his property destroyed. His parents had to watch it all and are not feeling very good. But I know all will be rebuilt again. Uttam's Father still remembered me from Davali celebration where I became his sister many years ago. It is on that day, if a man has not a sister, he can adopt a female friend. He still is using the reading glasses I send him 20 years ago.

We had the usual family Lunch later which is always the same, yoghurt, beaten rice, curry pasta and tea.

Back in Kathmandu again. What a country, life goes on again. Electricity is almost out for many hours. The police are very corrupt I am told. Being a policeman is particularly good. The get paid very well. All live in very fancy homes.

The market is brimming with food again. So many vegetables! And everybody is shopping. But underneath the long food stall tables raw sewage is flowing along, and it stinks. Like medieval times. A wonder one does not get some sickness. There are Roaches 2 inches long running all over. It is an animal always happy anywhere and will always thrive.

Found a dairy nearby which makes yak cheese. Love it. It sells out fast and one has to stand in line for it. It is an exceptionally good medicine for keeping a stomach settled. I found out it does a better job than Pepto Bismol.

Went by motorbike to downtown Katmandu. Traffic is so bad now that going by car takes too long.

At the Airline office I changed my return trip for earlier departure to the USA. Rumor has it that another Maoist uprising is coming about 28th of May. How can one plan that?

We had lunch at a Tibet Restaurant. Momo pasties filled with chicken and very delicious.

Watched Uttam fix around his property today too. He can almost do anything. Putting up solar fix gas or electric lines and water lines he is in charge of it and then sells his water time to people or gives it free to poorer tenants.

Last night was a noisy night. Some Roosters kept crowing, dogs barking. I just have a hard time going down the ladder for the toilet. Yes, my room has a ladder only. And then I just sit there and look over the city from my eagle nest.

Shanti cooks very native, she has been in the USA for 2 years and has seen how we do it. But she does it her way. All food gets prepared on the kitchen floor. Since there is no soap or dish detergent used, I am only hoping for my good stomach will last. Not many spices are used. The main dish is always Dhal (Lentils) and Rice.

I have tried flying to Mt. Everest Basecamp again, but the weather is not holding up and every day it gets canceled.

Hope my flight to Bhutan will have clear skies. Left early for the Airport to avoid traffic. Druk Air owned by Bhutan, is the only airline aloud to fly into Bhutan. Expensive but a beautiful plane. Spotless and a nice crew. I was directed into the most scenic window seat. And what a beautiful sight it was. There was Mount Everest so clear and I felt like touching it. It gave me Goosebumps flying along the Himalayan ridge. The plane had to pick its way around Mountains for a landing I had to congratulate the 2 pilots on landing. Wow.

Bhutan, 2010

For so many years I have dreamed of going to Bhutan, but since it is a closed country one has to get visa and pay the daily $200tax fee. The altitude was worrying me too.

And now I am in the country of "Gross National Happiness".

The Kingdom of Bhutan claims, it is a place on earth where man and nature exist in undisturbed harmony.

60% of the country is forest. Many festivals take place and are not tourist oriented but for the people. Not many tourists are there anyway. Since one has to pay a daily $200fee not many can afford to come here.

There are no traffic lights, no McDonald's and no tobacco.

Buddhism is the Religion and is always seen in the arts especially in the paintings and many prayer flags.

Welcome to Druk-Yul (Bhutan)

My guide Penmar and driver Karma were waiting for me. The Airport was so clean and beautiful, it is the only Airport in Bhutan.

It is near Paro at 7000feet. It took one-hour drive to the Capital Thimphu at 8500 feet, on a Road built in 1976 which was winding around Mountains and following a River. There is no garbage anywhere, not a plastic bag either. But it is dry, it has not rained enough. Passed many Peach Orchards in bloom. The cows standing in the fields did look skinny.

Bhutans economy is based on agriculture, forestry and the sale of hydroelectric power to India. One crop that cannot be found in Bhutan is tobacco, as Bhutan is the only country in the world to have banned the sale of tobacco.

Thimphu is a busy city with many beautiful traditional buildings. All buildings must conform to the Bhutanese building style. Signs are only aloud the size 2x4feet. And mostly in blue color with white lettering. My Hotel Phuntshopelri was nice but how can one pronounce it?

Traffic is well behaved; people listen to the only traffic policeman. There are parks and parking is provided.

One big stadium in the Country and very important. The main sport is Archery, and I went to a big competition.

I noticed right away the men wore the traditional skirt and long-sleeved jacket and the women wore all the long dresses. Very eye catching. It is a must to wear to business or school. The King does not like people to wear western clothing.

For Lunch at the Hotel Thimphu and delicious. Fried periwinkle, my first time, a very common food at this time of year. Young Ferns, which are seasonal, like asparagus. Picked in the woods and sold in the street stalls. A few hours later I was sick to my stomach and could pinpoint it to the ferns. And that was the beginning of my travails. I never got rid of the stomach ailment again.

My guys are showing me about, both are young and love to walk. Thimphu has a lot of little stores. Which is fun to investigate.

Went up to the Takin Sanctuary and saw my first Takin, a very strange animal. It is between a cow, horse, deer, goat and something else lives up in the Mountains.

Karma, she and friend invited me to Dinner at her house. Very good. Karma is related to the King family and is beautiful.

Saturday 12th

An awfully bad night now the altitude is getting to me. 6 hours of headache and loose toilet. I am weak today. My "boys" are taking me to the Herbal Hospital. Big pills and 3x a day.

By evening Karma called a real Doctor friend and he gave me Imodium and something else. Herbal Medicine did not work.

I did notice a lot of used Condoms lying near garbage receptacles!!

Walls are painted with large Penis very graphic especially at the entrance to a private home.

I am better now, and we are leaving for the long trip to Punakka. Fortified with Imodium but no appetite, which is not bad. Have tried to lose a few pounds.

A long drive and arrived at a beautiful Hotel Punarsangchu on the River. It could not be nicer. The view is fantastic from my room. Getting there was a very curvy Road and we had to drive slowly. There are many obstacles in the Roadways. Mudslides especially. I did like the slow driving and could enjoy it more.

Going over the Dochula pass to the 108 Stupas on top of the mountain. Built by volunteers at 4000meters or 12 000feet. Commemorate the victory in 2003 against India?

Going down to lower Altitude is better, and another hike to a nunnery again uphill was wearing me out. My head was drumming. I balked after that and just wanted to get to a place to sleep.

At the Wangdue Inn I got my rest. Again, a beautiful place on the River. There is a strong wind, but it is warm.

I finally ate a cracker and some soup and a potato. Having a rest on my Balcony now.

Traveling now to the Phobjikha/Gangteng Valley.

Karma, a he, Driver is a Champion Archer and has won the silver Medal in Barcelona in 2000. Very impressive. He promised me to show how it is done when I am better.

Have slept now but a bloody nose from the altitude. Taking now Motrin 800 hoping it will take all my pains away. Still have not eaten much.

Another 5-hour drive to Phuntshocholing. I am told there are no straight roads in Bhutan, all roads go either right or left.

Stopped at beautiful views and arrived at the Phuntshocholing

Farmhouse. A big very good cooked potato is all I wanted and ate.

This Valley called Phobjikha is the only Valley in Bhutan with lots of Rivers and some flat fields. It is dedicated to the Black necked Cranes who fly every winter from Tibet.

The fields are used as potato farms at an altitude of 8000 to 9000 feet. This is exhausting to work so high. The women look as if they have make-up on, but it is red skin burned from being outside in the cold.

It is summer but not at night. Very cold. My house does not have heat but lots of blankets. I am wearing all my warm cloth now. There is a nice toilet for which I am thankful since I am still troubled by my insides.

Today I was watching the children outside playing on their way home from school. Every time some adult passed them, they bowed their heads and stood at attention. As soon they passed, they were back to being children.

I am given lemon juice by the mother of the house. Something else was in it which made it taste horrible. Maybe it helped.

I went to bed with 2 big hot water bottles and one on my belly. Slept well. But still had to go to the toilet which was a trip! Since there is no electric, there was a candle in the hall, which was never going shorter, it burned 10 hours. I still had to find my way without disturbing or falling over stairwells. Stairs are very steep and the ceilings low. I called myself the stalker.

Getting into bed was the best. I counted 10 quilts on me.

There is a room in the house which is only used for praying. It is elaborate of woodcarvings, painted in all colors. It is like a shrine and many times a day somebody is in there using it.

Farmhouse morning is beautiful. The sun! The view over the Valley it is all glistening from dew. Hope that never will be here a Hotel. Since there is no electricity, I hope it stays natural. Then I am told that in Oct. Nov. many people come and stay in tents just to watch the migration of the Black cranes.

Went to Wangdue to see the head monk who blessed me and hoped to cure my ailment.

I can see why people send their children to the monastery. The get the best education and become teachers or anything they apply too. They have an incredibly good life. There are telephones and TV but no computers, run by solar.

The Government pays all. For Roads, Schools are free, Hospitals are free and the medicine. I guess that is where my $200 a day tax goes too.

In the Valley 2-foot-tall Bamboo grows, it looks like hay. The hills are covered by Rhododendron trees. In the winter, the Yaks come down from the top of the mountains to graze, right now only a few Horses are out there. They are used for trekking.

No dogs are around, and I was told the Leopard comes at night to eat anything especially dogs. I did not hear a sound all night silence.

Farmhouse living is not for everyone. It is simple. Dinner was potatoes and spinach with rice soup. My Cipro is working finally.

After walking today many hours I found an area were lots for future Hotels are being sold. Hidden away but still advertised.

I exclaimed to Pemar "you are Killing me" for so much walking, he just bowed his head and said I am sorry.

Saturday 15th

Ate today 2 eggs, 4 slices of toast tea and soup. And then we went on a 4-hour trek. It was long and I have no energy. I am just not enjoying it like I usually do, I must get healthy. There is a worry being so far away from a doctor and all at an altitude of 10 000 feet.

Lunch felt good and had 3 potatoes, 1egg, tea and butter and an apple with one homemade slice of cheese. Cheese is unpasteurized hope it will not make me sicker.

Went to the Nature Conservancy. And finally spied two more Cranes, one was so big and beautiful. Most have left for different places for the summer.

A good tea and a soak for my feet.

Watched how a house is being built nearby. All from mud. Anything made from wood is right there too. Never seen so beautiful carpenter work. No nails, it all fits together. Even the furniture is handmade.

The mud walls of houses are 2-foot-wide and stomped down by about 6-8 people for 10 minutes. Then a new layer is brought, and it is repeated. All is encased in a wooden wall of 8 feet long.

The persons perform the happiest dance while stomping and singing. The same people do move to another construction site when finished. It takes about 5 months for a big house to finish.

Today I traveled to Bumthay.

Question: What is the difference between a shooting diarrhea and a regular diarrhea?

But I woke with diarrhea again. Bloody nose now for 4 days and it is not getting better. I take cipro, motrin. No sleep, head hurts, nosebleed, cannot get air, diarrhea, weak, no appetite, looking like hell, stomach cramps, cough, and my ears hurt, my teeth hurt. I must return to Thimphu. I cannot go further away from Civilization. I ate an egg and some toast never thought to have a diet like that.

And the drive is again right and left, 7 hours! Karma took me right away to the Hospital and a checkup. I was much hydrated and got some new pills and fluids to drink, horrible stuff.

All made me feel better the next day and went to see the Lama at the Stupa for a blessing. He spoke fluent English and we could talk a little about his wanting to visit USA. I invited him to come which made him happy and I got a special blessing.

Well by now I even had a cake and some chocolate, let's hope it all will get better. But sleeping was difficult.

My pill I got was called Metronidazole, very bitter but it is helping.

We drove to Paro. Staying in the Dechen Hill Resort. I have an appetite again and had lunch.

Then attempted to go up to the "Tigers Nest". This monastic retreat is built into a sheer cliff face high above Paro Valley. Made it to a certain height and had to turn around. My head started to spin. It is good I did that. That height I found out is where many people have died going further there because of the altitude. It is at 11 000feet but very sudden. Karma told me stories about it and that was good enough for me.

Our Dinner was tonight Chicken Tikka and Roti with yoghurt. I love it. Karma took me to the Airport, and I felt I have a new friend in Bhutan. A special present was given to me by Karma two handbags, very beautiful. And a white silk scarf was wrapped around me as a farewell for a safe journey.

And into Druk Air, which owns two propeller planes. Over the Himalayans with the most fantastic view of Mt. Everest again.

Back now in Kathmandu and trying to go back to USA. Lucky for me Uttam is helping me to get my ticket changed. Had bad news now, Kevin has cancer and to return as soon as possible.

There was still no hygiene in the city. I got sick right away again and on arrival in the states found out I had dengue fever on top of all my ailments. All was cured except not my husband Kevin.

Camino de Santiago, Spain, June 2011

Walking the Way" or The Way of St. James.

The Camino de Santiago de Compostela pilgrimage route and retracing the medieval footpath into northern Spain. For more than 1000 years pilgrims come to pay homage and end in the Cathedral that hold the relics of St. James. There are different ways of walking there, but I choose the most medieval trail.

For me it was a walk alone. Besides, I carried the ashes of my husband Kevin. He was supposed to make this walk with me and we were prepared for it. But Cancer took him before he could accompany me.

I started near the Town of Leon. There are many Albergue and Refugio's, but I preferred to stay in B&B or small farms. My luggage was transferred every day to the next stop. From the start on I was called a peregrino (pilgrim).

I got my Camino Credentials or Pilgrims passport which can be stamped along the way that one is doing the pilgrimage. At the office in Santiago the passport will be examined before one is awarded the

Compostela completion certificate.

The stamp could be had by different individuals. Historic churches usually gave a stamp or just a farmer sitting on a stool near his field, or a shop owner and even from some of the bars along the way.

There was the scallop shell has long been the symbol of the Camino de Santiago. The grooves in the shell, which come together at a single point, represent the various routes pilgrims traveled. It was good for scooping water do drink.

Walking the Camino is an amazing way to meet people from all over the world and everybody had a story to tell why one is on the pilgrimage. Some people told me they came to find themselves or to solve problems to work out anything. It was meeting People from all over the world.

I did my fast walk but still stopped at many little cafes for a good cheese sandwich and coffee. And was always surrounded by people I had maybe met yesterday or before. Everybody had a different speed to the walk.

The landscape changed every day, rolling hills, wheat fields, broom sage with the yellow flowers. 6 hours a day was the average of walking. But then sometimes the Inn was out of the way and I had to add another hour getting there.

Mornings on the trail greeting from everyone, natives or pilgrim— Buen Camino. Have a good walk. And then one starts looking for the yellow arrow usually painted on the road or on a building. Scallop shells, which are imbedded in the walkways. Or a yellow arrow appears on a tree, bench, stop sign or anywhere dedicated to the Camino.

There is no rush and a stop at a café at 10am is mandatory. And one has to remember that everything closes in the middle of the day and has to calculate, or it is starving time.

I had very good weather and mostly blue sky.

All villages had water fountains in the main plaza to refill.

At the highest point on the trail is Ferro Cruz about 200 km before Santiago. It is a small iron cross that is affixed to the top of a tall wooden pole. It has been a tradition on the Camino to bring a stone from home, which I did, and deposit it here. It is supposed to take away all your sorrows, and regrets.

The ever-growing mound of stones.

There even was a place called O Cebreiro with a little snow. It was a long climb up. The village was all stone and very cold. I had to use heat that night. It was cold. Really cold.

From here it was 152km more. It went fast and if one looked from the hills one could see the big Cathedral of Santiago de Compostela.

Arriving in Santiago the first thing one does to get the certificate, then to the Cathedral for the celebration.

Every night is Pilgrim's Mass, and all arriving pilgrims are there. Names are announced and country of Origin.

Sometimes the huge silver-plated Botafumeiro one of the largest incense burners in the world is used. At 120 pounds heavy. I heard if one donates money it will be used right away, my first night I waited and no Burner. But on the second night! Smoke billows from it.

The Botafumeiro hangs on ropes 150 feet above and was used to get rid of all the aromas from the heavily clothed pilgrims. Some have taken a year or more to walk from their homes in Europe.

Seeing the incense burner in action and feeling it as it flew by moved many people. It was a spectacle and even I was moved and had tears running down my cheeks.

Restaurants served huge Octopus, Pulpa. Very disgusting to me. To tenderize it, it gets beaten, then boiled and served with oil and bread.

Scotland, October 26, 2012

I joined a group of 8 people from all over the world, going on a hiking trip.

I had come earlier to see Edinburgh. A very beautiful city and many old buildings and then the big Edinburgh Castle!

Guns go off at 1pm every day on the ramparts. Great to walk the Royal Mile-High Street. Right and left things to see. On the bottom the Palace of Holyrood house, the Queens place to stay.

Around Edinburgh are many hiking trails and I spend 2 days just walking around. There is History of Scotland.

Our Van left for the North, again so much to see. We stopped at little fishing towns! Dunkeld and naturally we all ate lots of Salmon. It is being raised in big open circles with netting in the open sea. Stopped at Loch Eelen.

There are so many castles and we stopped at everyone. Made it to Loch Ness and watched the water but no viewing of the Monster. Staring at it did not help. The monster did not come up for air. In Inverness we had Scottish language lesson. I never understood anybody.

On our hikes we run into my favorite cows, Scottish highlander. They look like out of a movie with their long Hair. More Lochs even a town called Lochinver. Andreck Castle nearby. Refreshments and group photo at Clachaig Inn.

Drove to Isle of Sky to the town of Broadford for overnight at the Portree Hotel.

Stopped at a few Whiskey Brewer's. But taste one, all taste the same to me. "Wee dram wisskey," at Talisker.

The north is very empty of people and once a while a small town. Dunvegan Castle of the McLead Clan on its own little Island.

The moors and the Mountains were just beautiful.

We hiked through Uig-Fairy Glen ointy hills with the heather blooming. Fairies are little people residing inside. James Bond movies had been filmed on a very hairpin curving Road he used.

Music at Eilean Donan Castle-Kyle of Lochal. Rest stop at Claichag and Castle Doune.

That country needs a longer trip.

Belgium and Germany, February 2013

Belgium was my next to discover. It was my first time I went to Brugges. I used Airbnb and was happy with it. My landlady even had a bicycle for me, and I could discover the countryside by bike. Went into Holland and never noticed till I came to a little town. Different language signs. No problem since all borders are open.

Brugge, (Bruges) has a great downtown with many chocolate stores. I think it was 60. I stopped at all of them. And all gave samples. All of them were great. It is a city of cobblestones and old buildings. One of my favorite movies was made here and it was always on my bucket list to see it. The two scoundrels from the Movie had a lot of fun. The Movie was called "In Bruges". Made in 2008.

One week to Germany to discover Wuppertal because of having been invited by friends. Wuppertal is famous for its train which runs on a hanging track. It is called Schwebebahn in German or suspension railway or floating train. It was built in 1900. It has always worked except once when somebody had the crazy idea and tried to transport an Elephant. He made a mess of it.

Sicily, April 15, 2013

A roundtrip through Sicily. 11 days by Bus. It was wonderful. I liked the way we got to see so much of the Island. The most preserved Temple of Segesta overlooking olive groves in Palermo is a sight to be seen. Sicily was a colony of Athens in 430b.c. and Romans built copies of all the Greece Temples. Sicily has so many Roman ruins too many to visit in a short trip.

I even climbed the Volcano Mt. Etna almost to the top. Only pouring rain stopped me finally, I was not prepared for it. Again, not enough time to see it all.

From Catania by Ferry to Malta.

Malta by Ferry from Sicily, 2013

Instead of flying I decided to take the Ferry to Malta. I met my Brother Bernd in Malta and we had a great time discovering this Island. It has a lot of Roman ruins. The beautiful old city of Valletta was a surprise. Balconies on all the private homes decorated with gorgeous flowers.

We stayed right on the Ramparts in a Hotel downtown with a great view of the forts against the African Marauders in old times, I was told.

In the countryside are many little café's which we visited and small farms. There are no big roads traffic must wind around donkey roads. I loved it. And many times, only one car fit the road. Who goes first?

Yucatan, Mexico, January 2014

A weeklong trip to Merida to Hacienda Petac to learn Mexican cooking and how to make great drinks.

In the 1900 hundreds all Haciendas had a thriving business with sugarcane and Agave Plants, Henequen. The fiber called sisal, is used to produce rope. When synthetic fiber was invented the Haciendas were abandonment. Big beautiful Haciendas were built by the owners and then that was over, and many Haciendas are now in ruins and overgrown by the jungle again.

Some have still museum style open house and the landowners try to keep the old life as an explanation to guests.

We stayed in a place which has been rebuilt and now has a cooking school for about 8 people. Great rooms with high ceilings and endless space. Bathrooms one can get lost in, and the service is perfect.

All ingredients came from the farm and we went shopping in the market of Merida.

Making Margaritas in the morning made us all happy early on and our food was always delicious.

There was some time to discover the countryside like swimming in a cenote. It is very slick going into them but the temperature of the water is great. The one near the Hacienda was small and had a very steep ladder, not very safe.

We visited some of the Mayan ruins nearby.

Dubai, United Arab Emirates, March 2014

Having heard and read about Dubai -I must go there. Since I am very much interested in Camels, I hoped to meet different ones there. What a surprise to me that almost all Camels are used there for racing. Many Camels one can see along the roadways practicing for the races

There is so much new to see. I was impressed with the whole country. One hundred miles across from the Gulf of Iran.

It is maybe one of the safest countries in the world and the newest city in the world.

In 1950 it was a cluster of mud huts and Bedouin tents along the Dubai Creek. Now that part is like an open Museum for people to see. It is surrounded by government Buildings.

Right now, Dubai has the tallest Building in the world called Burj Khalifa, at 2722 feet tall. 209 floors an observation floor at 555 meters. Besides, it is twice as tall as the Eiffel Tower in Paris.

One looks down at the most beautiful Dubai fountain. In the evening a big production with music at the same time when the fountain splashing to the music.

Dubai has the largest Mall with theme parks, Aquarium, an indoor ski run, which was fun but very cold. With real Penguins walking around. A dive center for diving right there.

I loved the waiting room sign "for Chauffeurs only". Women do not drive but have beautiful cars and are driven.

Arriving in the mall the women take off their black wraps and have on the most exquisite dresses and jewelry.

I noticed that the Metro had even a wagon labeled Women only. There are skyscrapers which look like they are going to topple any minute but built on purpose like this. And when you think about it, 6 years ago there was only Sand.

Crossing the Dubai Creek, it is a wide River with Abras, electric boats. Driven by foreign employees from the east.

On the other side is the Souk. It is the real middle east. Anything can be bought here. Especially Gold! There are over 100 Gold shops. The canopied streets are full of closet sized stalls. There are stalls selling plastic flowers, I guess with no rain that is all one gets.

Construction crews work 24 hours a day, seven days a week. The country is being built by these foreign workers, Asians who live in horrible homes sharing any space to save money.

Foreign people cannot own anything but if one has money, places are for rent. I saw many beautiful Villas. National people own and are always identified. The men wear white dishdashas and the women wear long black gowns and abayas.

Nearby is the world's only 7-star Burj Al Arab Hotel. It is built like a sail. A suite goes for $12 000 a night, maybe more now.

There are people I met who buy Falcons. Birds for $250 000, I went to see the Falcon Residence. All the Falcons are sitting on racks and it is interesting to watch at feeding time.

Naturally, a Dune buggy ride in the evening was included and Dinner at a Bedouin Camp.

I got to ride "my" Camel finally on the last day.

Cornwall, England, June 2015

Doc Martin! That is all I needed to know when I saw an Advertisement for a visit to Pt. Isaak in Cornwall.

Arrived early in London to see some of the city. Rented a bicycle and did see and bike much of it. It is always amazing what one gets to see from a bicycle.

An add with Dacey's Cornish Tours caught my attention.
10 people signed up and by Van from London to Cornwall.
Pt. Isaak first stop.

Since I am addicted to "Doc Martin" which is filmed in Port Isaak, I needed to see the whole Village. It is called Portwen in the TV show. And I was lucky, almost all the crew was there, and I hoped to be in the set but no it did not happen. Still I loved seeing the actors and meeting, especially Bert. It is strange that nobody from the film crew chased us away. Just silence was requested.

Cornwall is very windy and we did a lot of hiking over long fields. The chimneys of the old tin mines are well preserved. Traveled to many beautiful places till Lands' End. Cornwall is very tropical and most everything was in bloom. There are so many Gardens to visit. And the interesting Eden Project with all the worlds climates under 3 roofs. From Rainforest to Desert.

There was St. Michael's Mount Castle. At low tide one could walk across on a stone passage. It is the home of Lord St. Levan.

The Minacktheatre hanging on a cliff. And what a view from there to the open sea. The show tells about the woman Rowena Cade who built this theatre. Performances are late into the summer. It can be very cold sometimes, but Blankets are provided.

London again for two more days to see a concert in Royal Albert Hall. A place I have very fond memories from 1958 and 1959 when I spend some of my time living in London. A day trip to Windsor Castle and the Roman Bath in Somerset.

Germany, 2015

A short visit to see Family and friends.

Granada, Spain. Gibraltar, Malaga, Spain, 2015

A beautiful Condo overlooking the Mediterranean with the bluest sky for a week near Malaga.

Arriving late at night and did not see much but in the morning to look out from our large Balcony, this wonderful view! But then had discover the countryside. Alminecar was the little village to get supplies. The Beach is black sand, and many fishing Boats are beached there for the day.

Driving to the Sierra Nevada's, stopping at de San Miguel Castle. Many Orange Groves and Avocado trees. The roman waterways are still used for irrigation. Arriving in Frigiliana at 9000feet, and we are the only car. The income in this town is fabricating Ceramics, sugar and honey. There was no way for me to turn around but finally further a small place to turn. Was a little scary.

At night we had a flamenco show in town. The musicians were Gypsys and an interesting singer.

Now to the Alhambra in Granada very Moorish looking. The palace of Nazaries Carlos and the Santo Maria Palace from 1526 are hard to describe. All fountains there work without electricity.

Driving to Gibraltar, a 3-hour drive. It was different from what I expected. Driving to the top on the old Devils road with a lighthouse. On top is a Mosque given by Saudi Arabia.

Many signs-Monkeys! They used to live all over, but it got out of hand and are banned except some of the old Monkeys are still around.

Gibraltar was astounding. Never knew the big Mountain was hollow. There were tunnels, big rooms, restaurants and a big hall. All of that was used in the second world war for defense. And the Monkeys are still there but not allowed to beg for food. So, they walk around or sit in the middle of the Roads up there.

Surprising is the Airport which is in the middle of the city. When a plane arrives, police stop all traffic because some of the runway is the main Road.

In the square are many fish restaurants and all serve English dishes naturally we all had fish and chips.

My Balcony has the most beautiful sunset and one can only love it. More flamenco music and an Andres Segovia competion in town.

Cancun, Mexico, 2016

One week to relax after a cold winter. But it was not happening. It was very cold in Cancun and I should have stayed home because it turned into very warm weeks in Maryland. But I still got a rest of eating and reading and walk on the Beach.

Memphis, Tennessee, June 2016

It is not a foreign country but to me it was so. Since Elvis Presley died, I have been trying to visit Graceland and the places he walked and performed. Memphis is Elvis! One can still feel him everywhere. I even rented one of his pink Cadillac to spoil myself.

Hadrian's Wall Newcastle-upon-Tyne, May 28, 2016

Hadrian's Wall walk in England was on my Bucket list and finally got to do it with a very good friend Paula. Paula had friends in Newcastle who helped us very much to get to know many places we would not have seen. We signed up with a company who transferred our luggage every night.

Our walk was quite easy to follow since we had good instruction book and many signs were on the trail. We hoped to find lots of little cafes but not so. I was dreaming of scones and jam and had to dream about it. Most all the cafes were closed or nonexistent.

But we were there to see Hadrian's roman wall and lots of it is still there. There are stretches one has to go up very steep hills and down again. The view is always great. Sheep and cows, we encountered. And one day we were invited to a sheep shearing at a farm. The noise! Every sheep was screaming for help. It is amazing how fast the men can do the clipping a sheep.

People have been using the stones from the roman Wall for building anything. Fences, Buildings, paving. But some of the stones have been returned. We did get lost sometimes and even hitched a ride because of a long walk in the heat.

Our final miles are in open sun, no shade to the Atlantic and the little town Browness-on-Solway.

There we celebrated our walk with a good Beer and our friend Andie took us back to Newcastle.

Germany for biking, 2016

Berlin was Paula and my destination. My good friends Carlo and Tom had a lot of biking in Berlin planned. It is the only way to get to know the city especially with a native. I had not been in Berlin since the wall between East Germany and West was removed.

Potsdam, a beautiful city with the castle and so many lakes. There is the bridge from the spy movie and in real life was the exchange point for American and Russian spies.

Colombia, 2016

Colombia was my new interest because of the peace agreement signed by the Rebels. Venezuela is not travel save anymore I choose to visit Colombia.

A tour organized by Gate 1 was the best. Bogota was our first town and I loved it, so much to see there. Very much nightlife and one can walk the streets and visit the stores which are open late into the night.

Flying to the Coffee Triangle to see the countryside. What a surprise that was. Coffee growing wherever one looked. And so many beautiful waterfalls and hiking trails for me. At the Hacienda we got lessons how coffee is done. There we learned not to drink -caffeine free- because it is done with an ingredient not good for us.

Flying to Medellin, which turned into another great place. Medellin is called "The city of Eternal Spring" At 4000feet it has the best weather There are cable cars, escalators and Metro everywhere in town instead of roads. They all can be used even by the poorest person even if they have no money to get to anyplace in Medellin.

We used a very long cable car from Parke Arvi to go to Medellin from the top of the mountain which took almost one hour.

The great Museum downtown has many paintings of Fernand Botero outside statues are everywhere he made. All are enormous fat people or animals. Botero loved everything oversize.

Cartagena was the final stop with a beautiful cruise to a small Island for a day. Swimming in Cartagena was impossible. The sand was dirty grey and on the Beach was to busy by many sellers.

The biggest Fortress San Felipe de Baranjas is in Cartagena and in perfect condition. It is so large one needs hours to see all.

Visited a school in the poorest area which was right on the Beach. Most houses nearby were flooded by rainwater.

The school is fostered by Gate1, the Travel Tour Company. All the slum children come there for free education. When arriving, cloth and shoes were given to them but on leaving in the evening had to be left at the school. Most parents I was told were drug addicts and would have sold the cloth right away. We brought suitcases of knapsacks and shoes. The happy faces of the children were a delight.

Cruising, January 2017

Cruising from Baltimore with stops at St. Thomas St. John, St. Martin, St. Kitts. Love the service and relaxation. Get to read Books and eat when I want to.

Istanbul, Turkey, June 2017

Another trip with my friend Paula, since she had not been in Turkey, we decided to see Istanbul for 3 days. It is still one of the most exiting cities in the world. The old Architecture! The old buildings and the food. But one could hear the Loudspeakers from all the Mosques. I noticed all the dogs running around have ear tags and are looking healthy. We must have been the only tourists because many stores have been closing. We were told no tourists, no business. The Grand Bazaar was empty. A place I remember for masses of people. Our cruise on the Bosporus was good; the food was bad but I ate I was hungry. Could see a lot what was going on by the Water.

And we are getting ready to fly tomorrow to Rwanda Africa with

Turkish Airlines.

Rwanda, Africa, 2017

A late arrival in Kigali, Rwanda and driving through Kigali and no traffic at all. There was not a flat place we could see. All hills and Mountains. Our Step Town Hotel was on a ridge overlooking the city. It looked like the city was sprawling forever up and down the hills. Some call it the land of the thousand hills.

1994, horror swept through Rwanda and it had the biggest Genocide. History tells that it was coming on for a long time, but then brother turned against Brother. Now the Tutsis and Hutus are one, hopefully this has been resolved and but not forgotten. Wherever one goes there is a reminder of it. Monument, Museums places too many to tell. I did not know Germany colonized Rwanda in 1884. I did find museums with German heritage.

There is no spraying for anything in Rwanda all the food is Organic. No plastic bottles or plastic bags can be used. I liked the last Saturday of the month law. Everybody, even the President must help cleaning the country. It is clean.

We drove to some beautiful countryside. Saw after a long hike in the Nyungwe Natl. Park Chimpanzees in the wild. Colobus Monkeys in another preserve.

And so many tea plantations, Coffee and tea is the most important export.

Lake Kivu is the country's largest lake. It is also one of the world's deepest. There was an invisible line through the lake with the Congo Border. Near the top we went to Goma to see the Bordertown of the Congo. With the help of a friendly Policeman we could watch the many people trying to enter Rwanda. It was like a Zoo. One could see the difference of the 2 countries. Our Resort Hotel was Emeraude Resort.

But we came to see the Gorillas in the Mist.

After many stops and driving to beautiful places we arrived at our Villa Gorilla Inn in Ruhengeri.

In the morning we assembled at the Ranger place where we were assigned to a Gorilla group Mr. Lucky. It sounds all very simple to do but it takes Rangers to find the Gorilla groups and they do move and might be gone by the time one gets to the place last seen. 8 people can only go to the Gorillas a day to each Group. Our guides we hired carried our bags and water. And we needed every drop. We were lucky and the Ranger told us that Mr. Lucky was coming down the Mountain and so we only had 3 hours of climbing to do. This is steep and slippery. Nobody has ever heard of zig zagging that would have been too easy. It was straight up the Mountain.

And there was the Silverback! Mr. Lucky, Huge, and he was waiting for us.

One hour before, we were told all the ground rules we had to do should anything happen, stay 20 feet away from the gorillas and more stuff.

No Spitting, no coughing, voice low voice. Well the Gorillas seemed to want us in their mist. We relaxed and sat down and to the babies it was game time, over and under us, touching us, smelling us. I could not believe the feeling I got. It was the highlight of all my trips! The mothers just kept eating, there were 5 of them. The huge Silverback laid down next to me and just kept eating leaves and showed us how to peel a branch to get to the sweet stuff and once a while he would look around to check everything. Then he even lay down on his back and took a little nap. We 5 women loved every moment of it. After one-hour Mr. Lucky got up and looked at us. The Ranger explained that he had enough of us now and the hour was over.

It was hard for us to leave. Nothing can be like this experience of standing aside the huge silver back with his grey hair at his back.

The next day I climbed again to see Dian Fossey's Place. 1985 Dian was killed in her Cabin. She is buried with her beloved Gorillas. That was a difficult climb, very muddy and steep.

It cost now $1500 for one hour to see the Gorillas. But it does not guarantee for viewing if the Gorillas are gone. We all got a Gorilla trekking certificate.

The next days were spend at the Akagera Natl. Park. It is a very hilly Park, and the Animals are plentiful. Especially Zebras, Antelope, Giraffe. The Lake had more Birdlife I have ever seen. Currently there were only 5 Lions. And they were well fed.

Kigali is a tidy city with many colonial buildings and next to are gleaming million $ buildings.

There is the Genocide Memorial, it is a must see.

The now famous Hotel des Mille Collines (Hotel Rwanda) to see and have lunch there.

And to some of the stores and the market. The country is run mostly by women. Even in government more women then men.

All had to end finally, and we stopped on our way back to the states in Istanbul again.

Istanbul 3 more days

This time we had to see Topkapi which took many hours. There are a lot of buildings and we did not get to see the Jewells.

We ate ourselves sick trying all the dates and sugary desserts. I do not think I will eat another Date again. And to cleanse we went to a Haman for a Turkish experience.

Poland, 2017

Poland is a large country and roads are better. I wanted to see the North like Warsaw and Gdansk. The Baltic Region has so much history.

Warsaw was beautiful and in many places, I could listen to Chopin music hours. The Benches along the road had buttons to push and a piano concert could be heard.

Gdansk was famous for the Lech Walesa uprising and how it all came to the freedom of Poland.

The Hotels are all beautiful and hidden in old houses. From the outside one cannot see much of the modern inside. The Cities all have been rebuilt in the style before the war. I could only shake my head what a difference 5 years have been I was there, such prosperity now.

There is food, the markets are full. I remember when one could order only bread and cheese lots of sugar so cheesecake was another thing one could always buy. Nothing else was for sale.

I loved my bigos, had the best. And the biggest surprise in food was McDonald. Only the best there. There is no McDonald like that except in Poland. And always in the background music from Chopin, in Restaurants or on the streets or concert hall.

Auschwitz for a visit again. It has changed now, and it is not the cold place anymore. There is now a huge visitor center and it was crowded with people from all over the world. Especially young people. Krakow was very busy, and I loved seeing it again.

Germany, 2017

A quick trip to Germany for a visit to Munich and driving with my Brother Bernd to the Zugspitze. It was surprising how one got transported to the top. Inside of the Mountain was a train driven by a toothy chain.

On top one could see the most beautiful sight with 3 countries from the top.

Iceland, December 2017

I flew WOW Airline. A shoestring Airline. It was a beautiful plane but that was it. A glass of water cost $.

Iceland has been the most expensive country I have been too.

First of all, it was raining. It was cold. A coffee average $12. There was Dinner most reasonable to be had. $45! Whale meat, Puffins and fish was a choice in many Restaurants.

The Blue Hot Springs are overpriced. From the native's advice I found out that there are many Hot Springs in Reykjavik and are almost free for use or free for Pensioner.

My wanting to see the Northern lights was frustrating. Finally, on the 4th night the rains stopped and we drove way into the countryside. There we waited for hours and nothing happened.so much for the Northern lights. Many Icelandic ponies are in Iceland. But riding them is very expensive $95 for a half an hour. Since I have my own Horse and having had an Icelandic Pony it was not important to ride.

There are many Green houses and most everything growing inside are vegetables. Having their own heat, it can be regulated into different seasons. It is all volcanic heat.

It was a very wet visit. Back on the plane I noticed the Hostess was making a soup, Ramen Noodle, for a passenger. $12!!!!!

Costa Rica, December 2017

Two months in a warm climate! I loved it. Mostly swimming and hiking and just relaxing at my friends' pool.

Lanzarote, Spain, December-January 2018

Again 1 glorious month in a warm climate. Except the water is very cold. But there are many hiking trails and many Winery's to check out.

South Africa, Lesotho, Namibia, South Africa, February 2018

Resting after a long flight for a few days in the beautiful Tulbagh Valley.

Lesotho

Then with friends on a 4x4 Safari through Lesotho. The country has no flat area it is all mountains. It is surrounded by a wall or Mountains or river. There are only few entrances and one has to be at a certain time there or the Gates are closed. All Lodges had been interesting. Food was different but there always was wine with Dinner.

The Roads we drove were sometimes so bad I thought we would fall of the cliff. I did close my eyes sometimes.

Villages were connected by Horse transportation mostly. Saw plants and a different birdlife. There were Caves and cliffs with old paintings in many places.

Lesotho never was colonized and always a Monarchy and still has its own King.

Our 4x4 could drive through places I never knew we could pass. We forded Rivers and swamps easy. There was sometimes a nice place we could get out of the car and hike the hills.

Then back to Tulbagh again to repack for Namibia. Having been there in 1990 but not long enough.

Namibia

It was again a long drive, but I love looking out and watching the scenery. Getting closer to Namibia I noticed many Winery's. Amazing were all this wine might go?

At the Fish Canyon I finally got to see the 1500year old Welwitschia plant. Looks ugly like an old Agave.

At a road stop a donkey cart came along and was surprised that everything was handmade by the two young men. The invited me into the cart and I drove quite a way. One wonders what do the donkeys get to eat. Nothing was growing in that area, but the donkeys looked good.

Rest homes, Lodges are built to fit the country. Much dry wood and sand is building material.

When I finally saw Swakkopmund I fell in love with that town. Right on the Ocean and with many parks and lots of Restaurants by the sea.

I did ride a camel in the Red Dunes. The are the highest in the world. Many people come here to do Sandboarding.

Stopped at Erindi Game Reserve to watch from the balconies the wildlife in the waterhole. Elephants and many rhinos.

There even is a Duwisib Castle. Everything inside is if the owners just went away for a trip.

Going to Etosha is the final place to see wildlife. It is huge with many Animals and too many to describe. They all were there. There are German forts and are used now as Lodges. Since it is a flat area the outlook towers of the Forts are all open and come in handy to watch the great herds coming by.

There are always waterholes for attraction.

My friends had Relatives near Etoscha and we stayed there and had even better views from their Farm and Game Lodge.

Namibia is beautiful.

Back to Tulbagh and getting ready for Cederberg hiking.

Up and down the roads to the Cederberg Wilderness. There are no Gas stations, everything must be brought in. We had a nice little historic cottage but most people camp.

The rock formations are strange, and some are like Apartments, but the wind made them look like that. In the evening sun it was a painter delight in color. The spectacular rock formation some called: Maltese Cross, Wolfberg Cracks, The Arch, and especially Lot's wife.

There is even Rock art, some 3000years old left from the San bushmen. I saw only Baboons, but other animals live here. The trails are great and marked.

There even is a Kromrivier Winery at over 3000feet altitude. Supposed to be exceptionally good wine. Yes, I liked it.

On the way back we stopped at Langebaan with quick look at the Ocean and visiting family.

Russia, Estonia, Latvia, Lithuania, Poland, 2019

One last trip before going on my 5-month Cruise Jan4 2020. By Gate-1 Tour the classic Balkans. But starting in Moscow Russia. I knew I was going to like it because I love Russia, but the Balkans were new to me. My visa for Russia is good for many years and I am happy being a preferred guest.

Arriving as usually late at night so in the next 3 days I had to catch up on many places. I love the Metro stations it is an underground Museum with 44 stations recognized as cultural heritage.

The Kremlin is the center of Moscow. It is famous for especially the Dormition Cathedral built 1326, St. Basil's Cathedral with the Red Square. It was Christmas season, and many little lights were shining. Especially the famous GUM Department store on Red Square. 3 floors of shopping.

Day trip to the Holy Trinity Saint Sergius Lavra Monastery. Built 1423. Amazing how religion is so important again. The baroque style is beautiful. The Bell Tower is 88 meters high and contains 30 bells. The heaviest Zar-bell weighs 72 tons.

Now the train to St. Petersburg. It was daytime and wonderful to look out at the passing countryside.

One of my favorite walking cities. So much to see and the Hermitage first again. I never have enough time to see all. But being on a tour has its advantages. We did not have to stand in line.

A visit to the Peter and Paul Fortress, which houses the crypts of the last Czar and his family.

A visit to the Peterhof Summer Palace with magnificent fountains topped by gold statues on the Gulf of Finland.

Tallinn, Estonia

By Bus to Tallin, I like going by Bus, because one can see more of the countryside. What grows, how are the towns looking, the farms.

Tallin is a medieval city with very narrow streets. Can all be walked.

Visiting the old town square with the Gothic Town Hall and climbing up to the Toompea hill, the seat of Government.

Driving to KadriorgPalace a Baroque palace, it was a gift from Peter the Great of Russia.

Our Dinner that night was in a Olde Hansa Medieval Restaurant, supposed to have been in business since 1475 A.D . One dessert was called "A Swan is not a Goose". Never found out what it was.

Riga, Latvia

Arriving in the late afternoon in Riga. A beautiful skyline from the Hotel to the Banks of the Daugava River. The town dates to the 13th century. Baroque to Classic and Deco. It is there, the Art Nouveau Architecture is real. One has to stop all the time to look at the facades of buildings, supposed to be 750 of them in Riga. The fantastic Orthodox Cathedral. Outside Musicians playing music. Many miles I walked through the city. Old Riga is known also where the worlds first Christmas tree was erected.

Vilnius, Lithuania is next on our drive. Again, a beautiful countryside to there. Visiting the Hill of Crosses. Climbing Gedimino Castle Tower, The Church of Saints Peter and Paul.

A trip to the Trakai Castle on Galvo Lake it was once a home for the Lithuanian Dukes. I rented a boat with a driver and explored the lake.

Our drive to Poland with a few stops. Warsaw was next. This city is thriving. It is all reconstructed in the old style before the War. Most impressive is the Monument to the Heroes of the Warsaw ghetto. At night we all went to a Chopin Concert in a place fitting for a King. Champagne was served.

Our last day was spent at the Wilanow Palace. It is a Baroque Palace close to Versailles in looks. Built in the 17th century. With large Gardens and lakeside promenades. It was not destroyed in the 2nd world war. That was my quick trip through the Balkans.

My trips have been short only to San Francisco and Maine to visit Relatives because of my departure on a 5-month long trip around the World on the beautiful "Amsterdam".

January the 4th from Ft. Lauderdale Florida.

It all came to a halt because of the corona virus. It affected our cruise to a standstill March 24, 2020 in Freemantle Australia, when we all had to get off the ship and fly home to the USA.

Index

www.ingramcontent.com/pod-product-compliance
Lightning Source LLC
Chambersburg PA
CBHW020916140626
46545CB00015B/60